HERODIAN

II

BOOKS V–VIII

HERODIAN

IN TWO VOLUMES

II
BOOKS V–VIII

WITH AN ENGLISH TRANSLATION BY

C. R. WHITTAKER
UNIVERSITY OF ALBERTA

CAMBRIDGE, MASSACHUSETTS
HARVARD UNIVERSITY PRESS
LONDON
WILLIAM HEINEMANN LTD
MCMLXX

American ISBN 0–674–99501–5
British ISBN 0 434 99455 3

Printed in Great Britain

35-166

CONTENTS

HERODIAN

ΗΡΩΔΙΑΝΟΥ
ΤΗΣ ΜΕΤΑ ΜΑΡΚΟΝ ΒΑΣΙΛΕΙΑΣ ΙΣΤΟΡΙΑΣ ΒΙΒΛΙΟΝ ΠΕΜΠΤΟΝ

1. Ὅπως μὲν δὴ ὁ Ἀντωνῖνος ἦρξέ τε καὶ ἐτελεύτησε, δεδήλωται ἐν τῷ πρὸ τούτου συγγράμματι [ἥ τε πρὸ τούτου ἐπιβουλὴ καὶ διαδοχή].¹ γενόμενος δὲ ἐν τῇ Ἀντιοχείᾳ ὁ Μακρῖνος ἐπιστέλλει τῷ τε δήμῳ Ῥωμαίων καὶ τῇ συγκλήτῳ, 2 λέγων τοιάδε. " ἐν εἰδόσι μὲν ὑμῖν τοῦ τε βίου μου τὴν ἐξ ἀρχῆς προαίρεσιν τοῦ τε τρόπου τὸ πρὸς χρηστότητα ἐπιρρεπές, καὶ τὸ πρᾶον τῆς διοικηθείσης πρότερον πράξεως, οὐ πολύ τι ἐξουσίας καὶ δυνάμεως βασιλικῆς ἀποδεούσης, ὅπου γε καὶ αὐτὸς ὁ βασιλεὺς τοῖς ἐπάρχουσι τῶν

¹ del Wolf

---

¹ Accepting Wolf's deletion, which seems correct in removing a clumsy phrase; but see 3.1.1n for recapitulations at the beginning of new books.

² The date of M.'s return to Antioch can be fixed by his presence at Zeugma (if one assumes he was returning). Diadumenianus was acclaimed as Caesar by the army at Zeugma, Dio 78.19.1, 78.40.1. The senate had also declared him Caesar after the receipt of M.'s first letter; i.e. about early May, Dio

THE FIFTH BOOK OF HERODIAN'S HISTORY OF THE EMPIRE FROM THE TIME OF MARCUS AURELIUS

1. In the preceding book Antoninus' rule and death have been described [and before this, the intrigue and succession].[1] On arrival at Antioch,[2] Macrinus sent off a letter to the senate and Roman people with the following message. "You know what my disposi- 2 tion in life has been from the beginning, and how my character has inclined to what is morally good.[3] You are aware of the mildness of my previous administrative work, which is not too much different from the office and powers of an emperor (on the occasions when the emperor himself relies upon the

---

78.17.1. News of this senatorial honour must have reached M. about early June, but by this time, Dio seems to imply, M. had been forced to anticipate the senate, Dio 78.19.1. Thus the date for M. at Zeugma was about late May. If the news travelled by land, the letters would have taken a month longer each way; this is rather more consistent with Dio's report of a circus demonstration when news of Diadumenianus was known in Rome, since it was on Diadumenianus' *natalia*, 14th September; but the news of M.'s succession was known in Rome at the *ludi Martiales*, 14th May, Dio 78.18.3.

[3] The opening *sententia* is typical of a Thucydidean speech; Thuc. 1.68.3, 2.36.4, 4.59.2. The speeches were inevitably the place where the rhetoric of H. was on show; cf. Stein, *Dexip. et Herod.* 142 ff.

HERODIAN

στρατοπέδων πεπίστευται, περιττὸν νομίζω μακ-
ρηγορεῖν. ἴστε γάρ με καὶ οἷς ἐκεῖνος ἔπραττεν
οὐκ ἀρεσκόμενον, καὶ προκινδυνεύσαντα ὑμῶν ἐν
οἷς πολλάκις ταῖς τυχούσαις διαβολαῖς πιστεύων
3 ἀφειδῶς ὑμῖν προσεφέρετο. κἀμὲ μὲν κακῶς
ἠγόρευε, καὶ δημοσίᾳ πολλάκις τὸ μέτριόν μου καὶ
πρὸς τοὺς ἀρχομένους φιλάνθρωπον διαβάλλων
καὶ διασκώπτων ἐς ῥᾳθυμίαν καὶ τρόπων χαυνό-
τητα· κολακείαις δὲ χαίρων, καὶ τοὺς εἰς ὠμότητα
παροξύνοντας τῷ τε θυμῷ τὸ ἐνδόσιμον αὐτοῦ
διδόντας τήν τε ὀργὴν διαβολαῖς ἐγείροντας εὔνους
καὶ πιστοὺς ἐδοκίμαζε φίλους. ἐμοὶ δὲ ἐξ ἀρχῆς
4 τὸ πρᾷον καὶ μέτριον προσφιλές. τὸν γοῦν πρὸς
Παρθυαίους πόλεμον, μέγιστόν τε ὄντα καὶ ἐφ' ᾧ
πᾶσα ῾Ρωμαίων ἐσάλευεν ἀρχή, κατελύσαμεν καὶ
ἐν οἷς ἀνδρείως παραταξάμενοι οὐδέν τι ἡττήμεθα,
καὶ ἐν οἷς σπείσαντες μετὰ πολλῆς δυνάμεως
ἐλθόντα μέγαν βασιλέα πιστὸν φίλον ἀντ' ἐχθροῦ
δυσμάχου ἐποιήσαμεν. ἐμοῦ δὲ κρατοῦντος ἐν
ἀδείᾳ τε [1] καὶ ἀναιμωτὶ πάντες βιώσονται, ἀρι-
στοκρατίᾳ τε μᾶλλον ἢ βασιλείᾳ νομισθήσεται.

[1] μὲν Ogl

[1] Some of the more notorious informers under Caracalla are
noted by Dio 78.21; Ti. Manilius Fuscus (*Albo* 347), Julianus
(unknown, *PIR*² J 102), Sulpicius Arrienus (*Albo* 490) and C.'s
favourite, L. Lucilius Priscillianus (*Albo* 337, Oliver *AJA* 50
(1946) 247–50); but M. refused to reveal to the senate most
of the evidence about informers.

4

prefects of his troops). So I do not need to make a
long oration. As you know I did not like all that
Antoninus did and I took risks for you on many occasions when he was treating you without mercy,
because he believed any slanders that he heard. He 3
slandered me too and publicly jibed at my moderation and generosity towards his subjects, accusing
me of idleness and feebleness of character. He
took pleasure in flatterers, and approved as his loyal
friends and supporters those who spurred him on to
cruelty by pandering to his hot temper and stirring
up his anger with slanderous charges.[1] But I have
from the start favoured leniency and moderation.
Take the Parthian war; this was a very important 4
war and critical for the entire Roman empire. But
we have brought it to an end in two ways; by
fighting bravely without giving way in the slightest
and by signing a treaty [2] with the great king which
makes him into a faithful ally instead of a bitter
enemy, after he had come against us with a large
force. As long as I hold power, everyone shall live
free from fear and bloodshed, and this shall be a rule

[2] On the terms of the treaty, see 4.15.5n; Dio 78.26.3,
78.27.1 and 4. Artabanus accepted a good deal less than his
original demand; the establishment of Tiridates on the
Armenian throne, a Parthian nominee crowned by Rome, was
in the best Augustan tradition; but Tiridates had been the
choice of Vologaeses, though in Roman custody for the last
three years. The terms are far from a victory for the Parthians
or Artabanus, indicating that the battle had not been as dis-
astrous to M. as Dio suggests, but more as H. describes it.
H.'s account tends to be confirmed by the Syriac source,
Mšiha Zkha (quoted in Debevoise, Polit. Hist. of Parthia 267n,
Mingana, Sources syriaques 104).

5 μηδέ τις ἀπαξιούτω ἢ τύχης πταῖσμα νομιζέτω,
ὅτι δὴ ὄντα με ἐκ τῆς ἱππάδος τάξεως ἐπὶ τοῦτο
ἤγαγε.[1] τί γὰρ ὄφελος εὐγενείας, εἰ μὴ χρηστὸς
καὶ φιλάνθρωπος συνοικεῖ τρόπος; τὰ μὲν γὰρ
τῆς τύχης δῶρα καὶ ἀναξίοις περιπίπτει, ἡ δὲ τῆς
ψυχῆς ἀρετὴ ἰδίαν ἑκάστῳ δόξαν περιτίθησιν.
εὐγένεια δὲ καὶ πλοῦτος καὶ ὅσα τοιαῦτα μακαρίζε-
ται μέν, οὐκ ἐπαινεῖται δέ, ὡς παρ' ἄλλου δοθέντα·
6 ἐπιείκεια δὲ καὶ χρηστότης ἅμα τῷ θαυμάζεσθαι
καὶ τῶν ἐπαίνων τὴν ἀναφορὰν ἐς αὑτόν τινα ἔχει
τὸν κατορθοῦντα. τί γοῦν ὑμᾶς ὤνησεν ἡ Κομόδου
εὐγένεια ἢ 'Αντωνίνου ἡ πατρῴα διαδοχή; οἱ μὲν
γὰρ ὥσπερ ὄφλημα κληρονομίας εἰληφότες ἀπο-
χρῶνταί τε καὶ ἐνυβρίζουσιν ὡς ἄνωθεν ἰδίῳ
κτήματι· οἱ δὲ παρ' ὑμῶν λαβόντες χάριτός τε

---

[1] ἤγαγε θεός· A

[1] Aristocracy in contrast to tyranny is simply another aspect
of the theme of the ideal kingship of popular Stoic doctrine;
under the enlightened despotism of the *princeps*, the senate and
the *amici* hold an honourable position, contributing their
advice and authority to the imperial decisions; this was
respublica contrasted with *regnum*; cf. 2.3.10 (Pertinax),
2.14.3 (Severus), 6.1.2 (Alexander); a theme of obvious advantages to the new man and especially to the lowly born
equestrian emperor; cf. Tac. *A.* 2.35.2, *H.* 4.9, Dio 52.32.1,
Pliny, *Paneg.* 66 (*commune imperium*); emphasized by
sophists, Dio of Prusa, περὶ βασ. 1.32. Ps. Aristides *Or.* 35
(Keil) 5; contrasted with Commodus, 1.5.5.
[2] Anticipating the senatorial opposition that is illustrated
by Dio's class-conscious remarks, 78.11.1–4. Remarks about

6

of the aristocracy rather than a tyranny.[1] No one 5
should think I am unworthy or consider it a mistake
of fortune that I have risen from the equestrian
order to this position.[2] What is the good of noble
birth, if integrity and human behaviour do not go
with it? The gifts of good fortune are showered
even on those who do not deserve them, but the
goodness of a man's heart confers upon each person his own individual reputation.[3] Nobility and
wealth and such like are considered lucky, but they
are not qualities one praises, because they are inherited from someone else. But fairness and hon- 6
esty, while being admirable qualities, also attract
praise for the person who successfully practises
them. For instance, what benefit to you were
Commodus' noble birth or Antoninus' succession to
his father's rule? Some get possession of the empire as
though it were an inheritance they were owed; then
they misuse and make a mockery of it like a private
family heirloom. But others who receive the
power from you are always indebted to your

equestrian emperors are very relevant if H. was writing during
the time of Philip; see Introduction, p.xvii.

[3] Cf. Sall. *Cat.* 8 on the *vetus doctrina* of the capriciousness of
fortune and the counter-theme of *virtus*; the contrast between
virtus and *nobilitas* is dominant in the historical writings of
Sallust and Tacitus; cf. Earl, *Polit. Thought of Sallust* 32–5,
Roberts, *G & R* 6 (1936) 9–17. In the period after Nerva,
which made a virtue out of the necessity of succession by
adoption, the practice was made philosophically respectable
by hackneyed arguments of the kind used by H. here; cf. Tac.
H. 1.16.2 (the danger of succession by birth, *nam generari et
nasci a principibus fortuitum*). But the philosopher-emperor
M. Aurelius chose his own son, as did every earlier emperor
(except Claudius) who had a son.

αἰδίου εἰσὶ χρεῶσται καὶ πειρῶνται ἀμείψασθαι
7 τοὺς εὐεργεσίαις προειληφότας. καὶ τῶν μὲν
εὐπατριδῶν βασιλέων τὸ εὐγενὲς ἐς ὑπεροψίαν
ἐκπίπτει καταφρονήσει τῶν ὑπηκόων [1] ὡς πολὺ
ἐλαττόνων· οἱ δὲ ἐκ μετρίων πράξεων ἐπὶ τοῦτο
ἐλθόντες περιέπουσιν αὐτὸ [2] ὡς καμάτῳ κτηθέν,
αἰδῶ τε καὶ τιμὴν ἀπονέμουσιν, ἣν εἰώθεσαν, τοῖς
8 ποτὲ κρείττοσιν. ἐμοὶ δὲ σκοπὸς μηδέν τι πράττειν ἄνευ τῆς ὑμετέρας γνώμης, κοινωνούς τε καὶ
συμβούλους ἔχειν τῆς τῶν πραγμάτων διοικήσεως.
ὑμεῖς δὲ ἐν [3] ἀδείᾳ καὶ ἐλευθερίᾳ βιώσεσθε, ὧν
ἀφῃρέθητε μὲν ὑπὸ τῶν εὐπατριδῶν βασιλέων, ἀπο-
δοῦναι δὲ ὑμῖν ἐπειράθησαν πρότερον [4] μὲν Μάρκος
ὕστερον δὲ Περτίναξ, ἐξ ἰδιωτικῶν σπαργάνων
ἐπὶ τοῦτο ἐλθόντες. γένους γὰρ ἔνδοξον ἀρχὴν
αὐτὸν παρασχεῖν καὶ τῷ ὑστέρῳ γένει ἄμεινον ἢ
κλέος προγονικὸν παραλαμβάνοντα τρόπου φαυλό-
τητι καταισχῦναι."

[1] πολλῶν A
[2] om O
[3] om V μὲν for δὲ ἐν A
[4] πρῶτον

[1] Severus also stressed the theme; cf. 2.14.3. M. was able
to save a certain consular, Aurelianus, from execution by the
soldiers on the plea that it was " not right to kill a senator,"
Dio 78.12.2 (very fragmentary, cf. Boissevain 3. 414–15).

favour and try to repay you for the benefits they
received.   Nobility of birth in the case of patrician 7
emperors degenerates into haughtiness, because
they have a contempt for their subjects and think
them vastly inferior to themselves.   But those who
reach the power from moderate means treat it carefully as a reward for their labour, and continue to
respect and honour, as they used to, those who were
once more powerful than themselves.   It is my in- 8
tention to do nothing without your approval.   I
shall make you my partners and advisers in the administration of the state.   You shall live in security and freedom,¹ the rights which you lost under
the nobly born emperors but which Marcus first and
then Pertinax, both of them men who were born
of common cloth before they came to power, tried
to restore to you.²   It is better to be the distinguished founder of a line and leave this to one's descendants than to inherit a glorious past from one's
ancestors and disgrace it by corrupt behaviour."

Later, however, M. was unable or unwilling to save him, and
thereby roused senatorial hostility; Dio 78.19.1.   Note the
stress on *aequitas Aug(usti)* and δικαιοσύνη on coins of M.;
Vogt, *Alex. Münzen* 1.173 ff.
² M. Aurelius was hardly a new man, but he was an adopted
heir (see above for the importance of this). SHA, *Macr.*
11.2, says M. wished to bear the names of Severus and Pertinax,
but only Severus appears, and his son is named Antoninus;
thus a greater stress on the continuity with the Severans than
with Pertinax and M. Aurelius; SHA, *Macr.* 5.6–7, 12.1,
Petrikovits, *RE* (Opellius 2) 552.   This was partly necessitated
by the popularity of Caracalla among the soldiers, who
demanded another Antoninus; Dio 78.19.2; also the reason
why there was no *damnatio memoriae* of Caracalla; Dio 78.9.2,
78.17.2–3, SHA, *Macr.* 5.9.

HERODIAN

2. ἀναγνωσθείσης δὲ τῆς τοιαύτης ἐπιστολῆς,
εὐφημεῖ τε αὐτὸν ἡ σύγκλητος καὶ τὰς σεβασμίους
τιμὰς πάσας ψηφίζεται. οὐχ οὕτως δὲ εὔφραινε
πάντας ἡ Μακρίνου διαδοχή, ὡς ὑπερήδοντό τε
καὶ πανδημεὶ ἑώρταζον ἐπὶ τῇ Ἀντωνίνου ἀπαλ-
λαγῇ. ἕκαστός τε ᾤετο, μάλιστα τῶν ἐν ἀξιώσει
τινὶ ἢ πράξει καθεστώτων, ξίφος ἀποσεσεῖσθαι [1]
2 τοῖς αὐχέσιν ἐπαιωρούμενον. συκοφάνται τε ἢ
δοῦλοι, ὅσοι [2] δεσπότας κατήγγελον, [3] ἀνεσκολο-
πίσθησαν· ἥ τε Ῥωμαίων πόλις καὶ σχεδὸν πᾶσα
ἡ ὑπὸ Ῥωμαίους οἰκουμένη καθαρθεῖσα πονηρῶν
ἀνθρώπων, τῶν μὲν κολασθέντων τῶν δὲ ἐξωσθέν-
των, εἰ δέ τινες καὶ ἔλαθον, δι' εὐλάβειαν ἡσυχαζόν-
των, [4] ἐν ἀδείᾳ πολλῇ καὶ εἰκόνι ἐλευθερίας ἐβίωσαν
ἐκείνου τοῦ ἔτους οὗ μόνου ὁ Μακρῖνος ἐβασίλευσε.
3 τοσοῦτον δὲ ἥμαρτεν ὅσον μὴ διέλυσεν εὐθέως τὰ

---

[1] ἀποπεσεῖσθαι Oa
[3] κατήγγελλον Ai
[2] ὅσα φ om A
[4] ἡσυχάζοντες ἦσαν· A

---

[1] H. has confused two letters; the first sent on M.'s accession
in April 217 (news of which was in Rome by the middle of
May, 5.1.1n), in which M. committed the indiscretion of claiming imperial titles not yet voted to him; Dio 78.16.2, 78.17.1.
The second was in 218 after the peace with Artabanus, claiming
a Parthian victory; Dio 78.27.3. The titles of M. (according
to Dio) were *imperator Caesar pius felix Augustus procos.* as
well as the name Severus; he does not mention *trib. pot.* or
pontifex maximus (SHA, *Macr.* 7.2); coins do not show *pius*
and *felix* but inscriptions do (*ILS* III (index) 291); patrician

10

2. After the reading of this letter,[1] the senate acclaimed him emperor and voted him all the honours of an Augustus.[2] It was not Macrinus' accession that pleased them all, so much as their universal exultation and celebration at the fall of Antoninus. The feeling of everyone, but particularly of those of high distinction and office, was that a sword which was hanging over their heads had been removed. Informers and slaves who had de- 2 nounced their masters were crucified. Rome itself and nearly the whole of the Roman empire was purged of criminals; some were punished, some were exiled and, if some actually escaped, they were careful not to advertise themselves. Men lived in security and the semblance of freedom for that single year while Macrinus was emperor. But he 3

status and priesthoods were almost automatic; SHA, *Macr.* 7.1, *CIL* VI. 1984, 2009 5–8. Discussed by Salama (next note).

[2] Dio 78.13.1–2 says the senate voted M. *ornamenta consularia* as soon as he acceded, raising him from equestrian to senatorial status (cf. 4.12.1n); M. properly declined to count this as a true consulship in his titles (i.e. *cos.* II does not appear at first), and in theory in 218 his consulship with Adventus counted as his first. But coins of 218 appear with *cos.* II, *BMC* V. 503–4, indicating a change in resolve. Coins are in a series, with *trib. pot.* alone, *trib. pot. cos.*, *trib. pot.* II *cos.*, *trib. pot.* II *cos.* II, which might simply mean a change of *trib. pot.* on 10th December (like M. Aurelius) and normal assumption of *cos.* II on 1st January. But it could confirm Dio, if M. renewed his *trib. pot.* on 1st January; it is possible that in face of growing senatorial unpopularity, M. discarded constitutional scruples and attempted to raise his prestige by *cos.* II and a Parthian victory; the *victoria* coins appear in 218; a single inscription shows M. with *cos.* II and Parthicus Maximus, but, since it is on a milestone in Mauretania Caesariensis, this may be only local enthusiasm; Salama, *REA* 66 (1964) 334–52.

στρατόπεδα καὶ ἑκάστους ἐς τὰ ἑαυτῶν ἀπέπεμψεν,
αὐτός τε ἐς τὴν Ῥώμην ποθοῦσαν ἐπείχθη, τοῦ
δήμου ἑκάστοτε καλοῦντος μεγάλαις βοαῖς, ἐν δὲ
τῇ Ἀντιοχείᾳ διέτριβε γένειόν τε ἀσκῶν, βαδίζων
τε πλέον τοῦ δέοντος ἠρεμαίως, βραδύτατά τε καὶ
μόλις τοῖς προσιοῦσιν ἀποκρινόμενος ὡς μηδ᾽
ἀκούεσθαι πολλάκις διὰ τὸ καθειμένον τῆς φωνῆς.
4 ἐζήλου δὲ ταῦτα ὡς δὴ Μάρκου ἐπιτηδεύματα, τὸν
δὲ λοιπὸν βίον οὐκ ἐμιμήσατο, ἐπεδίδου δὲ ἑκάστοτε
ἐς τὸ ἁβροδίαιτον, ὀρχηστῶν τε θέαις καὶ πάσης
μούσης κινήσεώς τε εὐρύθμου [1] ὑποκριταῖς σχολά-
ζων, τῆς τε τῶν πραγμάτων διοικήσεως ἀμελῶς
ἔχων. προῄει τε πόρπαις καὶ ζωστῆρι χρυσῷ τε [2]
πολλῷ καὶ λίθοις τιμίοις πεποικιλμένος,[3] τῆς

---

[1] εὐθύμου a κιν. τε εὐρ. del Lange
[2] Nauck om φι καὶ χρ. A
[3] πεποικιλμένοις κεκοσμημένος i cf. 5.3.4

---

[1] Cf. 4.15.9n for an explanation of why M. did not return to
Rome at once and disband his army.

[2] Cf. 5.5.1n; support for M. at the *ludi Martiales* of 14th
May, but against M. at the *natalia* of Diadumenianus of 14th
September. No doubt much of this swing in feeling was due
to the organization by outraged senators; cf. Dio 78.15.1 ff.,
78.18.4 (for Dio's feelings); SHA, *Macr.* 2.4, 4.1 ff. But there
is no need to suppose that all senators thought in the same way
as Dio, as Dio himself admits; 78.13.1, 78.15.2; senators who
benefited from M. would have been his supporters; e.g. the
elder and younger Pomponius Bassus, since the latter had been
restored from exile (*Albo* 421, 422; from the heart of the old
Antonine families through the wife of the elder Bassus, Annia
Faustina; cf. Magie, *R. Rule in Asia Minor* 1326, 1573, for the
estate of the Ormelais); Q. Anicius Faustus (*Albo* 27);
Domitius Florus (*Albo* 204); a certain Flaccus (*Albo* 219).

was wrong in not disbanding his army at once [1] and
posting every man home, and in not making for Rome
himself where he was wanted and the people were
continually calling for him in noisy demonstrations.[2]
He should not have wasted his time in Antioch cultivating his beard [3] and walking about the place more
than necessary at a slow pace and speaking to
people at audiences very slowly and laboriously so
that frequently he could not even be heard because
of his low voice.   These were supposedly imitations 4
of Marcus' characteristics,[4] but the resemblance did
not extend to the rest of his life.   He indulged regularly in a life of luxury by wasting his time on
mime shows [5] and performers of all the arts and
rhythmic dancing.   Meanwhile he neglected government business.   He used to go out wearing brooches
and a belt and all decked out in gold and precious

---

[3] Cf. 5.4.7 for M.'s beard; coins show the beard dressed in
the archaic fashion (*barba promissa*), confirming H.'s suggestion
of an imitation of M. Aurelius; *BMC* V. ccxiii (" too unflatter-
ing to be regarded as an idealized portrait "). Beards as a
fashionable claim to wisdom caused Lucian to remark that
" if cultivating one's beard is acquiring wisdom, a goat with a
good beard is a fine Plato," *Epigr.* 45.

[4] Cf. 5.1.8n. M.'s dilemma was to court the favour of the
soldiers by stressing his continuity with Caracalla, but to re-
tain the loyalty of the senators who hated Caracalla by repeal-
ing many of the burdensome taxes of C. In the event he
pleased no one.

[5] Dancing was part of the mime shows. Assessments of
M.'s character vary widely; luxurious living (Dio 78.15.3,
SHA, *Macr.* 13.4), cruelty (SHA, *Macr.* 12.1 ff., *Elag.* 2.3)
austerity and old-fashioned severity (SHA, *Macr.* 11.1, Victor,
Caes. 22.3). Dio 78.40.3–41.4 is not unfair but is the view of
an outraged senator. H. is too concerned to find a moral cause
of failure.

τοιαύτης πολυτελείας παρὰ τοῖς Ῥωμαίων [1] στρατιώταις οὐκ ἐπαινουμένης, βαρβάρου δὲ μᾶλλον
5 καὶ θηλυπρεποῦς εἶναι δοκούσης. ἅπερ ὁρῶντες
οἱ στρατιῶται οὐ πάνυ τι ἀπεδέχοντο, ἀπηρέσκοντό
τε αὐτοῦ τῷ βίῳ ὡς ἀνειμένῳ μᾶλλον ἢ κατ'
ἄνδρα στρατιωτικόν· παραβάλλοντες δὲ τὴν μνήμην
τῆς [2] Ἀντωνίνου διαίτης ἐπιστραφείσης τε καὶ
στρατιωτικῆς γενομένης,[3] κατεγίνωσκον τῆς Μακ-
6 ρίνου πολυτελείας. ἔτι [4] τε ἠγανάκτουν αὐτοὶ μὲν
ὑπὸ σκηναῖς καὶ ἐν ἀλλοδαπῇ διαιτώμενοι, ἔσθ'
ὅτε καὶ σπανίζοντες τῶν ἐπιτηδείων,[5] ἔς τε τὰ
ἑαυτῶν οὐκ ἐπανιόντες εἰρήνης εἶναι δοκούσης·
ὁρῶντες δὲ τὸν Μακρῖνον ἐν [6] χλιδῇ καὶ τρυφῇ
διαιτώμενον, ἀφηνιάζοντες ἤδη πρὸς ἀλλήλους
αὐτὸν κακῶς ἠγόρευον, προφάσεώς τε ὀλίγης
λαβέσθαι εὔχοντο ἐς τὸ ἀποσκευάσασθαι τὸ λυποῦν.

3. ἐχρῆν δὲ ἄρα Μακρῖνον ἐνιαυτοῦ μόνου τῇ
βασιλείᾳ ἐντρυφήσαντα ἅμα τῷ βίῳ καὶ τὴν
ἀρχὴν καταλῦσαι, μικρὰν καὶ εὐτελῆ πρόφασιν
τοῖς στρατιώταις ἐς ἃ ἐβούλοντο τῆς τύχης παρα-

---

[1] Ῥωμαίοις Mendelss
[2] τῇ φι
[3] διαίτη ἐπιστραφείση (ἐπιστραφεῖ B) τε καὶ στρατιωτικῇ
γενομένη Oi corr Stav following Steph (ἐπιστρεφοῦς)
[4] ὅτι φ

14

stones. Such extravagance is not admired by the
Roman troops, appearing to be more appropriate to
barbarians and women. When the soldiers saw this, 5
they did not approve at all and were angry at
Macrinus' way of life because they thought it too
dissolute for a military man.[1] As they recalled
Antoninus' disciplined military habits in comparison,
they censured Macrinus' extravagance. They were 6
also angry because, while they were still living in
tents in a foreign country, sometimes even on short
supplies and not returning to their own countries in
spite of apparently peaceful conditions, Macrinus,
they noticed, was living in the lap of luxury. In
this state of unrest, and bitterly criticizing him
among themselves, they longed to find a slight
excuse for getting rid of the cause of their trouble.

3. After only one year of a life of ease as emperor
it was obviously inevitable that Macrinus would
lose the empire, and his life too, whenever chance
provided a small, trivial excuse for the soldiers to

[1] M.'s failure to win the army is emphasized in all sources;
Dio 78.19.2—M. forced to curry favour by naming his son
Antoninus; Dio 78.28.1–29.2—M.'s attempt to reduce the pay
and privileges causes discontent, magnified by his failure to
disperse the troops; SHA, *Macr.* 12—a highly coloured description of M.'s military discipline; Dio 78.34.2–3—M. was forced
to restore privileges and to promise a donative of 5,000
denarii, cf. SHA, *Macr.* 5.7; Dio 78.36.3—M. complains of the
impossibility of maintaining high rates of pay; the predominance of *fides militum* type coins, *BMC* V. 494, 497, 505.
There is no reason to believe the dress of M. offended the
soldiers, since many of them later supported Elagabalus who
was more extreme.

5 ἀναγκαίων Jo   6 Jo om Oi

2 σχούσης. Μαῖσα ἦν τις ὄνομα, τὸ γένος Φοίνισσα,
ἀπὸ Ἐμέσου [1] καλουμένης οὕτω πόλεως ἐν
Φοινίκῃ· [2] ἀδελφὴ δὲ ἐγεγόνει Ἰουλίας τῆς Σεβήρου
μὲν [3] γυναικὸς Ἀντωνίνου δὲ μητρός. παρὰ πάντα
οὖν τὸν τῆς ἀδελφῆς βίον ἐν τῇ βασιλείῳ διέτριψεν
αὐλῇ χρόνου πολυετοῦς, παρ' ὃν [4] Σεβῆρός τε καὶ
Ἀντωνῖνος ἐβασίλευσαν. τὴν δὴ Μαῖσαν ταύτην
ὁ Μακρῖνος, μετὰ τὴν τῆς ἀδελφῆς τελευτὴν
Ἀντωνίνου δὲ ἀναίρεσιν, προσέταξεν ἐς τὴν
πατρίδα ἐπανελθοῦσαν ἐν τοῖς οἰκείοις καταβιῶναι,
πάντα ἔχουσαν τὰ ἑαυτῆς. πλείστων δὲ ἦν
χρημάτων ἀνάπλεως ἅτε μακρῷ χρόνῳ βασιλικῇ
3 ἐξουσίᾳ ἐντεθραμμένη. ἐπανελθοῦσα δὲ ἡ πρεσβῦτις διέτριβεν ἐν τοῖς ἑαυτῆς. ἦσαν δὲ αὐτῇ
θυγατέρες δύο· Σοαιμὶς μὲν ἡ πρεσβυτέρα ἑκα-

---

[1] ἐμέσης A
[2] ἐν φοιν. om Jo
[3] Bekk² μὲν τῆς Σεβ. Oi
[4] οὗ O

---

[1] Julia Maesa; *PIR*² J 678; former wife of Julius Avitus (cf.
5.7.3), who had been suffect consul under Severus and proconsul of Asia, before serving under C. in some capacity in
Mesopotamia and Cyprus (Dio 78.3.2). Another of the same
family (brother?) was C. Julius Avitus Alexianus, *PIR*² J 192,
AE (1963) 42, an important and powerful *comes* of Severus and
Caracalla (in Britain 209–11). Thus the family had many
opportunities for building a strong client following among
soldiers and court officials. Maesa was the real power behind
the throne after 218 until her death (6.1.4n); she was named
Augusta as early as 30th May 218 (this date is on the records
of the *fratres Arvales*, *CIL* VI. 2104 23—obviously retro-

have their way. There was a woman called Maesa,[1] 2
a Phoenician from Emesa (which is the name of a
city in that country). She was the sister of Julia,
the wife of Severus and Antoninus' mother. For the
whole time her sister was alive during the many
years of the rule of Severus and Antoninus, Maesa
lived at the imperial court. After the death of the
sister and the assassination of Antoninus, Macrinus
ordered her to return to her own country and
live among her own people, though in full possession of her property. After a long period of
association with imperial power Maesa was an extremely wealthy person. The old lady returned 3
home and lived on her property. But she had two
daughters, Soaemis (the elder)[2] and Mamaea (the

spectively noted; cf. 5.4.5n) and *mater castrorum* in 218 (*AE*
(1955) 260).

[2] Julia Soemias Bassiana; *PIR*[2] J 704; the name varies in
the sources, but probably derives from the Syrian *Suhaim*
(cf. Symiamira, SHA, *Macr.* 9.2, etc.). Her husband
(probably dead in 217) was the powerful equestrian, Sex.
Varius Marcellus, for whose career see *ILS* 478, 8687, Dio
78.30.2, Klass, *RE* (Varius 16), Pflaum, *Carrières* no. 237; a
native of Apamea, he rose through the procuratorial service,
often (suggests Pflaum) acting in special responsibility posts as
agent for the absent emperor; e.g. *procurator aquarum* in
Rome while S. was in the East *c.* 195/6, procurator of Britain
after Albinus' defeat 197 (3.8.2n), *procurator rationis privatae*
and *vice praefect(orum) praetorio et urbi* during the absence of
S. in Britain; adlected into the senate by C. (to reduce his
power, says Pflaum), *c.* 211-17 he was made *praeses* of the
recently formed (see 3.10.2n) province of Numidia. Thus
another of the Syrian families with influence at the court.
Soaemias never seems to have been of great influence; she
was alleged to be having an affair with Gannys, Dio 79.6.2-3;
cf. 5.8.8n.

λεῖτο, ἡ δὲ ἑτέρα Μαμαία.[1] παῖδες δὲ ἦσαν τῇ
μὲν πρεσβυτέρᾳ Βασιανὸς ὄνομα, τῇ δὲ νεωτέρᾳ
'Αλεξιανός. ὑπὸ δὲ ταῖς μητράσι καὶ τῇ μάμμῃ
ἀνετρέφοντο, ὁ μὲν Βασιανὸς περὶ ἔτη γεγονὼς
τεσσαρεσκαίδεκα, ὁ δὲ 'Αλεξιανὸς δεκάτου ἔτους
4 ἐπιβεβηκώς. ἱέρωντο [2] δὲ αὐτοὶ θεῷ ἡλίῳ· τοῦτον
γὰρ οἱ ἐπιχώριοι σέβουσι, τῇ Φοινίκων φωνῇ
'Ελαιαγάβαλον [3] καλοῦντες. νεὼς δὲ αὐτῷ μέγιστος κατεσκεύαστο, χρυσῷ πολλῷ καὶ ἀργύρῳ
κεκοσμημένος λίθων τε πολυτελείᾳ. θρησκεύεται
δὲ οὐ μόνον πρὸς τῶν ἐπιχωρίων, ἀλλὰ καὶ πάντες
οἱ γειτνιῶντες σατράπαι τε καὶ βασιλεῖς βάρβαροι
φιλοτίμως πέμπουσι τῷ θεῷ ἑκάστου τοῦ [4] ἔτους
5 πολυτελῆ ἀναθήματα. ἄγαλμα μὲν οὖν, ὥσπερ
παρ' "Ελλησιν ἢ 'Ρωμαίοις, οὐδὲν ἔστηκε χειρο-

---

[1] Oi but many edit Μαμμαία also Βασσιανὸς (below) cf. Dio
78.30.3 etc.　　　　　　　　　　[2] ἱερῶντο AJo
[3] ἐλεαγ. A cf. ἐλεγ. ἐλεαγ. ἐλαγ. Dio *Heliog.* SHA and
Eutrop　　　　　　　　　　[4] om i

---

[1] Julia Avita Mamaea; *PIR²* J 649; her husband Gessius
Marcianus was another Syrian (from Arca), had also risen
through the procuratorial service (Dio 78.30.3) but possibly
not given senatorial status by Caracalla (*Dig.* 1.9.12 (Ulpian));
these families, very close to the emperor, are a remarkable
illustration of the changed social status of the equestrian
service under Severus; Stein, *Ritterstand* 193. For Mamaea,
see 6.1.8n.
[2] Dio 78.30.2 uses the name Avitus, i.e. Varius Avitus;
Lambertz, *RE* (Varius 10) 393, thinks H. has made an error;

younger),[1] both of whom had sons, called Bassianus [2]
and Alexianus [3] respectively. The two boys, Bassianus, aged about fourteen, and Alexianus, just
turned nine, were being raised by their mothers and
grandmother. Both boys were dedicated [4] to the
service of the sun god whom the local inhabitants 4
worship under its Phoenician name of Elagabalus.
There was a huge temple built there, richly ornamented with gold and silver and valuable stones.
The cult extended not just to the local inhabitants
either. Satraps of all the adjacent territories and
barbarian princes tried to outdo each other in sending costly dedications to the god every year.[5] There 5
was no actual man-made statue of the god, the sort
Greeks and Romans put up; but there was an enor-

but it seems possible that Elagabalus (as he is wrongly called)
deliberately stressed the name of his maternal great-grandfather, Julius Bassianus (*PIR*² J 202, *Epit. de Caes.* 23.2), in
order to publicize his link with Caracalla through their
common ancestor. According to Dio 79.20.2 (if exact), the boy
was born about March 204 (cf. 5.7.4n).

[3] Named Bassianus by Dio 78.30.3, etc.; *PIR*² A 1610.
Possibly the same as the *frater Arvalis* called M. Julius Gessius
Bassianus (*CIL* VI. 2086, 2103 dated 213–14, but more likely
this is a brother or an uncle); there is nothing improbable
about the name Alexianus, a family name (5.3.2n). The
birth date of 1st October 208 is consistent with what is said
here (cf. 5.7.4n), wrongly translated often as though he were
already ten now, but the Greek means " he had entered upon
his tenth year." Other dates are late and untrustworthy.

[4] Jo's reading (*app. critic.*) means the boys " were being
trained " (see below).

[5] The cult of Baal of Emesa is discussed at length by Gross,
Reallex. f. Antike u. Christentum IV. 987 ff. (Elagabal); the
cult was administered by the priest-kings of the principality
(descended from the Arab sheik, Samsiceramus) even after
the absorption of the state into Syria by Domitian.

19

HERODIAN

ποίητον, θεοῦ φέρον εἰκόνα· λίθος δέ τις ἔστι
μέγιστος, κάτωθεν περιφερής, λήγων ἐς ὀξύτητα·
κωνοειδὲς αὐτῷ σχῆμα, μέλαινά τε ἡ χροιά.
διοπετῆ[1] τε αὐτὸν εἶναι σεμνολογοῦσιν, ἐξοχάς τέ
τινας βραχείας καὶ τύπους δεικνύουσιν, εἰκόνα τε
ἡλίου ἀνέργαστον εἶναι θέλουσιν, οὕτω βλέποντες.[2]

6 τούτῳ δὴ τῷ θεῷ ὁ Βασιανὸς ἱερώμενος[3] (ἅτε
γὰρ πρεσβυτέρῳ ἐκείνῳ ἐγκεχείριστο ἡ θρησκεία[4])
προῄει τε σχήματι βαρβάρῳ, χιτῶνας χρυσοϋφεῖς
καὶ ἁλουργεῖς[5] χειριδωτοὺς καὶ ποδήρεις ἀνε-
ζωσμένος, τά τε σκέλη πάντα σκέπων ἀπ' ὀνύχων
ἐς μηροὺς ἐσθῆσιν ὁμοίως χρυσῷ καὶ πορφύρα
πεποικιλμέναις. τήν τε κεφαλὴν ἐκόσμει στέφα-

7 νος λίθων πολυτελῶν χροιᾷ διηνθισμένος. ἦν δὲ
τὴν ἡλικίαν[6] ἀκμαῖος καὶ τὴν ὄψιν τῶν κατ'
αὐτὸν ὡραιότατος μειρακίων πάντων. ἐς τὸ αὐτὸ
δὴ συνιόντων κάλλους σώματος, ἡλικίας ἀκμῆς,
ἁβροῦ σχήματος, ἀπείκασεν ἄν τις τὸ μειράκιον
Διονύσου καλαῖς εἰκόσιν.

[1] διπετῆ Α διηπετῆ φ
[2] βλέπ⟨ειν ἐθέλ⟩οντες Gedike Schwartz cf. 5.4.4
[3] ἱερώμενος (ἱεράομαι) Whit ἱερωμένος (ἱερόω) Οἱ
[4] θυσία Ο
[5] Αα g[1] (over -οῖς) -γοῖς l -γέσι Β -γίδας V -γίδα Jo
[6] τῇ ἡλικίᾳ Ο

[1] Illustrated on coins of E.; e.g. *BMC* V. 546, 560, no. 197–8
(pl. 89.7); the coins types are associated with the legend
conservator, an epithet of Jupiter.
[2] My emendation means that E. was already priest of the
cult; cf. 5.3.3n.
[3] The flowing long-sleeved tunic of Ionian and eastern dress,
discarded by most Greeks in the fifth century in favour of the

20

mous stone, rounded at the base and coming to a point on the top, conical in shape and black.[1] This stone is worshipped as though it were sent from heaven; on it there are some small projecting pieces and markings that are pointed out, which the people would like to believe are a rough picture of the sun, because this is how they see them. Bassianus, the 6 elder of the two boys, was a priest[2] of this god (as the elder of the two he had been put in charge of the cult). He used to appear in public in barbarian clothes, wearing a long-sleeved " chiton " that hung to his feet and was gold and purple.[3] His legs from the waist down to the tips of his toes were completely covered similarly with garments ornamented with gold and purple. On his head he wore a crown of precious stones[4] glowing with different colours. Bassianus was in the prime of his youth and the 7 most handsome of all the young men of his time.[5] With this combination of good looks, youth and splendid dress there was a possible resemblance between the young man and the magnificent statues of Dionysus.

short Dorian tunic (cf. Thuc. 1.6). H. stresses the dress and appearance of E., partly because the barbarities of dress are used as means to characterize emperors; e.g. 1.3.3 ff. (tyrants), 1.14.8 (Commodus), 4.7.3, etc. (Caracalla), 5.2.4 (Macrinus). The classic literary model of effeminacy and vice was the semi-mythical king Sardanapalus; e.g. Dio of Prusa, περὶ βασ. 1.3, 4.109–13, which must have influenced H. in his description of E., especially since Cassius Dio frequently calls him Sardanapalus, e.g. 79.1.1.

[4] The language is similar to Lucian, *Bis Acc.* 16.

[5] The good looks of E. are noted by SHA, *Macr.* 9.3, but are not confirmed by the portrait on the coins, *BMC* V. pl. 87.

8 ἱερουργοῦντα δὴ τοῦτον, περί τε τοῖς βωμοῖς
χορεύοντα νόμῳ βαρβάρων ὑπό τε αὐλοῖς καὶ
σύριγξι παντοδαπῶν τε ὀργάνων ἤχῳ, περιεργότερον ἐπέβλεπον οἵ τε ἄλλοι ἄνθρωποι καὶ μάλιστα
οἱ στρατιῶται, εἰδότες γένους ὄντα βασιλικοῦ, καὶ
τῆς ὥρας αὐτοῦ πάντων τὰς ὄψεις ἐς ἑαυτὴν
9 ἐπιστρεφούσης. ἐγειτνίαζε δὲ τῇ πόλει ἐκείνῃ τότε
μέγιστον στρατόπεδον, ὃ τῆς Φοινίκης προήσπιζεν·
ὕστερον δὲ μετηνέχθη, ὡς ἐν τοῖς ἑξῆς ἐροῦμεν.
φοιτῶντες οὖν οἱ στρατιῶται ἑκάστοτε ἐς τὴν
πόλιν, ἔς τε τὸν νεὼν ἰόντες θρησκείας δὴ χάριν, τὸ
μειράκιον ἡδέως ¹ ἔβλεπον. ἦσαν δέ τινες ἐξ
αὐτῶν καὶ ² πρόσφυγες οἰκεῖοί τε τῆς Μαίσης,
10 πρὸς οὓς ἐκείνη θαυμάζοντας τὸν παῖδα, εἴτε
πλασαμένη εἴτε καὶ ἀληθεύουσα, ἐξεῖπεν ὅτι ἄρα
Ἀντωνίνου υἱός ἐστι φύσει, τῇ δὲ ὑπολήψει ἄλλου
δοκοίη· ἐπιφοιτῆσαι γὰρ αὐτὸν ταῖς θυγατράσιν

¹ om l   ² om O

¹ Legio III Gallica, stationed at Raphaneae; the other
garrisons were at Antioch and Apamea. The legion was later
transferred with E. to Nicomedia (Dio 79.7.1–3) and then disbanded (ILS 2657; cf. 2314–17), but H. omits to mention it
again; another example of unrevised or hasty work, 4.8.5n.
The legatus of this legion may have been the Verus who later
aspired to the purple himself (Dio 79.7.1).
² The Greek is not clear; πρόσφυξ is explained by Stephanus,
Thes. Ling. Graec., q.v., as a client who seeks protection; but
does this mean some soldiers had fled from Rome (cf. Politian,
Roma profugi)? H. probably has in mind Gannys, who had

22

As Bassianus performed his priestly duties, danc- 8
ing at the altars to the music of flutes and pipes and
all kinds of instruments in the barbarian fashion,
everyone, especially the soldiers, viewed him with
fairly close interest because they knew he was a
member of the imperial family (apart from the fact
that his beautiful appearance attracted everyone's
attention). At the time there was a large military 9
garrison near the city of Emesa acting as a defence
for Phoenicia, though later it was transferred, as we
shall see.[1] The soldiers used to go regularly to the
city and to the temple, supposedly to worship, but
they enjoyed watching the lad. Some of them were
clients of Maesa and people who had fled to her for
protection.[2] Because they admired the boy, she 10
told them (what may or may not have been true) that
he was actually the natural son of Antoninus,[3]
although it was assumed he had a different father.
Antoninus, she said, had slept with her daughters
when they were young and able to bear children, at

been brought up in the household of Maesa; Dio 79.6 (but
fragmentary; cf. *PIR*[2] G 74, which does not accept the
identification of Gannys with Eutychianus); Gannys must
have had a remarkable influence over the soldiers to become
one of their commanders, Dio 78.38.3–4; there were only a
few freedmen and soldiers (and some equestrians?) and Emesan
citizens who began the plot, Dio 78.31.3.

[3] Cf. 5.4.3, SHA, *Car.* 9.2, *Macr.* 9.4, 14.2, 15.2, *Elag.* 1.4,
Dio 78.31.3, 78.32.2–3 (who says that there was some physical
likeness). The early coinage of E. stressed his descent from
Caracalla, as did his name of M. Aurelius Antoninus; *BMC*
V. ccxxxi–ii. The story had obvious political advantages;
e.g. SHA, *Elag.* 3.1 (*omni populo ad nomen Antoninum . . .
desiderium factum est*); cf. the inscriptions with *divi magni
Antonini f(ilius) divi Severi nepos*, etc., *ILS* III (index) 292.

αὐτῆς νέαις τε οὔσαις καὶ ὡραίαις, καθ᾽ ὃν καιρὸν
ἐν τοῖς βασιλείοις σὺν τῇ ἀδελφῇ διέτριβεν. ὅπερ
ἐκεῖνοι ἀκούσαντες, τοῖς συστρατιώταις [1] κατ᾽
ὀλίγον ἀπαγγέλλοντες διαβόητον ἐποίησαν τὴν
11 φήμην, ὡς ἐς πᾶν χωρῆσαι τὸ στρατιωτικόν. τῇ
δὲ Μαίσῃ ἐλέγετο σωροὺς εἶναι χρημάτων, ἐκείνην
δὲ ἑτοίμως [2] πάντα προέσθαι τοῖς στρατιώταις, εἰ
τὴν βασιλείαν τῷ γένει ἀνανεώσαιντο.[3] ὡς [4] δὲ
συνέθεντο,[5] νύκτωρ εἰ κατέλθοιεν λαθόντες, ἀνοίξειν
τὰς πύλας καὶ δέξεσθαι [6] πᾶν τὸ γένος ἔνδον
βασιλέα τε καὶ υἱὸν ἀποδείξειν Ἀντωνίνου, ἐπέδω-
κεν ἑαυτὴν ἡ πρεσβῦτις, ἑλομένη πάντα κίνδυνον
ἀναρρῖψαι μᾶλλον ἢ ἰδιωτεύειν καὶ δοκεῖν ἀπερ-
ρῖφθαι· νύκτωρ τε λάθρᾳ τῆς πόλεως ὑπεξῆλθε
12 σὺν ταῖς θυγατράσι καὶ τοῖς ἐγγόνοις. καταγαγόν-
των τε αὐτοὺς τῶν προσφυγόντων στρατιωτῶν
γενόμενοι πρὸς τῷ τείχει τοῦ στρατοπέδου ῥᾷστα
ὑπεδέχθησαν· εὐθέως τε τὸν παῖδα πᾶν τὸ

---

[1] στρατιώταις O
[2] ἑτοίμως ⟨ἔχειν⟩ conj Mendelss cf. 7.3.6
[3] -σαιτο i
[4] lac before ὡς conj Mendelss cf. 7.3.6
[5] -θετο i
[6] δέξασθαι AV ag

---

[1] As it happens there is evidence of Soaemias in Rome in
204 near the date of E.'s birth; she took part in the Secular
Games *inter mulieres equestres*, *AE* (1932) 70.
[2] The night of 15th May 218. For the chronology of these

the time when she was living in the palace with her sister.[1] When the soldiers heard this, they passed the news on gradually to their fellow soldiers, and soon made it so publicized that it got round the whole army. The story went that Maesa had loads 11 of wealth, all of which she was willing to distribute to the soldiers if they restored the empire to her family. The soldiers agreed that, if the family came secretly during the night, they would open the gates to take them all in and would declare the son of Antoninus emperor. The old woman agreed to this because she would rather have risked any danger than live as an ordinary person, apparently rejected. Quietly at night she slipped out of the city with her daughters and their children.[2] Guided by the 12 soldiers who were under her protection, the party reached the camp walls and were received without the slightest trouble. Immediately the whole garrison saluted him as Antoninus [3] and, putting the im-

events, see Petrikovits, *Klio* 31 (1938) 105–7; the eclipse of the sun which Dio 78.30.1 says happened just before these events must be an error (5.4.11n). Dio 78.31 is very fragmentary, but suggests that only Gannys (probably the same person as Eutychianus, see Boissevain 3.438), accompanied E. to the camp, but SHA, *Macr.* 9.6, says Maesa and her household went too; the immediate execution of a daughter and son-in-law of Mamaea by Macrinus' prefect, Ulpius Julianus, shows that Maesa and her daughters must have been in the camp very soon after.

[3] The full name and titles taken by E. (though perhaps not until after the final defeat of Macrinus) were *M. Aurelius Antoninus pius felix Augustus* (cf. 5.5.1). Dio calls him Avitus or Pseudantoninus or Assyrius or Sardanapalus or Tiberinus. The date of this salutation is given by Dio 78.31.4 as 16th May 218.

στρατόπεδον Ἀντωνῖνον προσηγόρευσαν, τῇ τε πορφυρᾷ[1] χλαμύδι περιβαλόντες εἶχον ἔνδον. πάντα δὲ τὰ ἐπιτήδεια καὶ παῖδας καὶ γυναῖκας, ὅσα τε[2] εἶχον ἐν κώμαις ἢ ἀγροῖς τοῖς πλησίον, εἰσκομίσαντες, τάς τε πύλας ἀποκλείσαντες, παρεσκεύαζον ἑαυτοὺς ὡς, εἰ δέοι, ὑπομενοῦντες πολιορκίαν.

4. ὡς δὲ[3] ταῦτα ἀπηγγέλη τῷ Μακρίνῳ ἐν Ἀντιοχείᾳ διατρίβοντι, ἥ τε φήμη διέδραμεν ἀνὰ τὰ λοιπὰ στρατόπεδα ὅτι τε Ἀντωνίνου υἱὸς εὑρέθη καὶ ὅτι ἡ Ἰουλίας ἀδελφὴ χρήματα δίδωσι, πάντα τὰ λεγόμενα καὶ ἐνδεχόμενα καὶ ἀληθῆ
2 πιστεύσαντες εἶναι τὰς ψυχὰς ἐξεπτόηντο. ἐνῆγε δ' αὐτοὺς καὶ ἀνέπειθεν ἐς πραγμάτων καινοτομίαν τό τε Μακρίνου μῖσος καὶ[4] τὸ[5] Ἀντωνίνου τῆς μνήμης πάθος,[4] καὶ πρό γε ἁπάντων ἡ τῶν χρημάτων ἐλπίς ὡς πολλοὺς καὶ αὐτομολοῦντας φοιτᾶν πρὸς τὸν νέον Ἀντωνῖνον. ὁ δὲ Μακρῖνος καταφρονῶν τοῦ πράγματος ὡς παιδαριώδους, χρώμενός τε τῇ συνήθει ῥαθυμίᾳ,[6] αὐτὸς μὲν οἴκοι μένει, πέμπει δὲ ἕνα τῶν ⟨ἐπ⟩αρχόντων[7] τοῦ στρατοπέδου, δύναμιν δοὺς ὅσην ᾤετο ῥᾷστα

---

1 AJo τήν τε πορφύραν Oi   2 om φgl καὶ ὅσα A
3 Jo δὴ Oi
4 καὶ ἡ ἀντ. μνήμη καὶ ὁ πόθος A
5 om Ogl   6 Jo προθυμία Oi
7 Mendelss ἀρχόντων Oi ἐπάρχων Jo

26

perial purple cloak on him, they kept him in the
camp. Then they moved all their supplies and
children and wives from the settlements and land
near by into the camp, before shutting the gates
and preparing to withstand a siege if necessary.

4. As the news reached Macrinus while he was delaying in Antioch, the rumours also spread throughout the rest of the army that a son of Antoninus had
been found and that the sister of Julia was distributing money. The soldiers accepted the likeli-
hood of all the rumours and believed them true. So
their spirits rose. But it was their hatred for Macri- 2
nus and devotion to the memory of Antoninus which
was a persuasive inducement for them to rebel.
And, of course, there was the lure of money, above all
else, which resulted in many of them going as deserters to join the new Antoninus. Macrinus discounted the affair as child's play and carried on with
his usual life of leisure,[1] personally remaining at home
and sending one of his prefects with a force he
thought was enough to wipe out the rebels easily.

[1] A good example of the way in which the stereotype of the
unsuccessful emperor distorts the truth. In fact M. seems to
have reacted immediately the news from Raphaneae reached
him about 18th May (ninety miles from Antioch); a message
was sent to the prefect Julianus who was in the vicinity of
Raphaneae, but he had already taken action and been defeated
(next note); this news probably reached M. about 20th May,
and he at once left for Apamea to secure the loyalty of legio II
Parthica. But soon after reaching Apamea he discovered
Julianus had been murdered (Dio 78.34.4) so he returned to
Antioch about 27th May (three days march each way and a
day at Apamea). This gave M. less than two weeks to collect
his forces for the final battle; cf. Petrikovits, *Klio* 31 (1938)
105–7 who varies from these dates slightly.

3 ἐκπορθήσειν τοὺς ἀφεστῶτας. ὡς δ' ἦλθεν Ἰου-
λιανός (τοῦτο γὰρ ἦν ὄνομα τῷ ἐπάρχῳ) καὶ
προσέβαλε [1] τοῖς τείχεσιν, ἔνδοθεν οἱ [2] στρατιῶται
ἀνελθόντες ἐπί τε τοὺς πύργους καὶ τὰς ἐπάλξεις
τόν τε παῖδα τῷ ἔξωθεν πολιορκοῦντι στρατῷ
ἐδείκνυσαν, Ἀντωνίνου υἱὸν εὐφημοῦντες, βαλάντιά
τε χρημάτων μεστὰ [3] δέλεαρ προδοσίας αὐτοῖς
4 ἐδείκνυσαν.[4] οἱ δὲ πιστεύσαντες Ἀντωνίνου τε
εἶναι τέκνον καὶ ὁμοιότατόν γε (βλέπειν γὰρ οὕτως
ἤθελον) τοῦ μὲν Ἰουλιανοῦ τὴν κεφαλὴν ἀποτέ-
μνουσι καὶ πέμπουσι τῷ Μακρίνῳ, αὐτοὶ δὲ πάντες
ἀνοιχθεισῶν αὐτοῖς τῶν πυλῶν ἐς τὸ στρατόπεδον
ἐδέχθησαν. οὕτως ἡ δύναμις αὐξηθεῖσα οὐ μόνον
ἦν πρὸς τὸ ἀπομάχεσθαι πολιορκίαν [5] ἀλλὰ καὶ
πρὸς τὸ συστάδην καὶ ἐξ ἀντιστάσεως ἀγωνίζεσθαι
ἀξιόχρεως· ἔτι τε καὶ τῶν αὐτομόλων τὸ πλῆθος
ἑκάστοτε, εἰ καὶ κατ' ὀλίγους προσιόν, τὴν δύναμιν
ηὔξησεν.

[1] -βαλλε φι   [2] οἱ ἔνδοθεν Jo ἔνδον οἱ A
[3] μετὰ a   [4] ἐδείκνυον Jo
[5] Schwartz πολιορκίᾳ Oi

[1] Ulpius Julianus; Pflaum, *Carrières*, no. 288; like his col-
league, Julianus Nestor, he had been *praefectus peregrinorum*
(Dio 78.15.1), then *a censibus* (perhaps in Syria) and had been
part of the *factio* that supported M. (4.12.8n). The details of
the attack are vividly recounted by Dio 78.32, who says that

28

When the prefect (whose name was Julianus)[1] 3
arrived at the camp, he made an assault on the walls,
but the troops inside came up on to the turrets and
battlements, and displayed the boy to the besieging
army, honouring him with the title of son of Antoninus and also showing the attackers their purses
full of money as a bait to make them desert. As 4
Macrinus' troops were convinced that the boy
was the son of Antoninus and even resembled him
closely (since this was what they wanted to see),
they cut off Julianus' head and sent it back to
Macrinus,[2] while the gates of the camp were thrown
open and the troops welcomed in. As a result, the
forces there were increased to a size which was able
not only to keep off a siege but also to fight a pitched
battle at close quarters. Every day the number of
deserters increased the total force, even though they
came in small groups.

the camp might have been taken if Julianus had pressed home
the advantage gained from his Moroccan soldiers; these
soldiers, specially raised by Caracalla, and naturally loyal to
their countryman, Macrinus, are probably the (*seniores* and)
iuniores regiments of *equites* and *pedites* recorded on *ILS* 1356;
cf. Pflaum, *Carrières* 810–11. Julianus was already near
Raphaneae, Dio 78.31.4.

[2] Julianus managed to escape from the battle, but on
arriving at Apamea was murdered by the soldiers of the legio
II Parthica; M. was shown the head soon after his arrival at
Apamea; Dio 78.34.4–5. The Parthian legion was rewarded
for its defection by the title of Antoniniana and later *c*. 220
with *pia fidelis felix aeterna*; Ritterling, *RE* (legio) 1479 ff.,
CIL XIV. 2257. Pflaum, *Carrières*, no. 290, plausibly suggests
(though on very little evidence) that the *praefectus* of the
legion was P. Valerius Comazon, later promoted to praetorian
prefect, consul and three times urban prefect; Dio 79.4.1–2
(who says he was " prefect of the camp ").

5 ὁ δὲ Μακρῖνος ὡς ταῦτα ἐπυνθάνετο, ἀθροίσας πάντα ὃν εἶχε στρατόν. ἐπῄει [1] ὡς δὴ πολιορκήσων τοὺς ἐκείνῳ προσκεχωρηκότας. ὁ δὲ Ἀντωνῖνος, οὐκ ἀναμενόντων τῶν σὺν αὐτῷ στρατιωτῶν πολιορκηθῆναι, θαρρησάντων δὲ μετὰ πάσης προθυμίας ἐξελθεῖν τε καὶ ὑπαντώμενοι τῷ Μακρίνῳ ἐκ παρατάξεως ἀγωνίζεσθαι, ἐξάγει τὴν αὑτοῦ

6 δύναμιν. συμμίξαντα δὲ ἀλλήλοις τὰ στρατόπεδα Φοινίκης τε καὶ Συρίας ἐν μεθορίοις, οἱ μὲν ὑπὲρ τοῦ Ἀντωνίνου προθύμως ἠγωνίζοντο, δεδιότες, εἰ ἡττηθεῖεν, τὴν ἐφ᾽ οἷς ἔδρασαν τιμωρίαν ἀναδέξασθαι· οἱ δὲ σὺν τῷ Μακρίνῳ ῥᾳθυμότερον προσεφέροντο τῷ ἔργῳ, ἀποδιδράσκοντες καὶ μετιόντες

7 πρὸς τὸν Ἀντωνῖνον. ἅπερ ὁρῶν ὁ Μακρῖνος, φοβηθείς τε μὴ παντάπασι γυμνωθεὶς τῆς δυνάμεως

---

[1] ἀπῄει Jo

---

[1] For M.'s movements, see 5.4.1n; on arrival at Apamea he tried to win the Parthian legion by naming his son, Diadumenianus, Augustus and distributing a massive donative (5.2.5n), as well as promising to restore privileges and ration allowances; Dio 78.34.2 ff. The soldiers took the money and then showed M. the head of Julianus. M. at once returned to Antioch and the Parthian legion soon after joined the troops at Raphaneae (perhaps the date was 30th May, recorded later by the *fratres Arvales* in honour of E. and Maesa; *CIL* VI. 2104 *b*. 23). M. must have sent for reinforcements from the other Syrian legions, but, apart from the fact that they were also canvassed by Elagabalus (Dio 78.34.6–7), the nearest

After the news of this further development, 5
Macrinus mustered his entire army [1] and advanced
with the intention of laying siege to the soldiers who
had defected. But Antoninus brought his force out of
the camp because the troops, without waiting for the
siege, were full of enthusiasm and confidence about
marching out to meet Macrinus in a pitched battle.
The two armies met on the borders of Phoenicia and 6
Syria.[2] Antoninus' forces put up an intense resistance because they were afraid that, if they were defeated, they would be punished for their past action.
Macrinus' troops by contrast brought little energy
to the fight and changed sides as deserters to Antoninus.[3] When he saw this, Macrinus was afraid 7
that, abandoned by all his troops, he would be taken

legion, IV Scythica, was 120 miles away at Zeugma; XVI
Flavia was at Samosata.
   [2] While M. mustered support in Antioch, E. was joined by
legio II Parthica and then marched North, obviously with the
intention of bringing M. to battle before reinforcements could
arrive; the battle was not on the border of Syria Coele and
Syria Phoenice, but at a village twenty-four miles outside
Antioch (Honigmann, *RE* (Syria) 1692, conjectures Immae).
Downey, *Hist. of Antioch* 249–50, argues from Dio 78.34.5
that there were two battles, but Dio explicitly says M. avoided
battle when in Apamea. The battle on 8th June 218 is
described by Dio 78.37.3–39.1.
   [3] M. probably relied mainly on the praetorian cohorts and
the special bodyguard of *equites singulares*, though he could
call upon the Moroccan auxiliaries too (5.4.3n). E. was supported mainly by two legions, probably slightly outnumber-
ing the opposition. Dio 78.38.4 says that E.'s troops, led by
Gannys, showed lack of fighting spirit, and would have been
defeated but for the flight of M. Is this credible? Much
more probably M. left the field after an indecisive battle in
order to rally support in Antioch (Dio 78.39.1), but the
praetorians defected in his absence.

αἰχμάλωτός τε ληφθεὶς αἰσχίστως ὑβρισθείη, ἔτι
τῆς μάχης συνεστώσης, ἑσπέρας ἤδη προσιούσης,[1]
ἀπορρίψας τὸ χλαμύδιον καὶ εἴ τι σχῆμα βασιλικὸν
περιέκειτο, λαθὼν ἀποδιδράσκει σὺν ὀλίγοις ἑκατοντάρχαις, οὓς πιστοτάτους ᾤετο, τὸ γένειον
ἀποκειράμενος, ὡς μὴ γνωρίζοιτο, ἐσθῆτά τε
ὁδοιπορικὴν λαβὼν καὶ τὴν κεφαλὴν ἀεὶ σκέπων.
8 νύκτωρ τε καὶ μεθ' ἡμέραν ὡδοιπόρει, φθάνων τὴν
φήμην τῆς ἑαυτοῦ τύχης, τῶν τε ἑκατοντάρχων
μεγάλῃ σπουδῇ τὰ ὀχήματα ἐπειγόντων, ὡς ἂν
ὑπὸ Μακρίνου ἔτι βασιλεύοντος ἐπί τινα σπουδαῖα
πεμφθέντων.

ὁ μὲν οὖν ἔφυγεν, ὡς εἴρηται· ὁ δὲ στρατὸς
ἑκατέρωθεν ἐμάχοντο, ὑπὲρ μὲν [2] τοῦ Μακρίνου οἱ
σωματοφύλακες καὶ δορυφόροι, οὓς δὴ πραιτωριανοὺς καλοῦσιν, οἳ γενναίως ἀνθεστήκεσαν παντὶ
τῷ ἄλλῳ στρατῷ ἅτε ὄντες μέγιστοί τε καὶ
ἐπίλεκτοι· τὸ δὲ ἐπίλοιπον πᾶν πλῆθος ὑπὲρ τοῦ
9 Ἀντωνίνου ἠγωνίζοντο. ὡς δὲ ἐπὶ πολὺ τὸν Μακρῖνον οὐκ ἔβλεπον οἱ ὑπὲρ αὐτοῦ μαχόμενοι οὐδὲ
τὰ τῆς βασιλείας σύμβολα, διηπόρουν δὴ [3] ποῦ
ποτὲ ἄρα εἴη, πότερον ἐν τῷ πλήθει τῶν κειμένων
ἢ ἀποδρὰς ᾤχετο, ἠγνόουν τε πῶς χρήσονται τῷ
πράγματι· οὔτε γὰρ μάχεσθαι ἤθελον ὑπὲρ τοῦ
μὴ παρόντος, παραδοῦναι δὲ [4] αὑτοὺς ἐκδότους

---

[1] ἑσπέρας—προσιούσης om P

prisoner and badly molested. So, while the battle
still continued, towards evening he took off his cloak
and the various imperial insignia he was wearing,
shaved off his beard to avoid recognition and put on
the clothes of an ordinary traveller,[1] keeping his head
covered all the time. With a few centurions who
he believed were completely trustworthy he quietly
ran away. Journeying night and day, he travelled 8
further than the news of his own disaster. The centurions energetically urged on the carriage as though
Macrinus were still emperor and had dispatched them
upon an important mission.

After Macrinus' flight (mentioned above) both
armies continued the battle. On Macrinus' side the
personal bodyguard and the palace soldiers (called
praetorians),[2] who were very tall, picked soldiers,
fought magnificently against the opposing army.
Otherwise the mass of soldiers took Antoninus'
side. But when, after a period, Macrinus' troops 9
failed to see him or the imperial standards, they
were in a quandary, wondering where he could be,
and whether he was among the many dead or had
taken to his heels. And how were they to react in
that case, since they were not willing to fight a battle
for someone not there, and were ashamed to surrender

[1] The black *paenula*, a cloak worn by private citizens and
plebeians. The disguise was that of a *tabellarius*, thereby
giving M. access to the imperial post.
[2] If this is not a gloss in the text, what kind of an audience
would not have known about the praetorian guard? Cf.
1.12.6 for H.'s commendable care in trying to distinguish
different bodies of imperial guard.

----

[2] om φi   [3] δὲ Bi om A   [4] τε A

10 καὶ [1] ὥσπερ αἰχμαλώτους ᾐδοῦντο. ὡς δὲ παρὰ
τῶν αὐτομόλων ἐπύθετο Ἀντωνῖνος τὴν τοῦ Μακρίνου φυγήν, πέμψας κήρυκας διδάσκει αὐτοὺς ὅτι
μάτην ὑπὲρ ἀνάνδρου καὶ φυγάδος μάχονται,
ἄδειάν τε καὶ ἀμνηστίαν ἐνόρκως ὑπισχνεῖται,
καλεῖ τε καὶ αὐτὸν δορυφορήσοντας. οἱ μὲν οὖν
πεισθέντες προσεχώρησαν,[2] ὁ δὲ Ἀντωνῖνος πέμπει
τοὺς διώξοντας [3] τὸν Μακρῖνον πολὺ προκεχωρη-
11 κότα. ἐν Χαλκηδόνι γοῦν τῆς Βιθυνίας κατελήφθη,
νοσῶν χαλεπώτατα ὑπό τε τῆς συνεχοῦς ὁδοιπορίας
συντετριμμένος. ἔνθα αὐτὸν εὑρόντες ἔν τινι
κρυπτόμενον προαστείῳ οἱ διώκοντες τὴν κεφαλὴν
ἀπέτεμον. ἐλέγετο δὲ σπεύδειν ἐς τὴν Ῥώμην,
θαρρῶν τῇ τοῦ δήμου περὶ αὐτὸν σπουδῇ· περαιού-
μενον δ’ αὐτὸν ἐς τὴν Εὐρώπην διὰ τοῦ στενοῦ τῆς
Προποντίδος πορθμοῦ, ἤδη τε τῷ Βυζαντίῳ προσ-
πελάζοντα, φασὶν ἀντιπνοίᾳ χρήσασθαι, ἐπανάγον-
12 τος αὐτὸν τοῦ πνεύματος ἐς τὴν τιμωρίαν. παρὰ
τοσοῦτον μὲν δὴ Μακρῖνος οὐκ ἐξέφυγε τοὺς
διώξαντας, τέλει τε ἐχρήσατο αἰσχρῷ ὕστερον

[1] ἐκδότους καὶ om φ
[2] προεχ. gl
[3] διώξαντας gl

---

[1] Dio 78.39.1 ff. says M. returned first to Antioch, claiming
a victory; when news of the praetorians' collapse came he left,

as prisoners of war ? When Antoninus heard from de- 10
serters the news of Macrinus' flight, he sent her-
alds to tell the troops that they were wasting their
time fighting for a cowardly fugitive. He gave a
solemn undertaking that they would be pardoned
under an amnesty, and called on them to serve him
too as guards. Convinced by the offer, they joined
his side, while Antoninus dispatched men to pursue
Macrinus, by now well in advance of them. In the 11
end he was captured at Chalcedon in Bithynia
suffering severe exhaustion from the continuous
travelling. His pursuers found him hiding in a district just outside the city and decapitated him.[1]
The information has it that he was hurrying to Rome,
confident of popular support for himself. But, they
say, after he had set sail for Europe across the narrow
straights of Propontis and had practically reached
Byzantium, he met a contrary wind which blew him
back to his fate; so near was Macrinus to escaping 12
his pursuers. The unhappy end he met was after
he later decided to do what he should have done in the

travelling through Cilicia, Cappadocia, Galatia and Bithynia
to Eribolon, the port of Nicomedia, from where he sailed to
Chalcedon. Arrested in Chalcedon, M. was escorted back, but
killed by one of his guard in Cappadocia. At the least M.'s
death must have been one month after the battle of 8th June;
Dio 78.40.1 says the body was seen by E. on the march north-
wards to winter quarters in Bithynia with two legions (III
Gallica and IV Scythica) some months later. A later
tradition says M. was killed at Archelaïs in Cappadocia; cf.
Mommsen, *Chron. Min*. I. 147, 435, etc. This suggests M.
was on the run for a long time, and may explain Dio's reference
to an eclipse of the sun (7th October 218); cf. 5.3.11n. It
would also explain why E. was so long returning to Rome
(5.5.8n).

θελήσας ἐς τὴν Ῥώμην ἀνελθεῖν, δέον ἐν ἀρχῇ
τοῦτο ποιῆσαι· ὁμοῦ δὲ ἔπταισε καὶ γνώμῃ καὶ
τύχῃ.

τέλει μὲν δὴ τοιούτῳ Μακρῖνος ἐχρήσατο,
συναιρεθέντος αὐτῷ καὶ τοῦ παιδός, ὃν ἦν
ποιήσας Καίσαρα, Διαδουμενιανὸν [1] καλούμενον·
5. ἐπεὶ δὲ ὅ τε στρατὸς πᾶς μετελθὼν πρὸς τὸν
Ἀντωνῖνον προσεῖπε βασιλέα, τά τε τῆς ἀρχῆς
ὑπεδέξατο,[2] διοικηθέντων αὐτῷ κατὰ τὴν ἀνατολὴν
τῶν ἐπειγόντων ὑπό τε τῆς μάμμης καὶ τῶν
συνόντων φίλων (αὐτὸς γὰρ ἦν νέος τε τὴν
ἡλικίαν, πραγμάτων τε καὶ παιδείας [3] ἄπειρος),
οὐ πολλοῦ χρόνου διατρίψας εἶχε περὶ ἔξοδον,
σπευδούσης μάλιστα τῆς Μαίσης ἐς τὰ συνήθη
2 ἑαυτῇ [4] βασίλεια Ῥώμης. ὡς δὲ τῇ τε συγκλήτῳ
καὶ τῷ Ῥωμαίων δήμῳ τὰ πραχθέντα ἐδηλώθη,
δυσφόρως μὲν πάντες ἤκουσαν, ὑπήκουον δὲ ἀν-

---

[1] διαδομενιανὸν O
[2] ⟨ἐκεῖνος⟩ ὑπεδέξ. Steph
[3] καὶ παιδείας om P
[4] ἑαυτῆς O

---

[1] See 4.15.9n for an explanation of M.'s delay. The conjecture that M. went to the Danube provinces is improbable;
but he did send two of his most trusted supporters, Aelius
Triccianus and Marcius Agrippa (cf. 4.14.2n) to Pannonia and

first place by returning to Rome.[1] Both his judgement and his luck failed.

And so Macrinus died. With him was executed his
son Diadumenianus, whom he had made Caesar.[2]
5. After the whole army had changed its allegiance to
Antoninus and proclaimed him as emperor,[3] he accepted the rule. The immediate business in the East
was dealt with by his grandmother and his circle of
advisers because he was young and without administrative experience or education. But he did not
delay long in setting out for Rome,[4] where Maesa
particularly was anxious to get to the imperial palace
she had been used to. When a report of the events 2
reached the senate and people of Rome, there was
general gloom at the news, but they were forced to

Dacia; Dio 78.13.3, cf. 78.27.5; his interest in the frontier
may also be illustrated by the appearance of a woman re-
presenting Moesia Inferior on coins; Gerassimov, *Bull. Inst.
Arch. Bulg.* 27 (1946) 251–3; cf. Mattingly, *Studies D. M.
Robinson* II. 965.

[2] M. Opellius Antoninus Diadumenianus was given the title
of Caesar and Antoninus in 217 (5.1.1n); H. seems not to
know of his elevation to Augustus, which had taken place
hurriedly at Apamea (5.4.5n); although the title Augustus
appears on coins, it was probably never confirmed by the
senate before M.'s defeat; the *congiarium* recorded by SHA,
Diad. 2.9, and *Chronog. of 354* (and on coins) was almost
certainly distributed in Antioch; *BMC* V. 511, no. 95,
McDonald, *Coins in the Hunterian Coll.* III. 174–5.

[3] The term used by H. is *basileus*; strictly the soldiers would
have declared him *imperator*; cf. 2.2.9n.

[4] Cf. 5.4.11n. Dio 79.3.1 says E. remained in Antioch for
some months. He seems to have been in no hurry either to
get to Asia Minor, or to leave Nicomedia for Rome; 5.5.8n,
Dio 79.3.2. The formal " haste " to get to Rome is noted in
1.7.2.

HERODIAN

ἀγκῇ τοῦ στρατοῦ ταῦτα ᾑρημένου. κατεγίνωσκόν
τε τοῦ Μακρίνου ῥᾳθυμίαν τε καὶ τρόπων χαυνό-
τητα, αἴτιόν τε οὐκ ἄλλον ἀλλ᾽ ἢ αὐτὸν ἑαυτῷ
γεγενῆσθαι ἔλεγον.

3 ὁ δὲ Ἀντωνῖνος ἀπάρας τῆς Συρίας ἐλθών τε [1]
ἐς τὴν Νικομήδειαν ἐχείμαζε, τῆς ὥρας τοῦ ἔτους
οὕτως ἀπαιτούσης. εὐθέως τε ἐξεβακχεύετο,[2] τήν
τε ἱερωσύνην τοῦ ἐπιχωρίου θεοῦ, ᾗ ἐντέθραπτο,
περιεργότερον ἐξωρχεῖτο,[3] σχήμασί τε ἐσθῆτος
πολυτελεστάτοις[4] χρώμενος, διά τε πορφύρας
⟨καὶ⟩[5] χρυσοῦ ὑφάσμένοις[6] περιδεραίοις τε καὶ
ψελίοις κοσμούμενος, ἐς εἶδος δὲ [7] τιάρας στεφά-
νην[8] ἐπικείμενος χρυσῷ καὶ λίθοις ποικίλην
4 τιμίοις.[9] ἦν τε αὐτῷ τὸ σχῆμα μεταξὺ Φοινίσσης

---

1 Steph δὲ Oi   2 ἐξ εβάκχευεν Jo
3 Sylb ἐξώρχητο Oi   4 Sylb -της Oi
5 Irmisc cf. 5.8.6 διαχρύσοις τε πορφύρας Reisk
6 Irmisc ὑφάσμασι Oi   7 om O
8 Steph -άνους Ogl -άνη a
9 Steph ποικίλοις τιμίοις i ποικίλοις O

---

1 Dio 79.1.2 says a letter was immediately sent to the
senate (soon after the battle of 8th June) in which E. reviled
M. and claimed for himself the titles of *imperator Caesar
Antonini filius Severi nepos pius felix Augustus* and *procos.
trib. pot.* before they were voted by the senate; the date of
E.'s co-option into the *frates Arvales* is given as 14th July 218
(*CIL* VI. 2104 *b.* 33), which may be the *dies imperii* of the
senate's confirmation of titles; cf. *CIL* VI. 2001, 2009 for the
titles of *procos.* and *pius felix* on the priestly records. The
consular title of M. was assumed by E., says Dio 79.8.1–2,
though the coins seem to indicate this did not happen at once;
BMC V. 530.
2 Initial enthusiasm for E. (SHA, *Elag.* 3.1 ff.) wore off by

submit to the course decided by the army.[1] They blamed Macrinus' lack of energy and moral fibre and said he had no one to blame but himself.

Setting out from Syria, Antoninus reached Nico- 3 media, where he was forced by the season of the year to spend the winter.[2] Straight away he began to practise his ecstatic rites and go through the ridiculous motions of the priestly office belonging to his local god in which he had been trained. He wore the most expensive types of clothes, woven of purple and gold, and adorned himself with necklaces and bangles. On his head he wore a crown in the shape of a tiara glittering with gold and precious stones. The effect 4

the winter (Dio 78.39.4). The disturbed state of the legions in the East is recorded by Dio 79.7.1–3; legio III Gallica, legio IV Scythica and the fleet at Cyzicus all produced claimants for the purple; Gannys, E.'s original supporter and choice for Caesar, was executed; legio III Gallica was disbanded (5.3.9n); legio IV Scythica was given an extraordinary equestrian legatus (Pflaum, *Carrières*, no. 293, a *comes* and *amicus* of E. who later became praetorian prefect). There was a wholesale removal of M.'s supporters from office for fear of armed rebellion—Fabius Agrippa (legatus of Syria Coele), Pica Caerianus (legatus of Arabia), Claudius Attalus (proconsul of Cyprus), Aelius Triccianus (legatus of Pannonia Inferior), M. Munatius Sulla Cerialis (legatus of Cappadocia). In Rome a number of the old aristocracy were executed— Seius Carus, L. Valerius Paetus, M. Silius Messala, Pomponius Bassus; two were from the old Antonine junta, two had strong connections in the East (cf. Introduction, p. lxxxi). In their places the Syrian princesses put a number of their own new equestrians; e.g. Ulpius Victor as procurator *agens vice praesidis* in Dacia Porolissensis (Pflaum, *Carrières*, no. 257), M. Aedinius Julianus procurator *agens vice praesidis* in Aquitania (Pflaum, *Marbre de Thorigny* 35–9), C. Furius Sabinus Aquila Timesitheus, the later prefect, as procurator *agens vice praesidis* in Arabia (Pflaum, *Carrières*, no. 317).

ἱερᾶς στολῆς καὶ χλιδῆς Μηδικῆς. Ῥωμαϊκὴν δὲ
ἢ Ἑλληνικὴν [1] πᾶσαν ἐσθῆτα ἐμυσάττετο, ἐρίου
φάσκων εἰργάσθαι, πράγματος εὐτελοῦς· τοῖς δὲ
Σηρῶν [2] ὑφάσμασι μόνοις ἠρέσκετο. προῄει τε
ὑπὸ αὐλοῖς καὶ τυμπάνοις, τῷ θεῷ δῆθεν ὀργιάζων.
5 ἡ δὲ Μαῖσα ταῦτα ὁρῶσα πάνυ ἤσχαλλε, πείθειν
τε λιπαροῦσα ἐπειρᾶτο μεταμφιέσασθαι τὴν
Ῥωμαίων στολὴν μέλλοντά [τε] [3] ἐς τὴν πόλιν
ἀφίξεσθαι καὶ ἐς τὴν σύγκλητον εἰσελεύσεσθαι, μὴ
ἀλλοδαπὸν ἢ παντάπασι βάρβαρον τὸ σχῆμα
ὀφθὲν εὐθὺς λυπήσῃ τοὺς ἰδόντας, ἀήθεις τε ὄντας
καὶ οἰομένους τὰ τοιαῦτα καλλωπίσματα οὐκ
6 ἀνδράσιν ἀλλὰ θηλείαις πρέπειν. ὁ δὲ καταφρονή-
σας τῶν ὑπὸ τῆς πρεσβύτιδος λεχθέντων, μηδ'
ἄλλῳ τινὶ πεισθείς (οὐδὲ γὰρ προσίετο εἰ μὴ τοὺς
ὁμοιοτρόπους τε καὶ κόλακας αὐτοῦ τῶν ἁμαρτημά-

---

[1] Steph ῥωμαϊκῆς δὲ ἢ ἑλληνικῆς Οἱ
[2] συρῶν a   [3] om Jo Mendelss

---

[1] The name Mede may indicate that H. is recalling a
classical model such as Xen. *Cyrop.* 1.3.2 or 4.5.54, which
suggests to him the vocabulary he is using (cf. 4.2.10n).
Similar passages are suggested by Irmisch *ad loc.*
[2] The Chinese name for silk was "sir", from which was derived the name for both Chinese (*Seres*) and silk (*sericum*).
In Rome (*sericum*) was not always pure silk, but a combination of silk, linen and cotton. Caligula appeared in
public wearing this silk (Suet. *Gaius* 52) which had been
forbidden by Tiberius (Tac. *A.* 2.33.1). SHA, *Elag.* 26.1, says
E. appeared wearing pure silk.
[3] The dominant position of Maesa is noted by all sources;

was something between the sacred garb of the Phoenicians and the luxurious apparel of the Medes.[1] Any Roman or Greek dress he loathed because, he claimed, it was made out of wool, which is a cheap material. Only seric silk was good enough for him.[2] He appeared in public accompanied by flutes and drums, no doubt because he was honouring his god with special rites.

Maesa [3] was extremely worried when she saw this, 5 and continually tried to persuade him to change into Roman clothes now that he was going to come to Rome and enter the senate house. If he was wearing a strange, completely barbarous dress, he would straight away offend the spectators who were not used to it [4] and considered this kind of finery more appropriate for women than men. But Antoninus 6 rejected the advice of the old woman and anyone else's attempts to persuade him. No one was admitted to his presence except men of similar habit and those who flattered his faults. However, he was

Dio (Xiph.) 79.17.2, SHA, *Elag.* 12.3 (4.2 seems an error), *BMC* V. ccxxxiii (the only Augusta to issue double denarii). She was named *mater castrorum* in 218; *AE* (1955) 260.

[4] There was nothing strange about eastern religious practices in Rome; cf. Caracalla's forshadowing of *sol* Elagabalus and Athena (Allāt), the moon goddess, by his coin issues; *BMC* V. 465, no. 195 (cf. Dio (Xiph.) 77.10.3), 486, no. 283. The solar symbol of a radiate lion may even be a particular reference to C.'s visit to Emesa in 215 (*BMC* V. ccvii, *RIC* IV. 3.204–5). E.'s real fault lay in making no concession to Roman tradition when introducing the local Syrian cult. Supersession of Jupiter Optimus Maximus, introduction of cult practices like circumcision, abstention from pork and foreign dress were bound to offend upper-class sensibilities.

των). βουλόμενος ἐν ἔθει γενέσθαι τῆς τοῦ
σχήματος ὄψεως τήν τε σύγκλητον καὶ τὸν δῆμον
Ῥωμαίων, ἀπόντος τε αὐτοῦ πεῖραν δοθῆναι πῶς
φέρουσι τὴν ὄψιν [τοῦ σχήματος],[1] εἰκόνα μεγίστην
γράψας παντὸς ἑαυτοῦ, οἷος προϊών [2] τε καὶ
ἱερουργῶν ἐφαίνετο, παραστήσας τε ἐν τῇ γραφῇ
τὸν τύπον τοῦ ἐπιχωρίου θεοῦ, ᾧ δὴ καλλιερῶν [3]
7 ἐγέγραπτο, πέμψας τε ἐς τὴν Ῥώμην, ἐκέλευσεν
ἐν τῷ μεσαιτάτῳ τῆς συγκλήτου τόπῳ ὑψηλοτάτῳ
τε τὴν εἰκόνα ἀνατεθῆναι ὑπὲρ κεφαλῆς τοῦ
ἀγάλματος τῆς νίκης, ᾧ [4] συνιόντες ἐς τὸ βουλευτήριον λιβανωτόν τε θυμιῶσιν ἕκαστος καὶ
οἴνους [5] σπένδουσι. προσέταξέ τε πάντας τοὺς
Ῥωμαίων ἄρχοντας, καὶ εἴ τινες δημοσίας θυσίας
ἐπιτελοῦσι, πρὸ τῶν ἄλλων θεῶν οὓς δὴ καλοῦσιν
ἱερουργοῦντες,[6] ὀνομάζειν τὸν νέον θεὸν Ἐλαιαγά-
βαλον.[7] ὡς δὲ ἐς τὴν Ῥώμην ἀφίκετο τῷ προειρημένῳ σχήματι, οὐδὲν παράδοξον εἶδον οἱ
8 Ῥωμαῖοι, τῇ γραφῇ ἐνειθισμένοι. δοὺς δὲ τὰς

---

[1] om? Mendelss πεῖραν—σχήματος om A
[2] Steph προσιών Oi
[3] καλλιεργῶν Bi
[4] Mendelss ὡς Oi
[5] οἴνου a
[6] P -οῦντας Oi
[7] Stav ἐλεγάβαλον Oi

anxious that the senate and people of Rome should get used to seeing his dress, and to test out their reactions to the sight before he arrived. So an enormous picture was painted of him as he appeared in public performing as a priest. Also in the picture was a portrait of the Emesene god, to whom he was represented making a favourable sacrifice. The 7 picture was sent to Rome with orders that it should hang right in the middle of the senate house, very high up over the head of the statue of Victory.[1] This was where all the members, on arrival for meetings at the house, burn an offering of incense and make a libation of wine. Instructions were also issued to every Roman magistrate or person conducting public sacrifices that the new god Elagabalus' name should precede any of the others invoked by the officiating priests.[2] When Antoninus arrived at Rome, dressed as has been described, the Romans, conditioned by the painting, found nothing strange in the sight. He paid the people the cash bonus normal at the ac- 8

[1] The statue of victory probably rested on the plinth discovered in the *curia Julia* on the podium of the presidential seat, just inside the doors; cf. Bartoli, *Rend. Pont. Accad.* 27 (1951/2) 47-54, who discusses a mutilated inscription to the *domus divina* set up perhaps in the senate at the same time. The religious " programme " coins do not begin in Rome until 220, though in the East the *sol* propaganda starts in 218/9; *BMC* V. 574 ff.

[2] This desire for supremacy of the Emesene god motivates most of E.'s policy, but not with any obvious political intention; cf. Dio (Xiph.) 79.11.1 (greater than Jupiter), SHA, *Elag.* 3.4, 6.7, 7.4 (other gods as slaves and E.'s desire for monotheism); hence the symbolic unions of various gods and the transfer of cult objects to Elagabalus; but E. never seems to envisage the cult as a means to imperial unity. See Gross, *Real. f. Antike u. Christentum* IV. 993-4.

HERODIAN

συνήθεις τῷ δήμῳ νομὰς ἐπὶ τῇ τῆς βασιλείας
διαδοχῇ, φιλοτίμως τε καὶ πολυτελῶς [1] ἐπιτελέσας
παντοδαπὰς θέας, νεών τε μέγιστον καὶ κάλλιστον
κατασκευάσας τῷ θεῷ, βωμούς τε πλείστους περὶ
τὸν νεὼν ἱδρύσας, ἑκάστοτε προϊὼν ἔωθεν ἑκατόμβας τε ταύρων καὶ προβάτων πολὺ πλῆθος
κατέσφαττε τοῖς τε βωμοῖς ἐπετίθει, παντοδαποῖς
ἀρώμασι σωρεύων, οἴνου τε τοῦ παλαιοτάτου καὶ
καλλίστου πολλοὺς ἀμφορέας τῶν βωμῶν προχέων,
ὡς ῥεῖθρα φέρεσθαι οἴνου τε καὶ αἵματος μεμιγμέ-
9 νου. περί τε τοὺς βωμοὺς ἐχόρευεν ὑπὸ παντοδαποῖς ἤχοις ὀργάνων, γύναιά τε ἐπιχώρια
ἐχόρευε σὺν αὐτῷ, περιθέοντα τοῖς βωμοῖς,
κύμβαλα ἢ τύμπανα μετὰ χεῖρας φέροντα· περιει-
στήκει δὲ πᾶσα ἡ σύγκλητος καὶ τὸ ἱππικὸν τάγμα
ἐν θεάτρου σχήματι. τὰ δὲ σπλάγχνα τῶν ἱερουρ-
γηθέντων τά τε ἀρώματα ἐν χρυσοῖς σκεύεσιν
ὑπὲρ κεφαλῆς οὐκ οἰκέται δή [2] τινες ἢ εὐτελεῖς
10 ἄνθρωποι ἔφερον, ἀλλ' οἵ τε ἔπαρχοι τῶν στρατοπέδων καὶ οἱ ἐν ταῖς μεγίσταις πράξεσιν,

---

[1] Bekk[2] Bergl φιλοτίμους (also Jo) τε καὶ πολυτελεῖς Oi P
(*omnifariam*)
[2] Steph δὲ φι om A

---

[1] Cf. 5.6.9n. The *congiarium* is recorded on late coins of 219
as *liberalitas* II, the first distribution being in E.'s absence at
his accession; *BMC* V. 546, 661 ff. Evidence for the date of
E.'s return to Rome is weak; Eutropius 8.22 says it was in
July 219, but a dedicatory altar set up by the *equites singulares*

cession of a new emperor,[1] provided lavish and various spectacles to win favour and built an enormous and magnificent temple to his new god, around which he set up many altars.[2] Each day at dawn he came out and slaughtered a hecatomb of cattle and a large number of sheep which were placed upon the altars and loaded with every variety of spices.[3] In front of the altars many jars of the finest and oldest wines were poured out, so that streams of blood and wine flowed together. Around the altars he and some 9 Phoenician women danced to the sounds of many different instruments, circling the altars with cymbals and drums in their hands. The entire senate and the equestrian order stood round them in the order they sat in the theatre. The entrails of the sacrificial victims and spices were carried in golden bowls, not on the heads of household servants or lower-class people, but by military prefects and important officials 10 wearing long tunics in the Phoenician style down to

[1] is dated 29th September *ob reditum domini nostri* (*ILS* 2188); *adventus* coins continue into the types of 220 but are undated, *BMC* V. ccxxxvii, 560, nos. 195–6, 608, *RIC* IV. 2.42, nos. 184–5.

[2] Not apparently the temple mentioned in 5.6.6. This temple here seems to be the temple on the Palatine noted in SHA, *Elag.* 3.4 (i.e. the Heliogabalium); another temple on the site of the old temple of Orcus (SHA, *Elag.* 1.6) is otherwise unknown. Cf. Mommsen, *Chron. Min.* I. 147, for the Heliogabalium.

[3] There are numerous representations of the emperor sacrificing on coins, together with titles such as *sacerd(os) dei solis Elagab(ali)*, *summum sacerdos Aug(ustus)*, etc., *BMC* V. 564–5, 569, 571. The Roman title of *pontifex maximus* is superseded and disappears. Cf. also the title *sacerdos amplissimus dei invicti solis Elagabali* on inscriptions, *ILS* 473, 475, *AE* (1908) 202; Jantsch, *JÖAI* 29 (1935) 265–8.

ἀνεζωσμένοι [οἱ] [1] μὲν χιτῶνας ποδήρεις καὶ
χειριδωτοὺς νόμῳ Φοινίκων, ἐν μέσῳ φέροντες
μίαν πορφύραν· ὑποδήμασι δὲ [2] λίνου πεποιημέ-
νοις ἐχρῶντο, ὥσπερ οἱ κατ᾽ ἐκεῖνα τὰ χωρία
προφητεύοντες. ἐδόκει δὲ τιμὴν μεγίστην νέμειν
οἷς ἐκοινώνει τῆς ἱερουργίας.

6. πλὴν καίτοι χορεύειν ἀεὶ καὶ ἱερουργεῖν δοκῶν,
πλείστους ἀπέκτεινε τῶν ἐνδόξων τε καὶ πλουσίων,
διαβληθέντας αὐτῷ ὡς ἀπαρεσκομένους καὶ σκώ-
πτοντας αὐτοῦ τὸν βίον. ἠγάγετο δὲ γυναῖκα τὴν
εὐγενεστάτην Ῥωμαίων, ἣν Σεβαστὴν ἀναγορεύσας
μετ᾽ ὀλίγον χρόνον ἀπεπέμψατο, ἰδιωτεύειν κελεύ-
2 σας καὶ τῶν τιμῶν παρελόμενος. μετ᾽ ἐκείνην δὲ
προσποιησάμενος ἐρᾶν, ἵνα δὴ καὶ τὰ τῶν ἀνδρῶν
πράττειν δοκοίη, παρθένου τῇ Ῥωμαίων Ἑστίᾳ [3]
ἱερωμένης ἁγνεύειν τε πρὸς τῶν ἱερῶν νόμων
κελευομένης καὶ μέχρι τέλους τοῦ βίου παρθε-
νεύεσθαι, ἀποσπάσας αὐτὴν τῆς Ἑστίας καὶ τοῦ

[1] om Steph and perhaps μὲν also
[2] Reisk from P (sed et) τε Oi
[3] Steph τῆς ῥωμ. ἑστίας Oi

---

[1] The *kalasiris*, described by Hesychius as a tunic with a
broad stripe; it was sometimes completely purple or purple
with a white stripe; the stripe ran from head to toe.

[2] The *phaikas* or *phaikasion* worn in Athens and Egypt,
Appian *BC* 5.11, Plut. *Ant.* 33 (not always made of linen).
The reference to *prophetai* by H. may be just a loose term for
priests.

46

their feet, with long sleeves and a single purple stripe in the middle.[1] They also wore linen shoes of the kind used by local oracle priests in Phoenicia.[2] It was considered a great honour had been done to anyone given a part in the sacrifice.

6. Although the emperor seemed to spend all his time dancing and performing sacrifices, he executed very many distinguished and wealthy men, after information was laid that they disapproved and made fun of his way of life. He married a woman from the most aristocratic family in Rome, whom he named as Augusta;[3] but soon he divorced her and, depriving her of her honours, told her to return to private life. Then, in order to provide a semblance of his virility, 2 he pretended to fall in love with a Vestal Virgin, a priestess of the Roman goddess Vesta, bound by sacral law to remain a pure virgin to the end of her life.[4] This girl was taken away from Vesta's service and the

[3] Julia Cornelia Paula; *PIR*[2] J 660; her name appears on Alexandrian coins before the end of August 219 (year 2 of E.) and continues until 220/1 (year 4); thus she married E. almost as soon as his return (5.5.8n), but since E.'s next wife also appears in year 4, she may have been divorced as early as September 220; cf. Dio (Xiph.) 79.9.1–3; it seems improbable from what H. says that she was related to the jurist (and later prefect?) Julius Paulus.

[4] Julia Aquila Severa; *PIR*[2] J 648; the fact that she was a Vestal Virgin doubtless provided E. with an opportunity to claim that the marriage with this *innupta Minerva* corresponded to the sacred marriage (*hieros gamos*) of the god Elagabalus; but E.'s claim to be in love with her is supported by her return to being his wife after Annia Faustina. E. first married her in year 4 of the Alexandrian coin series (i.e. before September 221), perhaps late in 220; the re-marriage was in year 5, probably between September and November 221; cf. Lederer, *Num. Chron.* (6) 3 (1943) 94–6.

ἱεροῦ παρθενῶνος γυναῖκα ἔθετο, ἐπιστείλας τῇ
συγκλήτῳ καὶ παραμυθησάμενος ἀσέβημά τε καὶ
ἁμάρτημα τηλικοῦτον, φήσας ἀνθρώπινόν τι πεπον-
θέναι πάθος· ἔρωτι γὰρ τῆς κόρης ἑαλωκέναι,
ἁρμόζοντά τε καὶ σεβάσμιον εἶναι γάμον ἱερέως τε
καὶ ἱερείας. πλὴν καὶ ταύτην αὖ [1] μετ᾽ οὐ πολὺ
ἀπεπέμψατο, τρίτην δὲ πάλιν ἠγάγετο, ἀναφέρου-
σαν τὸ γένος ἐς Κόμοδον.

3 ἔπαιζε δὲ γάμους οὐ μόνον ἀνθρωπείους, ἀλλὰ
καὶ τῷ θεῷ, ᾧ ἱεράτευε, γυναῖκα ἐζήτει· καὶ τῆς
τε Παλλάδος τὸ ἄγαλμα, ὃ κρυπτὸν καὶ ἀόρατον
σέβουσι Ῥωμαῖοι, ἐς τὸν ἑαυτοῦ θάλαμον μετή-
γαγε· καὶ μὴ κινηθὲν ἐξ οὗπερ ἦλθεν ἀπὸ Ἰλίου,
εἰ μὴ ὅτε πυρὶ κατεφλέχθη ὁ νεώς, ἐκίνησεν οὗτος,
καὶ πρὸς γάμον δὴ ἐς τὴν βασίλειον αὐλὴν τῷ θεῷ
4 ἀνήγαγε. φήσας δὲ ἀπαρέσκεσθαι αὐτὸν [2] ὡς
πάντα ἐν ὅπλοις καὶ πολεμικῇ θεῷ, τῆς Οὐρανίας
τὸ ἄγαλμα μετεπέμψατο, σεβόντων αὐτὸ ὑπερφυῶς
Καρχηδονίων τε καὶ τῶν κατὰ τὴν Λιβύην

---

[1] Stroth οὐ Oi om Sylb
[2] Gedike αὐτὸν ἢ αὐτῇ g[2] (mg) αὐτῷ Oi

---

[1] Annia Aurelia Faustina; *PIR*[2] A 710; daughter of Ti.
Claudius Severus Proculus (*cos.* 200) and Annia Faustina
(daughter of Ummidius Quadratus, *cos.* 167; cf. 1.8.4n), both
parents being related to M. Aurelius; her husband Pomponius
Bassus was executed by E. (5.5.3n). Some scandalous detail
about this marriage is recounted by Dio 79.5.3–5, but is cut
short by a lacuna. The marriage was in Alexandrian year 4

women's quarters of the temple to be installed as his wife. He sent a letter to the senate excusing his great impiety and sin, but saying he had fallen victim to manly passion and was smitten with love for the girl; marriage between a priest and a priestess, he added, was fitting and sacred. However, soon afterwards this girl too was sent away, and he made a third marriage with a woman who traced her family back to Commodus.[1]

It was not just human marriage that he made a mockery of. In an effort to find a wife for the god he served, he transferred the statue of Pallas to his own quarters. This statue is revered by the Romans but kept hidden out of sight and never moved since it came from Troy (apart from when the temple caught fire).[2] Now the emperor moved it and conducted it to the imperial palace to be married, one imagines, to his god. But then he declared that his god was displeased with such a war-like goddess who was always armed, and sent for the statue of Urania who is worshipped widely among the Carthaginians and

---

[1] (before September 221) and lasted just into year 5 (one coin with this date). Dio (Xiph.) 79.9.4 says there was a fourth and fifth marriage before E. returned to Aquila Severa. If so, they must have been very brief.

[2] Cf. 1.14.4n; according to Servius (on *Aen.* 7.188) there were seven *pignora* kept in the *penus Vestae*, which included the Palladium and the *ancilia* of the Salii; cf. SHA, *Elag.* 3.4, 6.6–9 (and Magie's note in the Loeb edition). Magie (*ibid.*) suggests that unpopularity in Rome forced E. to abandon the sacred marriage of Pallas (and his own with a Vestal Virgin) and to turn to Carthaginian and Syrian goddesses. The interest in Vesta and the other goddesses was part of the syncretism E. intended, to establish a monotheistic worship of which he was the head and the incarnation.

ἀνθρώπων. φασὶ δὲ αὐτὸ Διδὼ τὴν Φοίνισσαν
ἱδρύσασθαι, ὅτε δὴ τὴν ἀρχαίαν Καρχηδόνα πόλιν
ἔκτισε, βύρσαν κατατεμοῦσα.[1] Λίβυες μὲν οὖν
αὐτὴν Οὐρανίαν καλοῦσι, Φοίνικες δὲ Ἀστρο-
5 άρχην [2] ὀνομάζουσι, σελήνην εἶναι θέλοντες. ἁρμό-
ζειν τοίνυν λέγων ὁ Ἀντωνῖνος γάμον ἡλίου καὶ
σελήνης τό τε ἄγαλμα μετεπέμψατο καὶ πάντα τὸν
ἐκεῖθεν χρυσόν, χρήματά τε πάμπλειστα τῇ θεῷ [3]
ἐς προῖκα δὴ [4] ἐπιδοῦναι ἐκέλευσε. κομισθέν τε
τὸ ἄγαλμα συνῴκισε [5] δὴ τῷ θεῷ, κελεύσας
πάντας τοὺς κατὰ Ῥώμην καὶ Ἰταλίαν ἀνθρώπους
ἑορτάζειν παντοδαπαῖς τε εὐφροσύναις καὶ εὐωχίαις
χρῆσθαι δημοσίᾳ τε καὶ ἰδίᾳ ὡς δὴ γαμούντων
θεῶν.

6   κατεσκεύασε [6] δὲ καὶ ἐν τῷ προαστείῳ νεὼν

[1] Steph -σαν Oi	[2] Ἀστάρτην Reisk
[3] AP τὴν θεὸν φi	[4] om O
[5] συνῳκίσαι O	[6] κατασκευάσαι Oi

---

[1] Known also as Tanit and *Caelestis Afrorum dea* (cf.
Salambo also associated with this goddess, SHA, *Elag.* 7.3).
It is possible that Severus had already built a temple to the
goddess in Rome (cf. *ILS* 4438 for the temple later, *CAH*
XII. 413 (Nock)). *Venus Caelestis* appears on the coins of
Julia Soaemias, *BMC* V. ccxxxiii. Child sacrifices, formerly
a feature of this Carthaginian cult, are said by Dio to reappear
under E. (Xiph.) 79.11—but Dio is very unreliable on the
period, and depends chiefly on colourful stories from authors
hostile to E.

other people in Libya.[1] Tradition says that Dido
the Phoenician set up the statue at the time, presumably when she founded the ancient city of Carthage, after cutting up the hide.[2] The name used by
Libyans for the goddess is Urania, by the Phoenicians Astroarche;[3] they would also have it that she
is the moon goddess. A marriage between the sun 5
and the moon, Antoninus declared, was very appropriate, and he sent for the statue together with all the
gold from her temple. He also issued orders that a
very large sum of money should be contributed, supposedly as a dowry. When the statue had been
brought, he married it to the god, giving instructions
that all the inhabitants of Rome and Italy should celebrate in public and private with all kinds of festivities
and banquets, as though this were a real marriage of
the gods.

In the outlying district of the city he constructed a 6
vast, magnificent temple [1] to which he brought the

[2] The story is told by Virgil *A.* 1.367-8 describing the found-
ing of Carthage's citadel of Byrsa (Phoenician Bosra), supposedly named after the ceremony of measuring the land with
an ox hide (*byrsa*), but the etymology is incorrect. The point
of interest here is that, in spite of almost childlike explanations
about Roman antiquities earlier, H. expects his readers to
understand this reference. The use of δή suggests that
this is a marginal gloss that has crept into the text, but it
may be a sign of incompleteness, cf. 4. 8. 5n.

[3] Astarte (or Astargatis), often called *dea Syria* and like *dea
Caelestis* often equated with Magna Mater, Aphrodite, Venus;
a moon goddess, whose temple is described by Lucian, *de
Syr. dea* 4, not far from Emesa, at Sidon. The goddess was
specially venerated by Nero (Suet. *Nero* 56) and, also like
dea Caelestis, had a temple built at Rome. The spread of
oriental cults to the West, often by soldiers, is discussed in
CAH XII. 427 ff. (Nock).

μέγιστόν τε καὶ πολυτελέστατον, ἐς ὃν ἑκάστου
ἔτους κατῆγε [1] τὸν θεὸν ἀκμάζοντος θέρους.
πανηγύρεις [2] τε παντοδαπὰς συνεκρότει, ἱππο-
δρόμους τε κατασκευάσας καὶ θέατρα,[1] διά τε
ἡνιοχείας καὶ πάντων θεαμάτων τε καὶ ἀκροαμά-
των [3] πλείστων εὐωχούμενον τὸν δῆμον καὶ παν-
νυχίζοντα εὐφραίνειν ᾤετο. τόν τε θεὸν αὐτὸν
ἐπιστήσας ἅρματι χρυσῷ τε καὶ λίθοις τιμιωτάτοις
πεποικιλμένῳ [4] κατῆγεν ἀπὸ τῆς πόλεως ἐπὶ τὸ
7 προάστειον. τὸ δὲ ἅρμα ἦγεν ἐξάπωλον, ἵππων
λευκῶν μεγίστων τε καὶ ἀσπίλων, χρυσῷ πολλῷ
καὶ φαλάροις ποικίλοις κεκοσμημένων,[5] τάς τε
ἡνίας κατεῖχεν οὐδείς, οὐδὲ [6] τοῦ ἅρματος
ἄνθρωπος ἐπέβαινεν, αὐτῷ δὲ περιέκειντο ὡς
ἡνιοχοῦντι δὴ τῷ θεῷ. ὁ δ᾽ Ἀντωνῖνος ἔθεε [7]
πρὸ τοῦ ἅρματος ἀναποδίζων ἐς τοὐπίσω, ἔς τε
τὸν θεὸν ἀποβλέπων καὶ τοὺς χαλινοὺς ἀντέχων
τῶν [8] ἵππων· πᾶσάν τε τὴν ὁδὸν [8] ἤννε τρέχων
ἔμπαλιν ἑαυτοῦ ἀφορῶν τε ἐς [9] τὸ πρόσθεν τοῦ

---

[1] κατάγε (A[1] κατῆγε over κατάγε) O
[2] πανηγύρεις τε καὶ αὐτοῦ παντοδαπὰ συνεκρότει (ἐνεκρότει A)
θέατρα κατασκευάσας καὶ θέατρα O
[3] ἀκουσμάτων i   [4] P -μένον Oi
[5] AP -μένον Oi (A[1] over correct -μένων)
[6] Stav οὐδέπω δὲ Oi τάς τε ἡνίας κατεῖχεν om P and continues
neque enim quisquam mortalium eum inscenderat currum
[7] ἔθει Mendelss   [8] τῶν—ὁδὸν om O
[9] ἔμπαλιν ἑαυτοῦ· ἤννε τρέχων· ἀφορῶντος εἰς A εἰς τὸ
πρόσω ἤννε (ἤννε B) τρέχων ἔμπαλιν ἑαυτοῦ ἀφορῶν τε εἰς φ

---

[1] Nothing else is known of this temple, at one time thought
to be in the suburb, ad spem veterem, on the eastern side of the
city near the Porta Maggiore; this is now discounted, Platner-

god each year at mid-summer. He instituted many different festivals and constructed circuses (for horse-racing) and theatres, imagining that, if he provided chariot races and all kinds of spectacles and entertainments, and if he feasted the people all night long, he would be popular. The god was set up in a chariot studded with gold and precious stones and driven from the city to the suburb.[2] The chariot was 7 drawn by a team of six large, pure white horses which had been decorated with lots of gold and ornamented discs. No human person ever sat in the chariot or held the reins, which were fastened to the god as though he were driving himself. Antoninus ran along in front of the chariot, but facing backwards as he ran looking at the god and holding the bridles of the horses.[3] He ran the whole way backwards like this

Ashby, *Top. Dict. Rome* 199. It was in this district that E. was found by the soldiers in the first mutiny of 221, SHA, *Elag.* 13.5. The only known temple of Elagabalus was on the Palatine (5.5.8n). The short length of E.'s reign gives rise to doubts about the magnificence of such a construction; possibly the towers, mentioned in 5.6.9, were part of the structure like the corner towers of the temple of the sun at Kasr Raba in Arabia, suggests Domaszewski; quoted by Gross, *Real. f. Antike u. Christentum* IV. 995. The temple cannot have been completed much before the mid-summer of 221. Cf. Nash, *Pict. Dict. Anc. Rome* II. 384, for the large villa, amphitheatre and circus built in the gardens of Spes Vetus.

[2] The procession accompanying the black stone is recorded on Roman and Alexandrian coins in 220/1, Vogt, *Alex. Münz-* 1.181 f.; it is possible therefore that H. is only describing a single event (see previous note).

[3] Altheim, *Niedergang d. alt. Welt* II. 268, notes a relief from Palmyra on which a camel is carrying a sacred stone, and the man accompanying the animal is facing backwards.

8 θεοῦ. πρός τε τὸ μὴ πταῖσαι [1] αὐτὸν ἢ διολι-
σθαίνειν,[2] οὐχ ὁρῶντα ὅπου βαίνει, γῇ τε ἡ
χρυσίζουσα παμπλείστη ὑπέστρωτο, οἵ τε προ-
ασπίζοντες ἑκατέρωθεν ἀντεῖχον, τῆς ἀσφαλείας
τοῦ τοιούτου δρόμου προνοούμενοι. ὁ δὲ δῆμος
ἑκατέρωθεν παρέθει μετὰ παντοδαπῆς [3] δᾳδουχίας,
στεφάνους καὶ ἄνθη ἐπιρριπτοῦντες· ἀγάλματά τε
πάντων θεῶν, καὶ εἴ τι πολυτελὲς ἀνάθημα ⟨ἢ⟩ [4]
τίμιον, ὅσα τε τῆς βασιλείας σύμβολα ἢ πολυτελῆ
κειμήλια, οἵ τε ἱππεῖς καὶ ὁ [5] στρατὸς πᾶς προ-
9 επόμπευον τοῦ θεοῦ. μετὰ δὲ τὸ καταγαγεῖν
αὐτὸν καὶ ἱδρῦσαι ἐν τῷ ναῷ [6] τάς τε προειρημένας
θυσίας καὶ πανηγύρεις ἐπετέλει, πύργους τε μεγίστους καὶ ὑψηλοτάτους κατασκευάσας, ἀνιών τε
ἐπ᾽ αὐτούς,[7] ἐρρίπτει τοῖς ὄχλοις, ἁρπάζειν πᾶσιν
ἐπιτρέπων, ἐκπώματά τε χρυσᾶ καὶ ἀργυρᾶ
ἐσθῆτάς τε καὶ ὀθόνας παντοδαπάς, ζῷά τε πάντα,
ὅσα ἥμερα, πλὴν χοίρων· τούτων γὰρ ἀπείχετο

---

[1] πέσαι φ πεσεῖν Α
[2] διολισθαίνει φ-σθένειν Α
[3] Steph -οῦς Agl -οὺς aJo -ὰς φ
[4] Schwartz ⟨καὶ⟩ Steph τίμιον om Mendelss
[5] om φi
[6] νεὼ Α

54

looking up at the front of the god. But to stop him 8
tripping and falling while he was not looking where
he was going, lots of sand gleaming like gold was put
down, and his bodyguard supported him on either side
to make sure he was safe as he ran like this. Along
both sides of the route the people ran with a great
array of torches, showering wreaths and flowers on him.
In the procession, in front of the god, went images of
all the other gods and valuable or precious temple
dedications and all the imperial standards or costly
heirlooms. Also the cavalry and all the army joined
in.[1] After the god had been conducted and installed in 9
the temple, the emperor carried out the festival
sacrifices described above. Then he climbed on to
some very large high towers that had been constructed [2] and threw down on to the crowd, for anyone to catch, gold and silver cups, all kinds of clothes
and fine, linen garments and every kind of domestic
animal,[3] except pigs, which he did not touch by

[1] Obviously of the Roman garrison only.

[2] Cf. 5.6.6n.

[3] A practice of Gaius and Nero at the circus; the larger
objects were obviously distributed by tokens (*missilia*); cf.
Suet. *Gaius.* 18.2, *Nero* 11.2, SHA, *Elag.* 22.2 (calls them *sortes*).
Although these distributions are said to be for the sport of
seeing people scramble, they were also a means of reaching a
lower-class public than the *plebs frumentaria* who benefited
from the *congiaria*; E. distributed a *congiarium* every year of
his reign. See van Berchem, *Distribution de Blé et d'Argent*
129 and 161. The event described here took place, according
to SHA, *Elag.* 8.3, on E.'s entry into his consulship (i.e. either
January 220—*cos.* III, or 222—*cos.* IV), but H. is explicitly
contradictory, saying mid-summer was the date.

[7] αὐτοῦ Vg αὐτοῖς al

HERODIAN

10 Φοινίκων νόμῳ. ἐν δὴ ταῖς ἁρπαγαῖς πολλοὶ
διεφθείροντο, ὑπό τε ἀλλήλων πατούμενοι καὶ τοῖς
δόρασι τῶν στρατιωτῶν [1] περιπίπτοντες, ὡς τὴν
ἐκείνου ἑορτὴν πολλοῖς φέρειν συμφοράν. αὐτὸς
δὲ ἐβλέπετο πολλάκις ἡνιοχῶν ἢ ὀρχούμενος· οὐδὲ
γὰρ λανθάνειν ἤθελεν ἁμαρτάνων. προῄει τε
ὑπογραφόμενος τοὺς ὀφθαλμοὺς καὶ τὰς παρειὰς
ἐρυθραίνων,[2] φύσει τε πρόσωπον ὡραῖον ὑβρίζων
βαφαῖς ἀσχήμοσιν.

7. ὁρῶσα δὲ ταῦτα ἡ Μαῖσα, ὑποπτεύουσά τε
τοὺς στρατιώτας ἀπαρέσκεσθαι τῷ τοιούτῳ τοῦ
βασιλέως βίῳ, καὶ δεδοικυῖα μή τι ἐκείνου παθόν-
τος πάλιν ἰδιωτεύῃ, πείθει αὐτόν, κοῦφον ἄλλως
καὶ ἄφρονα νεανίαν, θέσθαι υἱὸν Καίσαρά τε [3]
ἀποδεῖξαι [4] τὸν ἑαυτοῦ μὲν ἀνεψιὸν ἐκείνης δὲ

---

[1] στρατῶν i
[3] Steph δὲ Oi
[2] ἐρυθραίνων AJo
[4] καίσ. τε ἀποδεῖξαι om P

---

[1] The worship of Elagabalus, like that of most semitic cults,
demanded abstention from pork, circumcision and other
rituals of purification and orgiastic mysticism; the Galli of
Astargatis and Cybele castrated themselves; temple prostitu-
tion and homosexuality were common; astrology and
astronomy and the reliance on Chaldean *magi* were at the
heart of the solar cults; cf. *CAH* XI. 643 ff. (Cumont).
None of the sources attempts to make any sense of the lurid
and obscene tales about E. which fall within these rituals; cf.
Dio (Xiph.) 79.11.1–2, 79.13.2–4, 79.17.1 (cf. Leo, p. 287),
SHA, *Elag.* 5.1–6.5, 8.1–2, 8.6, 24.2, etc. The origin of
these stories is only conjectural and obviously more than one (*ex
Graecis Latinisque*, SHA, *Elag.* 35.1, 18.4); Marius Maximus
is mentioned (SHA, *Elag.* 11.6) and was probably hostile after

Phoenician law.[1]   In the scramble lots of people were 10
killed, trampled to death by one another or impaled on
the spears of the soldiers.   Thus the festival of Elagabalus was fatal for many people.   The emperor himself was often to be seen driving his chariot or dancing,[2] making no attempt to conceal his vices.   He
used to go out with painted eyes and rouge on his
cheeks,[3] spoiling his natural good looks by using dis-
gusting make-up.

7. As she viewed these developments, Maesa suspected that the soldiers were revolted by this kind
of behaviour by the emperor.[4]   Her fears were that,
if anything happened to him, she would again be reduced to the status of an ordinary person.   So, since
he was in most matters a thoughtless, silly young man,
she persuaded him by flattery to adopt and appoint as

to being dismissed from the office of *praefectus urbi*; Claudius
Aelianus, the sophist author, wrote an *Indictment of Gynnis*
after E.'s death (Philos. *VS* 2.31.625(01)); cf. Barbieri, *RFIC*
32 (1954) 65.

[2] E. drove in the uniform of the Greens, Dio (Xiph.) 79.14.2.
For E.'s dancing, see SHA, *Elag.* 32.8, and Dio (Xiph.) 79.14.3.
A number of E.'s favourites were charioteers and athletes.

[3] For the phrase, cf. Pollux, 5.102, Lucian, *Bis Acc.* 31,
Athen. *Deipn.* 12.7.529A.   But H. may have in mind a
classical model like Xen. *Cyrop.* 1.3.2.   Various materials
were used for cosmetics—such as antimony (*stibium*) on the
eyes, and on the face the root of anchusa and white lead
(*psimythion*).

[4] The cult of *sol* was not offensive in itself, since it continued to be popular; the coinage of Severus Alexander
continues to show the predominance of the cult (though not
connected with Elagabalus), *BMC* VI. 30.   The chief cause
of the soldiers' complaint was over the extraordinary appointments of E. and the influence of men like Hierocles and
Zoticus (5.7.6n); Dio (Xiph.) 79.16.1, SHA, *Elag.* 15.1–2.

ἔγγονον [1] ἐκ τῆς ἑτέρας θυγατρὸς Μαμαίας,
2 εἰποῦσα αὐτῷ κεχαρισμένα, ὡς ἄρα χρὴ ἐκεῖνον
μὲν τῇ ἱερωσύνῃ καὶ θρησκείᾳ σχολάζειν τοῦ θεοῦ,
βακχείαις καὶ ὀργίοις τοῖς τε θείοις ἔργοις ἀνακεί-
μενον, εἶναι δὲ ἕτερον τὸν τὰ ἀνθρώπεια διοικοῦντα,
ἐκείνῳ δὲ παρέξοντα τῆς βασιλείας τὸ ἀνενόχλητόν
τε καὶ ἀμέριμνον· μὴ δεῖν τοίνυν ξένον ζητεῖν
μηδ' ἀλλότριον, ἀλλὰ τῷ ἀνεψιῷ ταῦτα ἐγχειρίσαι.
3 μετονομάζεται δὴ ὁ Ἀλεξιανός, καὶ Ἀλέξανδρος
καλεῖται, παραχθέντος αὐτῷ τοῦ παππῴου [2] ὀνόμα-
τος ἐς τὸ τοῦ Μακεδόνος ὡς πάνυ τε ἐνδόξου καὶ
τιμηθέντος ὑπὸ τοῦ δοκοῦντος πατρὸς ἀμφοτέρων
εἶναι· τὴν ⟨γὰρ⟩ [3] Ἀντωνίνου τοῦ Σεβήρου
παιδὸς μοιχείαν ἀμφότεραι αἱ Μαίσης θυγατέρες
αὐτή τε ἡ πρεσβῦτις ἐσεμνύνετο πρὸς τὸ τοὺς
στρατιώτας στέργειν τοὺς παῖδας, υἱοὺς [4] ἐκείνου
δοκοῦντας εἶναι.[4]

---

[1] ἔκγονον Ai   [2] Sylb πάππου Oi   [3] Steph
[4] υἱοὺς—εἶναι om P υἱοὺς om l

[1] The formal adoption took place in the senate, and seems
to have had full juridical validity (whatever the political
intentions); cf. Hammond, *Ant. Monarchy* 13–14. The date
of the event is disputed; a lacunose reading in the *Feriale
Duranum* shows the date as probably 26th June 221; [*vi kal.*]
iulias quod dominus nost[e]*r* [m]*arcus aure*[l]*ius severus
al*[e]*xa*[nder cae]*sar appe*[llat]*us sit*; A. also assumed the *toga
virilis* on the same day, though not yet in his fourteenth year.
But *CIL* VI. 3069 is a dedication by the *vigiles* to *imperatores*
(sic) *Antonino et Al*[e]*ssandro* which is dated 1st June 221—
possibly an error or back-dated. *CIL* VI. 2001 shows A.'s
co-option into the *sodales Antoniniani* on the 10th July.
Coins showing M. Aurelius Alexander Caesar and *princeps*

Caesar his cousin, her own grandchild by her daughter
Mamaea. Her argument was that of course the 2
emperor should keep himself free to carry out his
priestly office and worship the god, since he was
dedicated to his ecstatic and orgiastic rites and his
divine duties. Someone else should look after
wordly affairs so as to leave him free from the cares
and worries of the principate. This being so, rather
than looking for an outsider from another family,
the task should be put in the hands of his cousin.[1]
Alexianus changed his name from that inherited from 3
his grandfather to Alexander,[2] the name of the
Macedonian so admired and honoured by the alleged
father of the two cousins. Both the daughter of
Maesa, and the old lady herself, used to boast of the
adultery of Antoninus (Severus' son), to make the
troops think the boys were his sons and so favour them.

---

iuventutis are undated, but are probably from 221 to 222,
BMC V. ccxl, 571, 614. The tradition that A. was made
Caesar in 218 (e.g. SHA, *Alex.* 1.2, Victor *Caes.* 23.3) is
erroneous; cf. Jardé, *Études . . . Sévère Alexandre* 11n.

[2] Cf. 5.3.3n for A.'s name; Perhaps H.'s information is
garbled and, although he knew A. was named after his grandfather, he was unaware that the common name was Bassianus.
But "grandfather" here may mean "ancestor", since Alexianus or Alexio was a dynastic name of the Emesene priest-
kings. If so, H. appears unaware that Alexander was already
an accepted Hellenized alternative; cf. C. Julius Alexio,
father of C. Julius Samsigeramus (*PIR*² J 143), C. Julius Avitus
Alexianus, perhaps a brother of Mamaea (*PIR*² J 192), Alexander, king of Emesa and brother of Iamblichus who gained
Roman citizenship from Augustus (Dio 51.2.2). Note that
the Julius Alexander, executed by Commodus for conspiracy,
was also from Emesa, Dio (Xiph.) 72.14.1, SHA, *Comm.* 8.3.
The name was proposed by E.

4 ἀποδείκνυται δὴ [1] Καῖσαρ ὁ ᾿Αλέξανδρος, ὕπατός
τε σὺν αὐτῷ [2] ᾿Αντωνίνῳ. κατελθών τε ἐς τὴν
σύγκλητον ταῦτα ἐκύρωσε, γελοιότατα ψηφισαμέ-
νων πάντων ἃ ἐκελεύοντο,[3] πατέρα μὲν ἐκεῖνον
δοκεῖν ἔτη γεγονότα περί που [4] ἐκκαίδεκα,[5] τὸν
᾿Αλέξανδρον δὲ υἱὸν τοῦ δωδεκάτου ἐπιβαίνοντα.
ὡς δὲ Καῖσαρ ὁ ᾿Αλέξανδρος ἀπεδείχθη, ὁ ᾿Αντωνῖ-
νος αὐτὸν ἐβούλετο τὰ ἑαυτοῦ παιδεύειν ἐπιτηδεύματα, ὀρχεῖσθαί τε καὶ χορεύειν τῆς τε ἱερωσύ-
5 νης κοινωνεῖν καὶ σχήμασι καὶ ἔργοις ὁμοίοις. ἡ
δὲ μήτηρ αὐτὸν ἡ Μαμαία ἀπῆγε μὲν τῶν αἰσχρῶν
καὶ ἀπρεπῶν βασιλεῦσιν ἔργων, διδασκάλους δὲ [6]
πάσης παιδείας λάθρᾳ μετεπέμπετο, τοῖς τε
σώφροσιν αὐτὸν ἧκει μαθήμασι, παλαίστραις τε
καὶ τοῖς ἀνδρῶν γυμνασίοις εἴθιζε, παιδείαν τε τὴν

[1] P δὲ Oi   [2] τῷ i
[3] ἐκελεύετο O   [4] περί που om V
[5] ἐκκαιδεκατον (ἑξκ. A ἑξκ. B) O quatuordecim P
[6] Bergl τε OiJo

---

[1] The joint consulship was in 222. A.'s exact status is not
clear. Military diplomata of 7th January 222 record A. with
the praenomen imperatoris as well as the title of Caesar; AE
(1964) 269 confirming CIL XVI. 140, 141; Dušanić, Hist. 13
(1964) 490, believes the reading imper. Caes. is a genitive
referring to E., but cf. CIL XVI. 135 (Severus and Caracalla in
208) for a parallel. I agree with Forni, Archiv. stor. Lodigiano
(1959) 12 ff., and Hammond, Ant. Monarchy 3 f., that A.'s
name on the diplomata argues a legal status with secondary
imperium. Cf. 5.7.5n for consors imperii. A.'s name alone
on edicts as imp. Alexander before E.'s death (Cod. Just.
9.1.3, 4.44.1, 8.44.6) might be a retrospective addition.
[2] The ages given here are inconsistent with those in 5.3.3;
the former ages are partially confirmed by Dio (Xiph.) 79.20.2

Alexander was appointed Caesar and shared the 4
consulship with Antoninus.[1] When the latter entered the senate to have it ratified, everyone made a
complete farce of it by voting as they were told and
declaring the emperor himself to be a father at his
age of about sixteen, and Alexander his son, when
now in his twelfth year.[2] After Alexander's appointment as Caesar, Antoninus wanted him to be
trained in his own pursuits of leaping and dancing,
and to share in his priesthood by wearing the same
dress and following the same practices. But his 5
mother, Mamaea,[3] removed him from contact with
such activities which were shameful and unbecoming
for emperors. In private she summoned teachers
of all the arts, and trained him in the exercise of self-
control, introducing him to the wrestling schools and
manly exercises, and gave him both a Latin and a

who says E. was eighteen when he died (in March 222).
Although there are some verbal similarities between this
passage (especially 5.7.1) and Dio (Xiph.) 79.17.2 ff., in his
account Dio expressly states that his information is second-
hand (Dio (Xiph.) 80.1.2 ff.). According to Dio's account it
was E. who made a farce of the occasion, not the senate.

[3] Although later Christian writers praise Julia Mamaea for
her care of A. (e.g. Nicephoras Callistus 5.17), they are biased
in her favour by her supposed conversion to Christianity
(Syncell. 1.675 (B), Orosius 7.18.7), a story based on her
contact with Origen (Euseb. *HE* 6.21, etc., though the date
was not in 226 but 231-3). All sources make clear that the
dominant influence at this stage was Maesa, whose sponsor-
ship of A. was part of a palace struggle to overthrow Soaemias
and E.; Herzog, *RE* (Julia Maesa) 942-3. Thus Ulpian was
probably the choice of Maesa, not Mamaea (cf. SHA, *Alex.*
51.4) and advanced to become *praefectus annonae* (*Cod. Iust.*
8.37.4 dated a few days after E.'s death) and tutor to A. until
removed by E. (see below).

Ἑλλήνων καὶ Ῥωμαίων ἐπαίδευεν. ἐφ᾽ οἷς Ἀντωνῖνος πάνυ ἤσχαλλε, καὶ μετεγίνωσκε θέμενος
6 αὐτὸν υἱὸν καὶ κοινωνὸν τῆς ἀρχῆς. τούς τε οὖν
διδασκάλους αὐτοῦ πάντας ἀπεσόβει τῆς βασιλείου
αὐλῆς, τινάς τε αὐτῶν τοὺς ἐνδοξοτάτους οὓς μὲν
ἀπέκτεινεν οὓς δὲ ἐφυγάδευσεν, αἰτίας γελοιοτάτας
ἐπιφέρων, ὡς διαφθείροιεν αὐτῷ τὸν δοκοῦντα
υἱόν, οὐκ ἐπιτρέποντες χορεύειν ἢ βακχεύεσθαι,
σωφρονίζοντες [1] δὲ καὶ τὰ ἀνδρῶν διδάσκοντες.[1]
ἐς τοσοῦτον δὲ ἐξώκειλε παροινίας [2] ὡς πάντα [3] τὰ
ἀπὸ τῆς σκηνῆς καὶ τῶν δημοσίων θεάτρων μετα-
γαγεῖν ἐπὶ τὰς μεγίστας τῶν βασιλικῶν πράξεων,
καὶ τοῖς μὲν στρατοπέδοις ἔπαρχον ἐπιστῆσαι
ὀρχηστήν τινα γεγονότα καὶ δημοσίᾳ ἐν τῷ

---

[1] Mendelss -οντας Oi   [2] παρανοίας i
[3] ὡς ἂν πάντα Jo ὡς δὴ πάντα Suda

---

[1] SHA, *Alex.* 3.2–3, provides a list of teachers, but the whole
of the *vita* has to be treated with great caution, because of its
tendentious and "programmatic" features (cf. especially
Baynes, *The Historia Augusta* 57–67, 118–44, even if his thesis
is unproven, Momigliano, *Studies in Historiography* 158–9,
171). One name provided is Julius Frontinus, perhaps the
sophist, Fronto of Emesa, centre of a literary group in Athens
during H.'s time of writing; also he was a teaching rival of
Philostratus, *Suda* s.v. Φρόντων, Wellmann, *RE* (Fronto 13).
Another is said to be Scaurinus, perhaps the son of L. Verus'
tutor. The name of Silvinus is given by SHA, *Elag.* 16.4, as
one who was executed. Possibly Ulpian, the later prefect,
was employed at this stage too (cf. SHA, *Alex.* 51.4, *pro tutore
habuit* and *Cod. Just.* 4.65.4.1, naming him as *parens meus*),
but was driven away by E.; SHA, *Elag.* 16.4.
[2] The title *consors imperii* has been proposed for the lacuna
in *CIL* VI. 2001 and the military *diplomata* (5.7.4n), but *AE*
(1964) 269 contains the curious title *Caes(ar) imperi(i) et sacer-*

Greek education.[1]   Antoninus was absolutely furious about this and regretted the adoption of Alexander and his participation in the empire.[2]   He cleared out 6 all Alexander's teachers from the court, executing some of the extremely distinguished ones and driving others into exile.   Ridiculous charges were brought against them, that they were corrupting his adopted son by not allowing him to dance or go into a frenzy, but teaching him moderation and manly arts.   The emperor was driven to such extremes of lunacy that he took men from the stage and the public theatres and put them in charge of most important imperial business.[3]   A man, who in his youth had

dotis co(n)s(ul);   explained by Dušanić, *Hist.* 13 (1964) 495 ff., as a special title " Caesar of the state and Elagabalus," but what does this mean?   Far easier to assume the omission of *consors* by haplography.   If so, this confirms H. here and 5.7.4 (a share in the priesthood), and adds support to the argument that A. held some kind of secondary *imperium*.   Cf. *Orac. Sib.* 12.269 (ἔνθ' ὅτε νηπίαχος Καῖδαρ δὺν τῷ βαδιλεύδη).

[3] Cf. 5.5.3n for some of the appointments as rewards to supporters after the fall of Macrinus (Dio (Xiph.) 79.15.3); these were mostly equestrian posts.   Names and details of the more extraordinary appointments are provided by Dio (Xiph.) 79.15-16, 79.21, SHA, *Elag.* 6.1-5, 10.2 ff., 11.1, 12.1, 15.1-2. Protagenes (charioteer) became a close associate, Cordius (or Gordius) (charioteer) became *praefectus vigilum*, Aurelius Zoticus Avitus (son of a cook) became *a cubiculo*, though later dismissed and possibly appeared again under Alexander as *nomenclator a censibus* (*CIL* XIV. 3553, Jardé, *Sévère Alexandre* 59), Claudius (barber) became *praefectus annonae*, perhaps in place of Ulpian when he was dismissed in 221, Aurelius Eubulus became *procurator summarum rerum*, a mule driver, a courier, a locksmith became *procuratores vicesim. heredit.*; above all, Hierocles (charioteer) was considered as a candidate for Caesar.   It is almost impossible to tell which of these appointments are genuine.

'Ρωμαίων θεάτρῳ ὀρχησάμενον, ὅτε ἦν νέος·
7 πάλιν δὲ ἕτερον ὁμοίως ⟨ἐκ⟩ [1] τῆς σκηνῆς
βαστάσας,[2] παιδείας τῶν νέων καὶ εὐκοσμίας τῆς
τε ὑποστάσεως [3] τῶν [4] ἐς τὴν σύγκλητον βουλὴν
ἢ τὸ ἱππικὸν τάγμα κατατασσομένων προέστησεν.
ἡνιόχοις τε καὶ κωμῳδοῖς καὶ μίμων ὑποκριταῖς
τὰς μεγίστας τῶν βασιλείων πίστεων ἐνεχείρισε.
τοῖς [5] δὲ δούλοις αὐτοῦ ἢ ἀπελευθέροις, ὡς ἔτυχεν
ἕκαστος ἐπ᾽ αἰσχρῷ τινὶ εὐδοκιμήσας,[6] τὰς
ὑπατικὰς τῶν ἐθνῶν ἐξουσίας ἐνεχείρισε.[5]

8. πάντων δὲ οὕτως τῶν πάλαι δοκούντων
σεμνῶν ἐς ὕβριν καὶ παροινίαν ἐκβεβακχευμένων,

[1] Stav ⟨ἀπὸ⟩ Steph
[2] ἀποστήσας Stroth
[3] ἐξετάσεως Sylb
[4] Sylb τῆς Oi
[5] τοῖς—ἐνεχείρισε om O
[6] ἕκαστοις . . . εὐδοκιμήσασι i but corrected from P

[1] A clear reference to P. Valerius Comazon (Eutychianus?);
Hanslik, *RE* (Valerius 134); probably from a family of pro-
fessional dancers and actors, if the name is correct, though he
may not have actually been one himself, since he served, when
young (in the fleet?), in Thrace *c.* 181–3, where he was
punished by Claudius Attalus (3.1.6n); later he gained influence at court (probably accounting for the term *Caesarianus*
applied to him) and rose to be " prefect of the camp "—either
praefectus castrorum or prefect of the Parthian legion (cf.
5.4.4n; Howe, *Praet. Pref.* 97 ff., wrongly *c.* 182). In 218 he
was made praetorian prefect, and in 219 adlected *inter consu-
lares* replacing Marius Maximus as urban prefect; he was
consul in 220 (*cos.* II in *CIL* VI. 866 probably on the basis of
his earlier *ornamenta consularia*), but replaced by Leon as

64

been a dancer in public in the theatre at Rome, was appointed military prefect.[1] Similarly, another was 7 raised from the stage and put in charge of the training and morals of the youth and the census qualifications of members of the senatorial and equestrian orders.[2] He assigned positions of the highest responsibility in the empire to charioteers and comedy actors and mimers. His slaves and freedmen, who perhaps excelled in some foul activity, he appointed as governors of consular provinces.[3]

8. When all that was once held in respect was reduced in this way to a state of dishonour and frenzied madness, everyone, and particularly the soldiers,

[1] urban prefect (Dio (Xiph.) 79.14.2, though no date); a second tenure of the urban prefecture followed, perhaps in 221, but he was replaced by Fulvius (Diogenianus?; cf. 5.8.8n), whom he in turn replaced in A.'s reign.

[2] The function of *praefectura morum*, inherent in the censorial powers of the emperor (cf. Pliny, *Paneg.* 45.4–6) was given to a *procurator ad census* (or *a censibus*; the terms are synonymous; cf. *ILS* 1387 and *AE* (1945) 80, against Hirschfeld, *Kais. Verwalt.* 67n); this officer appears under the Antonines, but his grade was enhanced by Severus to eliminate equestrian opposition (cf. 2.11.6n, though Oliver, *AJP* 67 (1946) 316, doubts any new function). E. possibly extended this equestrian officer's functions to review senators also.

[3] This seems an exaggeration; slaves and freedmen certainly attained a degree of social mobility hitherto unprecedented, but I can find no example of a freedman appointed directly to a consular province; but there are some unusual appointments, such as that of Claudius Aelius Pollio, from centurion to governor of Germania Inferior (Dio 78.40.1 —the executioner of Diadumenianus) Dio 79.3.1, *CIL* XIII. 6807. Cf. Stein, *Ritterstand* 206 and 262, for the breakdown of distinctions between senators and equestrians, though the tendency to adlect and use equestrian procurators for military commands had been growing.

65

οἵ τε ἄλλοι πάντες ἄνθρωποι καὶ μάλιστα οἱ στρατιῶται ἤχθοντο καὶ ἐδυσφόρουν· ἐμυσάττοντο δὲ
αὐτὸν ὁρῶντες τὸ μὲν πρόσωπον καλλωπιζόμενον
περιεργότερον ἢ κατὰ γυναῖκα σώφρονα, περιδεραίοις δὲ χρυσίνοις [1] ἐσθῆσί τε ἁπαλαῖς ἀνάνδρως
κοσμούμενον, ὀρχούμενόν τε οὕτως ὡς ὑπὸ πάντων
2 ὁρᾶσθαι. ἐπιρρεπεστέρας τοίνυν τὰς γνώμας πρὸς
τὸν Ἀλέξανδρον εἶχον, καὶ ἐλπίδας κρείττους ἐν
παιδὶ κοσμίως καὶ σωφρόνως ἀνατρεφομένῳ.[2]
ἐφρούρουν τε αὐτὸν παντοίως ὁρῶντες ἐπιβουλευ-
όμενον ὑπὸ τοῦ Ἀντωνίνου. ἥ τε μήτηρ Μαμαία
οὔτε ποτὸν οὔτε ἐδώδιμόν τι εἴα τὸν παῖδα
προσφέρεσθαι τῶν ὑπ’ ἐκείνου πεμπομένων· ὀψο-
ποιοῖς τε καὶ οἰνοχόοις ὁ παῖς ἐχρῆτο οὐ τοῖς
βασιλικοῖς καὶ ἐν κοινῇ ὑπηρεσίᾳ τυγχάνουσιν,
ἀλλὰ τοῖς ὑπὸ τῆς μητρὸς ἐπιλεχθεῖσι πιστοτάτοις
3 τε εἶναι δοκοῦσιν. ἐδίδου δὲ καὶ χρήματα λανθά-
νουσα διανέμεσθαι τοῖς στρατιώταις κρύβδην, ὅπως
αὐτῶν τὴν πρὸς τὸν Ἀλέξανδρον εὔνοιαν καὶ διὰ
χρημάτων, ἐς ἃ μάλιστα ἀποβλέπουσιν, οἰκει-
ώσηται.[3]

ταῦτα δὴ ὁ Ἀντωνῖνος πυνθανόμενος παντὶ
τρόπῳ ἐπεβούλευε τῷ Ἀλεξάνδρῳ καὶ τῇ μητρὶ
αὐτοῦ· ἀλλὰ τὰς ἐπιβουλὰς πάσας ἀπεῖργέ τε καὶ

---

[1] χρυσοῖς Jo   [2] ἀναστρεφ. O   [3] -σεται O

[1] The account of the palace struggle between Soaemias and
Maesa is given by SHA, *Elag.* 13–15, a section of the *vita* which
is circumstantial and generally believed to be accurate; Lambertz, *RE* (Varius 10) 402–3, Jardé, *Sévère Alexandre* 10 ff.

began to grow bitterly angry. They were revolted at the sight of the emperor with his face made up more elaborately than a modest woman would have done, and effeminately dressed up in golden neck-laces and soft clothes, dancing for everyone to see in this state. So they inclined more favourably to- 2 wards Alexander, expecting better things of a boy who was receiving such a modest and serious educa-tion. And, realizing that Antoninus was plotting against the boy, they kept a close watch over him. Mamaea, his mother, would not allow him to taste any food or drink sent by the emperor. The boy did not make use of cooks and cupbearers who were in general employment in the palace—only men selected by Mamaea and approved for their complete loyalty. Mamaea also privately handed over some 3 money for a clandestine distribution to the soldiers. In this way she hoped to capture the loyalty of the soldiers with money as well, always the most attrac-tive inducement for the men.[1]

When Antoninus discovered this activity he began a full-scale campaign to plot against Alexander and his mother. But all his plans were frustrated and checked by Maesa, the two young men's grand-

If so, the first mutiny of the soldiers took place in late 221. It seems probable also that the dismissal of Ulpian (5.7.5n), Zoticus (whose name Avitus shows he was a freedman of Maesa) and Comazon (5.7.6n) had all taken place in 221 in an attempt by E. and Soaemias to supersede the authority of Maesa. Although E. was saved by the intervention of the praetorian prefect, Antiochianus (otherwise unknown), he was forced to dismiss some of his favourites, acknowledge A. as his true Caesar (i.e. not Hierocles, 5.7.6n) and permit a special guard for A., Mamaea and Maesa.

ἐκώλυεν [1] ἡ κοινὴ μάμμη ἀμφοτέρων Μαῖσα, γυνὴ
καὶ ἄλλως ἐντρεχὴς καὶ τῇ βασιλείῳ αὐλῇ πολλῶν
ἐτῶν ἐνδιαιτηθεῖσα [ἄτε τῆς Σεβήρου γυναικὸς
Ἰουλίας ἀδελφὴ γενομένη καὶ τὰ πάντα σὺν αὐτῇ
4 ἐν τοῖς βασιλείοις διατρίψασα].[2] οὐδὲν οὖν αὐτὴν
ἐλάνθανε τῶν ὑπὸ τοῦ Ἀντωνίνου βουλευομένων,
φύσει τε χαύνου τὸν τρόπον ὄντος, καὶ ἀφειδῶς
πάντα καὶ φανερῶς ἃ ἐβουλεύετο λέγοντος καὶ
πράττοντος. ὡς δὲ τὰ τῆς ἐπιβουλῆς αὐτῷ οὐ
προεχώρει, παραλῦσαι τῆς τοῦ Καίσαρος τιμῆς
ἠθέλησε τὸν παῖδα, καὶ οὔτε ἐν ταῖς προσαγο-
ρεύσεσιν [3] οὔτε ἐν ταῖς προόδοις Ἀλέξανδρος ἔτι
5 ἑωρᾶτο.[4] οἱ δὲ στρατιῶται ἐπεζήτουν τε αὐτόν,
καὶ ἠγανάκτουν ὅτι δὴ τῆς ἀρχῆς παραλυθείη.
διεσκέδασε δὲ ὁ Ἀντωνῖνος καὶ φήμην ὡς τοῦ
Ἀλεξάνδρου τεθνήξεσθαι μέλλοντος, ἐποιεῖτό τε
ἀπόπειραν ὅπως οἴσουσιν οἱ στρατιῶται τὸ θρυ-
λούμενον. οἱ δ᾽ ἐπεὶ μήτε [5] τὸν παῖδα ἔβλεπον
ὑπό τε τῆς φήμης τὰς ψυχὰς ἐτρώθησαν, ἀγανακτήσαντες οὔτε τὴν συνήθη φρουρὰν ἔπεμψαν τῷ
Ἀντωνίνῳ, κατακλείσαντές τε αὑτοὺς ἐν τῷ
στρατοπέδῳ τὸν Ἀλέξανδρον ἐν ⟨τῷ⟩ [6] ἱερῷ

[1] ἀπεσόβει O
[2] interpol conj Mendelss cf. 5.3.2, 5.3.10
[3] προαγορ. Ai
[4] AJo ἐτιμᾶτο φi
[5] μηκέτι Sylb
[6] Sylb

mother. She was a woman who, in addition to being enterprising had many years of experience of living at the imperial palace [as the sister of Julia, Severus' wife with whom she spent her entire time at the palace].[1] She missed none of Antoninus' machina- 4 tions, since his behaviour was naturally unsubtle and he was totally indiscreet about his plans in words and actions. With the failure of his contrivances, Antoninus planned to remove the boy from his position as Caesar, and no longer was he to be seen at public salutations or at the head of processions.[2] But the 5 soldiers demanded his presence, and were angry that he had been removed (so they said) from power. Antoninus spread a report to the effect that Alexander was on the point of dying, in an attempt to see how the soldiers would take the rumour. Since they failed to see the boy and were deeply upset by the news, the soldiers angrily refused to mount their usual guard over Antoninus. They shut themselves up in the camp and demanded Alexander's visible presence at their

[1] The repetitive phrase τὰ πάντα . . . βασιλείοις, and the use of a very similar phrase in 5.3.2 and 5.3.10 make it probable that Mendelssohn is correct in regarding this as a gloss.

[2] E. regretted the adoption and attempted to abrogate A.'s title of Caesar; after the first mutiny of the soldiers (see above) he continued to intrigue against A., and refused to participate in the consular procession on 1st January 222, when both were consuls, and should have been formally inducted at the temple of Jupiter Optimus Maximus on the Capitol. H., as he frequently does, generalizes from a particular incident. Coins of 222 show the *processus consularis* but E. and A. appear separately and alone; the cold war between the two extended to their rival *officinae* in the minting of coins; cf. *BMC* V. ccxli, 614–15, nos. 453, 456.

6 ἠξίουν ἰδεῖν. ὁ δ' Ἀντωνῖνος ἐν δέει πολλῷ
γενόμενος, παραλαβὼν τὸν Ἀλέξανδρον, συγκαθ-
εσθεὶς αὐτῷ ἐν τῷ βασιλικῷ φορείῳ, ὅπερ διὰ [1]
χρυσοῦ πολλοῦ καὶ λίθων τιμίων πεποίκιλτο,
κατῆλθεν ἐς τὸ στρατόπεδον [σὺν τῷ Ἀλεξάν-
δρῳ].[2] ὡς δὲ ἀνοίξαντες τὰς πύλας ἐδέξαντο
αὐτοὺς ἔς τε τὸν νεὼν τοῦ στρατοπέδου ἤγαγον,
τὸν μὲν Ἀλέξανδρον ὑπερφυῶς ἠσπάζοντό τε καὶ
εὐφήμουν, τῷ δὲ Ἀντωνίνῳ ἀμελέστερον προσεφέ-
7 ροντο. ἐφ' οἷς ἐκεῖνος ἀγανακτῶν, καὶ διανυκτε-
ρεύσας ἐν τῷ ἱερῷ τοῦ στρατοπέδου, πάνυ ἤσχαλλε
καὶ τοῖς στρατιώταις ὠργίζετο· ἐκέλευέ [3] τε τοὺς
παρασήμως [4] καὶ ὑπερφυῶς τὸν Ἀλέξανδρον
εὐφημήσαντας, τοὺς δὲ [5] αἰτίους δῆθεν στάσεως
8 καὶ θορύβου, συλλαμβάνεσθαι πρὸς τιμωρίαν. οἱ
δὲ στρατιῶται ἐπὶ τούτῳ ἀγανακτήσαντες, ἄλλως
μὲν μισοῦντες τὸν Ἀντωνῖνον καὶ ἀποσκευάσασθαι
θέλοντες ἀσχημονοῦντα βασιλέα, τότε δὲ καὶ τοῖς
συλλαμβανομένοις [6] ἐπαμύνειν δεῖν ἡγούμενοι, καιρὸν εὔκαιρον καὶ πρόφασιν δικαίαν νομίζοντες, τὸν
μὲν Ἀντωνῖνον αὐτόν τε καὶ τὴν μητέρα Σοαιμίδα
(παρῆν γὰρ ὡς Σεβαστή τε καὶ μήτηρ) ἀναιροῦσι,

<hr>

[1] δὴ l   [2] del Whit
[3] ἐκέλευσε AJo   [4] g[2] (mg) παρασήμους Oi
[5] δὲ om Agl ὡς instead of τοὺς δὲ Steph τοὺς—θορύβου
spurious? Mendelss   [6] AJo λαμβ. φι

<hr>

[1] Cf. 4.4.5; the temple of Mars, where the standards and the
statues of the emperors were kept, Tac. *H.* 1.36. The temple

shrine.[1] Antoninus in absolute terror got hold of Alex- 6
ander, sat beside him in the imperial litter, (which was
richly inlaid with gold and precious stones) and went
to the camp [with the boy]. The soldiers opened
the gates to receive them, before conducting
them to the camp shrine. But, whereas they greeted
Alexander with enthusiastic shouts of good wishes,
they ignored Antoninus. He was furious at such 7
treatment, and, after spending a night fuming and
raging at the soldiers in the camp shrine, he began to
issue orders that those who had openly and enthusiastically acclaimed Alexander should be seized for
punishment, as well as those supposedly guilty of
sedition and riot. This inflamed the soldiers, who were 8
already antagonistic to Antoninus and anxious to be
rid of an emperor who was a disgrace. Now they
also thought that they should give help to those
who were being held as prisoners. Believing the
opportunity was right and their case just, they
killed Antoninus and Soaemis (who was with him as
Augusta and his mother) and all his retinue [2] that

is illustrated on a coin of Claudius, and a priest is recorded on
ILS 2090. The increased importance of the cult of Mars in
this period inside the camp was perhaps a reaction to the
oriental cults (like that of Elagabalus) being introduced outside. The demand for A.'s presence at the shrine therefore
had a special point. See Durry, *Cohortes prét.* 321–3 and
pl. III B (a coin of Claudius).

[2] With E. were killed Hierocles, Aurelius Eubulus, Fulvius
(Diogenianus?) the urban prefect, and the praetorian prefects;
Dio 79.21.1. The names of the prefects are not certain;
Antiochianus (5.8.3n) may still have been in office; another
possible man is one whose name has been lost (. . . atus) but
who had been a close supporter of E. since 218, Pflaum,
Carrières, no. 293.

τούς τε περὶ αὐτὸν πάντας, ὅσοι ἔνδον κατελήφθη-
σαν [1] ὑπηρέται τε καὶ συνεργοὶ ἐδόκουν εἶναι τῶν
9 ἁμαρτημάτων. τὰ δὲ σώματα τοῦ τε Ἀντωνίνου
καὶ τῆς Σοαιμίδος παρέδοσαν σύρειν τε καὶ
ἐνυβρίζειν τοῖς βουλομένοις· ἅπερ ἐπὶ πολὺ διὰ
πάσης [2] τῆς πόλεως συρέντα τε καὶ λωβηθέντα ἐς
τοὺς ὀχετοὺς ἀπερρίφθη [3] τοὺς ἐς τὸν Θύβριν
ποταμὸν ῥέοντας.

10 Ἀντωνῖνος μὲν οὖν ἐς ἕκτον ἔτος ἐλάσας τῆς
βασιλείας καὶ χρησάμενος τῷ προειρημένῳ βίῳ,

---

[1] AJo κατελείφ. φι and A[1] (over ή)
[2] μέσης Jo
[3] -ερρίφη AJo

---

[1] From H.'s language, one would expect this to mean that
the supporters had entered the camp with E. Dio (Xiph.)
79.20.1 seems to confirm H. that the murder of the emperor,
his mother and the supporters took place in the camp, but
SHA, *Elag.* 17.1, says that the assassination happened in the
palace (a reliable section of the *vita*). H. almost ignores the
importance of Soaemias, yet much of the crisis of 221 was
probably due to her attempts to shake off the influence of
Maesa, who now sponsored Mamaea and Alexander. Right
up to the last the two sisters were vying for the favour of the
soldiers (Dio, *ibid.*). Soaemias appeared in the senate when
A. was named as Caesar (Dio (Xiph.) 79.17.2); she is named
on inscriptions as *mater Augusti* (e.g. *AE* (1954) 28—an erased
name), as *consors imperii* (*AE* (1936) 39) and perhaps even as
mater senatus (*AE* (1956) 144, Benario, *TAPA* 90 (1959)
11 ff.), an obvious challenge to Maesa's position.

were caught inside,[1] who were thought to be the attendants and confederates in his crimes. The bodies of Antoninus and Soaemis were handed over to those who wished to drag them around and desecrate them. After being dragged through the city for a long time and mutilated, they were thrown into the sewers which run down to the River Tiber.[2]

So in the sixth year of his rule,[3] after a life such as has been described above, Antoninus and his mother

---

[2] Dio (Xiph.) 79.20.2 ff. (cf. Zos. 1.11), SHA, *Elag.* 17.4–7; the ancient punishment for criminals. Only E.'s body was thrown into the Tiber. For the principle of *poena post mortem*, see Vittinghoff, *Staatsfeind in d. röm. Kaiserzeit* 43–6.

[3] The chronology of H. for the reigns of E. and A. are a puzzle. Both here and in 6.1.7 and 6.2.1 he appears completely to miscalculate the lengths of the reigns, but in 6.9.3 and 6.9.8 he is well aware of the correct date of A.'s death. Some errors may be explained by H.'s method of episodic narrative (cf. 6.2.1n), though that is impossible here. Either these are straightforward errors by a historian writing twenty-five years later, or the figures in the text have been corrupted by unskillful copyists (i.e. ϛ' for ε'). But it is interesting to note that all the figures are correct if calculated from the date of the death of Caracalla (April 217); thus E. would be in his sixth regnal year in 222 and A. in his fourteenth regnal year in 230. Although (as far as I am aware) never an official method of calculating regnal years, contemporaries may have been encouraged to date in this fashion by the *damnatio memoriae* of both Macrinus and E. (Dio 79.2.1–6, SHA, *Elag.* 17.4, *Alex.* 1.2) which propagated the fiction that the predecessor had never been emperor; e.g. *nec imperator nec Antoninus*, SHA, *Alex.* 7.4 (admittedly untrustworthy); cf. E.'s assumption of a fictional back-dated consulship belonging to Macrinus (5.5.2n), and his refusal to wait for senatorial confirmation of titles; this may also be the origin of the error that A. had been Caesar since 218 in Victor *Caes.* 23.3, SHA, *Alex.* 1.2.

οὕτως ἅμα τῇ μητρὶ κατέστρεψεν· [1] οἱ δὲ [2]
στρατιῶται αὐτοκράτορα τὸν Ἀλέξανδρον ἀναγορεύσαντες ἐς τὰ βασίλεια ἀνήγαγον, κομιδῇ νέον
καὶ πάνυ ὑπὸ τῇ μητρὶ καὶ τῇ μάμμῃ παιδ-
αγωγούμενον.

[1] aJo -στρεψαν Ogl
[2] P τε Oi

---

[1] The *dies imperii* is probably recorded on the *Feriale
Duranum* as 13th March (222), by the vote of the soldiers; on
the following day perhaps the senate added its vote of the
titles of Augustus, *pater patriae*, and *pontifex maximus* (Fink–
Hoey–Snyder, *YCS* 7 (1940) 85 ff., though see the reservations

were murdered. Alexander, though extremely young and very much under the tutelage of his mother and grandmother, was greeted as emperor by the soldiers [1] and conducted up to the palace.[2]

of Hoey about two separate days, *ibid.* 93–4). Dio 79.3.3 is in agreement that E. died on 13th March (see *YCS* 7 (1940) 86n for the method of calculation). SHA, *Alex.* 6.2 (dated 6th March), is incorrect. A.'s full name of M. Aurelius Severus Alexander probably dates from now (cf. *CIL* VI. 1454 dated 13th April), perhaps at the wish of the praetorians (SHA, *Alex.* 12.4, may be partially true).

[2] H. does not mention the senate's vote (cf. 2.6.13n) noted in SHA, *Alex.* 1.3. The interpretation of the *Feriale Duranum* which supposes two separate days for the vote of the soldiers and the senate is slightly supported by H.'s omission.

BOOK SIX

ΒΙΒΛΙΟΝ ΕΚΤΟΝ

1. Ὁποίῳ μὲν δὴ τέλει ὁ νέος[1] Ἀντωνῖνος ἐχρήσατο, ἐν τοῖς προειρημένοις δεδήλωται·[2] παραλαβόντος δὲ τὴν ἀρχὴν Ἀλεξάνδρου τὸ ⟨μὲν⟩[3] σχῆμα καὶ τὸ ὄνομα τῆς βασιλείας ἐκείνῳ περιέκειτο, ἡ μέντοι διοίκησις τῶν πραγμάτων καὶ ἡ τῆς ἀρχῆς οἰκονομία ὑπὸ ταῖς γυναιξὶ διῳκεῖτο, ἐπί τε τὸ[4] σωφρονέστερον καὶ σεμνότερον πάντα
2 μετάγειν ἐπειρῶντο. καὶ πρῶτον μὲν τῆς συγκλήτου βουλῆς τοὺς δοκοῦντας καὶ ἡλικίᾳ σεμνοτάτους καὶ βίῳ σωφρονεστάτους ἑκκαίδεκα ἐπελέξαντο συνέδρους εἶναι καὶ συμβούλους τοῦ βασιλέως· οὐδέ τι ἐλέγετο ἢ ἐπράττετο, εἰ μὴ κἀκεῖνοι αὐτὸ ἐπικρίναντες σύμψηφοι ἐγένοντο. ἤρεσκέ τε τῷ δήμῳ καὶ τοῖς στρατοπέδοις, ἀλλὰ καὶ τῇ συγκλήτῳ

---

[1] μέγας φgl maior P   [2] δηλωθεὶς a
[3] Bekk   [4] ⟨αῖ⟩ ἐπὶ τὸ Reisk

---

[1] A. was only thirteen years old; cf. 5.3.3n, 5.7.4n.
[2] Well illustrated by the title of A. on an inscription as *Juliae Mamaeae Aug(ustae)filio Juliae Maesae Aug(ustae)nepote*, *AE* (1912) 155. The coins issuing from the *officina* of Maesa lay stress on *pudicitia*; *BMC* VI. 51.

BOOK SIX

1. In the previous book a description was given of the death of the young Antoninus. After Alexander's accession to power[1] he possessed the trappings and the name of emperor, but the control of administration and imperial policy was in the hands of his womenfolk,[2] who tried to bring back a complete return to moderate dignified government. The first 2 reform was to choose sixteen senators as councillors and advisers to the emperor,[3] men who presented the appearance of greatest dignity in years and the most moderate way of life. No statement was made or action taken without their considered approval. This form of the principate, which changed from a high-handed tyranny to an aristocratic type of

---

[3] Cf. Zon. 12.15 (perhaps from Dio); the same body is referred to in 7.1.3, where they are said to be elected by the senate; although there are many references to the work of the *consilium* in the *vita*, it is suspect and in some case demonstrably false. Dio's references to the *consilium* in the famous speech of Maecenas, 52.15.1–4, 33.3–4 (which Millar unconvincingly says was addressed to Caracalla and not Alexander) were by definition describing a council not in existence. The council remained, as before, essentially an *ad hoc* advisory body drawn from the wider group of *amici*; if there were special committees of experts, their greater importance was not due to an increase in *de jure* powers, but to A.'s more pliable (and weaker) rule; see Crook, *Consilium Principis* 86–91, Millar, *Cassius Dio* 102 ff.

βουλῇ, τὸ σχῆμα τῆς βασιλείας ἐκ τυραννίδος
ἐφυβρίστου ἐς ἀριστοκρατίας τύπον μεταχθείσης.
3 πρῶτον μὲν οὖν τὰ ἀγάλματα τῶν θεῶν, ἅπερ
ἔτυχεν ἐκεῖνος κινήσας καὶ μεταγαγών, ἔπεμψαν
ἐς τοὺς ἰδίους καὶ ἀρχαίους ναούς τε καὶ σηκούς·
τούς τε ὑπ' ἐκείνου ἀλόγως, ἢ ἐφ' οἷς εὐδοκιμήκε-
σαν ἁμαρτήμασιν, ἐς τιμὰς καὶ ἐξουσίας προαχθέν-
τας τῶν δοθέντων ἀφείλοντο, ἑκάστους κελεύσαντες
ἐς τὴν προτέραν αὐτῶν ἐπανιέναι τῆς ἀξίας
4 αἵρεσιν. τάς τε πράξεις ἁπάσας καὶ τὰς διοι-

---

[1] If A.'s " aristocratic " policy is to be seen in such principles as that *nihil tamen tam proprium imperii est ut legibus
vivere* (*Cod. Just.* 6.23.3) and in the observance of the elaborate
protocol which permitted the senate a dignified appearance
(e.g. *Dig.* (Ulpian) 1.9.1, SHA, *Alex.* 17.3–4, 18.2–3, 27.3, 43.1),
it was also in A.'s reign that the autocratic position of the
emperor was formally defined by such principles as *licet lex
imperii sollemnibus iuris imperatorem solverit* (*Cod. Just.*
6.23.3) and *princeps legibus solutus est* (*Dig.* (Ulpian) 1.3.31).
The super-prefecture of Domitius Ulpianus (not even mentioned by H.), who became praetorian prefect by 1st December
222 (*Cod. Just.* 4.65.4), and the tight control of administration
under the regency of Maesa and Mamaea could not be concealed by the adlection of the praetorian prefect *inter con-
sulares*, supposedly to maintain the propriety *ne quis non
senator de Romano senatore iudicaret*; Jardé, *Sévère Alexandre*
35 ff., doubts whether other prefects were senators after
Ulpian, but Pflaum, *Marbre de Thorigny* 39 ff., argues for
T. Lorenius Celsus, L. Didius Marinus, L. Domitius Honoratus
and M. Aedinus Julianus as senatorial prefects; cf. Stein,
Eunomia 1 (1957) 6, for the last two after 223.
[2] Restoration of buildings and shrines occupies a prominent
place in the coinage of A.; e.g. the completion of the restoration of the Colosseum in 223 (cf. SHA, *Elag.* 17.8, *Alex.* 24.3,
BMC VI. 128–9, nos. 156–8); the Nymphaeum in 226; the
Mint in 228. The temple of Elagabalus on the Palatine may

government, was approved by the people and the soldiers as well as the senate.[1]

For a start the statues of the gods, which the pre- 3 vious emperor had moved from their places, were returned to their original ancient temples and shrines.[2] Those who had been advanced to positions of honour and power without justification, or who had been promoted for their notoriety in crimes, were deprived of their benefices and all instructed to return to their previous status and occupation.[3] All civil and legal 4

have been rededicated to Jupiter Ultor; Brown, *AJA* 42 (1938) 129, *BMC* VI. 57, though doubted by Ziegler, *RE* (Palatium). Dio (Xiph.) 79.21.2 says that the god Elagabalus was banished from Rome (though destined to return under Gallienus and Aurelian).

[3] Cf. SHA, *Alex.* 15.1–2. Some examples of men restored to positions of importance, previously dismissed or idle under E. are Marius Maximus (dismissed from the urban prefecture in 218, now made *cos.* II in 223), Comazon (dismissed by E. from the urban prefecture in 221, now re-employed as urban prefect for the third time in 222, 5.7.6n), perhaps the later emperor M. Antonius Gordianus, though his earlier career is almost unknown. (7.5.2n), Julius Flavianus, praetorian prefect 218, now restored to the same position (Pippidi, *Epig. Beitr. z. Gesch. Histrias* 163–77). But the break in continuity should not be exaggerated. Cassius Dio, said by Millar, *Cassius Dio* 25–7, to have been unemployed under E. must (according to the new date of Ulpian's downfall in 223/4, *P.Oxy.* 2565) have served in Africa and Dalmatia under E., but was given an important military province of Pannonia Superior *c.* 222/3 (cf. Dio (Xiph.) 80.4.2). Jardé, *Sévère Alexandre* 60n, gives a list of men serving both emperors, and the *album* of patrons of Canusium in 223 (some senators " les plus en vue " in the new régime) contains many previously honoured by E., and some who had been execrated by the senate after the death of Caracalla; Pflaum, *Marbre de Thorigny* 37–49. The continuity came from the Syrian Augustae.

κήσεις, τὰς μὲν πολιτικὰς καὶ ἀγοραίους ἐνεχεί-
ρισαν τοῖς ἐπὶ λόγοις εὐδοκιμωτάτοις καὶ νόμων
ἐμπείροις, τὰς δὲ [1] στρατιωτικὰς τοῖς ἐξετασθεῖσί
τε καὶ εὐδοκιμήσασιν ἐν εὐτάκτοις τε καὶ πολεμι-
καῖς πράξεσιν.

ἐπὶ πολὺ δ' οὕτω τῆς ἀρχῆς διοικουμένης, ἡ μὲν
Μαῖσα πρεσβῦτις ἤδη οὖσα ἀνεπαύσατο τοῦ βίου,
ἔτυχέ τε βασιλικῶν τιμῶν, καὶ ὡς νομίζουσι
5 Ῥωμαῖοι, ἐξεθειάσθη· ἡ δὲ Μαμαία μόνη τῷ
παιδὶ καταλειφθεῖσα ὁμοίως αὐτοῦ ἄρχειν τε καὶ
κρατεῖν ἐπειρᾶτο. ἤδη τε ὁρῶσα ἐν ἀκμῇ [2] τὸν
νεανίαν γενόμενον, καὶ δεδοικυῖα μὴ ἄρα ἡλικία
ἀκμάζουσα ὑπηρετούσης ἀδείας τε καὶ ἐξουσίας ἔς
τι τῶν γενικῶν [3] ἁμαρτημάτων ἐξοκείλῃ, πανταχόθεν ἐφρούρει τὴν αὐλήν,[4] οὐδέ τινα εἴα
προσιέναι τῷ μειρακίῳ τῶν ἐπὶ φαύλῳ βίῳ
διαβεβλημένων, μή πως τὸ ἦθος διαφθαρείη,
προκαλεσαμένων αὐτοῦ τῶν κολάκων τὰς ὀρέξεις

---

[1] P (autem) τε Oi   [2] Bekk[1] ἀρχῇ Oi
[3] συγγενικῶν Steph προγονικῶν Reisk   [4] ἀρχήν Jo

---

[1] Consultation with *prudentes* (some of whom were jurists)
had always been the practice of emperors, and from Hadrian's
time *iuris periti* had regularly been on the *consilium*; the great
jurist prefects, Ulpian and Julius Paulus were inevitably
close advisers *ex officio* (cf. SHA, *Alex.* 31.2–3). There may
therefore have been a legal committee of the council (SHA,
Alex. 16.1, looks like an anachronism).

[2] Like the legal experts, the *amici militares* were represented
among the advisers on the council; there is therefore nothing

business and administration was put in the charge
of the men with the highest rhetorical reputation and
legal skill.[1] Military affairs were entrusted to men
of proved reputations for maintaining discipline and
waging wars.[2]

After a long period of this type of government in
the empire, Maesa, already an old woman, died and
received imperial honours and deification,[3] according to Roman practice. Mamaea, left alone with 5
her son, still tried to control and dominate him.
Realizing that he was now a young man in his prime,
she was also afraid that his youthful vigour might
perhaps be encouraged by his unrestricted position
of power and drive him to commit some of the crimes
associated with his forebears.[4] Therefore the palace
was put under strict guard and no one with a reputation for loose living was allowed to come near the
young lad, for fear his morals would be corrupted if
sycophants directed his vigorous enthusiasms towards

improbable about a committee of such men to deal with
military matters and advise on action; cf. Crook, *Consilium
Principis* 114, Fink–Hoey–Snyder, *YCS* 7 (1940) 37.
Discipline in Rome and the provinces did not improve under
the experts (6.4.7n).

[3] H. appears to have exaggerated the length of time before
Maesa died. The weight of evidence shows that she died
sometime after November 224 (she does not appear deified in
the *acta Arvalium* of that date), but before August 226 (the
latest for A.'s marriage to Orbiana); the evidence is collected
by Fink–Hoey–Snyder, *YCS* 7 (1940) 22 and 113 f.; *consecratio*
coins are undated, but come about 225, *BMC* VI. 135 ff.

[4] This meaning of the much disputed Greek *genikos* is justified by Stroth; other suggestions are " sexual crimes " or
" general (i.e. greater) crimes." See the discussion in
Irmisch, *Herod. Hist. ad loc.*

HERODIAN

6 ἀκμαζούσας ἐς αἰσχρὰς ἐπιθυμίας. δικάζειν [τε] [1]
οὖν αὐτὸν ἔπειθε συνεχέστατα καὶ ἐπὶ πλεῖστον
τῆς ἡμέρας, ὡς ἂν ἀσχολούμενος περὶ τὰ κρείττονα καὶ τῇ βασιλείᾳ ἀναγκαῖα μὴ ἔχοι καιρὸν ἐς
τὸ ἐπιτηδεύειν τι τῶν ἁμαρτημάτων. ὑπῆρχε δέ
τι καὶ φυσικὸν ἦθος πρᾶον καὶ ἥμερον τῷ Ἀλεξάνδρῳ ἔς τε τὸ φιλάνθρωπον πάνυ ἐπιρρεπές, ὡς
7 ἐδήλωσε καὶ τῆς ἡλικίας προχωρούσης. ἐς τεσ-
σαρεσκαιδέκατον γοῦν [2] ἐλάσας τῆς βασιλείας ἔτος
ἀναιμωτὶ ἦρξεν [οὐδέ τις εἰπεῖν ἔχει ὑπ' ἐκείνου
φονευθέντα].[3] καίτοι τινῶν μεγίσταις αἰτίαις ὑπο-
πεσόντων, ὅμως ἐφείσατο ὡς μὴ φονεῦσαι, οὐ
ῥᾳδίως τοῦτο ἄλλου βασιλέως τῶν καθ' ἡμᾶς
ποιήσαντος ἢ παραφυλάξαντος μετὰ τὴν Μάρκου
ἀρχήν. ὑπ' Ἀλεξάνδρου δ' οὐκ ἄν τις εἰπεῖν ἔχοι
ἢ μνημονεῦσαι ἐν ἔτεσι τοσούτοις ἀκρίτως [4]
φονευθέντα.

8 ᾐτιᾶτο δὲ καὶ τὴν μητέρα καὶ πάνυ ἤσχαλλεν
ὁρῶν αὐτὴν οὖσαν φιλοχρήματον καὶ περὶ τοῦτο

[1] om Bekk[2]   [2] οὖν Jo
[3] om Jo Mendelss(?)   [4] ἀκριβῶς A

---

[1] See 5.8.10n for the problem of chronology.
[2] The reference is to senators, as was understood by the
author of SHA, *Alex.* 52.2, quoting H.; perhaps the word
βουλευτήν has dropped out, but, in view of what follows, I agree
with Mendelssohn that this clause is an interpolation. In view
of the execution recorded in 6.1.10, H. may only mean (as
is stated more generally below) that A. never executed a
senator *without trial*.

84

low desires. His mother urged him to occupy him- 6
self continually with judicial work for most of the
day, hoping that while he was busy on extremely
important business, essential to imperial rule, he
would have no chance to turn his attention to any
vice. Alexander's character was naturally gentle
and docile, always inclined to show sympathy. This
he demonstrated as he grew older. Certainly, up 7
to the fourteenth year [1] of his reign he ruled without
bloodshed [and one could not name anyone executed
by him].[2] Even though some people were guilty of
very serious crimes, Alexander spared them from
execution, an ideal which no other emperor of our
time has found easy to practise or preserve since
Marcus' reign.[3] But throughout the many years of
Alexander's rule it would be impossible to recall the
name of a person executed without trial.

Alexander also found fault with his mother [4] and 8
was very much upset to see her avarice and absolute

---

[3] Some confirmation is to be found in *Cod. Just.* 9.8.1 which
lightened the law of *maiestas*. The legislative activity of this
reign is illustrated by about 450 edicts and constitutions in
the *Codex*, not all of them in the direction of leniency.

[4] Cf. 5.3.3n, 6.5.9n. Herodian implies that Mamaea's
domination did not occur until after the death of Maesa.
Zon. 12.15 is too general (he does not mention Maesa) to be
understood as more than that Mamaea's power increased
after the death of E.; Mamaea's titles indicate that up to
224 she was on a par with Maesa (*mater Augusti et castrorum*),
but that by 227 she had increased her prestige considerably
(*mater Augusti et castrorum et senatus et patriae* and later *mater
universi generis humani*). Mamaea had probably intrigued to
obtain special powers for the praetorian prefect, Ulpian, whom
Zos. 1.11.2 says she intended to be *custos et consors imperii*;
cf. Pflaum, *Marbre de Thorigny* 41-4.

HERODIAN

ὑπερφυῶς ἐσπουδακυῖαν. προσποιουμένη γὰρ ἀθ-
ροίζειν αὐτὰ ἵνα ἔχοι τοῖς στρατιώταις ἀφθόνως
καὶ ῥᾳδίως ὁ Ἀλέξανδρος χαρίζεσθαι, ἰδίᾳ
ἐθησαύριζε· καὶ διέβαλλεν ἔσθ' ὅπῃ [1] τοῦτο τὴν
ἀρχήν, αὐτοῦ ἄκοντός τε καὶ ἀσχάλλοντος οὐσίας
τινῶν καὶ κληρονομίας ἐξ ἐπηρείας ὑφαρπασάσης
ἐκείνης.

9   ἠγάγετο δ' αὐτῷ καὶ γυναῖκα τῶν εὐπατριδῶν,
ἣν συνοικοῦσαν καὶ ἀγαπωμένην μετὰ ταῦτα τῶν
βασιλείων ἐδίωξεν· ἐνυβρίζουσά τε καὶ βασίλισσα
εἶναι μόνη θέλουσα, φθονοῦσά τε τῆς προσηγορίας
ἐκείνῃ, ἐς τοσοῦτον προεχώρησεν ὕβρεως ὡς τὸν
πατέρα τῆς κόρης, καίτοι ὑπ' Ἀλεξάνδρου γαμβροῦ
ὄντος πάνυ τιμώμενον, μὴ φέροντα τὴν Μαμαίαν
ἐνυβρίζουσαν αὐτῷ τε καὶ τῇ θυγατρὶ αὐτοῦ,
φυγεῖν ἐς τὸ στρατόπεδον, τῷ μὲν Ἀλεξάνδρῳ

---

[1] ὅποι A

[1] Gneia Seia Herennia Sallustia Barbia Orbiana; her full
name appears on Alexandrian coins in the years 225/6 and
226/7; Vogt, *Alex. Münzen* 1.127–8; cf. *ILS* 486. Roman
coins of *c.* 225 (special marriage issue) name her as Sallustia
Barbia Orbiana, *BMC* VI. 142 ff. The family may be connected with a Herennius Orbianus (under Pius) or Seius
Fuscianus (*amicus* of M. Aurelius) or the Barbii of Aquileia;
Fink, *AJP* 60 (1939) 329 ff., Pflaum, *Rev. Arch.* (1953) 72–6.
Nothing is known of a daughter of Macrinus (-rianus?) recorded in SHA, *Alex.* 49.3 (supposedly Dexippus), or of
Sulpicia Memmia in SHA, *Alex.* 20.3; cf. *Alex.* 58.1 (Varius
Macrinus, *adfinis eius*) and *ILS* 1355 (Q. Sallustius Macrinus,
rejected by Pflaum, *Carrières*, no. 227).

[2] Tentatively identified as Seius Caesar on the *Feriale
Duranum* by Fink, *AJP* 60 (1939) 326–32 (who gives him the
full name of L. (Cn.?) Seius Herennius Sallustius Barbius,

obsession with money. She alleged that she was saving it in order to enable Alexander to make a generous *ex gratia* payment to the troops without difficulty. But she was making a private hoard. This cast a certain cloud upon his reign, though Alexander opposed and deplored her forcible confiscation of some people's inherited property.

His mother provided a wife [1] for him from a patri- 9 cian family but, though he lived with her and loved her, Mamaea banished her from the palace with insults. Wishing to be the only empress, Mamaea was jealous of the title of Augusta going to the girl. The abuse went to such lengths that the father of the girl,[2] in spite of his high position of honour as father-in-law to Alexander, could not stand the insults Mamea offered him and his daughter. He took refuge in the military camp [3] and, though he acknowledged his gratitude to Alexander for his

though the identification is open to doubt; Weinstock, *JRS* 32 (1942) 128). If true that A.'s father-in-law was given the name of Caesar, this may have been what Dexippus referred to in SHA, *Alex.* 49.3–4; *CIL* VIII. 15524 (Thugga) is a damaged inscription of *c.* 224/5 recording someone as Caesar. *ILAlg* I.2095, which may also refer to the father-in-law, is too badly damaged to restore with any certainty; cf. *Albo* 340.

[3] The second attempt in the reign to rouse the praetorians to riot. In 223 or early 224 (see *P.Oxy.* 2565 for the date) there were three days of rioting between guards and populace, from " some small cause," Dio (Xiph.) 80.2.2–4, Zon. 12.15; though probably due to discontent caused by Ulpian's removal of the prefects Julius Flavianus and (Geminius?) Chrestus, Zos. 1.11. Control over the praetorians appears to have been tenuous in 229, when Alexander advised Cassius Dio, consul for that year, not to spend his time in Rome for fear of his unpopularity with the guards. Evidently the reign was far from the ideal described by H.

χάριν εἰδότα ἐφ' οἷς ἐτιμᾶτο, τὴν δὲ Μαμαίαν
10 αἰτιώμενον ἐφ' οἷς ὑβρίζετο. ἐκείνη δὲ ἀγανακτή-
σασα αὐτόν τε ἀναιρεθῆναι ἐκέλευσε, καὶ τὴν
κόρην ἐκβληθεῖσαν τῶν βασιλείων ἐς Λιβύην
ἐφυγάδευσε. ταῦτα δὲ ἐπράττετο ἄκοντός τε καὶ
ἀναγκαζομένου τοῦ Ἀλεξάνδρου· ἦρχε γὰρ αὐτοῦ [1]
ὑπερβαλλόντως ἡ μήτηρ, καὶ πᾶν τὸ κελευόμενον
ἐκεῖνος ἐποίει. τοῦτο δ' ἄν τις μόνον ἔσχεν
ἐγκαλέσαι αὐτῷ, ὅτι δὴ ὑπὸ περιττῆς πραότητος
καὶ αἰδοῦς πλείονος ἢ ἐχρῆν τῇ μητρί, ἐν οἷς
ἀπηρέσκετο, ὅμως ἐπείθετο.

2. ἐτῶν μὲν οὖν τρισκαίδεκα [2] οὕτως, ὅσον ἐπ'
αὐτῷ, τὴν βασιλείαν ἀμέμπτως διῴκησε· τῷ δὲ
[τεσσαρεσκαι]δεκάτῳ [3] ἔτει αἰφνιδίως ἐκομίσθη
γράμματα τῶν κατὰ Συρίαν τε καὶ Μεσοποταμίαν
ἡγεμόνων, δηλοῦντα ὅτι Ἀρταξέρξης [4] ὁ Περσῶν
βασιλεὺς μετὰ τὸ Παρθυαίους καθελεῖν καὶ τῆς
κατὰ τὴν ἀνατολὴν ἀρχῆς παραλῦσαι, Ἀρτάβανόν

---

[1] αὐτοῦ καὶ αφ

[2] originally γ' (i.e. 3) corrupted to ιγ' (i.e. 13) and (below) δ' (i.e. 4) corrupted to ιδ' (i.e. 14) conj Dändliker

[3] [τεσσαρεσκαι] om Cassola τῷ τεσσ. ἔτει om P

[4] Ἀρταξάρης Stav (throughout) from Agathias *Hist.* 2.26 f., 4.23 f. but Dio (Xiph.) 80.3.2 as here

---

[1] I have accepted the emendation of Cassola, *RAAN* 38 (1963) 141–3, though with some hesitation; cf. 5.8.10n. In 6.9.3 and 6.9.8 H. knows that A. ruled for fourteen years; it is inconceivable therefore that he imagined two major campaigns, against Persia and the Germans, to have taken place within one year (even if he had not been a contemporary). It is also typical of H.'s technique that he allows the episodic narrative to overlap with the chronological, which a copyist,

honours, he laid charges against Mamaea for her
insults. Furious at this, the empress ordered him 10
to be executed and the girl, already turned out of
the palace, was exiled to Libya. These actions were
done in face of the opposition of Alexander, who was
compelled to acquiesce. Completely dominated by
his mother, he did exactly as he was told. This was
the one thing for which he can be faulted; that he
obeyed his mother in matters of which he disapproved because he was over-mild and showed
greater respect to her than he ought to have done.

2. So for thirteen years Alexander ruled without
cause for complaint as far as he himself was concerned. But in his tenth [1] year unexpected letters
came from the governors of Syria and Mesopotamia
with information that Artaxerxes, king of the
Persians, had defeated the Parthians, broken up their
eastern kingdom and killed Artabanus, the previous
great king who wore the double crown.[2] He had also

failing to understand, has attempted to rationalize. But the
error may simply be due to careless writing and two different
chronological systems. The year mentioned here was 230,
the year in which A. celebrated his *decennalia* (even though
trib. pot. IX), reckoning from 221 as Caesar, *BMC* VI. 74.

[2] In 208 Ardashir (=Artaxerxes) seized control over the Sass-
anians in Persis, a vassal state under the Arsacids, and began to
expand his power over neighbouring states, doubtless assisted
by the rivalry between Artaban V and Vologaeses V for the Parthian throne. Artaban established his primacy at Susa by 5th
September 221, the date of a recently discovered relief
(Girshman, *Mon. et Mém. Acad. Inscr. et Belles-Lett.* 44 (1950)
97-107). Almost immediately he engaged Ardashir in a
series of battles and was finally defeated in early 224 (6.2.7n).
Since the coinage of Vologaeses in Seleucia terminates
abruptly in 222/3, it can be assumed he too had been defeated
by Ardashir the year before.

HERODIAN

τε τὸν πρότερον καλούμενον μέγαν [1] βασιλέα καὶ
δυσὶ διαδήμασι χρώμενον ἀποκτεῖναι, πάντα τε τὰ
περίοικα βάρβαρα χειρώσασθαι καὶ ἐς φόρου
συντέλειαν ὑπαγαγέσθαι,[2] οὐχ ἡσυχάζει οὐδ' ἐντὸς
Τίγριδος ποταμοῦ μένει, ἀλλὰ τὰς ὄχθας ὑπερβαί-
νων καὶ τοὺς τῆς Ῥωμαίων ἀρχῆς ὅρους Μεσοπο-
2 ταμίαν τε κατατρέχει καὶ Σύροις ἀπειλεῖ, πᾶσάν
τε τὴν ἀντικειμένην ἤπειρον Εὐρώπῃ καὶ διαι-
ρουμένην Αἰγαίῳ τε καὶ τῷ πορθμῷ τῆς Προποντίδος, Ἀσίαν τε πᾶσαν καλουμένην προγονικὸν
κτῆμα ἡγούμενος τῇ Περσῶν ἀρχῇ ἀνακτήσασθαι
βούλεται, φάσκων ἀπὸ Κύρου τοῦ πρώτου τὴν
ἀρχὴν ἐκ Μήδων ἐς Πέρσας μεταστήσαντος μέχρι
Δαρείου τοῦ τελευταίου Περσῶν βασιλέως, οὗ τὴν
ἀρχὴν Ἀλέξανδρος ὁ Μακεδὼν καθεῖλε, πάντα
μέχρις Ἰωνίας καὶ Καρίας ὑπὸ σατράπαις Περσι-
κοῖς διῳκῆσθαι· προσήκειν οὖν αὐτῷ Πέρσαις
ἀνανεώσασθαι πᾶσαν ὁλόκληρον, ἣν πρότερον
ἔσχον, ἀρχήν.

<hr>

[1] τὸν μέγαν φι   [2] Steph ὑπάγεσθαι Οἱ

<hr>

[1] Ardashir had to contend with the sons of Artaban, by
whom he was temporarily checked in Media and Armenia
(Dio (Xiph.) 80.3.3); after this he was preoccupied with
conquest of the eastern territories of the Parthian kingdom;
CAH XII. 109–10 (Christensen). It is difficult to believe
that Vologaeses actually reoccupied Seleucia in 228/9, as suggested by Simonetta, *Num. Chron.* (6) 16 (1956) 77–82; cf.
BM Parthia 241–3, nos. 1–36. The interval between Artaban's
death in 224 and the apparent " year of accession " of Ardashir

gained complete control over the neighbouring bar-barians and reduced them to tributary status.[1] He was causing unrest by refusing to be contained by the River Tigris and was crossing the banks which were the boundary of the Roman empire. Mesopotamia was being overrun and Syria threatened.[2] Believ- 2 ing that the entire mainland facing Europe contained by the Aegean Sea and the Propontis Gulf (the whole of what is called Asia) belonged to him by ancestral right, he was intending to recover it for the Persian empire. He alleged that from the rule of Cyrus, who first transferred the kingdom from the Medes to the Persians, up to Darius, the last of the Persian kings, whose kingdom Alexander of Macedon had des-troyed, the whole country as far as Ionia and Caria had been under the government of Persian satraps.[3] So it was his right to restore and reunite the whole empire as it had once been.

c. 227 may perhaps be explained by the time spent in securing his conquests; the chronological difficulties are discussed by Taqisadeh and Henning, *Asia Major* 6 (1957) 106–21, sum-marized by Walser-Pekáry, *Krise d. röm. Reiches* 36.

[2] Zon. 12.15 and Syncellus 1.674 (Bonn) say that Ardashir advanced into Cappadocia and captured Nisibis and Carrhae in Mesopotamia, but he failed to take Hatra (Dio (Xiph.) 80.3.2). It is not clear whether the northern Mesopotamian cities were recovered; the absence of coinage from them under Maximinus suggests that they were not; cf. SHA, *Gord.* 26.6, *BM Arabia* 88 ff., 120 ff.

[3] From Cyrus the Great in the sixth century B.C. to the final defeat of Darius at Gaugamela in 331 B.C. Ardashir's claims are repeated in Dio (Xiph.) 80.4.1, though Dio suggests the threat of the Persians was only serious because of serious disorder among the Roman troops, many of whom joined the Persians, rather than fight. A mutiny in Mesopotamia resulted in the assassination of the governor (6.4.7n).

3 τοιαῦτα ¹ τοίνυν δηλωσάντων καὶ ἐπιστειλάντων
τῶν ὑπὸ ταῖς ἀνατολαῖς ἡγεμόνων, πρὸς τὴν
αἰφνίδιον καὶ παρ' ἐλπίδα κομισθεῖσαν ἀγγελίαν
οὐ μετρίως ὁ Ἀλέξανδρος ἐταράχθη, καὶ μάλιστα
εἰρήνῃ ἐκ παίδων ἐντραφεὶς ² καὶ τῇ κατὰ τὴν
πόλιν ἀεὶ σχολάσας τρυφῇ. τὰ μὲν οὖν πρῶτα
ἔδοξεν αὐτῷ κοινωσαμένῳ τοῖς φίλοις πρεσβείαν
πέμψαι καὶ διὰ γραμμάτων κωλῦσαι ³ τὴν ὁρμὴν
4 καὶ ἐλπίδα τοῦ βαρβάρου. ἔλεγε δὲ τὰ γράμματα ⁴
δεῖν μένειν τε αὐτὸν ἐν τοῖς τῶν ἰδίων ὅροις καὶ
μὴ καινοτομεῖν μηδὲ ματαίαις αἰωρούμενον ⁵ ἐλπίσι
μέγαν ἐγείρειν πόλεμον, ἀγαπητῶς δ' ⁶ ἔχειν
ἕκαστον τὰ αὑτοῦ· μηδὲ γὰρ ὁμοίαν ἔσεσθαι
μάχην αὐτῷ πρὸς Ῥωμαίους οἵαν σχεῖν πρὸς τοὺς
γειτνιῶντας καὶ ὁμοφύλους βαρβάρους. ὑπεμίμ-
νησκε δὲ τὰ γράμματα τῶν τε τοῦ Σεβαστοῦ καὶ

¹ τοιαῦτά τινα Agl   ² Steph ἐκτρ. Oi
³ λῦσαι A καταλῦσαι conj Mendelss from Thuc. 2.89.8
³⁻⁴ κωλῦσαι — γράμματα om φ
⁵ ἀμιρούμενον (-μοιρ- V) φ   ⁶ δὲ a τε Wolf

¹ There is no real evidence of any important campaigns in
A.'s reign before this date, though there are military themes
and *victoria* type coins in 225; cf. Jardé, *Sévère Alexandre*
76n, *BMC* VI. 60, 61.   From 229 A. bore the title of *invictus*
(e.g. *AE* (1899) 7), but this may be an attempt by A. to give
himself a military image in a period of dangerous military in-
subordination.   There was probably some minor activity on
the northern frontier; SHA, *Alex.* 58.1, *CIL* XIII. 8017.
² Cf. 6.7.10 for A.'s love of chariot-racing and luxury.

With this news from the dispatches of the eastern 3
governors, Alexander was badly upset at the sudden-
ness and unexpectedness of the report that had come.
Since childhood he had been brought up in conditions of peace [1] and had always been attached to the
comforts of the city.[2] Therefore his first decision
after communicating with his councillors was to send
a diplomatic representative, and put a halt to the
aggression of the barbarian and check his expectations by means of a letter.[3] In it he said Artaxerxes 4
must remain in his own territory without stirring up
trouble; he must not incite a war because he was
carried away by foolish optimism; everyone should
be content with their lot; for he would not find a war
against the Romans the same proposition as one
against neighbours and barbarians like himself. The
letter further reminded the king of the victories

[3] Because the cowardice of A. is part of H.'s explanation
for the failure of A.'s rule, he tends to underestimate the extent
of A.'s resistance to Ardashir (6.6.6n). There are indications
of a vigorous reaction to the crisis; an outbreak of piracy in
the Mediterranean, probably as a result of Rome's damaged
prestige, led to the appointment of a special officer to ensure
troop and supply movements and overall control of all sea
operations; *IGRR* IV. 1057 (P. Sallustius Sempronius; cf.
Domaszewski, *RhM* 58 (1903) 384). The extensive issue of
silver coins in Syria indicates the size of the military con-
centration; Bellinger, *Dura-Europos, Final Report* VI. 207–8.
The appointment of Rutilius Pudens Crispinus to Syria
Phoenice may be another preparatory move, since he was a
competent soldier (6.5.2n). Note also the appointment of the
later praetorian prefect, C. Furius Sabinus Aquila Timesitheus,
as procurator of Palestine and organizer of the supply train
for the expedition (*ILS* 1330, *exactori reliquor(um) annon(ae)
sacrae expeditionis*); cf. 5.5.3n, 6.7.6n, Pflaum, *Marbre de
Thorigny* 55–6.

τῶν [1] Τραϊανοῦ Λουκίου τε καὶ Σεβήρου κατ'
αὐτῶν τροπαίων. τοιαῦτα μὲν δή τινα ὁ Ἀλέξανδρος ἐπιστείλας ᾤετο πείσειν ἢ φοβήσειν ἐς τὸ
5 ἡσυχάζειν τὸν βάρβαρον· ὁ δ' οὐδέν τι φροντίζων
τῶν ἐπεσταλμένων, ὅπλοις ἀλλ' οὐ λόγοις οἰόμενος
δεῖν τὰ πράγματα διοικεῖσθαι, ἐνέκειτο ἄγων καὶ
φέρων τὰ Ῥωμαίων ἅπαντα, κατατρέχων τε καὶ
καθιππεύων Μεσοποταμίαν λείας τε ἀπήλαυνε, καὶ
τὰ ἐπικείμενα στρατόπεδα ταῖς ὄχθαις τῶν ποταμῶν προασπίζοντά τε τῆς Ῥωμαίων ἀρχῆς
ἐπολιόρκει. φύσει δ' ὢν ἀλαζών, καὶ ταῖς παρ'
ἐλπίδας εὐπραγίαις ἐπαιρόμενος, πάντα ῥᾳδίως
6 χειρώσεσθαι [2] προσεδόκα. ἦν δὲ αὐτὸν τὰ ἀνα-
πείθοντα οὐ μικρὰ ἐς ἐπιθυμίαν ἀρχῆς μείζονος.
πρῶτος γὰρ [3] ἐτόλμησε τῇ Παρθυαίων ἀρχῇ
ἐπιθέσθαι Πέρσαις τε τὴν βασιλείαν ἀνανεώσασθαι.
μετὰ γὰρ Δαρεῖον τὸν ὑπ' Ἀλεξάνδρου τοῦ Μακεδόνος τῆς ἀρχῆς παραλυθέντα, παμπλείστοις ἐν
ἔτεσι Μακεδόνες μὲν καὶ Ἀλεξάνδρου διάδοχοι
τῶν [4] ὑπὸ ταῖς ἀνατολαῖς ἐθνῶν καὶ [5] κατ' Ἀσίαν
ἅπασαν, νειμάμενοι [4] κατὰ χώρας, ἐβασίλευσαν.
7 ἐκείνων δὲ πρὸς ἀλλήλους διαφερομένων, πολέμοις
τε συνεχέσι τῆς Μακεδόνων δυνάμεως ἐξασθενού-
σης, πρῶτος Ἀρσάκης λέγεται, τὸ γένος Παρθυ-
αῖος, ἀναπεῖσαι τοὺς ἐπέκεινα βαρβάρους ἀποστῆναι

---

[1] τοῦ ABi
[2] Mendelss -σασθαι Oi (cf. gloss A φειρώσεσθαι)
[3] πρῶτος γὰρ περσῶν O

94

won over them by Augustus, Trajan, Lucius and
Severus.[1] With this letter Alexander hoped to persuade or frighten the barbarian into docility. But 5
Artaxerxes paid no attention to what was written,
since he believed that it was weapons not words that
must settle the issue. He pressed forward, ravaging
the entire Roman territory, overrunning Mesopotamia
with infantry and cavalry, and carrying off plunder.
The garrison on the river banks to protect the
Roman empire were besieged. Naturally vain, and
elated by his unexpected successes, Artaxerxes
assumed that everything would easily fall under
his control. There were important considerations 6
which encouraged his ambitions for a bigger empire;
he was the first that dared to attack the Parthian
kingdom and restore it to the Persians. After Darius
had lost the kingdom to Alexander the Macedonian,
the nations of the East and throughout Asia were
divided up and ruled for very many years by the
Macedonians and Alexander's successors. But as 7
they fell out with each other and Macedonian
strength was sapped by continual wars, the Parthian
Arsaces, according to accounts, was the first to urge
the barbarians in those countries to rebel from Mace-

[1] The recovery of the Parthian standards by Augustus,
20 B.C., Trajan's capture of Ctesiphon, A.D. 115, L. Verus'
triumph for his Parthian victory, A.D. 166. All of these events
were against the Parthians. It is ironic that Augustus' diplomatic triumph should be called a victory by H., since one of
the themes of his history is the need for military action against
barbarians.

---

[4] τῶν—νειμάμενοι om O
[5] om a ἐθνῶν τὴν ᾿Ασίαν Sylb

HERODIAN

Μακεδόνων· περιθέμενός τε τὸ διάδημα ἑκόντων Παρθυαίων καὶ τῶν προσχώρων βαρβάρων αὐτός τε ἐβασίλευσε, καὶ τοῖς ἐξ ἐκείνου τοῦ γένους ἐπὶ πλεῖστον παρέμενεν [1] ἡ ἀρχή, μέχρις Ἀρταβάνου τοῦ καθ᾽ ἡμᾶς γενομένου, ὃν Ἀρταξέρξης ἀποκτείνας Πέρσαις τὴν ἀρχὴν ἀνεκτήσατο, τά τε γειτνιῶντα ἔθνη βάρβαρα χειρωσάμενος ῥᾳδίως ἤδη καὶ τῇ Ῥωμαίων ἀρχῇ [2] ἐπεβούλευσεν.

3. ὡς δὲ τῷ Ἀλεξάνδρῳ ἐδηλώθη διατρίβοντι ἐν τῇ Ῥώμῃ τὰ κατὰ τὰς ἀνατολὰς ὑπὸ τοῦ βαρβάρου τολμώμενα, οὐκ ἀνασχετὰ ἡγούμενος, καλούντων δὲ αὐτὸν καὶ τῶν ἐκεῖσε ἡγεμόνων, ἀσχάλλων μὲν καὶ παρὰ γνώμην, ὅμως δ᾽ ἔσχε περὶ ἔξοδον. ἔκ τε οὖν αὐτῆς Ἰταλίας καὶ τῶν ὑπὸ Ῥωμαίοις πάντων ἐθνῶν λογάδες ἐς τὴν στρατιὰν ἠθροίζοντο, ὅσοι σώματος εὐεξίᾳ [3] καὶ ἡλικίας ἀκμῇ ἐς μάχην ἐπιτήδειοι ἐνομίζοντο.

---

[1] -έμεινεν O [2] τὴν Ῥ. ἀρχὴν O
[3] εὐεξιάς φ εὐευξία A

---

[1] "The day on which the dominion of the Parthians, the sons of mighty Arsaces, came to an end" was 28th April 224 according to the Chronicle of Arbela, though Agathias 4.24 says Ardashir seized power in 225 (the fourth year of A.'s rule). Dio (Xiph.) 80.3.2 says there were three battles before Artaban was defeated, which is confirmed by the Chronicle of Tabari (see Nöldeke, *Gesch. d. Pers. u. Arab. Zeit d. Sassanides* 12). The scene of the final battle is depicted on a relief in the gorge at Firouzabad.

[2] Preparations for a campaign were under way by 230; the coinage of 230 shows a preponderance of military themes, including *adlocutio Augusti* (not necessarily to be taken literally,

donia. As it was the wish of the Parthians and the
neighbouring barbarians, Arsaces himself ruled as
their crowned head. Power remained in the hands
of his heirs for a very long time, right up to our contemporary Artabanus. By killing him Artaxerxes
gained the throne for the Persians.[1] Now, after
subduing the neighbouring barbarian people, it was
a natural step to make plans to subvert the Roman
empire.

3. While Alexander was lingering in Rome the
news of the bold action of the barbarian in the East
came to him. Such acts, he believed, could not be
tolerated, and his eastern governors were demand-
ing his presence. So, though he regretted the decision which went against his inclinations, he made
preparations to leave.[2] From Italy[3] and all the
Roman provinces special levies were recruited for the
army, all of men passed as physically fit and of the

but perhaps indicating that the speech before A. left Rome is
not simply a rhetorical device of H.; cf. SHA, *Alex.* 53.1, for
a speech in Antioch); *BMC* VI. 75. Signs of road repairs in
Cilicia and Cappadocia are evident in 230–1; Magie, *R.
Rule in Asia Minor* 694, 1560.

[3] A badly damaged inscription recording A.'s appointment
of a certain L. Fulvius Gavius Numisius Petronius Aemilianus
may be correctly restored *ad [dilect(um) habend(um)] per
regionem Tra[nspadanum]*; if so, the levy was probably on
this occasion; but obviously this cannot be counted as strong
evidence, *ILS* 1173. The recruiting does not imply the
formation of a new legion, as has been suggested on the basis
of the appearance of a legio IV in SHA, *Max.* 5.5; rightly
rejected by Instinsky, *Klio* 34 (1942) 118–20. More probably
A. was bringing the existing legions up to full strength (cf.
6.8.8n), but see the arguments in Ritterling, *RE* (legio) 1329–
30, who favours the formation of a legio IV Italica (based on
ILS 487; but see 8.4.1n).

97

2 κινησίς τε μεγίστη πάσης [1] τῆς [2] ὑπὸ Ῥωμαίοις
ἐγένετο, δυνάμεως ἰσορρόπου ἀθροιζομένης πρὸς
τὸ ἀγγελλόμενον τῶν ἐπιτρεχόντων [3] βαρβάρων
πλῆθος. ὁ δὲ Ἀλέξανδρος ἀθροίσας τοὺς ἐν
Ῥώμῃ στρατιώτας, συνελθεῖν [4] τε πάντας κελεύσας
ἐς τὸ σύνηθες πεδίον, ἐπὶ βήματος [5] ἀνελθὼν ἔλεξε
τοιάδε.

3   " ἐβουλόμην μέν, ἄνδρες συστρατιῶται, τοὺς
συνήθεις πρὸς ὑμᾶς ποιεῖσθαι λόγους, δι' ὧν αὐτός
τε ἐκοσμούμην δημηγορῶν ὑμᾶς τε ἀκούοντας
εὔφραινον· εἰρήνης γὰρ πολυετοῦς ἀπολαύσαντες
εἴ τι καινὸν νῦν [6] ἀκούοιτε, ἴσως ἂν ὡς [7] παρ'
4 ἐλπίδα λεχθέντι ἐκπλαγείητε. χρὴ δ' ἄνδρας
γενναίους τε καὶ σώφρονας εὔχεσθαι μὲν ὑπάρχειν
τὰ βέλτιστα, φέρειν δὲ [8] τὰ προσπίπτοντα· τῶν
μὲν γὰρ δι' ἡδονῆς πραττομένων ἡ ἀπόλαυσις
γλυκεῖα, τῶν δ' ἐξ ἀνάγκης κατορθουμένων ἔνδοξος
ἡ ἀνδρεία. καὶ τὸ μὲν ἄρχειν ἀδίκων ἔργων οὐκ
εὐγνώμονα ἔχει τὴν πρόκλησιν, τὸ δὲ τοὺς
ἐνοχλοῦντας [9] ἀποσείεσθαι ἔκ τε τῆς ἀγαθῆς
συνειδήσεως ἔχει τὸ θαρραλέον, καὶ ἐκ τοῦ μὴ
5 ἀδικεῖν ἀλλ' ἀμύνεσθαι ὑπάρχει τὸ εὔελπι. Ἀρτα-

---

[1] Schwartz following edit. Ox (mg) πᾶσι Oi
[2] τοῖς φl
[3] τῶν ἐπιτρ. om OP
[4] ἐξελθεῖν V
[5] βῆμα Mendelss
[6] om O
[7] om O
[8] P (sed) τε Oi
[9] ὀχλοῦν. iA

98

right age for battle. The whole Roman empire was 2
in a state of complete upheaval,[1] gathering together
a force to match the reported size of the barbarian
invasion. Alexander mustered the Roman garrison with orders to meet on the usual open space.
Then, mounting the tribunal, he said:[2]

" Fellow soldiers, I would have preferred to make 3
the usual kind of speech to you which would be a
credit to my ability as a speaker and a pleasure for
you to listen to. After enjoying peace for many
years, you may possibly be astounded to hear something novel on this occasion coming unexpectedly
in my speech. But brave and balanced men must 4
hope for the best while taking what comes. One
gets fine pleasure from doing what one enjoys, but
the reputation for bravery is won from successfully
carrying out a necessary task. To be the initiator of
an unjust action is not the way to offer a sound challenge. Conversely, the elimination of trouble-
makers creates confidence because one is acting with
a good conscience Optimism is bred from not com-
mitting a wrong but preventing one. Artaxerxes, 5

---

[1] The vocabulary refers back to the words of the *prooemium*,
1.1.4; cf. 1.7.1, 3.7.7. The language may also be an un-
conscious or conscious reflection of the famous introduction
in Thuc. 1.1.2, though the context is very different there;
Stein, *Dexip. et Herod.* 141.

[2] Needless to say, the string of aphorisms in this speech are
a display of the rhetoric of H. not of A. This is one of only
two speeches in Books 4-6, probably a sign that the work was
intended for further revision before final publication; cf.
2.1.6n. The *campus* where A. addressed the soldiers was
probably that adjoining the *castra praetoria*, Tac. *A.* 12.36,
Durry, *Cohortes prét.* 54 ff.

ξέρξης [1] ἀνὴρ Πέρσης, τὸν ἑαυτοῦ δεσπότην
Ἀρτάβανον ἀποκτείνας τήν τε ἀρχὴν ἐς Πέρσας
μεταστήσας, ἀλλὰ καὶ τῶν ἡμετέρων [2] ὅπλων
καταθαρρήσας καὶ τῆς Ῥωμαίων δόξης κατα-
φρονήσας, πειρᾶται κατατρέχειν καὶ λυμαίνεσθαι
τὰ τῆς ἡμετέρας [2] ἀρχῆς κτήματα. τοῦτον ἐπει-
ράθην τὸ μὲν πρῶτον γράμμασι καὶ πειθοῖ παῦσαι
τῆς ἀπλήστου μανίας καὶ τῆς ἀλλοτρίων ἐπιθυμίας·
ὁ δὲ βαρβάρῳ φερόμενος ἀλαζονείᾳ οὔτε μένειν
6 οἴκοι βούλεται, προκαλεῖταί τε ἡμᾶς ἐς μάχην. μὴ
δὴ μέλλωμεν μηδὲ ὀκνῶμεν, ἀλλ' οἱ μὲν πρεσβύτε-
ροι ὑμῶν ὑπομνήσατε ἑαυτοὺς [3] τροπαίων ἃ μετὰ
Σεβήρου καὶ Ἀντωνίνου τοῦ ἐμοῦ πατρὸς ἡγείρατε
πολλάκις κατὰ βαρβάρων, οἱ δ' ἐν ἀκμῇ ὄντες
δόξης καὶ κλέους ἐπιθυμήσαντες δείξατε [4] ὅτι
ἄρα καὶ εἰρήνην ἄγειν [5] πράως καὶ μετ' αἰδοῦς
ἐπίστασθε καὶ τὰ πολεμικὰ τῆς χρείας ἀπαιτούσης
7 γενναίως κατορθοῦτε. τὸ δὲ βάρβαρον πρὸς μὲν
τὰ ὑπείκοντα καὶ ὀκνοῦντα θρασύνεται,[6] τῷ δ'
ἀντιπίπτοντι οὐκέθ' ὁμοίως ἀντέχει, ἐπεὶ μὴ ἐκ
συστάσεως αὐτοῖς ἡ μάχη [7] κατὰ τῶν ἀντιπάλων
ὑπισχνεῖται τὸ εὔελπι, ἀλλ' ἐξ ἐπιδρομῆς ἢ φυγῆς
κερδαίνειν νομίζουσιν ὅπερ ἂν σχῶσι δι' ἁρπαγῆς.
ἡμῖν δὲ [8] καὶ τὸ εὔτακτον ἅμα τῷ κοσμίῳ ὑπάρχει,
καὶ νικᾶν αὐτοὺς ἀεὶ δεδιδάγμεθα."

4. τοιαῦτά τινα εἰπόντα τὸν Ἀλέξανδρον πᾶς ὁ
στρατὸς ἀνευφήμησε, προθυμίαν τε πᾶσαν ἐς τὸ

---

[1] ἀρταξάρης gl (cf. 6.2.1)
[2] ὑμετέρων Ai and ὑμετέρας i

the Persian, murdered his own master, Artabanus, and transferred the rule to the Persians; but then he gained confidence against our own armed power and, contemptuous of our reputation, is trying to overrun and plunder the possessions of our empire. I attempted first by letters and persuasion to deter him from this utter madness and greed for other people's property. But because of his barbarian vanity, he refused to stay in his own land. He is challenging us to battle. We must not hesitate or 6 falter. Those of you who are more senior, remember the many triumphs you won against the barbarians under Severus or Antoninus, my father. And you in the prime of your youth, who are longing to win fame and glory, show them that, although you can be gentle and respectful in keeping the peace, you are successful and brave in war, if that is what necessity demands. Barbarians are bold when others retreat 7 or hesitate, but put up a very different fight if met by resistance. The reason for this is that it is not from set battles that they expect success against an enemy. They believe that it is from hit and run tactics that they gain what plunder they get. We believe in properly disciplined battle tactics and we have learned how to defeat them every time."

4. As Alexander finished speaking, the whole army cheered him, promising him their full support in the

---

3 *illum* P
4 ἐπιθυμήσατε δείξαντες i
4 ἄγειν ἔχειν O
6 θαρσύν εται i θρασὺν ἐστι Macar
7 ἡ ἐκ συστ. μάχη αὐτοῖς conj Mendelss
8 P (*at*) τε Oi

πολεμεῖν ὑπισχνεῖτο. ὁ δ' ἐπιδοὺς αὐτοῖς χρήματα
μεγαλοφρόνως, εὐτρεπίζεσθαι [1] τὰ πρὸς τὴν ἔξοδον
ἐκέλευσε.[2] κατελθών τε ἐς τὴν σύγκλητον βουλήν,
καὶ τοῖς προειρημένοις ὅμοια διαλεχθείς, ἐπήγγειλε
2 τὴν ἔξοδον.[2] καταλαβούσης δὲ τῆς ὡρισμένης
ἡμέρας θύσας τε τὰς ἐπὶ ταῖς ἐξόδοις [3] νενομισμέ-
νας ἱερουργίας, παραπεμφθείς τε ὑπὸ τῆς συγκλήτου καὶ παντὸς τοῦ δήμου, τῆς Ῥώμης ἀπῆρεν,
ἐπιστρεφόμενος ἀεὶ πρὸς τὴν πόλιν καὶ δακρύων.
ἀλλ' οὐδὲ τῶν δημοτῶν ἦν τις ὃς ἀδακρυτὶ
παρέπεμπεν αὐτόν· πόθον γὰρ ἑαυτοῦ τῷ πλήθει
ἐμπεποιήκει ἀνατραφείς τε ὑπ' αὐτοῖς [4] καὶ μετρίως
3 ἄρξας τοσούτων ἐτῶν. μετὰ πολλῆς δὲ σπουδῆς
ποιησάμενος τὴν πορείαν, τά τε Ἰλλυρικὰ ἔθνη καὶ
στρατόπεδα ἐπελθών, πλείστην τε δύναμιν κἀκεῖθεν
ἀθροίσας, ἐς Ἀντιόχειαν ἀφίκετο. ἐκεῖ δὲ γενόμε-

---

1 εὐτρεπίζει O εὐτρεπίζειν? Whit
2 ἐκέλευσε—ἔξοδον om O
3 ἐπὶ—ἐξόδοις om P
4 αὐτῶν AP (ab ipsis)

---

1 Probably like a popular *acclamatio* in response to the
contio; cf. 3.6.8 for similar wording. On acclamations in
general, see Hammond, *Ant. Monarchy* 284–5, and the
references there quoted.
2 An issue of coins and medallions in 231 record the
profectio and a series of military slogans; *RIC* IV. 2.112, no.
524, 124, no. 666A; *BMC* VI. 76–9. The title of proconsul
which appears in the *acta Arvalia* in 231 (*CIL* VI. 2108; also
on another inscription, *AE* (1950) 154) may denote that the
emperor had left Rome, though the title appears earlier also
(*AE* (1941) 163 from Cappadocia; but I am sceptical about
this inscription which records *trib. potest. imp. II* (sic) *cos.*
also; the *II* has been misplaced and should stand after *cos.*,

war.[1] For his part he made a generous distribution
of money to them and ordered preparations for departure to be put in hand. He went to the senate
and announced his departure to them in terms similar
to what he had already said to the soldiers. Then, 2
as the planned date came, he made the proper sacrifices for departures and, escorted by the senate and
all the people, he set out from Rome,[2] continually
looking back to the city with tears in his eyes. Not
one of even the ordinary people in the procession
was without tears either. Brought up under their
eyes [3] and after so many years of fair rule, he had
made himself loved by the people. The journey was 3
completed with all speed, first to the garrisons in the
Illyrian provinces, where he collected a large force;
then on to Antioch.[4] On arrival in Antioch he made

thus dating the inscription to 226–8, though omitting *trib. pot.*
numerals). A. probably left Rome in late spring 231,
arriving in Antioch by the late summer.

[3] Cf. 1.7.4 for the same observation about Commodus.

[4] Attempts to trace the route of A. and to define his troops
by means of dedications for the emperor's well-being are
rightly regarded by Jardé, *Sévère Alexandre* 78n, with
scepticism; nor can much confidence be placed in SHA, *Alex.*
50.5, describing A.'s special Macedonian phalanx dressed in
special Macedonian armour. The presence of an officer of
legio XXX Ulpia (from Vetera on the Rhine) in Ephesus
c. 232–5 may be an indication of *vexillationes* from that legion,
AE (1957) 161. At least some of the soldiers from the legio
VII Claudia in Moesia Superior took part in the expedition,
since the grave of one of them records him as *interfectus in
expeditione Partica et Ar(meniaca)*; *JÖAI* 8 (1905) 19, no. 58;
cf. Ritterling, *RE* (legio) 1332. Signs of A.'s presence in
Thrace are claimed by Instinsky, *Sitzungsb. d. Preuss. Akad.
d. Wiss.* philol.-hist. Kl. (1938) 421–2 on the grounds that a
milestone appears there with the name of Mamaea upon it—

νος τὰ πρὸς τὸν πόλεμον ἐξήρτυε, γυμνάζων τε
τοὺς στρατιώτας καὶ τὰ πολεμικὰ ἀσκῶν.

4 ἔδοξε δὲ αὐτῷ πρεσβείαν πάλιν πέμψαι πρὸς
τὸν Πέρσην καὶ περὶ εἰρήνης καὶ φιλίας διαλέγε-
σθαι· ἤλπιζε γὰρ αὐτὸν πείσειν ἢ φοβήσειν αὐτὸς
παρών. ὁ δὲ βάρβαρος τοὺς μὲν πρέσβεις τῶν
Ῥωμαίων ἀπέπεμψεν ἀπράκτους, αὐτὸς δὲ ἐπιλε-
ξάμενος τετρακοσίους Περσῶν τοὺς μεγίστους,
ἐσθῆσί τε πολυτελέσι καὶ χρυσῷ κεκοσμημένους
ἵππων τε καὶ τόξων παρασκευῇ, πρέσβεις ἔπεμψε
δὴ πρὸς τὸν Ἀλέξανδρον, καταπλήξειν οἰηθεὶς
τοὺς Ῥωμαίους τῇ τε ὄψει καὶ τῷ σχήματι τῶν
5 Περσῶν. ἔλεγε δ' ἡ πρεσβεία ὅτι [1] κελεύει μέγας
βασιλεὺς Ἀρταξέρξης [2] ἀφίστασθαι Ῥωμαίους τε
καὶ τὸν ἄρχοντα αὐτῶν Συρίας τε πάσης τε [3]
Ἀσίας τῆς Εὐρώπῃ [4] ἀντικειμένης, ἐᾶσαι δὲ
ἄρχειν Πέρσας μέχρις Ἰωνίας τε καὶ Καρίας καὶ
ὅσα Αἰγαίῳ καὶ Πόντῳ [5] ἔθνη διαιρεῖται· εἶναι [6]
6 γὰρ αὐτὰ Περσῶν [7] προγονικὰ κτήματα.[6] τοιαῦτά
τινα τῶν τετρακοσίων πρέσβεων ἀπαγγειλάντων,
κελεύει ὁ Ἀλέξανδρος τοὺς τετρακοσίους συλ-
ληφθῆναι, καὶ παρελόμενος πάσης τῆς περικειμένης
σκευῆς ἐς Φρυγίαν ἐξέπεμψε, δοὺς κώμας τε
οἰκεῖν καὶ χώραν γεωργεῖν, τοσαύτην αὐτοῖς

---

[1] ὅτι δὴ i   [2] ἀρταξάρης g (cf. 6.2.1)
[3] Mendelss from 6.2.2. and Zon. 12.15B πάσης ἀσίας τε Oi
[4] εὐρώπης AVg
[5] πάντα l προποντίδι conj Mendelss from 6.2.2
[6] εἶναι—κτήματα om P   [7] περσικὰ A om φ

---

the first recorded case of a milestone with the name of an
empress. The governor of Thrace before the expedition was

preparations for war, training the soldiers and prac-
tising manoeuvres.

He decided to send another diplomatic mission 4
to the Persians to discuss a peaceful alliance, in the
hopes of persuading them or frightening them by
his actual presence. But the barbarian king sent
back the representatives empty-handed, and in return chose four hundred of his tallest Persians,
decked in gold and sumptuous clothing and equipped with horses and bows, whom he sent supposedly
as his diplomatic representatives to Alexander,
thinking that the sight of Persians and their equipment would overawe the Romans. The mission 5
declared that by order of the great king the Romans
and their ruler must abandon Syria and the whole of
Asia opposite Europe, allowing Persian rule to extend
as far as Ionia and Caria and the peoples contained
within the Aegean–Pontus seaboard. For these were
the traditional possessions of Persians. Upon hear- 6
ing this ultimatum from the four hundred emissaries,
Alexander ordered them all to be seized. They
were stripped of their equipment and sent to Phrygia, where they were permitted to settle in villages
and farm the land.[1] They were punished only to the

---

probably Rutilius Pudens Crispinus, who then accompanied
A. to Syria (6.5.2n). SHA, *Alex.* 50.5, may contain a garbled
reference to six legions moved from the northern frontier for the
war, suggests Ritterling, *RE* (legio) 1330–1. The several
references to *exauctoratio* (Eutrop. 8.23, SHA, *Alex.* 52.3, 54.7)
probably refer to cuts in the army before this date for economic
rather than disciplinary reasons; cf. Domaszewski (in 6.8.8n).

[1] This piece of information, repeated by Zon. 12.15
(probably from H.), may well be local information picked up
by H. while in retirement.

ἐπιθεὶς τιμωρίαν ὡς οἴκαδε μὴ ἐπανελθεῖν·
ἀποκτεῖναι γὰρ ἀνόσιον καὶ οὐ πάνυ ἀνδρεῖον
ἡγήσατο μήτε μαχομένους καὶ τὰ κελευσθέντα
ὑπὸ τοῦ ἑαυτῶν δεσπότου ἀγγείλαντας.

7 τούτων δὴ οὕτως πραττομένων, παρασκευαζομέ-
νου τε τοῦ Ἀλεξάνδρου καὶ διαβῆναι τοὺς ποταμοὺς
ἔς τε τὴν βάρβαρον γῆν τὸν στρατὸν διαγαγεῖν,
ἐγένοντό τινες καὶ ἀποστάσεις στρατιωτῶν, ἀπό
τε Αἰγύπτου ἐληλυθότων, ἀλλὰ μὴν καὶ τῶν κατὰ
Συρίαν, καινοτομῆσαί τινα ἐπιχειρησάντων περὶ
τὴν βασιλείαν· οἳ ταχέως φωραθέντες ἐκολάσθησαν.
ἀλλὰ καί τινα τῶν στρατοπέδων μετέστησεν ὁ
Ἀλέξανδρος ἐς ἕτερα χωρία, ἐπιτηδειότερα δοκοῦντα εἶναι πρὸς τὸ κωλύειν τὰς τῶν βαρβάρων
ἐπιδρομάς.

5. τούτων δὴ αὐτῷ διοικηθέντων, τῆς τε στρα-
τιᾶς παμπληθοῦς συνειλεγμένης, ὅτε [1] δὴ ἀντίπαλα
καὶ ἰσόρροπα ᾠήθη εἶναι τὰ ἑαυτοῦ στρατεύματα
τῷ πλήθει τῶν βαρβάρων, σκεψάμενος σὺν τοῖς
φίλοις ἔνειμε τὸ στρατιωτικὸν ἐς τρεῖς μοίρας,

[1] ὅτι φ

[1] The Euphrates and the Tigris, though the geographic
details are so vague it is difficult to know whether A. actually
crossed the Tigris at all.

[2] The presence of Egyptian troops from legio II Traiana is
confirmed by the log book of the *strategos* of the nome of Ombos
and Elephantine, Wilcken, *Chrest.* no. 41, dated 232/3.

extent of not being allowed to return home, since Alexander believed it would violate their sacrosanctity and be rather cowardly to execute them when they were not combatants and simply delivering their master's message as ordered.

After this the emperor prepared to cross the 7 rivers[1] and invade barbarian territory with his army. But some of the Egyptian-based troops,[2] joined by some of the Syrians, mutinied in an attempt to cause a change of emperor.[3] The rebels were quickly caught and punished; but Alexander transferred some of the army to other countries where he thought there was more gainful employment for them in checking barbarian raids.

5. After completing these arrangements and collecting together a vast army, Alexander finally estimated that his force was equal in strength to meet the numbers of the enemy.[4] Meeting with his coun-

---

[3] H. may have misplaced here the mutiny of the Mesopotamian troops, in which the commander Flavius Heraclio was killed; noted by Dio (Xiph.) 80.4.1–2 and apparently dated c. 228; but Dio (Xiph.) 80.3.1 says there were many other revolts. Zos. 1.12 tells of a certain Antoninus who was proclaimed emperor by the troops; also a man called Uranius made a bid for the purple; Syncellus 1.674–5 (Bonn) indicates Edessa as the centre of the trouble. Later writers record another pretender, Taurinus (*Epit. de Caes.* 24; *Polemii Silvii laterculus*, Mommsen, *Chron. Min.* I. 521). The conspirators may all have been one and the same person, though the names are suspiciously like the pretender of 253/4, L. Julius Aurelius Sulpicius Uranius; cf. Jardé, *Sévère Alexandre* 66.

[4] On the preparatory measures, see 6.2.3n. The preliminary movements occupied most of 231, and the main expedition was probably launched in 232. The hasty repair of roads into Cappadocia in 231 was doubtless ordered as A. passed through Asia (see below).

καὶ τὴν μὲν μίαν ἐκέλευσε πρὸς τὰ ἀρκτῷα μέρη
ἀφορῶσαν, δι᾽ Ἀρμενίας ἐπελθοῦσαν φιλίου Ῥωμαίοις δοκούσης, κατατρέχειν τὴν Μήδων χώραν·
2 τὴν δὲ ἑτέραν ἔπεμψε πρὸς τὰ ἑῷα [1] μέρη τῆς
βαρβάρου γῆς βλέπουσαν, ἔνθα συρρέοντας τὸν
Τίγρητα καὶ τὸν Εὐφράτην ἕλη πυκνότατα
ὑποδέχεσθαι λέγουσι καὶ λανθάνειν ποταμῶν ἐκείνων μόνων [2] διὰ τοῦτο τὰς ἐκβολάς· τὴν δὲ τρίτην
μοῖραν καὶ γενναιοτάτην τοῦ στρατοῦ αὐτὸς ἔχων
ὑπέσχετο ἐπάξειν τοῖς βαρβάροις κατὰ μέσην τὴν
πορείαν.[3] οὕτω γὰρ ᾤετο διαφόροις ἐφόδοις
ἀφυλάκτως τε καὶ ἀπροόπτως αὐτοῖς ἐπελεύσεσθαι,
καὶ τὸ πλῆθος τῶν Περσῶν ἀεὶ πρὸς τοὺς ἐπιόντας

---

[1] ἀρκτῷα φi

[2] ἐκεῖνον μόνον A (but -ων μόνων A[1])

[3] μέσην τὴν πορείαν (πορίαν B) Οἱ Μεσοποταμίαν Mendelss

---

[1] The similarity between this strategy and that of Severus
in 195 does not prove it is untrue; cf. Dio (Xiph.) 75.2.3. The
question of how H. gained his information is impossible to
answer, but his account is the most detailed one we possess,
and seems trustworthy. He may have had access to the
ephemerides of A. (cf. *ILS* 1575 recording a freedman Theo-
prepes who was *proc(urator) ab ephemeride*) or H. may have
been present himself in the East; the latter seems more
probable in view of his criticisms of A.'s conduct of the war.

[2] The northern column probably crossed the Euphrates near
Melitene, judging from the repairs carried out on the Amaseia–
Melitene road in 231; *AE* (1905) 132–3, Wilson, *Anatolian
Studies* 10 (1960) 135. According to Msiha Zkha (Mingana,
Sources syriaques 105) the son of Artabanus (Artavasdes) who
had been resisting in the mountains of Armenia and Media

cil he divided the army into three columns,[1] the first
with orders to reconnoitre the northern regions and,
marching through Armenia (ostensibly Roman
allies), to overrun the territory of Media.[2] The 2
second was sent to spy out the eastern marches of
the barbarian territory, where reports say the Rivers
Tigris and Euphrates at their confluence drain into
extensive marshes, making them the only rivers whose
mouths are concealed.[3] The third column, the
cream of the army, Alexander undertook to accompany and lead in person against the barbarians by the central route.[4] He reckoned that
by these different lines of advance he would catch
the enemy off their guard when they were not expecting him. Also, the Persian force would be con-

(Zon. 12.15) had been captured and executed some years
before this (cf. 6.2.1n).

[3] The second column was probably intended to sail down
the Euphrates from Dura-Europos; the appearance of a *dux
ripae* at Dura about this time was perhaps connected with
this activity; Welles–Fink–Gilliam, *Dura-Europos, Final
Report* V. 1.23–4. It may have been intended to by-pass
Ardashir's reconstructed capital of Seleucia-Ctesiphon (Veh-
Ardashir) and enter Elymaïs and Persis from the flank (cf.
6.5.6–7).

[4] Almost nothing is heard of this column. A.'s presence at
Palmyra (ἐπιδημία θεοῦ 'Αλεξάνδρου) and the service of
Aurelius Zenobius with his Palmyrene cohorts under the
governor of Syria Phoenice, Rutilius Pudens Crispinus (*IGRR*
III. 1033), suggest that A. did not intend to enter north
Mesopotamia, but to cross the difficult terrain to Hatra.
The Roman presence at Hatra and record of work on the road
from Singara to the Khabur River in 232 (Oates, *Sumer* 11
(1955) 39–43) confirm that Hatra, which had come under
attack from Ardashir in *c.* 229, was now a Roman ally and
received a garrison of Moroccan auxiliaries.

διαιρούμενον ἀσθενέστερόν τε ἔσεσθαι καὶ ἀτακτό-
3 τερον [1] μαχεῖσθαι.[2] οὐ γὰρ δὴ μισθοφόροις χρῶνται στρατιώταις οἱ βάρβαροι ὥσπερ Ῥωμαῖοι,
οὐδὲ στρατόπεδα ἔχουσι συνεστῶτα καὶ μένοντα,
πολέμου τέχναις ἐγγεγυμνασμένα· ἀλλὰ πᾶν τὸ
πλῆθος τῶν ἀνδρῶν, ἔσθ' ὅπῃ καὶ τῶν γυναικῶν,
ἐπὰν κελεύσῃ βασιλεύς, ἀθροίζεται. διαλυθέντος
δὲ τοῦ πολέμου ἕκαστος ἐς τὰ ἑαυτοῦ ἐπανέρχεται,
τοσοῦτον ἀποκερδήσας ὅσα ἂν ἐξ ἁρπαγῆς αὐτῷ
4 περιγένηται. τόξοις τε καὶ ἵπποις οὐκ ἐς τὸ
πολεμεῖν μόνον χρῶνται ὥσπερ Ῥωμαῖοι, ἀλλ' ἐκ
παίδων σὺν αὐτοῖς ἀναστρέφονται [3] καὶ θηρῶντες
διαιτῶνται, οὔτε τὰς φαρέτρας ποτὲ ἀποτιθέμενοι
οὔτε τῶν ἵππων ἀποβαίνοντες, ἀεὶ δὲ αὐτοῖς
χρώμενοι ἢ κατὰ πολεμίων ἢ κατὰ θηρίων.

Ἀλέξανδρος μὲν οὖν, ὡς ᾤετο, ἄριστα βεβού-
5 λευτο· ἔσφηλε δὲ αὐτοῦ τὴν γνώμην ἡ τύχη. τὸ
μὲν γὰρ πεμφθὲν δι' Ἀρμενίας στρατιωτικόν,
μόλις καὶ χαλεπῶς ὑπερβαλὸν τὰ τῆς χώρας ὄρη
τραχύτατά τε ὄντα καὶ κρημνωδέστατα (πλὴν ἔτι
θέρους ὄντος ἀνεκτὴν εἶχε τὴν πορείαν), ἐμβαλὸν

[1] -τερα Ogl
[2] Steph -εσθαι Oi
[3] ἀνατρέφ. ABi

---

[1] The army was based on the feudal society, with peasant-
soldiers providing infantry forces for the feudal lord and an

stantly split facing the invading forces, and thus be
weaker and less co-ordinated in battle. It should 3
be explained that the barbarians do not have a paid
army like the Romans, nor do they have permanent,
standing garrisons,[1] trained in military techniques.
Instead there is a general muster of all males, and
sometimes women, too, when the king gives the
order. At the end of the war everyone returns to
his own home enriched by his share of the plunder.
They do not use their horses and their bows only in 4
war as the Romans do, since they are brought up
using both from childhood; they spend their lives
hunting animals, and never let their quivers out of
their hands or get off their horses. Both are in con-
stant use, whether in war or in hunting.

Alexander believed he had devised a sound plan of
campaign. But chance upset his calculations.[2] The 5
force which had been sent through Armenia, after an
almost impossibly difficult crossing of the country's
mountain ranges, which were extremely rough and
precipitous (though, because it was still summer,[3]

aristocratic class of warriors (artēshtārān) providing the
skilled horsemen; cf. *CAH* XII. 114–15 (Christensen).

[2] Cf. 1.13.6n on the use of fortune and chance in H. This
passage provides a good contrast between chance as opposed
to human calculations. But later H. attributes the failure of
A. to lack of care, cowardice and lack of discipline; the army
accused A. of failing to carry out his plan; then in 6.6.3 H.
reverts to his original theme, saying that the destruction of
the army was due to bad luck and bad judgement.

[3] If A. left Rome in early 231, he would have arrived in
Antioch in late summer; the rest of the year was spent in
diplomatic exchanges and training. The summer mentioned
here was that of 232.

ἐς τὴν Μήδων χώραν ἐπόρθει τε αὐτὴν καὶ πολλὰς [1]
ἐνέπρησε κώμας λείαν τε ἀπήγαγεν. ὁ δὲ Πέρσης
μαθὼν ἐπήμυνε κατὰ δύναμιν, ἀπείργειν δὲ τοὺς
6 Ῥωμαίους οὐ πάνυ τι ἐδύνατο· τραχεῖα γὰρ οὖσα
ἡ χώρα τοῖς μὲν πεζοῖς καὶ τὴν βάσιν εὐπαγῆ καὶ
τὴν πορείαν εὐμαρῆ παρεῖχεν, ἡ δ' ἵππος τῶν
βαρβάρων ὑπὸ τῆς τῶν ὀρῶν τραχύτητος ὁμοῦ
καὶ πρὸς δρόμον ἐπείχετο [2] καὶ καθιππεύειν ἢ
ἐπιέναι [3] ἐκωλύετο. ἧκον [3] δέ τινες ἀγγέλλοντες
τῷ Πέρσῃ ὡς ἄρα φαίνοιτο Ῥωμαίων στρατὸς
ἕτερος ἐν τοῖς ἑῴοις μέρεσι Παρθυαίων, τά τε
7 πεδία κατατρέχουσι. διόπερ φοβηθεὶς ἐκεῖνος [4] μὴ
τὰ ἐν Πάρθοις ῥᾳδίως λυμηνάμενοι ἐς Πέρσας
ἐμβάλωσι, καταλιπών τινα δύναμιν, ὅσην αὐτάρκη
ᾤετο ῥύεσθαι Μηδίαν, αὐτὸς σὺν παντὶ τῷ στρατῷ
ἐς τὰ ἑῷα μέρη ἠπείγετο. ἡ δὲ τῶν Ῥωμαίων
στρατιὰ τὴν πορείαν ἀμελέστερον ἐποιεῖτο μήτε
τινὸς φαινομένου μήτε ἀνθεστῶτος, ἤλπιζέ τε τὸν
Ἀλέξανδρον σὺν τῇ [5] τρίτῃ μοίρᾳ, γενναιοτάτῃ
οὔσῃ καὶ μεγίστῃ, ἐς μέσους ἐμβεβληκέναι τοὺς
βαρβάρους, κἀκείνους ἀνθελκομένους ἀεὶ πρὸς τὸ
ἐνοχλοῦν σχολαιτέραν αὐτοῖς καὶ ἀδεεστέραν παρ-
8 έξειν τὴν ἔφοδον. προείρητο γὰρ πᾶσι τοῖς στρατοῖς ὑπεράραι εἰς τὴν ⟨γῆν⟩,[6] καὶ τόπος ὥριστο ἐς

---

[1] καὶ πολλὰς om φP   [2] ἠπείγετο A
[3] ἐπιέναι κατὰ τῶν ἐναντίων ῥᾳδίως οὐχ εἶχε· ἧκον A
[4] ἐκεῖνα Oag   [5] om φi

the route was traversible), broke through into Media
and devastated the country, burning and plundering
many settlements. The Persian king was kept informed and resisted as forcibly as he could, but was
not really able to block them because the terrain 6
was broken. This provided firm and easy going for
infantry movement, but the barbarian horses were
stopped by the rough mountainous ground from
galloping, and so prevented from making any cavalry
attacks and charges. Then came the news to the
king that yet another Roman army had appeared in
eastern Parthia and was sweeping through the territory.[1] Fearing that the Romans, after devastating 7
the Parthian lands without difficulty, would invade
Persia, the king left behind what he considered
an adequate force to defend Media and hurried
off to the eastern districts at the head of his
entire army. Since there was no sign of anyone
or any resistance, the Roman army began to
grow somewhat careless on the march, expecting
that Alexander with the third column (which
was the strongest and biggest group) had invaded the central sector of the barbarians, and
that, because the enemy were being diverted to the
trouble-spot all the time, it would leave them an
easier and safer advance. All the troops had pre- 8
viously been instructed to make a flanking move-

[1] Cf. 6.5.2n.

---

[6] Whit from Stav (⟨πολεμίαν⟩ for ⟨γῆν⟩) ὑπεραρίστη (two
words B or hyphen V) glφ ὑπερτρέχειν a στρατοῖς, ἐπὰν αὐτοῖς
δηλώσῃ τὴν τοῦ βασιλέως κατὰ βαρβάρων ἔφοδον, τότ᾽ ἤδη
προσεγγίζειν αὐτῶ ἑκάτερα τὰ στρατεύματα, παρ᾽ ἑκατέρων τῶν
μερῶν. ἔσφηλε interpol A

113

ὃν [καὶ ὅπου] [1] συνελθεῖν ἔδει, παντὰ τὰ ἐμπίπ-
τοντα καὶ ἐν μέσῳ χειρουμένους. ἔσφηλε δὲ
αὐτοὺς ὁ Ἀλέξανδρος μήτε εἰσαγαγὼν τὸν στρατὸν
μήτε εἰσελθών, ἢ διὰ δέος, ἵνα μὴ δὴ αὐτὸς κινδυ-
νεύοι ψυχῇ καὶ σώματι ὑπὲρ τῆς Ῥωμαίων ἀρχῆς,
ἢ τῆς μητρὸς ἐπισχούσης γυναικείᾳ δειλίᾳ καὶ
9 ὑπερβαλλούσῃ φιλοτεκνίᾳ. ἤμβλυνε γὰρ αὐτοῦ τὰς
πρὸς ἀνδρείαν ὁρμάς, πείθουσα δεῖν ἄλλους ὑπὲρ
αὐτοῦ κινδυνεύειν, ἀλλὰ μὴ αὐτὸν παρατάττεσθαι·
ὅπερ τὸν εἰσελθόντα Ῥωμαίων στρατὸν ἀπώλεσεν.
ὁ γὰρ Πέρσης σὺν πάσῃ τῇ δυνάμει ἐπελθὼν οὐ
προσδοκῶντος τοῦ στρατοῦ, ἐκπεριελθὼν καὶ
ὥσπερ σαγηνεύσας, πανταχόθεν τε τοξεύων, διέ-
φθειρε τὴν δύναμιν τῶν Ῥωμαίων, ὀλίγων τε πρὸς
πολλοὺς ἀνθίστασθαι μὴ δυναμένων, καὶ ἀεὶ τὰ
γυμνὰ ἑαυτῶν, ἐς ἃ ἐτοξεύοντο, φραττόντων τοῖς
ὅπλοις· ῥύεσθαι γὰρ αὐτοῖς τὰ σώματα, οὐ
10 μάχεσθαι ἀγαπητὸν ἦν· ἔστε δὴ πάντες ἐς τὸ αὐτὸ
συναλισθέντες καὶ τῇ τῶν ἀσπίδων προβολῇ ὥσπερ
τειχίσαντες ἀπεμάχοντο ἐν σχήματι πολιορκίας
καὶ [2] πανταχόθεν βαλλόμενοι καὶ τιτρωσκόμενοι,

---

[1] [καὶ ὅπου] φi del Steph [καὶ] ἅπαντας Stav αὐτοὺς Wolf
[2] om i

---

[1] Cf. 6.1.8 for Mamaea's dominant position. It is typical
of H.'s interpretation of history that he should look for the
moral causes underlying the failure of A., whose rule was,
after all, one of which he approved. A ready answer lay to
hand in the domination exercised over A. by his mother;
this is the reason why such a disproportionate number of

ment into the territory, and a rendezvous had been
fixed where they should meet, once the territory between them was also under control. But Alexander
failed them by not invading with his army. Perhaps it
was due to fear—no doubt he wanted to avoid risking
his own life and limb for the Roman empire. Or his
mother may have restrained him because of her
womanly timidity and excessive love for her son.[1]
She used to blunt Alexander's efforts to behave 9
bravely by convincing him that it was other people's
job to take risks for him, not his to get involved
in the battle. It was this which brought about the
end of the invading Roman army. The Persian king
attacked the army with his entire force, catching
them by surprise and surrounding them in a trap.
Under fire from all sides, the Roman troops were destroyed, because they were unable to stand up to the
superior numbers and were continually having to
shield with their weapons their exposed sides that
formed a target for the enemy.[2] Under the circumstances saving one's skin was preferable to
fighting. In the end they were all driven into a 10
huddle and fought from behind a wall of shields, as
though they were in a siege. Bombarded from every
angle and suffering casualties, they held out bravely
for as long as they could. But finally they were all

chapters are devoted to the last four years of A.'s life, compared to the single chapter covering the first nine years of rule.

[2] While there is no reason to doubt the general facts of this
defeat of the Roman column the actual battle is described in
conventional clichés; thus, " few against many " (cf. 1.12.7
for a similar jingle); exposed sides in battle was a typical
feature of hoplite warfare (cf. Xen. *de Rep. Lac.* 11.9); a " wall
of shields," etc.

ἀντισχόντες ἐς ὅσον ἐνεδέχετο ἀνδρείως, τὸ τελευταῖον πάντες διεφθάρησαν. μεγίστη τε αὕτη
συμφορὰ καὶ οὐ ῥᾳδίως μνημονευθεῖσα Ῥωμαίους
ἐπέσχε, δυνάμεως μεγίστης διαφθαρείσης, γνώμῃ
καὶ ῥώμῃ μηδεμιᾶς τῶν ἀρχαίων ἀποδεούσης· τόν
τε Πέρσην ἐς ἐλπίδα μειζόνων πραγμάτων ἐτύφωσε
τηλικούτων ἔργων εὐπραγία.

6. ὡς δὲ ταῦτα τῷ Ἀλεξάνδρῳ ἐδηλώθη χαλεπῶς νοσοῦντι εἴτε διὰ δυσθυμίαν εἴτε διὰ τὴν τοῦ
ἀέρος ἀήθειαν, αὐτός τε δυσφόρως ἤνεγκε, καὶ ὁ
λοιπὸς στρατὸς ἠγανάκτησε πρὸς τὸν Ἀλέξανδρον
καὶ ἐχαλέπαινεν, ὅτι δὴ ψευσαμένου αὐτοῦ καὶ μὴ
τηρήσαντος τὰ συνθήματα προδοθείη ὁ εἰσελθὼν
2 στρατός. πλὴν ὁ Ἀλέξανδρος μήτε τὴν νόσον
φέρων καὶ τὸ πνιγῶδες τοῦ ἀέρος, τοῦ τε στρατοῦ
παντὸς νοσοῦντος, καὶ μάλιστα τῶν Ἰλλυρικῶν
στρατιωτῶν, οἳ ὑγρῷ καὶ χειμερίῳ ἀέρι ἐνειθισμένοι τροφάς τε πλείονας συνήθως εἰσφερόμενοι
χαλεπῶς νοσοῦντες διεφθείροντο, ἐπανελθεῖν τε ἐς
τὴν Ἀντιόχειαν ἐβουλεύσατο, καὶ πέμψας τὸν ἐν
3 Μηδίᾳ στρατὸν ἐπανελθεῖν ἐκέλευσεν. ἐκεῖνος μὲν
ὁ στρατὸς ἐπανιὼν πλεῖστος ἐν τοῖς ὄρεσι διεφθάρη,
καὶ ἠκρωτηριάσθησαν οὐκ ὀλίγοι ἐν δυσχειμέρῳ
χώρᾳ, ὡς ὀλιγίστους [1] πάνυ ἐκ πολλῶν ἐπανελθεῖν·
τὸ δὲ σὺν αὐτῷ πλῆθος ὁ Ἀλέξανδρος ἐς τὴν
Ἀντιόχειαν ἐπανήγαγε, πολλῶν καὶ ἐξ ἐκείνης τῆς
μοίρας ἀπολωλότων, ὡς μεγίστην ἐνεγκεῖν δυσθυμίαν τῷ στρατῷ καὶ Ἀλεξάνδρῳ ἀδοξίαν, σφαλέντι

[1] ὀλίγους a

destroyed. This terrible disaster, which no one likes to remember, was a set-back to the Romans, since a vast army, matching anything in earlier generations for courage and toughness, had been destroyed. Success in this important engagement fired the Persians with greater ambition.

6. The news came to Alexander while he was seriously ill, either from melancholia or lack of acclimatization to the atmosphere,[1] and made him bitterly depressed. But the rest of the army was absolutely furious with Alexander because the invading army had been betrayed by his deception and failure to keep to the plan. But the emperor could 2 not bear his illness or the stifling atmosphere. His whole army was suffering from sickness, but particularly the Illyrian troops, who were seriously ill and dying because they were used to a healthy, wintry climate and normally ate more food. So he decided to return to Antioch, and sent orders to the army in Media to return. But very few of the many soldiers 3 in this army survived the return trip, most of them dying in the mountains and several suffering mutilation of the hands and feet from the wintry conditions of the country. Alexander led his own body of men back to Antioch, but many of this section too had died, causing both the soldier's morale and the emperor's reputation to sink to their lowest point. Both Alexander's judgement and his luck had failed, with

---

[1] For the diseases of the atmosphere, see Hippoc. *de nat. hom.* 9; those in colder climates eat more, Hippoc. *de aer.* 3–4. Quoted by Leisner in Irmisch, *Herod. Hist. ad. loc.* (with many other examples of current medical views); cf. Arist. *de gen. anim.* 4.2.767a for diet and climate.

καὶ γνώμῃ καὶ τύχῃ, καὶ τῶν τριῶν μοιρῶν τοῦ
στρατοῦ ὧν ἔνειμε τὸ πλεῖστον ἀποβαλόντι διαφόροις συμφοραῖς, νόσῳ πολέμῳ [1] κρύει.

4 γενόμενος δὲ ἐν τῇ Ἀντιοχείᾳ ὁ Ἀλέξανδρος
αὐτός τε ῥᾳδίως ἐπερρώσθη τῷ εὐψυχεῖ καὶ
ἐνύδρῳ [2] τῆς πόλεως μετὰ τὸν ἐν Μεσοποταμίᾳ
ξηρὸν αὐχμόν, τούς τε στρατιώτας ἀνεκτᾶτο, καὶ
ἐφ᾽ οἷς λελύπηντο παρεμυθεῖτο μεγαλοδωρίᾳ
χρημάτων· τοῦτο γὰρ μόνον ἐς εὐνοίας ἀνάκτησιν
στρατιωτῶν ἐνόμιζε φάρμακον. δύναμίν τε ἤθροιζε
καὶ παρεσκεύαζεν ὡς δὴ πάλιν ἐπάξων [3] Πέρσαις,
5 εἰ ἐνοχλοῖεν καὶ μὴ ἡσυχάζοιεν. ἀπηγγέλλετο δὲ
καὶ ὁ Πέρσης λύσας τὴν δύναμιν καὶ ἑκάστους ἐς
τὰ ἑαυτῶν ἀποπέμψας. εἰ γὰρ καὶ ἐκ τοῦ κρείτ-
τονος ὑπέρτεροι [4] ἐδόκουν [5] γεγενῆσθαι οἱ βάρβαροι, πλὴν ὅμως ἐτετρύχωντο ταῖς τε κατὰ Μηδίαν
πολλάκις γενομέναις συμβολαῖς τῇ τε ἐν Παρθίᾳ
μάχῃ, πολλῶν μὲν πεσόντων παμπλείστων δὲ
τετρωμένων. οὐ γὰρ ἀνάνδρως οἱ Ῥωμαῖοι [6]
ἡττήθησαν, ἀλλὰ καὶ αὐτοὶ τοὺς πολεμίους ἔσθ᾽

---

[1] λιμῷ? cf. SHA *Alex.* 57.3   [2] εὐύδρῳ A
[3] ἐπανήξων O   [4] καὶ ὑπερ. O
[5] om φ   [6] γενναῖοι φ ἐκεῖνοι A

---

[1] SHA, *Alex.* 57.3, claims to be quoting H. in saying that the
army died by hunger, cold and disease (cf. *app. critic.*); but

the result that of the three originally established army groups he had lost the greater part in a series of different disasters, disease, war [1] and cold.

On his return to Antioch [2] Alexander made an easy 4 return to health in the refreshing atmosphere of the city with its plentiful water supply after the arid drought of Mesopotamia. He attempted to restore the morale of the soldiers and passify their annoyance by a generous distribution of money, believing this to be the only remedy which would restore his popularity with them. He also mobilized a force in preparation for another attack on the Persians if they gave trouble and did not remain peaceful. But a 5 report came that the Persian king too had demobilized his troops, dispersing them all to their respective homes. Even though the barbarians seemed to have emerged the victors by some superior force,[3] yet they had been damaged by the frequent skirmishes in Media and the battle in Parthia, because of the heavy list of losses and even greater number of wounded. The Romans, far from having retreated ignominiously, had in some cases actually inflicted

the *vita* claims this is contrary to the general reports, which were that A. had won a great victory (*Alex.* 55.1).

[2] During the winter of 232/3. It was probably during this time that Julia Mamaea met Origen, from whom, according to Eusebius, she received instruction while he stayed at court; Euseb. *HE* 6.21.3–4, Downey, *Hist. of Antioch* 305–6.

[3] An ambiguous phrase which editors have taken mean either " by some divine aid " (*forte quadam divinitus*); Bergler, Leisner, Stephan; or " from superior force of arms " (*ex meliore*); cf. Irmisch for references. Though the latter is tautologous, it is typical of H. to repeat himself. But cf. 8.3.9 for the claim that divine force had intervened if one was worsted in battle.

ὅπη κακώσαντες, παρὰ τοῦτο δὲ ἀπολόμενοι παρ'
6 ὅσον πλήθει ἐλάττους εὑρέθησαν, ὡς σχεδὸν
ἰσαρίθμου γενομένου τοῦ ἑκατέρωθεν πεσόντος
στρατοῦ τὸ περιλειφθὲν τῶν βαρβάρων πλήθει
ἀλλ' οὐ δυνάμει δοκεῖν [1] νενικηκέναι. δεῖγμα δὲ
τοῦτο οὐ μικρὸν τῆς τῶν βαρβάρων κακώσεως·
ἐτῶν γοῦν τριῶν ἢ τεττάρων ἡσύχασαν οὐδ' ἐν
ὅπλοις ἐγένοντο. ἅπερ μανθάνων ὁ Ἀλέξανδρος
καὶ αὐτὸς [2] ἐν τῇ Ἀντιοχείᾳ διέτριβεν· εὐθυμότε-
ρος δὲ καὶ ἀδεέστερος γενόμενος ἀνειμένης αὐτῷ
τῆς περὶ τὲ πολεμικὰ φροντίδος, ταῖς τῆς πόλεως
ἐσχόλαζε τρυφαῖς.

7. οἰομένου δὲ αὐτοῦ τὰ ἐν Πέρσαις ἐν εἰρήνῃ
μὲν ⟨μὴ⟩ συγκειμένῃ [3] ἡσυχάζειν, ἔχειν [4] δὲ ἀνα-
κωχὴν καὶ μέλλησιν τῷ βαρβάρῳ πρὸς τὸ πάλιν
ἐπάγειν τὸν στρατόν, ὃς ἅπαξ διαλυθεὶς οὐ ῥᾳδίως
ἠθροίζετο ἅτε [5] μὴ συντεταγμένος μηδὲ συνεστώς,
ἀλλ' ὄχλος μᾶλλον ἢ στρατὸς ὑπάρχων, καὶ τῶν
ἐπισιτισμῶν αὐτοῖς τοσούτων ὄντων ὅσον ἂν
ἕκαστος ἀφικνούμενος πρὸς τὸ ἑαυτοῦ χρειῶδες
ἐπενέγκηται, καὶ δυσαποσπάστως τε καὶ δυσόκνως

---

[1] δοκεῖ Aa   [2] Sylb οὗτος Oag οὗτ' l
[3] Whit τὰ ἐν π. ἐν εἰρήνῃ συγκείμενα (-κείμενος l) Oi ἐν εἰρήνῃ
μὲν οὐ κείμενα corr Steph ⟨μὴ⟩ μὲν ἐν εἰρήνῃ συγκειμένῃ Schwartz
[4] παρέχειν Lang Mendelss   [5] ὅτε φ οὗτε A

[1] Very similar to the language of Herodot. 2.169, though it
is clear that H. is not directly copying Herodotus. Once
again it is as though H. has a model in mind which uncon-

serious damage too on the enemy, and had only been
destroyed in so far as they were fewer in number.[1]
Practically the same number of soldiers fell on each 6
side, making the barbarian survivors appear to have
won by force of numbers and not sturdiness. Fairly
clear evidence of the damage to the barbarians lies
in the fact that for three or four years they remained
quiet without resorting to arms.[2] Learning of this,
Alexander also stayed in Antioch and devoted himself to the pleasures of the city, growing more cheer-
ful and more confident as his worries about the war
relaxed.

7. The emperor calculated that, since Persian
affairs were dormant in an unofficial peace, this acted
as an obstacle to the barbarian king and caused him
to hesitate in making a second invasion with
his army. For, if once the Persian disbanded
his army, it was difficult to reassemble, because
it was not an organized standing force. Being
really a horde of men rather than an army, with
as much food supplies as each person on arrival
brought for his own needs, they were difficult

sciously suggests to him a train of vocabulary; cf. 4.2.10n for
another Herodotean model.

[2] Indicating that A.'s campaign had not been entirely unsuccessful. H. was probably alive to witness, and here refers
to, the serious danger caused by the invasion of the Roman
empire by Shapur, successor of Ardashir, c. 241/2. Un-
fortunately H.'s vague " three or four years " make it impossible to place much confidence in this, one of the few pieces
of evidence H. produces for the length of his own lifetime.
Cf. 2.15.7n and Introduction, pp. xii–xix. SHA, *Max. et
Balb.* 13.4–5, and Zon. 12.18 suggest that the Persians were
again active in the reign of Maximinus, but the case is far from
proved; cf. *CAH* XII. 130 (Ensslin).

καταλειπόντων [1] τέκνα καὶ γυναῖκας καὶ τὴν
2 οἰκείαν χώραν, αἰφνιδίως ἄγγελοί τε καὶ γράμματα
ἐτάραξε τὸν ᾿Αλέξανδρον καὶ ἐς μείζονα φροντίδα
ἐνέβαλεν, ἐπιστειλάντων αὐτῷ τῶν ἐμπεπιστευμέ-
νων τὴν ᾿Ιλλυρίδος ἡγεμονίαν ὅτι ἄρα Γερμανοὶ
῾Ρῆνον καὶ ῎Ιστρον διαβαίνοντες [2] τὴν ῾Ρωμαίων
πορθοῦσιν ἀρχὴν καὶ τὰ ἐπὶ ταῖς ὄχθαις στρατόπεδα ἐπικείμενα πόλεις τε καὶ κώμας πολλῇ
δυνάμει κατατρέχουσιν, εἴη τε οὐκ ἐν ὀλίγῳ
κινδύνῳ τὰ ᾿Ιλλυρικὰ ἔθνη ὁμοροῦντα καὶ γειτνι-
3 ῶντα ᾿Ιταλίᾳ· δεῖσθαι τοίνυν τῆς αὐτοῦ παρουσίας
καὶ τοῦ στρατοῦ παντὸς ὃς ἦν σὺν αὐτῷ. δηλωθέν-
τα δὴ ταῦτα τόν τε ᾿Αλέξανδρον ἐτάραξε καὶ τοὺς
ἐκ τοῦ ᾿Ιλλυρικοῦ στρατιώτας ἐλύπησε,[3] διπλῇ
δοκοῦντας κεχρῆσθαι συμφορᾷ,[3] ἔκ τε ὧν πεπόν-
θεσαν Πέρσαις μαχόμενοι, ἔκ τε ὧν ἐπυνθάνοντο
τοὺς οἰκείους ἕκαστοι ὑπὸ Γερμανῶν ἀπολωλότας.

---

[1] P -λιπόντων Oi   [2] διαβάντες Jo
[3] ἐλύπησε—συμφορᾷ om A

[1] Cf. 6.5.3n; the reference is evidently to the feudal,
peasant-farmer infantry force used by the Persians.
[2] For the ambiguity of the term " Illyrian," see 2.9.9, but
H. evidently refers here to the dangers threatening Noricum
and Raetia, territories which were sometimes included in the
term "Illyrian"; cf. Appian Ill. 6. Yet judging from the first
point of A.'s expedition (later completed by Maximinus) it was
the Rhine not the Danube where the more serious danger lay.
Nevertheless H. is correct about the extensiveness of the crisis
on the front. The destruction of the forts of Zugmantel and
Saalburg on the Taunus salient and of Pfünz and Böhming just
west of Regensburg in the years c. 233/4 show that the entire

and reluctant to be torn away and leave their
wives and families or their own land.[1] But no 2
sooner had Alexander made this calculation than
dispatch-carriers and their communiqués de-
moralized him and threw him in a greater state of
anxiety. The message from the governors in Illyria
was that the Germans were on the march across the
Rhine and Danube, devastating the Roman empire,
over-running the garrisons on the river banks, and
also the cities and villages, with a large force and
putting the Illyrians who bordered Italy as neighbours in considerable danger.[2] Therefore, they 3
said, the presence of Alexander and the entire army
he had with him was essential. This news dis-
mayed Alexander and caused distress to the soldiers
transferred from Illyricum. They felt they had
suffered a double tragedy, first in their misfortunes
of the Persian war and then in the reports they received individually about the destruction of their
families by the Germans.[3] They turned their anger

Rhine–Danube link was in danger of collapse through the intrusion of the Alammani; cf. Franke, *Saalburg-Jahrb.* 15
(1956) 5–28, Forni in Ruggiero, *Diz. Epig.* (limes) 1216.
Later Maximinus was preoccupied with the lower Danube
tribes who may also have broken through at this time.

[3] The regional attachments of the legions had always been
strong; cf. Tac. *H.* 2.80 (the Syrian legions' fear of being
transferred to Germany). Severus' reforms accelerated the
process of localization and the growth of permanent military
attachments (3.8.5n). One of the causes of the discontent of
the Rhine troops in 235 was a fear that they might be transferred to the East (SHA, *Alex.* 63.5–6, *Max.* 7.5–6). Signs of
local frontier militia in the Odenwald and Wetterau along the
German *limes* as early as the late second century and the same
along the African frontier (probably about the same date) does

ἠγανάκτουν οὖν, καὶ τὸν Ἀλέξανδρον εἶχον ἐν
αἰτίᾳ ὡς τὰ ὑπὸ ταῖς ἀνατολαῖς δι' ἀμέλειαν ἢ
δειλίαν προδεδωκότα, πρός τε τὰ ἀρκτῷα μέλλοντα
4 καὶ ὀκνοῦντα. ἦν δὲ καὶ αὐτῷ δέος τῷ Ἀλεξάνδρῳ
τοῖς τε συνοῦσι φίλοις ἤδη καὶ περὶ αὐτῆς Ἰταλίας.
οὐ γὰρ ὅμοιον ἡγοῦντο τὸν ἐκ Περσῶν κίνδυνον
οἷον τὸν [1] ἐκ Γερμανῶν· οἱ μὲν γὰρ ὑπὸ ταῖς
ἀνατολαῖς κατοικοῦντες, μακρᾷ γῇ καὶ θαλάττῃ
πολλῇ διῃρημένοι, τὴν Ἰταλῶν χώραν μόλις
ἀκούουσι, τὰ Ἰλλυρικὰ δὲ ἔθνη στενὰ ὄντα καὶ οὐ
πολλὴν ἔχοντα [2] τὴν ὑπὸ Ῥωμαίοις γῆν, παρὰ
τοσοῦτον ὁμόρους καὶ γείτονας ποιεῖ Γερμανοὺς
5 Ἰταλιώταις.[3] ἐπαγγέλλει δὴ ἄκων μὲν καὶ ἀσχάλλων τὴν ἔξοδον, πλὴν τῆς ἀνάγκης αὐτὸν κα-

---

[1] A om φι   [2] ἀπέχοντα A
[3] γερμανοὺς τοῖς ἰταλιώταις, παρ' ὅσον αἱ ἄλπεις ἀλλήλους
διαφράττουσιν. ἐπαγγέλλει A

---

not, of course, support the statement of SHA, *Alex.* 58.4, that
A. began the system of hereditary *limitanei*; cf. Schleiermacher, *Bericht d. röm-germ. Kommission, 1942–50* (1953)
146–8; Baradez, *Fossatum Africae* 165 ff.

[1] An important statement for understanding part of the
reason for H.'s explanation of Roman institutions to his
audience.

[2] The reading may be corrupt here; the sense is that the
territory held by the Illyrians within the Roman empire is so
narrow that the frontier with the Germans is close to the
borders of Italy. The interpolation by the Monacensis MS
(A) assumes that H. is discussing the area of Raetia and

on Alexander, blaming him for his betrayal of their cause in the East through his negligence or cowardice and his hesitant procrastination over the northern crisis. Alexander and the advisers who accompanied **4** him were by this time even concerned about Italy, rating the German menace as very different from the Persians. The inhabitants of the eastern territories, separated as they are by a wide stretch of land and sea, hardly hear about Italy.[1] But the Illyrian provinces are a narrow stretch of land that do not occupy much of Roman territory.[2] This makes the Germans practically adjacent neighbours of the Italians. Reluctantly and sadly (through sheer necessity) Alex- **5** ander issued the proclamation of an expedition.[3] **A**

Noricum. The original home of the Illyrians in Bohemia, Moravia and N. Hungary lay across the Danube from Raetia and Noricum. They had been driven from their homes southwards and eastwards, or assimilated by the invading Celts and Germans over the centuries. Cf. Anderson, *Tacitus, Germania* 216–17, Fluss *RE* suppl. 5 (Illyrioi) 312–26.

[3] H. fails to make clear that A. returned to Rome in 233, when he celebrated a triumph and distributed his fifth *congiarum*. Although A. did not assume a title, he is described on an African milestone as *Partico max(imo)* [*Persico*]*max(imo)*; Jardé, *Sévère Alexandre* 81–2. The references to *Mars ultor* on coins, reminiscent of Augustus' dedication of the Parthian standards, may reflect a genuine victory (cf. SHA, *Alex.* 56.7 *signis relictis*). Acclamations of the senate are purported to have taken place on 23rd September 233 (*ibid.* 56.2); cf. Victor *Caes.* 24.2, Eutrop. 8.23, which allege victories. A medallion of 233 shows the emperor crowned by victory and trampling on the Tigris and Euphrates, Gnecchi, *Medagl. Rom.* II. 81, no. 17. A number of inscriptions also mention victory (collected by Jardé, *op. cit.* 83n; e.g. *CIL* VI. 186 *pro salute et reditu et victoria*); cf. *BMC* VI. 82 f., SHA, *Alex.* 56.1, 57.1. The German expedition did not begin until 234.

λούσης. καταλιπών τε δύναμιν ὅσην ᾤετο αὐτάρκη
ῥύεσθαι τὰς Ῥωμαίων ὄχθας, τά τε στρατόπεδα
καὶ τὰ φρούρια ἐπιμελέστερον τειχίσας καὶ
πληρώσας ἕκαστα τοῦ ὡρισμένου στρατοῦ, αὐτὸς
ἐς Γερμανοὺς ἠπείγετο ἅμα τῷ λοιπῷ πλήθει.
6 ἀνύσας δὲ τὴν ὁδὸν μετὰ πολλῆς σπουδῆς ἐπέστη
ταῖς τοῦ Ῥήνου ὄχθαις, καὶ τὰ πρὸς τὸν Γερμανι-
κὸν[1] πόλεμον παρεσκευάζετο, τόν τε ποταμὸν
ναυσὶ διελάμβανεν, ὧν[2] πρὸς ἀλλήλας συνδεθεισῶν
γεφυρωθέντα εὐμαρῆ τὴν διάβασιν τοῖς στρατιώταις
παρέξειν ᾤετο. μέγιστοι γὰρ δὴ οὗτοι ποταμῶν
ὑπ' ἄρκτῳ ῥέουσι, Ῥῆνός τε καὶ Ἴστρος, ὁ μὲν
Γερμανοὺς ὁ δὲ Παίονας παραμείβων· οἳ θέρους

---

[1] om P   [2] Steph διαλαμβάνων ὡς Oi

---

[1] A change in the disposition of the legions was made to
cover the route from south Mesopotamia; legio III Gallica
(reconstituted after Elagabalus) went nearer Palmyra
(Danada); VI Ferrata went to Syria Phoenice from Palestine,
Dura was probably strengthened and Hatra received a
garrison (6.5.2n). On the strength of the legions see 6.8.8n.

[2] Signs of A.'s activities are evident in the Taunus salient,
north of Moguntiacum, where the frontier had been strengthened as early as 223 and again after 229; cf. Schleiermacher,
op. cit. and *Hist.* 2 (1953/4) 103–4, Forni in Ruggiero, *Diz.
Epig.* (limes) 1198. Timesitheus, who had organized some of
the supply lines for A. in the Persian war, is recorded about
this time as *proc(urator) patrimon(i) prov(inciarum) Belgic(ae)
et duarum Germaniar(um) ibi vice praesid(is) prov(inciae)
German(iae) inferior(is)*, a remarkable office for an equestrian
official during the German war, and indicating the extent to
which A.'s doctrinaire devotion to senatorial appointments

126

force was left behind, sufficiently large, in his opinion,
to defend the Roman side of the river; the camps
and outposts were given more efficient defences [1] and
their full complement of soldiers. The rest of the force
Alexander himself took with him and marched against
the Germans. After completing the journey at 6
great speed, the emperor reached the banks of the
Rhine,[2] where he began to prepare for the German
war. The river was filled with boats, which, when
lashed together, he believed would provide the
troops with a convenient crossing by way of a bridge.[3]
The Rhine and the Danube are the two largest northern rivers, the one bordering Germany and the other
Pannonia.[4] In summer their depth and breadth pro-

was modified in practice; *ILS* 1330, Domaszewski, *RhM* 58
(1903) 227–8.

[3] The use of διαλαμβάνω in the sense of " intersect " is frequently used by Herodotus with the word " river "—thus to
divide up and fill up the river (e.g. 1.190, 1.202, etc.). A
medallion of 235 (*trib. pot. xiv*) shows A. crossing a bridge of
boats; the obverse portrays both A. and Mamaea with the
legend *mater Aug(usti)*; *BMC* VI. 209, no. 967 (pl. 31). In
7.1.7 H. appears to forget that A. has already bridged the
Rhine and makes Maximinus build another bridge; but I
doubt whether we know enough of the circumstances to affirm
that this is another sign of lack of revision on H.'s part, since a
bridge of boats might well have been dismantled and reconstructed in a relatively short space of time; cf. Poblocki, *de
Herod. vita* 22.

[4] A.'s activities appear to be confined to the Rhine, though
Maximinus later went on to the Danube. All of the information about the two rivers is simply repetition of literary
commonplaces; e.g. Ovid, *Trist.* 3.10.29 ff. (*undas frigore
concretas ungula pulsat equi*), *Pont.* 1.2.80, 4.7.9–10, Pliny,
Paneg. 12.3, 82.4–5 (*eadem illa nunc rigentia gelu flumina aut
campis superflua*); later repeated by Claudian, *Bell. Get.* 338,
Rutil. *de red.* 1.485 (see next note).

μὲν ναυσίπορον ἔχουσι τὸ ῥεῖθρον διὰ βάθος τε
καὶ πλάτος, τοῦ δὲ χειμῶνος παγέντες [1] ὑπὸ τοῦ
7 κρύους ἐν πεδίου σχήματι καθιππεύονται. ἀντιτυ-
πὲς δὲ οὕτω καὶ στερρὸν γίνεται τό ποτε ῥεῖθρον
ὡς μὴ μόνον ἵππων ὁπλαῖς καὶ ποσὶν ἀνθρώπων
ἀντέχειν, ἀλλὰ καὶ τοὺς ἀρύσασθαι θέλοντας μὴ
κάλπεις ἐπ' αὐτὸ [2] μηδὲ κοῖλα σκεύη φέρειν,
πελέκεις δὲ καὶ δικέλλας, ἵν' ἐκκόψαντες γυμνόν τε
σκεύους ἀράμενοι τὸ ὕδωρ φέρωσιν ὥσπερ λίθον.
8   φύσις μὲν δὴ τῶν ποταμῶν αὕτη· ὁ δὲ Ἀλέξανδρος Μαυρουσίους [3] τε πλείστους καὶ τοξοτῶν
ἀριθμὸν πολὺν ἐπαγόμενος ἀπὸ τῆς ἀνατολῆς [3] ἔκ
τε τῆς Ὀσροηνῶν χώρας, καὶ εἴ τινες Παρθυαίων
αὐτόμολοι ἢ χρήμασιν ἀναπεισθέντες ἠκολουθήκε-
σαν [4] αὐτῷ βοηθήσοντες, ἐξήρτυε δὴ [5] Γερμανοῖς
ἀντιτάξων. μάλιστα γὰρ τοιοῦτος στρατὸς ὀχληρὸς
ἐκείνοις γίνεται, τῶν τε Μαυρουσίων πόρρωθεν
ἀκοντιζόντων καὶ τὰς ἐπιδρομὰς τάς τε ἀναχωρή-
σεις κούφως ποιουμένων, τῶν τε τοξοτῶν ἐς
γυμνὰς τὰς κεφαλὰς αὐτῶν καὶ σώματα ἐπιμήκη
ῥᾷστα καὶ πόρρωθεν κατὰ [6] σκοποῦ τοξευόντων.[7]

[1] παγέντος Ogl   [2] Reisk αὐτῶ φι ἐς αὐτὸ A
[3] Μαυρουσίους—ἀνατολῆς om A   [4] ἠκολούθησαν O
[5] δὲ Oag   [6] ⟨ὡς⟩ κατὰ Steph
[7] lacuna after τοξευόντων Mendelss Stav

[1] A typical conceit of the kind favoured by the sophistic
schools (cf. Ovid, *Trist.* 3.10.23–4), who delighted in expanding

128

vide a navigable channel, but in winter they are frozen over because of the low temperatures, and are used by horses as though they were firm ground. So hard 7 and solid does the river, at one time a flowing current, now become that it does not just support the weight of horses' hooves and men's feet but, if anyone wants to draw water, they do not bring waterjugs and empty bowls but axes and mattocks to hack it out and carry it home like a stone in their hands without a bowl.[1]

So much for the description of the rivers. Alex- 8 ander had brought with him very many Moroccans and a huge force of archers from the East;[2] the latter came from Osrhoene, though some were Parthian deserters and mercenaries that had enlisted to serve the emperor. This force Alexander began to train to use against the Germans. An army of this kind is particularly harassing to them because the Mauretanians, with their long-range javelin throwing, used their tactics of light-armed attack and withdrawal, and the archers found the Germans' bare heads and large bodies an easy long-distance target for their arrows.

a theme by means of these picturesque *schemata ennoias*. The whole of this passage on the rivers (which is not obviously relevant to the history—winter on the Danube?) bears all the character of a *melete* (a practice declamation) with its use of antithesis, parisa, assonance and chiasmus. The inclusion of this material was not to give information to an ignorant audience but to please a sophisticated public. Cf. Introduction, pp. xxviii ff.

[2] Evidence of the presence of eastern troops is confirmed by *CIL* XI. 3104, XIII. 6677a (the name of the Osrhoenians has been obliterated, probably because of their subsequent revolt, 7.1.9–10). For other troops, see 7.2.3n.

129

ἐπιθέοντες δὲ πρὸς¹ τὴν συστάδην² μάχην,
ἀντιτυπεῖς³ καὶ ἰσόρροποι πολλάκις Ῥωμαίοις
ἐγίνοντο.⁴

9 Ἀλέξανδρος μὲν ἐν τούτοις ἦν· πλὴν ἔδοξεν
αὐτῷ πρεσβείαν πέμψαι πρὸς αὐτοὺς καὶ περὶ
εἰρήνης διαλέγεσθαι. πάντα τε ὑπισχνεῖτο παρέξειν ὅσων δέονται, καὶ χρημάτων ἀφειδῶς ἔχειν.⁵
τούτῳ γὰρ μάλιστα Γερμανοὶ πείθονται, φιλάργυ-
ροί τε ὄντες καὶ τὴν εἰρήνην ἀεὶ πρὸς Ῥωμαίους
χρυσίου καπηλεύοντες· ὅθεν ὁ Ἀλέξανδρος ἐπειρᾶτο ὠνήσασθαι μᾶλλον τὰς πρὸς αὐτοὺς⁶ σπονδὰς
10 ἢ διὰ πολέμου κινδυνεύειν. οἱ μέντοι στρατιῶται
χαλεπῶς ἔφερον διατριβῆς τε ματαίας ἐγγινομέ-
νης, καὶ μηδέν τι γενναῖον ἢ πρόθυμον ἐς τὸ
πολεμεῖν παρέχοντος τοῦ Ἀλεξάνδρου, ἀλλ᾽ ἡνιοχεί-
αις καὶ τρυφαῖς προσέχοντος,⁷ δέον ἐπεξελθεῖν
καὶ τιμωρήσασθαι Γερμανοὺς ἐπὶ τοῖς προτετολ-
μημένοις.⁸ 8. ἦν δέ τις ἐν τῷ στρατῷ Μαξιμῖνος

¹ ἐπιθέοντες δὲ πρὸς Stroth ἐπέθεόν τε πρὸς φι ἐπεὶ δὲ ὄντες
πρὸς A ἐπέθεόν ⟨ἐσθ᾽ ὅτε⟩ πρὸς Sylb
² συσταδὸν i   ³ ⟨ἐν ᾗ⟩ ἀντιτυπ. Steph   ⁴ ἐγένοντο Aal
⁵ ἔξειν Steph perhaps ὑπισχ. ὅσων δέονται χρημ. καὶ ἀφειδῶς
παρέξειν Whit
⁶ αὐτοῦ φ   ⁷ σχολάζοντος Jo   ⁸ τετολμ. Vl

¹ The phrase may refer to the Germans, not the *auxilia*;
cf. *app. critic.* for a conjectured lacuna in the text.
² Cf. 1.6.9 for the same implied criticism of Commodus and
the same comments on barbarian avarice. SHA, *Alex.* 63.5–6,
Max. 7.5–6, expand the theme to a typical rumour that A. and
his mother were anxious to return to the East. The story,
says the *vita*, was put out by the *amatores Maximini*. A.'s
problem must have been to gain time along a frontier which
had been penetrated in several places (cf. 6.7.2n).

If they charged into close combat, they were stubborn fighters and often the equals of the Romans.[1]

Such was Alexander's position. He decided, 9 however, to send a mission to the Germans to discuss peace terms, with a promise to meet all their requirements and saying that he had plenty of money.[2] This was the most effective bargaining counter with the Germans, who were avaricious and always ready to trade peace with the Romans in exchange for gold. That was why Alexander attempted to buy terms from them rather than risk the danger of war. But 10 the soldiers bitterly resented this ridiculous waste of time. In their opinion Alexander showed no honourable intention to pursue the war and preferred chariot-racing and a life of ease, when he should have marched out to punish the Germans for their previous insolence.

8. In the army there was a man called Maximinus,[3]

---

[3] C. Julius Verus Maximinus; *PIR*[2] J 407. The *vita* draws heavily upon H. but may contain some information from Dexippus, a near contemporary, and other less trustworthy sources. M. was born *c.* 172/3 (Zon. 12.16), probably a non-citizen (next note), who was recruited into the *auxilia* (cf. SHA, *Max.* 2.2 ff., for the possibility of transfer into the *equites singulares* in 196, though the passage is suspect, 3.6.9n). At some stage he gained his citizenship, perhaps for service in the field under the governor of Dacia *c.* 198/203, C. Julius Maximinus (*CIL* III. 1127). He transferred to the legions (by 211, SHA, *Max.* 4.4), rising through the ranks to be perhaps a *primus pilus*; from this position he may well have been transferred to the equestrian rank and a tribunate in the praetorian guard (cf. Birley, *R. Britain and the R. Army* 119–24, for the normality of such a progression), as suggested by SHA, *Max.* 5.1, under Elagabalus. After a number of equestrian *praefecturae* (see below), he was appointed *praefectus tironibus*. Although this was an age in which distinctions

HERODIAN

ὄνομα, τὸ μὲν γένος τῶν ἐνδοτάτω Θρακῶν καὶ
μιξοβαρβάρων, ἀπό τινος κώμης, ὡς ἐλέγετο,[1]
πρότερον μὲν ἐν παιδὶ ποιμαίνων, ἐν ἀκμῇ δὲ τῆς
ἡλικίας γενόμενος διὰ μέγεθος καὶ ἰσχὺν σώματος
ἐς τοὺς ἱππεύοντας στρατιώτας καταταγείς,[2] εἶτα
κατ᾽ ὀλίγον αὐτὸν χειραγωγούσης τῆς τύχης ἐλθὼν
διὰ πάσης τάξεως στρατιωτικῆς, ὡς στρατοπέδων
τε ἐπιμέλειαν τῶν ἐθνῶν τε ἀρχὰς πιστευθῆναι.
2 τὸν δὴ Μαξιμῖνον τοῦτον διὰ τὴν προειρημένην
στρατιωτικὴν ἐμπειρίαν ὁ Ἀλέξανδρος ἐπέστησε
πάσῃ τῇ τοῦ στρατοῦ νεολαίᾳ, ὡς ἀσκοίη τε αὐτοὺς
τὰ στρατιωτικὰ καὶ ἐς τὸ πολεμεῖν ἐπιτηδείους
παρασκευάζοι. ὁ δὲ μετὰ πάσης ἐπιμελείας ποιού-

[1] ὡς ἐλέγ. om P
[2] ταγείς Jo καταλεγείς lex Vindob

between senators and equestrians were rapidly losing their
rigidity, there is no good reason for believing M. ever reached
the rank of senator; all his posts can be explained in terms of
equestrian military appointments; Bang, *Hermes* 41 (1906)
300–3.
[1] The Greek almost exactly corresponds to the Latin *in
pueritia*. A list of H.'s Latinisms proves not that he drew
upon a Latin source, but that he was influenced by Latin;
cf. 1.12.2n. There is no reason to mistrust the story of M.'s
lowly origin, though H. (7.1.7) later admits it is a scandalous
story. The Greek " semi-barbarous " means semi-Romanized,
says Hohl, *Klio* 34 (1942) 264–89, and tales of Gothic or
German parentage are later inventions; cf. SHA, *Max.* 1.6
(parents called Micca and Hababa, corruption of *mixo-barbaros*),
Syncellus 1.674, 681 (Bonn) says he was a *Mysos* = Moesian,

132

from one of the semi-barbarous tribes of the in-
interior of Thrace. He is reported to have come
from a village where he was a shepherd-boy [1] once.
As he grew to manhood, he was drafted into the army
as a horseman because of his size and strength.
Soon, with the help of a bit of luck, he progressed
through all the ranks in the army and was given
charge of legions and commands over provinces.[2]
Because of this military experience, Alexander put 2
Maximinus in charge of all the recruits to give them
military training and turn them out fit for battle.
He discharged his trust extremely conscientiously,

which Altheim, *RhM* 91 (1942) 350–3 relates to a native of the
ripa Thracica in the Dobrudja, but this seems unlikely.

[2] The exact offices held by M. are difficult to determine
from H.'s Greek. The best interpretation seems to be that
after the praetorian tribunate M. became an auxiliary *praefectus* or *tribunus* (cf. Zos. 1.13 which says M. was *praefectus
alae* in 235); then he probably became a kind of local military
governor, perhaps *praefectus civitatium Moesiae et Treballiae*
(cf. *ILS* 1349 for the office and Victor, *Caes.* 25.1, describing
M. as *praesidens Trebellicae*), which might be described
generically as *praefectus gentium*, an office held by ex-auxiliary
officers (cf. *ILS* 2750 *tribunus militiis perfunctus proc(urator)
Aug(usti) ad curam gentium*); about 230 M. may have been
appointed as *praefectus legionis II Traianae* in Egypt, an
office sometimes described as *praefectus castrorum* and not in-
frequently held by an ex-*primus pilus* (Passerini in Ruggiero,
Diz. Epig. (legio) 580–5); there is some evidence for M. and
his son in Egypt in 232 in Wilken, *Chrest.* no. 41, though only
a restored text. From Egypt M. went to Mesopotamia either
as *praefectus legionis* or *praefectus castrorum* (the terms are
used much as in Egypt), the latter possibly indicating that
M. co-ordinated the legions in the province. The office of
praefectus castrorum was an important post in this period,
one grade below a praetorian prefect (*CIL* III. 99; cf.
Vegetius 2.9–10). See the discussion in Dobson–Domaszewski,
Rangordnung xxxi–iv.

μενος τὰ ἐγκεχειρισμένα εὔνοιαν πολλὴν παρὰ
τῶν στρατιωτῶν ἐκτήσατο, οὐ μόνον διδάσκων
αὐτοὺς τὰ ποιητέα, ἀλλὰ καὶ τοῖς ἔργοις πάντων
προηγούμενος, ὡς μὴ μαθητὰς εἶναι μόνον ἀλλὰ
καὶ ζηλωτὰς καὶ μιμητὰς τῆς ἐκείνου ἀνδρείας.
3 ἔτι τε καὶ δώροις αὐτοὺς καὶ παντοδαπαῖς τιμαῖς
ᾠκειώσατο. ὅθεν οἱ νεανίαι, ἐν οἷς ἦν τὸ πολὺ
πλῆθος Παιόνων μάλιστα, τῇ μὲν ἀνδρείᾳ τοῦ
Μαξιμίνου ἔχαιρον, τὸν δὲ Ἀλέξανδρον ἐπέσκωπτον
ὡς ὑπὸ τῆς μητρὸς ¹ ἀρχόμενον, καὶ διοικουμένων
τῶν πραγμάτων ὑπ' ἐξουσίας τε καὶ γνώμης
γυναικός, ῥᾳθύμως τε καὶ ἀνάνδρως τοῖς πολεμικοῖς προσφερομένου ἐκείνου. ὑπεμίμνησκον δὲ
ἀλλήλους τῶν τε ὑπὸ ταῖς ἀνατολαῖς διὰ μέλλησιν
αὐτοῦ πταισμάτων, καὶ ὅτι μηδὲν ἀνδρεῖον μηδὲ
4 νεανικὸν ² παρέχοιτο ἐς Γερμανοὺς ἐλθών. ὄντες
οὖν καὶ ἄλλως πρὸς τὸ καινοτομεῖν ἐπιτήδειοι, καὶ
τὸ μὲν παρὸν τῆς ἀρχῆς βαρὺ διὰ μῆκος ἐξουσίας
ἡγούμενοι ἀκερδές τε ἤδη πάσης προανηλωμένης

¹ τε μητρὸς φag   ² μηδὲ νεανικὸν om Jo

¹ The office of *praefectus tironibus*, apart from being concerned with training of recruits, may well have been of much
wider responsibilities; it was sometimes connected with the
census; cf. Ensslin, *RE* (praefectus) 1336. But in this case
M. may have been responsible for mustering the forces re-
quired for the campaign; cf. *ILS* 487 which records a body of
M.'s recruits who had been engaged on improving the com-
munications to Aquileia, a key town for the Danube front—
*viam quoque geminam a porta usque ad pontem per tirones
iuvent(utis) novae Italicae suae dilectus . . . munivit* (sc.

earning great popularity among the troops because
he did not confine himself only to teaching them what
to do but also took the lead in all the tasks.[1] As a
result they were not just pupils but copied his example of courage.[2] He also won their allegiance 3
still more by awarding them prizes and all kinds of
honours. So the young men, of whom the greater
majority were Pannonians, admired Maximinus'
courage and despised Alexander for being under his
mother's control and for the fact that business was
conducted on the authority and advice of a woman,
while he himself presented a picture of negligence
and cowardice in his conduct of war.[3] They reminded themselves of the eastern disasters due to
his procrastination and how he had shown no sign
of bravery or enthusiasm when he came to Germany.
On top of their general inclination to revolt, the 4
soldiers found the current state of the empire an-
noying because of the length of Alexander's rule,
and unprofitable now that all his munificence had

Maximinus) *ac restituit*—though the date may be after M.
became emperor; cf. 8.4.1n.

[2] A hackneyed rhetorical antithesis; cf. Xen. *Mem.* 1.6.3,
Isoc. *ad Dem.* 12 (Drerup), Joseph, *BJ* 5.314.

[3] There is little reason to believe that one of the causes of
the mutiny was A.'s excessive severity, which is part of the
idealized portrait of A. in the *vitae*; SHA, *Alex.* 12.5, 25.2,
50.1, 59.6, *Max.* 7.6. In fact A. seems to have been unable
to exercise any real discipline over the troops (e.g. SHA, *Max.*
7.2); cf. 6.4.7n. Although it is stated that M.'s initial support
came from the Pannonian recruits, Syncellus I.674 (Bonn)
speaks of the Celtic army (i.e. the German Rhine army) as
supporters of M. In this context, note that another equestrian, Timesitheus, was controlling the legions of the lower
Rhine (6.7.6n, 7.1.4n).

φιλοτιμίας, τὸ δὲ μέλλον καὶ προσιὸν ἔς τε [1] τὸ
κερδαλέον αὐτοῖς εὔελπι καὶ τῷ κτωμένῳ παρὰ
προσδοκίαν τίμιόν τε [2] καὶ περισπούδαστον, ἐβου-
λεύσαντο ἀποσκευάσασθαι μὲν τὸν Ἀλέξανδρον,
ἀνειπεῖν δὲ αὐτοκράτορα καὶ Σεβαστὸν τὸν Μαξιμῖνον, συστρατιώτην τε αὐτῶν ὄντα καὶ σύσκηνον,
ἔς τε τὸν παρόντα πόλεμον δι᾽ ἐμπειρίαν καὶ
5 ἀνδρείαν ἐπιτήδειον δοκοῦντα. ἀθροισθέντες οὖν
ἐς τὸ πεδίον ὡπλισμένοι ὡς δὴ ἐπὶ τὰ συνήθη
γυμνάσια, προελθόντα καὶ ἐπιστάντα αὐτοῖς τὸν
Μαξιμῖνον, εἴτε ἀγνοοῦντα [3] τὸ πραττόμενον εἴτε
καὶ λάθρα τοῦτο προκατασκευάσαντα, πορφύραν
ἐπιβαλόντες [4] βασιλικὴν αὐτοκράτορα ἀναγορεύου-
6 σιν. ὁ δὲ τὰ μὲν πρῶτα παρῃτεῖτο καὶ τὴν πορφύραν ἀπερρίπτει· ὡς δὲ ἐνέκειντο ξιφήρεις ἀποκτενεῖν ἀπειλοῦντες, τοῦ παρόντος κινδύνου τὸν
μέλλοντα [5] προελόμενος ἀνεδέξατο τὴν τιμήν, πολλάκις αὐτῷ πρότερον, ὡς ἔλεγε, χρησμῶν καὶ
ὀνε ι ράτων τὴν τοσαύτην τύχην προειρηκότων,
εἰπὼν πρὸς τοὺς στρατιώτας ὅτι ἄκων μὲν καὶ οὐ
βουλόμενος ἀναδέχεται, πειθόμενος τῇ ἐκείνων

---

[1] ἔσται φι   [2] τι O   [3] P Steph καὶ νοοῦντα Oi
[4] πορφύρᾳ περιβαλόντες Jo   [5] Jo τὸ μέλλον Oi

---

[1] Alternatively translated, " . . . and unprofitable because
his sense of ambition had spent itself". But, since H. indicates (6.3.1.) that A. never possessed military ambitions, it
is more consistent to regard this as another reference to the
parsimony of the reign (cf. 6.8.8n). Clearly a reduction of
largess was not the concern of new recruits alone.
[2] For the *commilito* theme, see, e.g., 1.5.3, 4.14.4, etc.

dried up.[1] But they were optimistic that the near
future would be profitable for them and bring desir-
able honours to the man who unexpectedly benefited.
They planned to do away with Alexander and declare Maximinus emperor and Augustus, because he
was their fellow soldier and camp-mate,[2] and seemed
the ideal choice for the present war with his experience and courage. They gathered in the open, 5
wearing their armour as though for their usual training,
and, as Maximinus came forward to supervise them,
they threw the purple, imperial cloak over him and
proclaimed him emperor, though it is not clear whether
Maximinus himself was unaware of what was happening or whether he had planned this secretly. His 6
first reaction was to refuse [3] and throw off the purple
cloak, but when they insisted at the point of the
sword, threatening to kill him, he preferred to avoid
the immediate danger rather than one in the future,
and accepted the honour (though the story is that
oracles and dreams had frequently in the past pre-
dicted such a fortune for him). He addressed his
soldiers and advised them that, although he accepted
under protest in spite of himself, because he bowed 7
to their desire, they must back up their decisions by

[3] H. rightly expresses some scepticism over the refusal of
power, though no doubt it was considered a means for testing
the enthusiasm and real support a candidate possessed among
the troops; cf. 2.3.4n. A number of sources record that the
revolt was not initiated by M., but by some officers; SHA,
Max. 7.4 (*tribuni barbari*). Zos. 1.13.1 says that the revolt
began among the legions from Pannonia and Moesia, who had
already taken up a hostile attitude to A. (6.7.3n). Jardé,
Sévère Alexandre 90n, believes that Zosimus' account derives
in part from Dexippus.

7 βουλήσει, παραγγέλλει δ' αὐτοῖς ἔργῳ βεβαιῶσαι
τὰ δόξαντα ἀραμένους τε τὰ ὅπλα σπεύδειν
ἐπιστῆναι τῷ Ἀλεξάνδρῳ ἀγνοοῦντι, τὴν φήμην
φθάσαντας, ἵν' ἐκπλήξαντες τοὺς συνόντας ἐκείνῳ
στρατιώτας καὶ φρουροὺς τοῦ σώματος ἢ πείσαιεν
ὁμογνωμονῆσαι ἢ ῥᾷστα βιάσαιντο ἀπαρασκεύους
8 τῷ μηδὲν προσδοκᾶν. ὡς δ' αὐτοὺς ἐς εὔνοιαν καὶ
προθυμίαν πάνυ [1] προκαλέσαιτο,[2] τά τε σιτηρέσια
ἐπεδιπλασίασε, νομάς τε καὶ δόσεις μεγίστας
ὑπέσχετο, τιμωρίας τε καὶ κηλῖδας πάσας αὐτοῖς
ἀνῆκεν, ἐπί τε τὴν πορείαν ἐξήγαγεν· οὐ πολὺ δ'
ἀφειστήκει τὸ χωρίον ἔνθα ἐσκήνου ὁ Ἀλέξανδρος
καὶ οἱ σὺν αὐτῷ.

[1] μᾶλλον A
[2] (or προσ-) Nauck προεκαλέσατο Vag προυκαλέσατο A
προσεκαλέσατο 1 προσκαλέσαντο B

---

[1] Very similar vocabulary is used by Zos. 1.13.1, indicating
that the writer was at least attempting to amalgamate H. with
his other sources. If so, he has misunderstood the significance
of the Pannonian references and assumed that M. was actually in
Pannonia when the revolt broke out. He then adds that when
A., who was on the Rhine, heard of the news he set out for
Rome, forgave the conspirators, was joined by Mamaea and
the prefects from Rome, who had come to settle the mutiny,
and was finally killed. But there is no reason to believe this
is true, since it stems from an explanation of how it was that
M., who was in Pannonia, and A., who was in Germany, could
have met.
[2] On the question of rises in pay and the meaning of
siteresion, see 3.8.4–5n, 4.4.7n. The three kinds of military
payments described here seem to be the *stipendium* (pay,

action. They must get hold of their arms and quickly
overpower Alexander before the news arrived, while
he was still in the dark. The object was to overcome
his attendant soldiers and his bodyguard, and either
persuade them to acquiesce or compel them to do so
without difficulty, catching them unprepared by the
unexpectedness of the event.[1] To assure his 8
popularity and their enthusiasm, Maximinus doubled
their pay,[2] promised an enormous bonus of cash and
kind, and cancelled all punishments and marks of
disgrace against them. Then he marched them out
on their journey. The position of the camp of Alexander and his retinue was not far away.[3]

siteresion), *donativum* (bonus cash payments) and other kinds
of *dona* (originally called *congiaria*, but the term was usually
reserved for payments to the city populace) which were payments in kind, such as oil, wine, etc. It is impossible that M.
doubled the salary, that had already been raised so high by
Caracalla. Therefore Domaszewski, *RhM* 58 (1903) 383,
suggested that Alexander and Mamaea had reduced the
stipendium to pre-Caracalla levels, thereby being able to afford
to bring the legions up to full strength (cf. 6.7.5); a measure
unsuccessfully attempted by Macrinus (5.2.5n). The theory
is attractive because it explains the reasons for Mamaea's
reputation for miserliness (6.1.8, 6.9.4) and the serious unrest
among the legions (6.8.3n). But Passerini, *Athen.* 24 (1946)
158, discounts the theory, and believes that H. here means
that the recipients of double pay were limited to the mutinous
legions, who thus became *duplicarii*, as had perhaps happened
to the soldiers who had supported Elagabalus in 217 (cf. *CIL*
VIII. 2584). In either case the increased military expendi-
ture was responsible for an added severity on the part of
provincial procurators in collections of taxes and the *annona
militaris*, as in Africa (7.4.4n).

[3] SHA, *Max.* 7.4, says the camp was *non longe ab urbe quadam*
in Gaul (i.e. Germany); the town was Moguntiacum; cf.
6.9.8n, Syncellus 1.674 (Bonn).

9. ὡς δ' ἀπηγγέλη [1] ταῦτα τῷ Ἀλεξάνδρῳ, ἐν [1]
μεγίστῃ ταραχῇ γενόμενος καὶ τῷ παραδόξῳ
τῆς ἀγγελίας ἐκπλαγείς, προπηδήσας τῆς βασιλείου
σκηνῆς ὥσπερ ἐνθουσιῶν, δακρυρροῶν καὶ τρέμων
τοῦ τε Μαξιμίνου ὡς ἀπίστου καὶ ἀχαρίστου
κατηγόρει, πάσας τὰς ἐς ἐκεῖνον εὐεργεσίας κατα-
2 τεθείσας πρὸς αὐτοῦ διηγούμενος, τούς τε νεανίας [2] ᾐτιᾶτο ὡς προπετῶς καὶ ἐπιόρκως ταῦτα
τετολμηκότας, δώσειν τε πάντα ὑπισχνεῖτο ὧν
δέοιντο, καὶ ἐπανορθώσεσθαι [3] εἴ τι μέμφοιντο.
οἱ δὲ σὺν αὐτῷ στρατιῶται ἐκείνης τῆς ἡμέρας
εὐφημήσαντες αὐτὸν παρέπεμψαν, ὑποσχόμενοι
3 παντὶ σθένει προασπίσειν [4] αὐτοῦ. τῆς νυκτὸς δὲ
διαδραμούσης, κατὰ τὸ περίορθρον ἀγγειλάντων
τινῶν ὅτι δὴ Μαξιμῖνος πρόσεισι [5] κόνις τε πόρρωθεν ἐγειρομένη φαίνεται βοῆς τε ἦχος πλήθους
ἐξακούεται, πάλιν προελθὼν ἐς τὸ πεδίον ὁ
Ἀλέξανδρος, συγκαλέσας τε τοὺς στρατιώτας,
ἐδεῖτο προμαχεῖν καὶ σώζειν ὃν ἀνεθρέψαντο καὶ
ὑφ' ᾧ βασιλεύοντι τεσσαρεσκαίδεκα ἔτεσιν ἀμέμπτως βεβιώκεσαν, πάντας τε ἐς οἶκτον καὶ ἔλεον
προκαλούμενος [6] ὁπλίζεσθαι ἐκέλευσεν καὶ ἐξελθόν-
4 τας ἀντιτάττεσθαι. οἱ δὲ στρατιῶται τὰ μὲν
πρῶτα ὑπισχνοῦντο, κατ' ὀλίγους [7] δὲ ἀνεχώρουν
οὐδ' ὅπλα λαβεῖν ἤθελον. οἱ δέ τινες τὸν ἔπαρχοντα [8] τοῦ στρατοῦ καὶ τοὺς οἰκείους Ἀλεξάνδρου

[1] ἀπηγγέλη τὰ περὶ τοῦ Μαξιμίνου ὁ Ἀλέξανδρος ἐν a
[2] JoP νεανίας συστρατιώτας Oi
[3] -σασθαι A -θῶσαι φ
[4] Steph -ζειν Oi

9. When Alexander was told what had happened,
he was panic-stricken and utterly dumbfounded by
the extraordinary news. He came rushing out of the
imperial tent like a man possessed, weeping and
trembling and raving against Maximinus for being
unfaithful and ungrateful, recounting all the favours
that had been showered upon him. He blamed the 2
recruits for daring to do such a rash thing in violation of their oaths of allegiance; he promised he
would give them anything they wanted and put
right any complaint. All that day Alexander's own
soldiers stood by him with expressions of loyalty and
promising they would protect him with all their
strength. After the passage of the night, at dawn 3
reports came in to say that Maximinus was approach-
ing, because there was a cloud of dust in sight a long
way off and a sound could be heard from the shouts
of a sizeable body of men. Going out on to the
parade ground again, Alexander mustered his troops
and begged them to fight for him and protect the
emperor whom they had brought up [1] and under
whose rule they had lived for fourteen years without
complaint. After appealing to everyone's sympathy
and pity, he gave the order to arm and take up
positions out in the battle line. In spite of their first 4
promises, the soldiers began to back out one by one
and refuse to take up their weapons. Some of them
demanded the execution of the military prefect and

---

[1] Cf. 6.4.2, 1.7.4.

---

[5] AP (*adesse*) πρόεισι φι   [6] προσκαλούμενος i
[7] ὀλίγον from P (*paulatim*)
[8] ἔπαρχόν τε al ἔπαρχον τὲ g (ὲ over erasure g²)

ἤτουν πρὸς ἀναίρεσιν, πρόφασιν ποιούμενοι αἰτίους
τῆς ἀποστάσεως γεγενῆσθαι. οἱ δὲ τὴν μητέρα
ἐμέμφοντο ὡς φιλάργυρον καὶ τὰ χρήματα ἀπο-
κλείουσαν, διά τε μικρολογίαν καὶ τὸ πρὸς τὰς
ἐπιδόσεις ὀκνηρὸν τοῦ Ἀλεξάνδρου μεμισημένου.[1]
5 καὶ μέχρι μέν τινος τοιαῦτα διαφόρως βοῶντες
προσέμενον· ὡς δὲ τοῦ Μαξιμίνου ὁ [2] στρατὸς
ἤδη τε ἐν ὄψεσιν ἦν, καὶ [3] βοῶντες οἱ νεανίαι
προυκαλοῦντο τοὺς [3] συστρατιώτας [4] καταλιπεῖν
μὲν γύναιον μικρολόγον καὶ μειράκιον δειλὸν [5]
μητρὶ δουλεῦον, προσιέναι δὲ ἀνδρὶ γενναίῳ καὶ
σώφρονι συστρατιώτῃ τε ἐν ὅπλοις ἀεὶ καὶ
πολεμικοῖς ἔργοις διητημένῳ, πεισθέντες οἱ στρατιῶται τὸν μὲν Ἀλέξανδρον καταλιμπάνουσιν,[6]
αὐτοὶ δὲ προσίασι τῷ Μαξιμίνῳ, αὐτοκράτωρ τε
6 ὑπὸ πάντων ἐκεῖνος ἀναγορεύεται. ὁ δὲ Ἀλέξανδρος τρέμων καὶ λιποψυχῶν [7] μόλις ἐς τὴν σκηνὴν
ἐπανέρχεται· τῇ τε μητρὶ περιπλακείς, καὶ ὥς
φασιν, ἀποδυρόμενός τε καὶ αἰτιώμενος ὅτι δι᾽
ἐκείνην ταῦτα πάσχει,[8] ἀνέμενε τὸν φονεύσοντα.[9]
ὁ δὲ Μαξιμῖνος ὑπὸ παντὸς τοῦ στρατοῦ Σεβαστὸς

---

[1] quae . . . invisum cunctis Alexandrum reddiderit P (leading
to many emendations) ὀκνηρὸν ⟨αἰτίαν⟩ τοῦ Ἀλεξάνδρου μίσους
Mendelss
[2] Aa om φgl   [3] καὶ—τοὺς om i but not P
[4] στρατιώτας i commilitones P   [5] μικρὸν i
[6] καταλείπουσι ag (but καταλιμπάνουσι g¹ in mg)
[7] Bekk² λειποψυχῶν Oi   [8] a -ειεν A-οι φgl
[9] -σαντα φJo

Alexander's household[1] on the grounds that they had been responsible for the retreat. Others criticized his mother's rapacity and miserliness over money.[2] As a result of this parsimonious attitude and unreadiness to distribute largess Alexander was disliked. Thus the soldiers remained where they were for some 5 time shouting out different complaints. Maximinus' army was by now in sight and the young recruits began to call out, urging their fellow soldiers to desert their " mean little sissy " or " their timid little lad tied to his mother's apron strings " and to come over to the side of a man who was brave and moderate, always their companion in battle and devoted to a life of military action. The soldiers were persuaded, and abandoning Alexander, they joined Maximinus, who was universally acclaimed as emperor. Trembling and terrified out of his wits, 6 Alexander just managed to get back to his tent. There, the reports say, he waited for his executioner, clinging to his mother and weeping and blaming her for his misfortunes. After Maximinus had been hailed with the title of Augustus by the whole army,

[1] H.'s language does not make it clear whether it is the praetorian prefect who was the subject of hatred or another official, though one naturally assumes it was the former. Names of A.'s later prefects are not known; perhaps the jurist, Julius Paulus was in office at this time; Pflaum, *Marbre de Thorigny* 44 ff., thinks he was the successor of Ulpian, though there is no proof that he was ever prefect (Howe, *Praet. Pref.* 105 f.). Possibly M. Attius Cornelianus, prefect about 230 was still in office and is the prefect referred to on *CIL* II. 2664 (234); cf. Howe, *op. cit.*, no. 39. Zos. 1.13.2 says that the prefects (i.e. both) were killed in 235.

[2] For a possible explanation of Mamaea's motives, see 6.8.8n.

προσαγορευθεὶς πέμπει χιλιάρχην ἑκατοντάρχας τέ
τινας τοὺς φονεύσοντας τὸν Ἀλέξανδρον καὶ τὴν
μητέρα καὶ εἴ[1] τινες ἀνθίσταντο τῶν σὺν αὐτῷ.
7 οἱ δὲ ἀφικόμενοι καὶ ἐπιπηδήσαντες τῇ σκηνῇ
αὐτόν τε ἀναιροῦσι καὶ τὴν μητέρα καὶ[1] εἴ τινες
ἐδόκουν ἐκείνῳ φίλοι καὶ τίμιοι, πλὴν τῶν πρὸς
ὀλίγον φυγεῖν ἢ λαθεῖν δυνηθέντων, οὓς πάντας
μετ' οὐ πολύ Μαξιμῖνος συλλαβὼν ἀπέκτεινεν.
8 τέλος μὲν δὴ τοιοῦτο κατέλαβε τὸν Ἀλέξανδρον
[καὶ τὴν μητέρα],[2] βασιλεύσαντα ἔτεσι τεσσαρεσκαίδεκα, ὅσον πρὸς τοὺς ἀρχομένους, ἀμέμπτως
καὶ ἀναιμωτί· φόνων τε γὰρ καὶ ὠμότητος
ἀκρίτων τε ἔργων ἀλλότριος ἐγένετο, ἔς τε τὸ
φιλάνθρωπον καὶ εὐεργετικώτερον[3] ἐπιρρεπής.
πάνυ γοῦν ἂν ἡ Ἀλεξάνδρου βασιλεία εὐδοκίμησεν
ἐς τὸ ὁλόκληρον, εἰ μὴ διεβέβλητο αὐτῷ τὰ τῆς
μητρὸς ἐς φιλαργυρίαν τε καὶ μικρολογίαν.

[1] εἴ τινες—καὶ om A
[2] om Cassola
[3] εὐεργετικὸν AJo

---

[1] Cassola, *RAAN* 38 (1963) 143, rightly points out that the
phrase " and his mother " has crept in from 6.9.6 and 6.9.7,
through the hand of a careless copyist. It does not fit here
grammatically.
[2] The exact date is not known for A.'s death. SHA, *Alex.*
59–60 (corrected by Lécrivain, *Études sur l'Histoire Aug.* 229)
means he died on 22nd March (235) at Bretzenheim bei Mainz;
the other literary evidence for the length of his reign is col-

he sent a tribune with some centurions to kill Alexander and his mother and any of his entourage that showed resistance. On arrival they burst into the 7 tent and slaughtered the emperor, his mother and all those thought to be his friends or favourites. Some of them managed to escape or hide for a brief time, but Maximinus soon caught them and killed them all.

So Alexander [and his mother] [1] met his end after 8 a rule of fourteen years which, as far as his subjects were concerned, was without fault or bloodshed.[2] Murder, cruelty and injustice were not part of his nature; his inclination was towards humane and benevolent behaviour. Indeed, his reign would have been notable for its complete success, but for the blame he incurred through his mother's faults of avarice and meanness.

lected in *CIL* XIII. 2.1, p. 298, though Eutrop. 8.23, Victor, *Caes.* 24.7, and *liber generationis* (Mommsen, *Chron. Min.* 1.138) all more or less agree that A. ruled almost exactly thirteen years from the death of Elagabalus. An attempt by van Sickle, *CP* 22 (1927) 315–17, and Schwartz, *CÉ* 30 (1955) 124–6, to date A.'s death to 8th January 235 is based on the insecure evidence of *P.Oxy.* 912, whose date is partially missing. News of Maximinus' accession was known in Rome by 25th March (*CIL* VI. 2001), in Numidia by 3rd May (*AE* (1948) 209), but not known—or at least unrecorded—in Egypt on 4th April (*Stud. Pal.* 20, no. 35) nor in Dura-Europos on 21st June (*Dura-Europos, Prelim. Report* V. 1.298). A date about 10th March would be consistent with the evidence; cf. Gilliam, *CÉ* 31 (1956) 149–51.

BOOK SEVEN

ΒΙΒΛΙΟΝ ΕΒΔΟΜΟΝ

1. Τίνι μὲν βίῳ Ἀλέξανδρος ἐχρήσατο τέλει τε
ὁποίῳ βασιλεύσας ἐτῶν τεσσαρεσκαίδεκα, ἐν τοῖς
προειρημένοις ἐδηλώσαμεν· ὁ δὲ Μαξιμῖνος παραλαβὼν τὴν ἀρχὴν [1] πολλὴν τὴν μεταβολὴν ἐποιή-
σατο, τραχύτατα καὶ μετὰ πολλοῦ φόβου τῇ
ἐξουσίᾳ χρώμενος, ἔκ τε πραείας καὶ πάνυ ἡμέρου
βασιλείας ἐς τυραννίδος ὠμότητα μετάγειν πάντα [2]
ἐπειρᾶτο, δυσμένειαν [3] ἑαυτῷ συνειδώς, ὅτι [4]
πρῶτος ἐξ εὐτελείας τῆς ἐσχάτης ἐς τοσαύτην
2 τύχην ἤλασε. φύσει δὲ ἦν τὸ ἦθος, ὥσπερ καὶ τὸ
γένος, βάρβαρος· τό τε φονικὸν πάτριον ἔχων καὶ
ἐπιχώριον, πρόνοιαν ἐποιεῖτο τὴν ἀρχὴν δι'
ὠμότητος βεβαιῶσαι, δεδιὼς μή τι τῇ [5] συγκλήτῳ
καὶ τοῖς ὑπηκόοις εὐκαταφρόνητος γένηται, οὐκ
ἐς τὴν παροῦσαν αὐτοῦ τύχην ἀφορῶσιν, ἀλλ' ἐς
τὰ τῆς γενέσεως [6] εὐτελῆ σπάργανα. τεθρύλητο
γὰρ παρὰ πᾶσι καὶ διεβέβλητο, ὅτι δὴ ποιμαίνων

---

[1] iJo βασίλειαν O   [2] om O
[3] δυσγένειαν Sylb cf. SHA Max. 8.9 propter humilitatem
generis barbari a nobilitate contemneretur
[4] ὅτι τε i   [5] μήτε τῇ a μή τοι τῇ A μή τῇ τε g
[6] γεννήσεως φ

BOOK SEVEN

1. In the last book I described the life and death of Alexander in a reign of fourteen years.[1] Once Maximinus had taken over the empire, he caused a great change, exercising his power cruelly and causing widespread fear. He tried to make a complete transformation from a mild tolerant autocracy to a savage tyranny,[2] conscious of the hatred against him for being the first man to rise from the most humble origins to such a fortunate position. But by his birth and normal behaviour he was a bar- 2 barian. Possessing the bloodthirsty temperament derived from his ancestors and his country, he devoted himself to strengthening his rule by cruel actions. He was afraid that the senate and his subjects would despise him, forgetting his present good fortune and fixing their attention on the humble circumstances of his birth. There was a scandalous story widely circulated that he was supposed

---

[1] For the recapitulation of chapter headings, see 3.1.1n.

[2] H. is at pains to fit M. into the schematic form of ideogrammatic language that he has used throughout the history; cf. 1.1.4n. So he contrasts *tyrannos* and *basileus*, savagery and gentleness, barbarian and Roman, military and senatorial. The subject was obviously one of political importance as H. wrote, and therefore H. is in danger of exaggerating the extent of the *metabole* that took place in the empire. See the comments of Townsend, *YCS* 14 (1955) 52 ff., and Introduction, pp. lxxii ff.

ἐν τοῖς Θρᾳκίοις ὄρεσιν, ἐπιδούς τε αὐτὸν διὰ
μέγεθος καὶ ἰσχὺν σώματος ἐς [1] εὐτελῆ καὶ
ἐπιχώριον στρατείαν, ὑπὸ τῆς τύχης ἐπὶ τὴν
3 Ῥωμαίων ἀρχὴν κεχειραγώγητο. εὐθέως οὖν τούς
τε φίλους πάντας, οἳ συνῆσαν τῷ Ἀλεξάνδρῳ
σύνεδροί τε [2] ὑπὸ [3] τῆς συγκλήτου βουλῆς ἐπιλε-
χθέντες, ἀπεσκευάσατο, καὶ οὓς μὲν ἐς τὴν Ῥώμην
ἀπέπεμψε, τινὰς δὲ ἐπὶ προφάσει διοικήσεως
ἀπεσείσατο, μόνος εἶναι βουλόμενος ἐν τῷ στρατῷ
καὶ μηδένα [4] αὐτῷ παρεῖναι ἐκ συνειδήσεως
εὐγενοῦς κρείττονα, ἀλλ' ἵν' ὥσπερ ἐξ ἀκροπόλεως,
μηδενὸς αὐτῷ παρόντος ᾧ [5] νέμειν αἰδῶ ἀνάγκην
4 ἔχοι, τοῖς τῆς τυραννίδος ἔργοις σχολάζοι. τήν τε

1 P καὶ Oi
2 om Reisk but see Crook, (*Consilium Principis* 87)
3 ἀπὸ Mendelss
4 μηδὲν φJο μηδέν' Mendelss
5 ὃν AV

---

1 Cf. 6.8.1, where the same details are related as facts; it is
clear that H. accepts them as true, since they fit in with his
stereotype. M. would have enlisted in the *auxilia*, since
Thrace was technically a *provincia inermis*. The famous
petition by the villagers of Skaptopare in Thrace show the
rapacity of these troops in 238, *IGRR* 1.674. A large number
of Thracian auxiliaries also served outside the province; cf.
Cheesman, *Auxilia of the R. Army* 178–9 and 81 (*equites
singulares*).
2 See 6.1.2n and Crook, *Consilium Principis* 87. It is not
clear from H.'s rather loose construction whether he means

to have been a shepherd in the Thracian mountains
until he offered himself for service in the small, local
army because of his physical size and strength.[1] It
was the hand of chance that had brought him to
rule the Roman empire. He immediately disposed of 3
all the friends accompanying Alexander, members
of his council selected by the senate;[2] some were
sent to Rome, others he removed from the administration on some excuse. He wanted to be left on his
own surrounded by his army,[3] without anybody
being near him who had the advantage of being
aware of their own nobility. Like a man living in a
fortress untroubled by the presence of anyone to
whom he would have to pay respect, he could then be
free to carry out his tyrannous activities. The en- 4

that both the *comites* and the members of the *consilium* were
part of the same group chosen by the senate, or whether it is
only the latter who were chosen for A.

[3] H. does not clarify the issue of whether the senate
officially recognized M.'s principate, though it is almost inconceivable he should fail to mention so important a matter if
there were anything but the normal procedure. Bersanetti,
Massimino 9–20, believes the senate recognized M.'s ursurpa-
tion, and only in 238 repudiated his title; but Altheim,
Niedergang d. alt. Welt II. 236, is sceptical about senatorial
recognition, basing his view upon Victor, *Caes.* 25.1, *primus e
militaribus potentiam cepit suffragiis legionum*; but Victor's
interests in the case render him more, not less, suspect. *CIL*
VI. 2001, 2009 both record M.'s inclusion in the *sodales
Antoniniani* (though the name is later erased) with the title
pro cos ex s(enatus) c(onsulto). Nor is there any reason to
doubt that M.'s son received the title of Caesar in 236 and
M.'s wife, Caecina Paulina, was deified soon after in the usual
way with senatorial decrees; cf. *RIC* IV. 2.153, *AE* (1964)
220 and 236. Victor also says that the senate recognized M.,
dum periculosum existimant inermes armato resistere.

θεραπείαν πᾶσαν, ἣ συγγεγόνει τῷ Ἀλεξάνδρῳ
τοσούτων ἐτῶν, τῆς βασιλείου αὐλῆς ἀπέπεμψε.
τοὺς δὲ πλείστους αὐτῶν καὶ ἀπέκτεινεν, ἐπιβουλὰς
ὑποπτεύων· ᾔδει γὰρ ἀλγοῦντας ἐπὶ τῇ ἐκείνου
ἀναιρέσει.

ἔτι δὲ καὶ μᾶλλον αὐτὸν ἐς ὠμότητα καὶ τὴν
πρὸς ἅπαντας ὀργὴν προυκαλέσατο συνωμοσία τις
διαβληθεῖσα κατ' αὐτοῦ συγκροτουμένη, πολλῶν
τε ἑκατοντάρχων συμπνεόντων καὶ τῶν ἀπὸ τῆς
5 βουλῆς ἁπάντων. Μάγνος τις ὄνομα ἦν τῶν
εὐπατριδῶν τε καὶ ὑπατευκότων· οὗτος διεβλήθη
συνάγειν κατ' αὐτοῦ χεῖρα, καὶ στρατιώτας τινὰς
πείθειν ἐς αὐτὸν τὴν ἀρχὴν μετάγειν. ἡ δὲ
συσκευὴ τοιαύτη τις ἐλέγετο ἔσεσθαι. γεφυρώσας
τὸν ποταμὸν ὁ Μαξιμῖνος ἔμελλεν ἐπὶ Γερμανοὺς
6 διαβήσεσθαι· ἅμα γὰρ τῷ τὴν ἀρχὴν παραλαβεῖν
εὐθέως πολεμικῶν ἔργων ἤρξατο, καὶ διὰ σώματος

---

[1] There is a danger of exaggerating the break. Though not
a servant, Quartinus was alive later (7.1.9n); several of A.'s
senatorial supporters continued to serve in office (7.3.4n).
One of A.'s most trusted equestrian partisans, Timesitheus
(cf. 5.5.3n, 6.2.3n, 6.7.6n), though removed from the German
legions, was promoted to an extensive procuratorial office in
Bithynia and Pontus which included acting as governor of
the (senatorial?) province; he later went on to a similar
position in Asia, controlling the entire finances of the province
and acting as proconsul; *ILS* 1330, Dobson-Domaszewski,
Rangordnung 273, Pflaum, *Marbre de Thorigny* 65 ff.

[2] Almost certainly C. Petronius Magnus; *Albo* 1125, whose
name is still legible, though erased, on the famous *album* of
the patrons of Canusium that was set up in 223 (*CIL* IX.

tire serving staff, who had been with Alexander for many years, were dismissed from the court. Most of them were executed on suspicion of treason since Maximinus knew they mourned the loss of Alexander.[1]

The disclosure of a plot formed against him, in which many centurions and people from the senate downwards joined, encouraged him to show still more brutality and bitterness towards everyone. A man 5 called Magnus,[2] a patrician consular, was accused of gathering together a group round himself and prompting some soldiers to transfer power to himself. It was alleged that his plan was to be as follows. Once Maximinus bridged the river,[3] he was on the point of crossing to attack the Germans. For no 6 sooner had he gained power, than he began his military campaign. Since he had apparently been

338 = *ILS* 6121); the list of senators prominent immediately after the accession of A. provides a rough guide to the group who now supported Magnus, though there is a danger of exaggerating their homogeneity (cf. Pflaum, *Marbre de Thorigny* 37 ff., Jardé, *Sévère Alexandre* 123–5). Among them are several members of the old Antonine aristocracy (Appius Claudius Julianus, L. Bruttius Crispinus, C. Bruttius Praesens), some of the new Severan élite (L. Didius Marinus—who married M. Aurelius' daughter, Cornificia, L. Aedinius Julianus, L. Domitius Honoratus, L. Lucilius Priscillianus), ex-equestrians adlected into the senate. Magnus is probably the praetor in the reign of Caracalla mentioned in the *Dig.* 23.4.30. Cf. SHA, *Max.* 10.1, *Trig. Tyr.* 32.1.

[3] See 6.7.6n for the bridge over the Rhine. H. seems to assume that the enemy lay immediately across the Rhine, whereas the Taunus front was some fifteen miles north of the river; criticized by Sievers, *Philol.* 31 (1872) 658, but it is now known that the Taunus frontier posts had been damaged and may well have been overrun; cf. 6.7.6n.

μέγεθος καὶ ἰσχὺν [στρατιωτικὴν] [1] καὶ ἐμπειρίαν
πολεμικὴν δοκῶν ἐπιλελέχθαι ἔργοις τὴν δόξαν καὶ
τὴν τῶν στρατιωτῶν ὑπόληψιν ἐπιστοῦτο,[2] τήν τε
Ἀλεξάνδρου μέλλησιν καὶ τὴν πρὸς τὰ πολεμικὰ
ἔργαο δειλίαν ἐλέγχειν ἐπειρᾶτο εἰκότως κατ-
εγνωσμένην. ἀσκῶν τε οὖν καὶ γυμνάζων τοὺς
στρατιώτας οὐ διέλειπεν,[3] αὐτός τε ἐν ὅπλοις ὢν
7 καὶ τὸν στρατὸν [4] παρορμῶν. τότε τοίνυν τὴν
γέφυραν ζεύξας ἔμελλεν ἐπὶ Γερμανοὺς διαβήσε-
σθαι. ὁ δὲ Μάγνος ἐλέγετο στρατιωτῶν μὲν [5]
ὀλίγους, ἀλλὰ τοὺς ἐξοχωτάτους καὶ μάλιστα τοὺς
τὴν φρουρὰν τῆς γεφύρας καὶ τὴν ἐπιμέλειαν
πεπιστευμένους,[6] ἀναπεῖσαι μετὰ τὸ διαβῆναι τὸν
Μαξιμῖνον λύσαντας τὴν γέφυραν προδοῦναι τοῖς
βαρβάροις, οὐχ ὑπαρχούσης αὐτῷ ἐπανόδου· πλάτει
γὰρ καὶ βάθει μέγιστος ὁ ποταμὸς ῥέων ἄβατος
⟨ἂν⟩ [7] αὐτῷ ἐγίνετο, οὔτε νεῶν οὐσῶν ἐν ταῖς
8 πολεμίαις ὄχθαις τῆς τε [8] γεφύρας λυθείσης. ἡ
μὲν τῆς διαβολῆς [9] φήμη τοιαύτη ἐγένετο, εἴτε
ἀληθὴς ὑπάρξασα εἴτε ὑπὸ τοῦ Μαξιμίνου συσκευα-
σθεῖσα· ἀκριβὲς δὲ εἰπεῖν οὐ ῥᾴδιον, ἐπεὶ ἔμενεν

---

[1] del Mendelss Stav   [2] ἐπὶ τοῦτο A
[3] old correction Mendelss for διέλιπεν Oi
[4] στρατὸν ἀεὶ i   [5] Steph οὐκ Oi
[6] Steph from P (*custodia pontis . . . fuerat demandata*)
πεποιημένους Oi
[7] Mendelss   [8] om i   [9] ἐπιβουλῆς Reisk

---

[1] One of the many passages which is translated almost
literally by the SHA, *vitae Max. duo* (cf. *Max.* 10 *passim*);

selected for his size, strength and military experience, he wanted to confirm his reputation and the soldiers' opinion of him by action, thus attempting to prove that Alexander's hesitation and timidity over military operations had been justifiably censured. As a result he never stopped training and exercising the men, even getting into arms himself and urging the troops on. That was the position when he 7 completed the bridge and was set to cross over against the Germans.[1] Magnus was alleged to have influenced some soldiers, not many of them, but key men whose particular duty was to keep a vigilant watch over the bridge; the men were induced to cut the bridge after Maximinus' crossing and betray him to the barbarians by denying him his return route. The tremendous breadth and depth of the river's course would have made a crossing impossible for Maximinus, since he would be without boats on the enemy shore and the bridge would be broken. 8 Such was the story of the plot, which may have contained some truth, or was possibly manufactured by Maximinus. It is difficult to say with accuracy,[2] because it remains unproven. Maximinus gave no

the author is believed by Homo, *Rev. Hist.* 131 (1919) 209–64 and 132 (1919) 1–38 to be following a Latin summary of H., but there seems no good reason why the author of the *vita* himself should not be summarizing H. and unskilfully conflating him with other sources; cf. Pasoli, *L'Uso di Erod. nella V. Max.* 16. SHA, *Trig. Tyr.* 32.1, which also mentions this episode, quotes Dexippus, but little confidence can be placed in authors quoted in the *vitae*; the episode is not mentioned in Zosimus or Zonaras.

[2] A conventional tribute to an historiographic ideal; e.g. Caes. *BG* 7.5, etc.

ἀνεξέλεγκτος. μήτε γὰρ κρίσεώς ¹ τινι μεταδοὺς
μήτε ἀπολογίας,² πάντας οὓς ὑπώπτευεν αἰφνιδίως
συναρπασθέντας ἀφειδῶς ἐφόνευσεν.

9 ἐγένετο δέ τις καὶ Ὀσροηνῶν τοξοτῶν ἀπόστασις,
οἳ πάνυ ἀλγοῦντες ἐπὶ τῇ Ἀλεξάνδρου τελευτῇ,
περιτυχόντες τῶν ἀπὸ ὑπατείας καὶ φίλων Ἀλεξάνδρου τινί (Κουαρτῖνος ³ δὲ ἦν ὄνομα, ὃν
Μαξιμῖνος ἐκπέμψας ἦν τοῦ στρατοῦ) ἁρπάσαντες
ἄκοντα καὶ οὐδὲν προειδότα στρατηγὸν ἑαυτῶν
κατέστησαν, πορφύρᾳ ⁴ τε καὶ πυρὶ προπομπεύ-
οντι,⁵ ὀλεθρίοις τιμαῖς, ἐκόσμησαν, ἐπί τε τὴν
10 ἀρχὴν ἦγον οὔ τι βουλόμενον. ἐκεῖνος μὲν οὖν ἐν
τῇ σκηνῇ καθεύδων ἐπιβουλευθεὶς νύκτωρ αἰφνιδίως ἀνῃρέθη ὑπὸ τοῦ συνόντος αὐτῷ καὶ δοκοῦντος
φίλου, τῶν τε Ὀσροηνῶν πρότερον ἡγουμένου
(Μακεδὼν ἦν ὄνομα αὐτῷ), καίτοι τῆς ἁρπαγῆς
καὶ τῆς ἀποστάσεως ἀρχηγοῦ καὶ ὁμογνώμονος ⁶
τοῖς Ὀσροηνοῖς γενομένου· ὃς οὐδεμίαν αἰτίαν

---

¹ Steph κρίσει Oἱ   ² ἀπολογία i
³ κουαρτίωνι Jo (κουαρτίνωι?)   ⁴ -φυραν al
⁵ Steph from P πομπεύοντα Oag πομπεύσαντα l
⁶ καὶ ὁμογ. om OP

---

¹ According to SHA, *Max.* 8.6, 4,000 were executed, a ludicrous exaggeration.

² Some evidence of the trouble among the Osrhoenian
auxiliaries is provided by the erasure of their name from *CIL*
XIII. 6677a, and the name of the centurions from a cohort on
CIL XI. 3104. But the Osrhoenians were used during the
German campaign, and, unless one supposes that M. disgraced
them later after the expedition, which seems improbable, the

one a chance to make a defence before a court, since everyone under suspicion was suddenly seized and ruthlessly executed.[1]

There was also trouble among the Osrhoenian 9 archers,[2] who bitterly regretted Alexander's death. When they found one of Alexander's consular friends called Quartinus,[3] who had been dismissed from the army by Maximinus, they seized upon him, and, even though it was against his wishes and unplanned, they set him up as their leader. He was fitted out with the fatal trappings of power, the purple and a procession of fire,[4] and, in spite of his wishes, brought to imperial rule. While he was sleeping in his tent 10 one night, he was suddenly and treacherously assassinated by his companion, who was supposedly one of his friends, and formerly the leader in charge of the Osrhoenians. This man, whose name was Macedo,[5] had been the ringleader in the mutinous seizure of Quartinus, working in co-operation with the Osrhoenians. Yet, in spite of this, and with-

incident of the mutiny was later, possibly in 236, and misplaced by H. who is following a cataloguing rather than chronological order. Though unreliable, SHA, *Trig. Tyr.* 32.1, says the revolt lasted six months, though ending just after Magnus' plot.

[3] Probably Titius Quartinus; *Albo* 1144, *PIR*[2] C 327; the name of a *legatus* of legio I Minervia in Germania Inferior has been erased some time after 225, perhaps the name of Quartinus. If so, he may have been a provincial governor by 235 when removed by M.; cf. SHA, *Trig. Tyr.* 32, *Max.* 11.1–6, Jardé, *Sévère Alexandre* 89, *CIL* XIII. 8728, 8811.

[4] Cf. 2.3.2n.

[5] Nothing is known of him; he was perhaps *praepositus numeri sagittariorum Osrhoenorum*, suggests Stein, *RE* (Macedo) 127.

ἔχθρας οὐδὲ [1] μίσους ἔχων ἀπέκτεινεν ὃν αὐτὸς [2]
ἥρπασέ τε καὶ ἀνέπεισεν, οἰόμενός τε μεγάλα
χαρίζεσθαι τῷ Μαξιμίνῳ τὴν κεφαλὴν ἀποτεμὼν
11 ἐκόμισεν. ὁ δὲ ἥσθη μὲν ἐπὶ τῷ ἔργῳ, στερηθεὶς
δὴ [3] πολεμίου, ὡς ᾤετο. ἐκεῖνον μέντοι,[4] καίτοι
μεγάλα ἐλπίζοντα καὶ δοκοῦντα ἀμοιβῆς ἐξαιρέτου
τεύξεσθαι, ἀπέκτεινεν ὡς καὶ τῆς ἀποστάσεως
γεγονότα ἀρχηγὸν καὶ ἀποκτείναντα ὃν αὐτὸς
ἄκοντα ἀνέπεισεν, ἄπιστόν τε γενόμενον περὶ τὸν
φίλον.
12 τοιαῦται μὲν δή τινες αἰτίαι ἔτι μᾶλλον ἐς
τραχύτητα καὶ ὠμότητα ἠκόνησαν τὴν τοῦ
Μαξιμίνου ψυχήν, καὶ πρότερον οὕτω πεφυκυῖαν.
ἦν δὲ καὶ τὴν ὄψιν φοβερώτατος, καὶ μέγιστος τὸ
σῶμα, ὡς μὴ ῥᾳδίως αὐτῷ τινα μήτε Ἑλλήνων
τῶν σωμασκούντων μήτε βαρβάρων τῶν μαχιμωτά-
των ἐξισοῦσθαι.

2. διοικήσας δὲ τὰ προειρημένα, πάντα τε τὸν
στρατὸν ἀναλαβών, καὶ διαβὰς ἀφόβως τὴν
γέφυραν, εἴχετο τῆς πρὸς Γερμανοὺς μάχης. μέγα

[1] Nauck οὔτε Oi
[2] Reisk from P αὐτὸς ὃν ABi (αὐτὸν V)
[3] A om a δὲ φgl
[4] μέντοι A μέν φι ᾤετο ⟨φλαύρου⟩ or ⟨εὐκαταφρονήτου⟩,
ἐκεῖνον, καίτοι Reisk ᾤετο ⟨οὐκ εὐκαταφρονήτου⟩. ἐκεῖνον μέντοι,
καίτοι conj Mendelss

[1] M. had some justification for bitterness after the plots since
he appears to have tried to placate the senate; coins were

out any reason for his hostility or hatred, he murdered the man he had forcibly persuaded to become
emperor. Assuming that Maximinus would be
enormously grateful, he cut off Quartinus' head and
took it to him. The emperor was pleased at the 11
action, believing, as he did, that he was rid of a
personal enemy, but, though Macedo had high hopes
and expectations of gaining a fine reward, Maximinus
executed him on charges of being a ringleader of the
mutiny, of murdering the unwilling victim of his
own prompting and proving to be a false friend.

This sort of provocation embittered Maximinus' 12
feelings,[1] making him even harsher and more
savage than he was instinctively before. He was in
any case a man of such frightening appearance and
colossal size that there is no obvious comparison to be
drawn with any of the best-trained Greek athletes
or warrior élite of the barbarians.[2]

2. After settling the business mentioned above,
Maximinus crossed the bridge [3] confidently with his
whole army, determined to fight the Germans. It

issued with *indulgentia Aug(usti)* and *Mars pacifer*. There is
no evidence to show that M. discarded " all pretence of
constitutionality " as Hammond says, *MAAR* 24 (1956)
124; cf. 7.1.3n. M. would hardly have bothered to send
letters to the senate if this were so. According to Amm.
Marc. 14.1.8 M.'s wife exercised a considerable restraining
influence over him, though she died soon after his accession
(7.1.3n).

[2] Some magnificent stories of M.'s size are provided in SHA,
Max. 6.8–9.

[3] Presumably in the vicinity of Mainz, where A. had been
murdered; the repair of the forts of Zugmantel and Saalburg
(6.7.2n) in the Taunus salient were the work of M. The troops
with M. are discussed by Ritterling, *RE* (legio) 1333 ff.

δέ τι πλῆθος καὶ σχεδὸν ἅπασαν τὴν ῾Ρωμαίων [1]
δύναμιν σὺν ἑαυτῷ εἰσήγαγε, Μαυρουσίων τε
ἀκοντιστῶν ἀριθμὸν πάμπλειστον καὶ τοξοτῶν [2]
᾽Οσροηνῶν τε καὶ ᾽Αρμενίων, ὧν ἦσαν οἱ μὲν ὑπή-
κοοι οἱ δὲ φίλοι καὶ σύμμαχοι, καὶ εἴ τινες
Παρθυαίων ἢ χρήμασι πεισθέντες καὶ αὐτομολή-
σαντες ἢ ληφθέντες αἰχμάλωτοι ῾Ρωμαίοις ἐδούλευ-
2 ον. τὰ δὲ πλήθη ταῦτα τοῦ στρατοῦ καὶ πρότερον
ὑπ᾽ ᾽Αλεξάνδρου ἤθροιστο, ηὐξήθη δὲ ὑπὸ τοῦ
Μαξιμίνου καὶ ἐς πολεμικὴν ἄσκησιν συγκεκρότητο.
μάλιστά τε [3] οἱ ἀκοντισταὶ καὶ οἱ τοξόται πρὸς τὰς
Γερμανῶν μάχας ἐπιτήδειοι δοκοῦσιν, ἐπιτρέχοντές
τε αὐτοῖς κούφως οὐ προσδοκῶσι καὶ ἀναχωροῦντες
3 ῥᾳδίως. γενόμενος δὲ ἐν τῇ πολεμίᾳ Μαξιμῖνος
πολλὴν γῆν ἐπῆλθεν, οὐδενὸς αὐτῷ ἀνθεστῶτος,
ἀλλὰ τῶν βαρβάρων ἀνακεχωρηκότων. ἐδῄου τε οὖν
πᾶσαν τὴν χώραν, μάλιστα τῶν ληίων ἀκμαζόντων,
τάς τε κώμας ἐμπιπρὰς διαρπάζειν ἐδίδου τῷ
στρατῷ. εὐμαρέστατα γὰρ τὸ πῦρ ἐπινέμεται τάς

---

[1] barbarorum P   [2] τοξότην i
[3] δὲ P (ceterum) om A

---

[1] SHA, Max. 12.1, says that M. advanced a distance of
about thirty or forty miles into hostile territory; but he seems
to have moved south along the frontier from the Taunus
Mountains to the area of Württemberg; there are signs of the
graves of men from an oriental ala kataphractaria at both
Rödelheim bei Frankfurt and Cannstatt (cf. ILS 9148,

was an enormous host that he was leading, practically the entire Roman fighting strength. Added to them was a very large number of Mauretanian spearmen and Osrhoenian and Armenian archers, some of whom were there as subjects and others under the terms of a friendly alliance; also some Parthians, either serving for pay or deserters and captured prisoners of war, now slaves of the Romans. This large body of troops had been assembled earlier by Alexander, but then augmented and trained up to war fitness by Maximinus. The most effective troops against German tactics seem to be the spearmen and archers who make their surprise, light-armed raids and then retire without difficulty. Once he had reached hostile territory, Maximinus advanced deep into the country,[1] not meeting any resistance because the barbarians had fallen back in front of him. He devastated all the countryside, particularly the ripening corn,[2] and set fire to the villages, which he allowed his army to plunder. Fire spreads very

Goessler, *Germania* 15 (1931) 10 ff.; Persian cataphracts were said by SHA, *Alex.* 56.5; to be part of A.'s force). M.'s presence is also supported by inscriptions from near Tübingen, *CIL* XIII. 6375, 9083. From here the forts near Regensburg were repaired (cf. 6.7.2n for references). The whole Rhine–Danube *limes* was repaired, *CIL* XIII. 6547, 9121.

[2] In 7.1.6 H. says that M. planned to set out on his expedition as soon as possible after A.'s assassination; i.e. about April; there may have been a delay after the conspiracy of Magnus, so that it was not until mid-summer that M. invaded Germany, as is suggested here. This would be consistent with a major battle late in 235 (as suggested in 7.2.6n); there is nothing to suggest M. postponed the invasion of Germany until 236, as stated by Schmidt, *Gesch. d. deutsch. Stämme* II. 1.246 ff.

τε πόλεις αὐτῶν ἃς ἔχουσι, καὶ τὰς οἰκήσεις ἁπάσας·
4 λίθων μὲν γὰρ παρ' αὐτοῖς ἢ πλίνθων ὀπτῶν σπάνις,
ὗλαι δ' εὔδενδροι,[1] ὅθεν ξύλων οὔσης ἐκτενείας συμ-
πηγνύντες αὐτὰ καὶ ἁρμόζοντες σκηνοποιοῦνται. ὁ
δὲ Μαξιμῖνος ἐπὶ πολὺ μὲν προεχώρησε, πράττων
τε τὰ προειρημένα καὶ λείας ἀπελαύνων, διδούς τε
5 τὰς ἀγέλας τῷ στρατῷ αἷς περιετύγχανον. οἱ δὲ
Γερμανοὶ ἀπὸ μὲν τῶν πεδίων, καὶ εἴ τινες ἦσαν
χῶραι ἄδενδροι, ἀνακεχωρήκεσαν, ἐν δὲ ταῖς ὕλαις
ἐκρύπτοντο περί τε [2] τὰ ἕλη διέτριβον, ὡς ἐκεῖ
τὰς μάχας καὶ τὰς ἐφόδους ποιοῖντο,[3] τῆς συνεχείας
τῶν φυτῶν ἀπασχολούσης ἐς ἑαυτὴν τὰ βέλη καὶ
τὰ ἀκόντια τῶν πολεμίων, τοῦ τε ἀγχιβαθοῦς τῶν
ἑλῶν Ῥωμαίοις μὲν δι' ἄγνοιαν τῶν τόπων ἐπισφα-
λοῦς ἐσομένου, ἑαυτοῖς δὲ δι' ἐμπειρίαν τῆς
χώρας [4] ἐγνωκόσι τὰ [5] ἄβατα καὶ ἀντιτυπῆ τῶν
τόπων ἐς γόνυ τε βρεχομένοις διατρέχειν ῥᾳδίου.[6]
6 εἰσὶ δὲ καὶ πρὸς τὸ νήχεσθαι γεγυμνασμένοι ἅτε
μόνῳ λουτρῷ τοῖς ποταμοῖς χρώμενοι.

περὶ ἐκεῖνα οὖν μάλιστα τὰ χωρία αἱ συμβολαὶ
ἐγίνοντο· ἔνθα καὶ γενναιότατα αὐτὸς ὁ βασιλεὺς

[1] εὔενδροι O   [2] P δὲ Oi   [3] ἐποιοῦντο O
[4] χώρας ⟨συμμάχου ὡς⟩ Reisk   [5] om φι
[6] ῥᾳδίως Aa (over -ου) ῥᾴδια Reisk

[1] After mentioning villages, H. suddenly changes to cities;
Tac. Germ. 16 denies there were cities in Germany in his day;
also he states that the houses in Germany were not built
162

easily through such cities[1] and through all the houses
as the Germans have, because they are short of stone 4
and baked bricks. However, there are thick forests,
and from them there is a plentiful supply of wooden
beams that are built up into a frame and jointed together to make a house.[2] Maximinus advanced a
long way, acting as described, carrying off plunder
and giving the flocks they came across to his soldiers.
The Germans retreated from the plains and any un- 5
wooded areas, but hid in the forests and waited in
the marshes, so as to launch their attack and fight in
this area. Here the thick foliage formed a barrage
against the arrows and missiles of the enemy, and
the deep marshes were dangerous for the Romans
because they were unfamiliar with the locality. For
the Germans, with their experience of the country
and their knowledge of which places were unfordable
and which provided firm standing, it was easy to cross
by wading up to their knees in water. They were 6
also adept swimmers, since the rivers were the only
places they used for washing.

It was mostly in these regions that the skirmishes
took place, and here that the emperor took charge

contiguously in order to prevent fires spreading. It is
probable that H. was influenced in his description by the
account of the sack of Sardis in Herod. 5.101 (πῦρ ἐπενέμετο
τὸ ἄστυ).

[2] A description of daub-and-wattle houses, either round or
rectangular, which have been found in excavations in the
middle west and south-west of Germany; cf. Anderson,
Tacitus, Germania 102–3. The word ἐκτένεια is disapproved
of by Pollux 3.119, but quoted by Cic. *Att.* 10.17.1 and used in
New Testament *koine* (e.g. *Acta* 26.7); for the relationship
between H. and Pollux, see 1.2.1n.

τῆς μάχης ἦρξεν. ἐπὶ γάρ τινι ἔλει μεγίστῳ, τῶν
μὲν Γερμανῶν ἐς αὐτὸ [1] ἀναχωρούντων ἐς φυγήν,
ἐς δίωξιν δὲ Ῥωμαίων ἐπεισελθεῖν ὀκνούντων,
πρῶτος ὁ Μαξιμῖνος ἅμα τῷ ἵππῳ ἐμβαλὼν ἐς τὸ
ἔλος, καίτοι ὑπὲρ γαστέρα τοῦ. ἵππου βρεχομένου,
7 τοὺς ἀνθεστῶτας ἐφόνευσε βαρβάρους, ὡς τὸν
λοιπὸν στρατὸν αἰδεσθέντα προδοῦναι μαχόμενον
ὑπὲρ αὐτῶν [2] βασιλέα τολμῆσαί τε καὶ τοῖς
ἔλεσιν [2] ἐπεισελθεῖν, πολὺ δέ τι πλῆθος ἑκατέρωθεν
πεσεῖν, καὶ Ῥωμαίων μὲν ⟨πολλοὺς⟩ [3] τῶν δὲ
βαρβάρων [4] σχεδὸν τὴν τότε παροῦσαν δύναμιν, [4]
ἀριστεύοντος αὐτοῦ, ὡς τὸ τέναγος [5] σωμάτων
πληρωθῆναι, τήν τε λίμνην αἵματι κερασθεῖσαν
πεζομαχοῦντι στρατῷ ναυμαχίας ὄψιν παρασχεῖν.
8 ταύτην τὴν μάχην καὶ τὴν ἀριστείαν αὐτοῦ οὐ
μόνον διὰ γραμμάτων τῇ τε συγκλήτῳ καὶ τῷ
δήμῳ ἐδήλωσεν, ἀλλὰ καὶ γραφῆναι κελεύσας

[1] αὐτὸν φi
[2] αὐτῶν θρασύτερον τολμῆσαι κἂν τῷ βάθει τῶν ἐλῶν (sic)
ἔπεισ. A
[3] or ⟨οὐκ ὀλίγους⟩ Stroth ⟨συχνὸν⟩ Sylb Ῥωμ. μὲν om P
[4] βαρβάρων ἐπὶ πολὺ καὶ σχεδὸν (sic) τε τὴν τότε παρ. δύν.
αὐτῶν A perhaps καὶ Ῥωμ.—δύναμιν interpol Whit
[5] τό τε ἔλος a

[1] There is no specific geographic feature that identifies the
site of this major battle, which could equally well be in

of the battle in person with great bravery.[1] At a
very large swamp, to which the Germans were
retreating in flight and the Romans were hesitating
to follow them, Maximinus took the lead by
plunging into the marsh on horse-back (even
though the level of the water came over the
horse's belly), and killed many of the barbarians
that resisted. The effect of his action was that 7
the rest of the army grew ashamed to betray an
emperor who was fighting for them, and they gained
the courage to wade into the swamp. Both sides
lost a lot of men, many Romans but practically the
whole existing army of the barbarians, as a result of
Maximinus' distinguished action. The shallow water
was filled with bodies and, as the swamp became
stained with blood, it looked like a naval battle [2]
to the infantry fighting there. The emperor made 8
a report on the battle and his own distinguished part
in a dispatch to the senate and the people. But

Germany or in the Bohemian plain. It is usually assumed
that H. is describing the climax to his campaign in the Württemberg area, where there are signs of his presence (7.2.3n).
If so, the date of the battle was probably late 235, though the
first evidence of M.'s *imp.* II salutation and the title of
Germanicus Maximus do not appear until 236 (7.2.8n);
Bersanetti, *Epig.* 3 (1941) 7-8, Carson, *ANS Centennial
Public.* (1958) 192-3, *BMC* VI. 92. This does not prove that
the German expedition was waged in 236 and is consistent
with a victory late in the year 235. If M. was to go on and
fight a campaign on the Danube in 236, it would seem best to
assume he left the Germanies after 235.

[2] A classical *locus communis* with a difference; cf. Thuc.
1.49 (a land battle by sea), Diod. Sic. 13.16 (the same). Since
this is so characteristic of H., I do not agree with Mendelssohn's
suggestion that the passage is an interpolation.

μεγίσταις εἰκόσιν ἀνέθηκε πρὸ τοῦ βουλευτηρίου,
ἵνα μὴ μόνον ἀκούειν τὰ γενόμενα ἀλλὰ καὶ
βλέπειν ἔχωσι ʽΡωμαῖοι. τὴν δ᾽ εἰκόνα ὕστερον
καθεῖλεν ἡ σύγκλητος μετὰ τῶν λοιπῶν αὐτοῦ
τιμῶν. γεγόνασι δὲ καὶ ἕτεραι συμβολαί, ἐν αἷς
ὡς αὐτουργός τε καὶ αὐτόχειρ τῆς μάχης ἀριστεύων
9 τε πανταχοῦ ἐπῃνεῖτο. πολλοὺς δὲ χειρωσάμενος
αὐτῶν αἰχμαλώτους καὶ λείαν ἀπελάσας, χειμῶνος
ἤδη καταλαμβάνοντος ἐπανῆλθεν ἐς Παίονας, ἔν
τε Σιρμίῳ διατρίβων, τῇ μεγίστῃ ἐκεῖ πόλει
δοκούσῃ, τὰ πρὸς τὴν εἴσοδον ἐς τὸ ἔαρ παρεσκευ-

---

[1] This naturally poses the question of how much of H.'s own description derived from seeing these pictures; his description falls roughly into four scenes: (1) crossing the bridge; (2) burning the villages; (3) barbarians hiding in the forests and marshes; (4) M. and the battle of the marshes. None of the scenes are described with the kind of detail to suggest H. had been present himself or had a first-hand informant. Cf. 1.7.5n, 2.9.4, 2.9.6, 3.9.12, 5.5.6–7, SHA, *Max.* 12.10.

[2] The title of *Germanicus* was officially recognized in Rome. It is recorded on *CIL* VI. 2001 (see 7.1.3n) when M.'s son was elected to the sacerdotal colleges in 236; although it is conceivable that the title was only given to the heir to start with, it seems likely that the senate officially voted the honour to M. as well. It was probably at the same time that M.'s son (see 8.4.9n) was formally recognized as Caesar. The *abolitio* of these honours took place in 238 (7.7.2n).

[3] H. has characteristically compressed two or three years' campaign into a few words (cf. 4.7.2n); the chronology of the German and Dacian–Sarmatian wars of M. are perhaps as follows: at Moguntiacum spring 235; in the Wetterau midsummer 235 (7.2.3n); in the Württemberg area late 235, where he probably spent the winter 235/6 (Regensburg?); move to the lower Danube and a major campaign in 236, after

he went further, and ordered huge pictures[1] of it to be
painted and set up in front of the senate house, so
that Romans would be able to see as well as hear
about his exploits.   Later the picture was destroyed
by the senate along with the rest of his honorary
dedications.   There were other engagements, too,
in which Maximinus personally took a leading part
in the battle and was always commended for bravery.[2]
After capturing many prisoners and loads of plunder, 9
he returned to Pannonia because winter had set in.[3]
At Sirmium,[4] which is considered to be the biggest
town, he spent his time making preparations for his

which he assumed the titles *Dacicus Maximus* and *Sarmaticus
Maximus* with the *imp.* III salutation (all appear on *CIL* III.
10649 with M.'s *trib. pot.* II; cf. V. 8076, XI. 1176), and
possibly also the *imp.* IV salutation (cf. Bersanetti, *Epig.* 3
(1941) 9); therefore winter at Sirmium 236/7; more fighting
against the Sarmatians and Dacians in 237 and addition of
imp. V and perhaps *imp.* VI salutations; after which M.
" returned " to Sirmium for winter 237/8.   A different view is
put forward by Siena, *RFIC* 33 (1955) 281, who prefers to
believe that *imp.* II and the *Germanicus* title were won in 235,
that M. then " returned " to Sirmium (where he had been
praefectus tironum before 235) and fought against the Dacians
and Sarmatians for two full years.   Against this view is the
fact that not a single coin or inscription shows the Germanicus
title or *imp.* II in 235, indicating that the battle occurred too
late in the year for inclusion in the titles, or that it was not
fought until spring 236, but in neither case making it plausible
that M. would winter at Sirmium 235/6; cf. *CIL* III. 5742,
11316; *RIC* IV. 2.139, no. 4, 143, nos. 35-6; but *BMC* VI.
224, nos. 25-30 give examples of *victoria Aug(usti)* on undated
coin types of 235.

[4] Increasingly used as the permanent base by emperors on
the Danube; the city on the River Save controlled the major
routes along the Danube frontier, and was an obvious base for
operations in the Hungarian plain.

HERODIAN

ἄζετο. ἠπείλει γάρ (καὶ ποιήσειν ἔμελλεν)
ἐκκόψειν τε καὶ ὑποτάξειν τὰ μέχρις ὠκεανοῦ
Γερμανῶν ἔθνη βάρβαρα.

3. τὰ μὲν οὖν πολεμικὰ τοιοῦτος ἦν· καὶ ἐς
δόξαν ἤρθη ἂν ἡ πρᾶξις αὐτοῦ, εἰ μὴ τοῖς οἰκείοις
καὶ τοῖς ὑπηκόοις βαρύτερος ἐγεγόνει καὶ φοβερώ-
τερος.¹ τί γὰρ ἦν ὄφελος βαρβάρων ἀναιρουμένων,
πλειόνων γινομένων ² φόνων ἐν αὐτῇ τε Ῥώμῃ
καὶ τοῖς ὑπηκόοις ἔθνεσιν; ἢ λείας ⟨καὶ⟩ ³
αἰχμαλώτους ⁴ ἀπάγειν τῶν ἐχθρῶν, γυμνοῦντα
2 καὶ τὰς οὐσίας ἀφαιρούμενον τῶν οἰκείων; ἄνεσίς
[τε] ⁵ γὰρ πᾶσα, μᾶλλον δὲ καὶ πρόκλησις δέδοτο
συκοφάνταις ⁶ ἐς τὸ ἐπηρεάζειν καὶ κινεῖν πράγματα προγονικά, εἰ τύχοι, καὶ ἄγνωστα καὶ
ἀνεξέλεγκτα. μόνον τέ τις κληθεὶς ἐς δικαστήριον
ὑπὸ συκοφάντου εὐθέως ἡττημένος ἀπῄει καὶ τῶν
3 ὑπαρχόντων πάντων στερηθείς. ἑκάστης γοῦν ἡμέ-

¹ φοβ. ⟨ἢ τοῖς πολεμίοις⟩ translated P
² Steph from P γενομ. Οἱ   ³ Reisk ⟨ἢ⟩ from P (aut)
⁴ om Wolf   ⁵ om Reisk
⁶ συκ. ⟨τε καὶ δούλοις⟩ perhaps in Jo cf. Exc. Val. 833

---

¹ Cf. 1.5.6n for the expression in relation to the expeditions
of M. Aurelius and Commodus. The same phrase is quoted
by SHA, *Max.* 13.3–4, where the allegation is made that H.
was biased in favour of M.—a most improbable proposition.
Although the phrase had a wide rhetorical currency, it is
possible that M. intended to revive the plan of M. Aurelius to
open up a frontier line north of the Danube.

168

spring offensive. He intended (and would have achieved) the total defeat and subjection of all the German barbarian tribes as far as the ocean.[1]

3. So much for Maximinus' military exploits. His achievement would have won him a reputation, if he had not proved so oppressive and fearsome to his own people and his subjects. There is little point in destroying barbarians, if even more people are being murdered actually in Rome and the subject nations;[2] nor in carrying off prisoners and plunder from the enemy, when the people at home are stripped bare of their possessions.[3] Informers were given 2 complete licence, even encouragement, to damage people and stir up old troubles, if there was a chance, without the cases being heard or any real evidence. A person simply had to receive a court summons from an informer, and straight away he lost his case and his property was confiscated. Men 3

[2] For the various meanings of *ethnos*, in addition to that of "province", see 1.1.3n.

[3] The rapacity of M. is mentioned in every source, but is very much part of the stereotype of the tyrant; H. discards the obvious military necessity for added money (7.3.3) because he is obsessed with questions of individual morality. It is no coincidence that the emperors who most successfully maintained the frontiers (Severus, Caracalla, Maximinus) also had to rely on confiscations to pay the bill. There is little evidence to suggest a deliberate policy by M. to exterminate the bourgeois urban classes (Rostovtzeff, *SEHRE* 452), but no doubt that the growing pluralism of the Roman empire made M. less sympathetic to the established interests of the prosperous middle classes (of whom H. himself was one); coin hoards, such as those found at Cologne or in Britain do not prove M.'s rapacity; *RIC* IV. 2.130, *Num. Chron.* (6) 6 (1946) 147–51.

ρας ἦν ἰδεῖν τοὺς χθὲς πλουσιωτάτους τῆς ἐπιούσης
μεταιτοῦντας· τοσαύτη τις ἦν τῆς τυραννίδος ἡ
φιλοχρηματία ἐπὶ προφάσει τῆς περὶ τοὺς στρατιώτας χρημάτων συνεχοῦς χορηγίας· ἦν δὲ καὶ
τοῖς ὠσὶ κοῦφος ἐς διαβολάς, ἡλικίας τε καὶ
ἀξιώματος ἀφειδῶς ἔχων. πλείστους γοῦν τῶν
ἔθνη καὶ στρατόπεδα πεπιστευμένων, μετὰ ὑπατείας
τιμὴν ἢ δόξαν ἐπὶ τροπαίοις προσγενομένην, ἐκ
μικρᾶς καὶ εὐτελοῦς διαβολῆς ἀναρπάστους ἐποίει,
4 καὶ ἐκέλευέ ¹ τε ² ἄνευ ὑπηρεσίας μόνους ὀχήμασιν
ἐπιτεθέντας ³ ἄγεσθαι νύκτωρ καὶ μεθ' ἡμέραν
ὁδεύοντας ἐξ ἀνατολῶν ἢ δύσεως, εἰ τύχοι, ἀπό τε
μεσημβρίας ἐς Παίονας, ἔνθα διέτριβε· σκύλας δὲ
καὶ ὑβρίσας φυγαῖς ἢ θανάτοις ἐζημίου.

ἐς ὅσον μὲν οὖν ἐς ⁴ τοὺς καθ' ἕνα ταῦτα ἐπράττετο καὶ μέχρις οἰκείων ⁵ ἔμενεν ἡ συμφορά, οὐ
πάνυ τι τοῖς δήμοις τῶν πόλεων ἢ τοῖς ἔθνεσι
5 διέφερε· τὰ γὰρ τῶν εὐδαιμονεῖν ⁶ δοκούντων ἢ
πλουσίων πταίσματα πρὸς τῶν ὄχλων οὐ μόνον
ἀμελεῖται, ἀλλά τινας τῶν κακοήθων καὶ φαύλων
ἔσθ' ὅτε καὶ εὐφραίνει φθόνῳ τῶν κρειττόνων καὶ

¹ ἐκέλευσέ φι
² γε or om Steph
³ ἐπιτιθ. φα
⁴ om φι
⁵ οἴκων conj Gedike ἰδιωτῶν Mendelss corrupt Stav
⁶ εὐδοκιμεῖν Exc. Val. from Jo perhaps

who were rich one day and beggars the next
were a daily sight, so tremendous was the
tyrant's greed for wealth, though he pretended
he needed a continuous supply of money to pay
the troops. His ears were quick to pick up
charges, sparing neither a person's age or position.
Many men in posts of trust in the provinces and the
army, who had held the honourable office of consul
or earned the distinction of a triumph, he caused to be
whisked away on some stifling, petty charge. Orders 4
were issued that they should be put in a carriage on
their own, without any attendants, and brought to
him, travelling night and day from East or West, as
the case might be, or from the South to Pannonia
where he was staying. Then, after tormenting and
insulting them, he punished them with exile or death.

As long as this treatment was confined to individuals,[1] and the tragedy went no further than the
immediate household, it made little difference to the
people in the cities or the provinces. Disasters that 5
occur to those who are apparently fortunate and rich
do not concern the common people and sometimes
even cause pleasure to certain worthless, malicious
individuals, because they envy the powerful and

[1] Christians in both Rome and the provinces had been
persecuted in the reign of M., including the deportation of
Hippolytus and Pontianus from the church in Rome and
threats being offered to Origen; cf. Zon. 12.16, Zos. 1.13.3,
Euseb. *HE* 6.28. But there is no evidence that this was more
than a reaction to the political favour enjoyed by certain
Christians under A. and localized action in the provinces due
to civil unrest (as in Cappadocia); cf. *CAH* XII. 75 ff.
(Ensslin), Besnier, *Hist. Rom.* IV. 144 f., Grégoire, *Les
persécutions dans l'empire rom.* 40-2.

εὐτυχούντων. ἐπεὶ δὲ ὁ Μαξιμῖνος τοὺς πλείστους
τῶν ἐνδόξων οἴκων ἐς πενίαν περιστήσας,[1] ἃ δὴ
μικρὰ καὶ ὀλίγα οὐδ' αὐτάρκη τῇ αὐτοῦ βουλήσει
ᾤετο, μετῆλθεν ἐπὶ τὰ δημόσια, καὶ εἴ τινα ἦν
χρήματα πολιτικὰ ἐς εὐθηνίας ἢ νομὰς τῶν
δημοτῶν[2] ἀθροιζόμενα[3] εἴτε θεάτροις ἢ πανηγύρε-
σιν ἀνακείμενα, ἐς ἑαυτὸν μετῆγε, ναῶν τε
ἀναθήματα θεῶν τε ἀγάλματα καὶ ἡρώων τιμάς,
καὶ εἴ τις ἦν κόσμος δημοσίου ἔργου ἢ καλλώπι-
σμα[4] πόλεως ἢ ὕλη νόμισμα ποιῆσαι δυναμένη,[10]
πᾶν ἐχωνεύετο. ὅπερ καὶ μάλιστα τοὺς δήμους
6 ἐλύπησε.[5] πένθος τε δημόσιον ἐνεποίει δίχα

[1] περισ. ⟨καὶ χρήματα ἀφελόμενος⟩ Reisk
[2] πολιτῶν a
[3] ἠθροισμένα Jo
[4] καλλωπίσματος πόλεως ἢ ὕλης . . . δυναμένης Oi corr
Bekk² Sylb
[5] ἐλύπει Jo

[1] An indication of the economic and political interests of
H. and the audience for whom he was writing; H. was not in
sympathy with those who stimulated the events of 7.10.5,
calling forth lower-class plebeian support; cf. 1.14.3n, 7.12.6
and Cassola, *NRS* 41 (1957) 221–3.
[2] It is doubtful whether by these acts of oppression M. extended his attention as widely as H. suggests, or that he had
a conscious policy of *Gleichshaltung*. Townsend, *YCS* 14
(1955) 58 ff., argues that M. intended the elimination of the
senate and of all supporters of the previous regime. But note
that L. Marius Perpetuus (son of a staunch Severan and
supporter of A., 6.1.3n) was made *cos. ord.* in 237; Rutilius
Pudens Crispinus, who had served A. loyally and was to lead

prosperous.[1] But after Maximinus had reduced
most of the distinguished families to penury,[2] he then
began to think it was an unimportant, insignificant
activity and not enough to satisfy his desire. So he
turned to the public treasury and began to expropriate
any money in the city being collected for food supply [3]
and cash distribution to the common people,
and funds put aside for theatres and festivals.
Temple dedications, statues of the gods, honorary
presentations to the heroes, any ornamentation
on public buildings or city decorations, or material
that could be turned into coin was all melted
down. That was what the people particularly 6

the opposition at Aquileia (6.5.2n, 8.2.5n), was perhaps *cos.
suff.* in 235/6 and certainly allowed to be proconsul of Achaia;
L. Flavius Honoratus Lucilianus, who was one of the patrons
of Canusium in 223 (supposedly the " party " of A.; 7.1.5n)
was appointed by M. to the key military province of Moesia
Inferior in 237 (see *Albo* 1042 for references); T. Clodius
Saturninus Fidus, appointed governor of Thrace by M., went
on to serve Gordian III in Cappadocia (*Albo* 1008); cf.
Bersanetti, *Massimino* 83 f., for a list of unharmed senators.
If M. had adopted an outright policy of suppression many of
these would not have been appointed, a mistake for which M.
paid (as is demonstrated by the events in Africa, where an
appointee of A. was left in command; 7.5.2n). Cf. Spigno,
Rend. Accad. Linc. (Cl. sc. moral. stor. filol.) 3 (1948) 127-9.

[3] Translated by Politian as *ad annonam* and supported by
Irmisch, *Herod. Hist. ad loc.*; cf. *IG* IV. 795 and *Thes. Ling.
Lat.* " annona " IV. This money may be not only that in
the official treasuries but also the private contributions of
poorer people to *collegia* funds that were also stored in temples,
and were distributed as *sportulae.* Hence the anger of the
plebs infima in addition to the opposition of the middle class;
cf. Whittaker, *Hist.* 13 (1964) 359-60, Waltzing, *Corporations
professionelles* 1.234-5, *CIL* VI. 10234, 12-13 (the *collegium*
of Aesculapius and Hygeia).

μάχης καὶ ἄνευ ὅπλων ὄψις [1] πολιορκίας, ὡς
τινας τῶν δημοτῶν καὶ χεῖρας ἀντιθεῖναι [2] καὶ
τοὺς νεὼς φρουρεῖν, ἑτοίμως τε ἔχειν πρότερον
ἀναιρεθέντας πρὸ τῶν βωμῶν πεσεῖν ἢ σκῦλα τῶν
πατρίδων ἰδεῖν. ἐντεῦθεν δὴ καὶ μάλιστα κατά τε
πόλεις καὶ κατὰ ἔθνη διοίδαινον τῶν ὄχλων αἱ
ψυχαί. ἀπηρέσκοντό τε καὶ οἱ στρατιῶται τοῖς
πραττομένοις, ὀνειδιζόντων αὐτοῖς ἐπιφθόνως συγ-
γενῶν τε καὶ οἰκείων ὡς δὴ δι᾽ αὐτοὺς ταῦτα
πράττοντος τοῦ Μαξιμίνου.

4. αἰτίαι μὲν δὴ αὗται, οὔτι γε ἄλογοι, ἐς μῖσος
καὶ ἀπόστασιν τοὺς ὄχλους [3] παρώξυνον. καὶ
πάντες μὲν εὔχοντο καὶ θεοὺς τοὺς ἀδικουμένους
ἐπεκάλουν, ἄρξασθαι δὲ οὐδεὶς ἐτόλμα, ἔστε
συμπληρουμένης αὐτῷ τριετοῦς βασιλείας ἐκ

---

[1] ὄψις φglJo
[2] ἀνατιθ. a ἀνατιθῆναι φ contra resistere P καὶ εἰς χεῖρας
ἐλθεῖν Jo ἀνατείνειν Wolf
[3] τοὺς πάντας O ἅπαντας Jo

---

[1] Exploitation of the provinces was nothing new under M.
CIL VIII. 17639 from Numidia is a complaint by the inhabitants against the rapacity of fiscal and military officials
of the province in the time of Alexander; Birley, *JRS* (1950)
60–8.
[2] An important consideration in the political attitude of
the soldiers must have been the attitude of their wives and
families; cf. 8.5.8 for the way the Alban legion was affected;
Whittaker, *Hist.* 13 (1964) 364n. How far the Severan
reform legalizing cohabitation for soldiers had increased this
pressure (3.8.5n) is illustrated by these references.
[3] Lit. " as his third year of rule was being filled out."
Taken literally this would mean a date in early March 238,
though little confidence can be placed in H.'s precision. The
whole discussion about the chronology of the year 238 is based

resented; the appearance of a siege, when there
was no fighting and no one armed, caused public
concern. Some of the lower classes turned to opposition and set a guard round the temples, prepared to
be slaughtered and killed in front of the altars rather
than see their country plundered. Throughout the
cities and the provinces [1] popular emotion rose to
a high pitch at this point. The soldiers were not in
favour of what was happening either, because their
relatives and families bitterly upbraided them, alleging that it was their fault that Maximinus was acting
in this way.[2]

4. These provocations quite justifiably accentu-
ated the bitterness and unrest among the populace.
Although everyone began praying and calling upon
the injured gods, none had the courage to take any
initiative until Maximinus was nearing the end of his
third year of reign,[3] and then for a trivial, insigni-

on inadequate evidence and arbitrary interpretations; the best
collection of the evidence is in Townsend, *YCS* 1 (1928)
231–8, *AJP* 51 (1931) 62–6; cf. Carson, *ANS Centennial
Publication* (1958) 134–57, more or less repeating Townsend;
van Sickle, *CP* 24 (1929) 285–89, produces no new evidence
but shows how arbitrary the interpretations are; Vitucci,
RFIC 32 (1954) 372–82, examines some of the inscriptions
and papyri and concludes they are inconclusive. The
following points are important: (1) only one date is certain—
29th August 238, by which time Gordian III was sole Augustus;
Vogt. *Alex. Münz*-1.193, *P.Oxy.* 1433.ii; hence the chronology
of Piganiol, *Hist. de Rome* (4) 430 cannot be accepted; (2)
Egyptian papyri dates are only reliable for a *terminus ante
quem* of an emperor's reign; (3) the time taken for news to
travel from Africa–Egypt–Pannonia–Rome is no precise guide
since it varied by the season, climate and urgency; (4) the
headings of the rescripts in the *Codex* are unreliable and only
give a rough indication of an emperor's date by their accumu-

μικρᾶς καὶ εὐτελοῦς προφάσεως, οἷα τυραννίδος
σφάλματα, πρῶτοι ὅπλα ἐκίνησαν ἔς τε ἀπόστασιν
εὐσταθῶς ὥρμησαν Λίβυες, ἐξ αἰτίας τοιᾶσδε.
2 ἐπετρόπευέ τις τῆς Καρχηδονίας χώρας τραχύτατα,
καὶ μετὰ πάσης ὠμότητος καταδίκας τε ἐποιεῖτο
καὶ χρημάτων εἰσπράξεις, βουλόμενος εὐδοκιμεῖν
παρὰ τῷ Μαξιμίνῳ. ἐκεῖνός τε γάρ, οὓς ᾔδει
ἁρμόζοντας τῇ ἑαυτοῦ γνώμῃ, ἐπελέγετο· οἵ τε
προεστῶτες τοῦ ταμείου ¹ τότε, εἰ καὶ σπανίως
χρηστοὶ ἐμπεπτώκεσαν, τόν τε κίνδυνον προῦπτον
ἔχοντες καὶ τὴν ἐκείνου φιλοχρηματίαν εἰδότες,
3 ἄκοντες ὅμως τοὺς λοιποὺς ἐμιμοῦντο. ὁ τοίνυν
κατὰ τὴν Λιβύην ἐπίτροπος τοῖς τε ἄλλοις πᾶσι ²
βιαίως προσεφέρετο, καὶ νεανίσκους τινὰς τῶν
παρ' ἐκείνοις εὖ γεγονότων καὶ πλουσίων καταδί-
καις περιβαλὼν εἰσπράττειν τὰ χρήματα εὐθέως
ἐπειρᾶτο, πατρῴων τε καὶ προγονικῶν οὐσιῶν
αὐτοὺς ἀφαιρεῖσθαι. ἐφ' οἷς ἀλγήσαντες οἱ νεανίσκοι τὰ μὲν χρήματα αὐτῷ ἀποδώσειν ὑπέσχοντο,
τριῶν ἡμερῶν αἰτήσαντες ἀνάθεσιν· συνωμοσίαν

---

¹ ταμείου i   ² om i

---

lation; (5) no confidence can be placed in the dates in the
SHA *vitae*. For what it is worth, I believe the revolt of
Gordian took place in the last days of February or early March
(cf. 7.5.7, 7.6.5).

¹ For M.'s avarice, see 7.3.1n, SHA, *Max.* 13.5, *Epit. de
Caes.* 25.1–2, Zos. 1.13.3, Zon. 12.16. In time of economic
emergency Africa Proconsularis provided easy pickings and
naturally the richer landowners suffered first.

² Apart from being the chief landowners, the local African
aristocracy also controlled the organizations of the *iuventutes*,

ficant reason—the kind of thing that proves the
undoing of a tyrant. The Libyans were the first to
take up their weapons and steadily move towards
rebellion. The causes of defection stemmed from 2
a severe procurator in the district of Carthage, who
used to exact absolutely savage sentences and confiscations from the people, hoping his name would
be favourably noted by Maximinus, since the emperor used to select men known to be in accord with
his own policy. Even if the imperial treasury officials
of this period were honest (which was rarely the case),
they reluctantly copied the rest, because of the
danger they faced and their knowledge of the
emperor's avarice.[1] As part of the Libyan pro- 3
curator's generally coercive behaviour was his
attempt to extort quick money from some young
men belonging to rich, noble Carthaginian families,
whom he had fined in the courts, and to strip them
of their ancestral, family property.[2] Smarting
under this treatment, the young men undertook to
pay him the money, but asked for a postponement of

evidence of which is found in several African towns; e.g. *AE*
(1928) 38—Saldae, *IL Alg.* II. 3606—Cirta, *AE* (1913) 22 and
159—Cuicul, *AE* (1921) 21—Thuburnica, etc.; these groups
of men of military age were probably the younger men, who
served in a kind of ephebate, acting as a local militia, guarding
the grain routes, and checking raiders. Their hostility could
have paralysed M.'s supplies and therefore he attempted to
control them, breaking their domination by the hostile
aristocracy. Significantly, Gordian I is said to have culti-
vated the support of such groups in Italy (cf. 7.10.7n); SHA,
Gord. 4.6. They are discussed at length, in relation to
evidence found at Mactar, by Picard, *Karthago* 8 (1957) 77–95.
It is against this background that the hostility of the young
nobles of Carthage and Thysdrus should be seen.

HERODIAN

δὲ ποιησάμενοι, πάντας τε οὓς ᾔδεσαν ἢ πεπονθότας
τι δεινὸν ἢ παθεῖν δεδοικότας ἀναπείσαντες,
κελεύουσι νύκτωρ κατελθεῖν [1] τοὺς ἐκ τῶν ἀγρῶν
[νεανίσκους],[2] ξύλα τε καὶ πελέκεις ἐπιφέρεσθαι.
4 οἱ δὲ πεισθέντες κελεύουσι τοῖς δεσπόταις πρὸ τῆς
ἕω συνῆλθον [3] ἐς τὴν πόλιν, κρύπτοντες ὑπὸ ταῖς
ἐσθῆσιν ἃ ἔφερον αὐτοσχεδίου πολέμου ὅπλα.
μέγα δέ τι πλῆθος ἠθροίσθη· φύσει γὰρ πολυάνθρωπος οὖσα ἡ Λιβύη πολλοὺς εἶχε τοὺς τὴν γῆν
5 γεωργοῦντας. ἅμα δὲ τῷ παραδραμεῖν τὸ περίορθ-
ριον [4] προελθόντες [5] οἱ νεανίσκοι τὸ μὲν πλῆθος
τῶν οἰκετῶν κελεύουσιν αὐτοῖς ἕπεσθαι ὡς ὄντας
μέρος τοῦ λοιποῦ ὄχλου, προστάξαντες τότε
ἀποκαλύπτειν ἃ ⟨ἐπ⟩εφέροντο [6] ὅπλα καὶ γενναίως
ἀνθεστάναι, εἴ τινες ἢ στρατιωτῶν ἢ δημοτῶν
αὐτοῖς ἐπίοιεν ἔκδικοι τοῦ γενησομένου ἔργου·

---

[1] ἐπελθεῖν O   [2] om Whit οἰκέτας Gedike
[3] συνελθόντες O   [4] iJo -ορθρον O
[5] Reisk προσελ. Oi   [6] Mendelss ἔφερον Oag cf. 7.4.4

[1] H. makes clear below that the supporters were not just
young men, but the tenant farmers (*coloni*) of the landowners;
cf. SHA, *Gord.* 7.3–4 (*rusticos vel Afros* and *plebem rusticam*);
possibly support also came from local peasants. The *coloni*
and peasants had long been exploited by both imperial
agents and rich landowners (cf. 7.3.6n and e.g. the complaints
of the tenants of the *saltus* Burunitanus or at Henchit
Mettich; Kotula, *Eos* 50 (1959/60) 264 ff.). Though the rift
between urban and rural society was growing wider (cf.
Frend, *Donatist Church* 99 ff., for Numidia) H. demonstrates

three days. A conspiracy was formed of all those who
were known to have suffered ill-treatment or feared
they would in the future.   They told their [young] [1]
supporters from the countryside to come into town
by night, armed with clubs and axes.   In obedience 4
to the orders of their landlords, the country folk
gathered in the city, hiding the weapons for their
improvised war under the clothes they were wearing.
A very large crowd gathered, for Libya is a heavily
populated country with many farmworkers on the
land.[2]   Soon after dawn the young men appeared 5
and told their mass of retainers to follow them as
though they were part of the rest of the crowd,
but, they added, the men should keep the weapons
they had brought hidden for the time being and
firmly resist any soldier [3] or common person who
might attack them in revenge for the deed they were

that the grievances of the lower classes in the rural area
could be used to political effect by the wealthier decurion
class; cf. 7.5.3n.

[2] The increasing burdens placed on the agricultural workers
by the *annona militaris* and compulsory service in the construction of the Severan *limes* must have been the basic cause
of the unrest; e.g. *AE* (1948) 109 from Banasa, showing the
back payments of taxes that were due.   By raising the
soldiers' pay (6.8.8n), M. had yet further imposed upon the
farmers.   Kotula, *Eos* 50 (1959/60) 200 ff., believes that under
M. the extensive repair of roads leading to Carthage, Hadrumetum and Leptis Magna were in order to facilitate the
speedier transport of higher corn levies; thus conditions were
ripe for revolt, as H. says, 7.3.6. Cf. Romanelli, *Province rom.
Africa* 447 f.

[3] Probably members of the Carthaginian urban cohort;
SHA, *Max.* 14.1, says that the defenders of the procurator
were so *in honorem Maximini*, though later they appear to
have joined Gordian (7.6.2n).

HERODIAN

6 αὐτοὶ δὲ λαβόντες ἐγχειρίδια ὑποκόλπια προσίασι
τῷ ἐπιτρόπῳ ὡς δὴ περὶ τῆς ἀποδόσεως τῶν
χρημάτων διαλεξόμενοι, προσπεσόντες τε αἰφνιδίως οὐ προσδοκῶντα παίσαντες φονεύουσι. τῶν
δὲ περὶ αὐτὸν στρατιωτῶν γυμνωσάντων τὰ ξίφη
τῷ τε φόνῳ ἐπεξελθεῖν θελόντων, οἱ ἐκ τῶν ἀγρῶν
κατεληλυθότες προβαλόμενοι ¹ τά τε ξύλα καὶ τοὺς
πελέκεις, ὑπερμαχόμενοι τῶν δεσποτῶν, τοὺς
ἀνθεστῶτας ῥᾳδίως ἐτρέψαντο.

5. οὕτως δὴ προχωρήσαντος τοῦ ἔργου, οἱ
νεανίσκοι ἅπαξ ἐν ἐπιγνώσει ² γενόμενοι μόνην
ᾔδεσαν ἑαυτοῖς σωτηρίαν ὑπάρχουσαν, εἰ τὰ
τολμηθέντα αὐτοῖς αὐξήσαιεν ἔργοις μείζοσι
καὶ κοινωνὸν τοῦ κινδύνου τὸν ἡγούμενον τοῦ
ἔθνους παραλάβοιεν, πᾶν τε τὸ ἔθνος ἀναπείσαιεν
ἐς ἀπόστασιν· ὅπερ ᾔδεσαν πάλαι μὲν εὔχεσθαι ³
2 μίσει Μαξιμίνου, φόβῳ δὲ κωλύεσθαι. σὺν
παντὶ τοίνυν τῷ πλήθει ἤδη μεσαζούσης
ἡμέρας ⁴ ἐπίασιν ἐπὶ τὴν τοῦ ἀνθυπατεύοντος
οἰκίαν. Γορδιανὸς δὲ ⁵ ἦν ὄνομα, κλήρῳ

---

¹ Bekk -βαλλόμενοι Oi   ² ἀπογνώσει AiP
³ εὐχ. ⟨πάντας⟩ translated P   ⁴ nocte intempesta P
⁵ Jo μὲν Oi

---

¹ The governors of senatorial provinces were still normally
chosen by lot; in the case of Africa and Asia the choice was
made from consulars who had held the consulship some twelve
to fifteen years earlier; Mommsen, *StR* (3) 2.1.255–6, Wadding-
ton, *Fastes d. prov. asiatiques* 13, Thomasson, *Statthalter d.
röm. Prov. Nordafrikas* 1.30 f. SHA, *Max.* 14.2. says that G.
had been appointed in the reign of Alexander *ex senatus
consulto*, but this is unlikely to be true; cf. SHA, *Gord.* 2.4,
5.2, where a forged letter shows the weakness of the informa-

going to do. They themselves went up to the 6
procurator with daggers under the folds of their
garments, pretending they were going to discuss
the payment of their fines.   Then they rushed at him
all of a sudden, while he was off his guard, and
stabbed him to death.   As the procurator's guards
drew their swords in an effort to avenge the assassination, the labourers in from the countryside bran-
dished their clubs and axes in defence of their
masters and easily routed the opposition.

5. After this success, once the young men had
examined their position, they realized there was
only one way to save themselves, which was to add
to their audacity by still more extreme actions.
They must make the provincial governor a partner
in their predicament and induce the whole province
to revolt.   They knew that such a move had been
approved for a long time because people hated
Maximinus, although they were restrained by
fear of him.   It was mid-day when they reached 2
the proconsul's house, accompanied by the whole
crowd.   Gordian, the name of the governor who had
obtained the proconsulship by sortition,[1] was an

tion. M. Antonius Gordianus Sempronianus was born *c.* 159
(if H. is right about his age; cf. Zon. 12.17); his family was
related to that of Ti. Claudius Atticus Herodes, the Athenian
millionaire (Philos. *VS* praef. 480(01), but otherwise no
details are known of his life and career except what is contained in the untrustworthy *vita*. In spite of his nobility, he
did not reach the consulship until late in life (SHA, *Gord.* 18.5;
the information about the dates of two consulships in SHA,
Gord. 4.1, is not confirmed by any inscriptions). His presence
in Antioch, where he met Philostratus for a literary discussion,
probably indicates G. was *comes* of Caracalla and friend of

μὲν τὴν ἀνθυπατείαν λαχών, πρεσβύτης δὲ ἐς ἔτος
ἤδη περί που ὀγδοηκοστὸν ἐληλακώς, πολλῶν δὲ
πρότερον ἄρξας ἐθνῶν ἔν τε πράξεσι μεγίσταις
ἐξετασθείς. ὅθεν αὐτόν τε ἡδέως ὑποδέξεσθαι [1]
τὴν ἀρχὴν ᾤοντο ὥσπερ κορυφαῖον τέλος τῶν
προγενομένων πράξεων, τήν τε σύγκλητον καὶ τὸν
Ῥωμαίων δῆμον ἀσμένως δέξεσθαι [1] ἄνδρα εὖ
γεγονότα καὶ ἐκ πολλῶν ἡγεμονιῶν ὥσπερ κατ'
3 ἀκολουθίαν ἐπὶ τοῦτο ἐλθόντα. συνέβαινε δὲ
ἐκείνης τῆς ἡμέρας, ἧς ταῦτα ἐπράττετο, οἴκοι τὸν
Γορδιανὸν διατρίβειν ἡσυχάζοντα, δεδωκότα τοῖς
καμάτοις ἀνάπαυλαν ἀργίαν τε ταῖς πράξεσιν. οἱ
δὲ νεανίσκοι ξιφήρεις σὺν παντὶ τῷ πλήθει,
βιασάμενοι τοὺς ταῖς αὐλείαις [2] ἐφεστῶτας, εἰσπη-
δήσαντες καταλαμβάνουσιν αὐτὸν ἐπί τινος σκιμπο-
δίου ἀναπαυόμενον, περιστάντες δὲ χλαμύδι πορφυρᾷ περιβάλλουσι σεβασμίαις [3] τε τιμαῖς προσαγο-
4 ρεύουσιν.[4] ὁ δὲ τῷ παραδόξῳ τοῦ πράγματος
ἐκπλαγείς, ἐνέδραν καὶ συσκευὴν ἐξ ἐπιβουλῆς
καθ' ἑαυτοῦ νομίζων, ῥίψας ἀπὸ τοῦ σκίμποδος ἐς
γῆν αὐτὸν ἐδεῖτο φείδεσθαι γέροντος μηδὲν αὐτοὺς
ἀδικήσαντος, σώζειν δὲ τὴν πίστιν καὶ τὴν εὔνοιαν

---

[1] Steph -ασθαι Oi   [2] Wolf αὐλίαις Oi   [3] -οις Mendelss
[4] πάσαις γεραίρουσιν conj Mendelss

Julia Domna c. 214–17. If so, he may have owed his late
advance to the favour of the Syrian empresses Julia Domna,
Maesa and Mamaea (cf. the career of Cassius Dio). Possibly
praetorian *legatus* of Britannia Inferior in 216, proconsul of
Achaia (cf. Philos. *VS loc. cit.*) and suffect consul in 222; for
dates and references, see recently A. Birley, *Britain and Rome*
56 ff., who also suggests Asian origins. On the tendentious

old man of about eighty. He had held many other
previous provincial commands and proved his ability
in important achievements. It was assumed therefore that he would be glad to accept the empire as
the crowning achievement of his eventful career, and
that the senate and people of Rome would welcome a
man who was nobly born and had held many commands in a sort of regular promotion. It so happened 3
on the day of the event that Gordian was spending
time quietly at home,[1] having a break from work
and giving himself some time off from his business.
Forcing their way past the guards in the outer
courtyard, the young men and the mob [2] burst in with
drawn swords and caught the governor resting on a
couch. Crowding round him, they clothed him in a
purple cloak and hailed him with the titles of
Augustus. Gordian was shattered by the surprise 4
event, and thought that a treacherous intrigue had
been planned against him. He threw himself off the
couch down at their feet and begged them to spare
the life of an innocent old man, remembering his

biographical details in the *vita Gordianorum*, see Syme, *H.–
A. Colloquium Bonn 1964/5* 268 ff.
  [1] It has been plausibly suggested that G. himself held
property at Thysdrus and had been responsible for the construction of the vast theatre (holding about 25,000–30,000
people) in the city; Lézine, *Cahiers de Tunisie* 8 (1960) 29–50.
  [2] Cf. 7.4.3n for the question of the extent to which this was
a genuine mass movement; here and elsewhere H. seems to
make it clear that the revolt was primarily a well-organized
group of wealthy landowners of the decurion class. A leader
called Mauricius is described as *potens apud Afros decurio* in
SHA, *Gord.* 7.5, 8.1–4 (though the name is obviously suspect).
Later the *plebs urbana* of Thysdrus and Carthage joined in the
movement (7.5.7, 7.9.4).

τῷ βασιλεύοντι. ἐπεὶ δὲ οἱ μὲν ξιφήρεις ἐνέκειντο,
ἐκεῖνος δὲ [1] ὑπὸ δέους καὶ ἀγνοίας [2] οὐκ ᾔδει τὸ
πεπραγμένον οὐδὲ τὸ τῆς παρούσης τύχης αἴτιον,
εἷς τῶν νεανίσκων, ὃς ἦν αὐτῶν γένει καὶ δυνάμει
λόγων προύχων, τοὺς λοιποὺς κατασιγάσας ἡσυχάζειν τε προστάξας,[3] ἔχων πρόκωπον [4] τὴν δεξιὰν
5 ἔλεξε πρὸς αὐτὸν τοιάδε· " δύο κινδύνων προκει-
μένων, τοῦ μὲν παρόντος τοῦ δὲ μέλλοντος, καὶ τοῦ
μὲν ἤδη προδήλου τοῦ δὲ ἐν ἀμφιβόλῳ τύχῃ,
ἑλέσθαι [5] σε δεῖ σήμερον σώζεσθαι μεθ' ἡμῶν καὶ
πιστεῦσαι σεαυτὸν ἐλπίδι κρείττονι, ᾗ πάντες
πεπιστεύκαμεν, ἢ τεθνάναι ἤδη πρὸς ἡμῶν. εἰ
μὲν οὖν τὰ παρόντα ἕλοιο, πολλὰ τὰ ἐφόδια ἐς
ἀγαθὰς ἐλπίδας, τό τε Μαξιμίνου παρὰ πᾶσι μῖσος,
πόθος [6] τε τυραννίδος ὠμῆς ἀπαλλαγῆς,[7] καὶ ἐν
ταῖς προγενομέναις πράξεσιν εὐδοκίμησις,[8] ἔν τε
συγκλήτῳ καὶ τῷ Ῥωμαίων δήμῳ γνῶσις [9] οὐκ
6 ἄσημος καὶ τιμὴ [10] ἔνδοξος ἀεί. ἀντειπόντι δέ σοι
καὶ μὴ συμπνεύσαντι ἡμῖν τήμερον [11] τέλος ἐπι-
κείσεται· ἀπολούμεθα δὲ καὶ αὐτοί, εἰ δέοι,
προαπολέσαντες [12] ⟨σέ⟩.[13] ἔργον γὰρ ἡμῖν τετόλμη-
ται μείζονος ἀπογνώσεως δεόμενον· κεῖται γὰρ ὁ
τῆς τυρρανίδος ὑπηρέτης, καὶ δίκας ὠμότητος
παρέσχε φονευθεὶς ὑφ' ἡμῶν. ἐφ' οἷς ἦν μὲν

<hr />

[1] τε Agl
[2] καὶ ἀγν. Οἱ ἀπεμάχετο, οὐ γὰρ ᾔδει conj Mendelss
καταγνύμενος? Whit

loyalty and goodwill to the emperor. As they pressed around him with their swords, the governor was in a state of panic and ignorance, without any idea of what had happened or the reason for this present turn of events.[1] One of the young men, noted for his high birth and rhetorical ability, made them quiet by calling for silence, and then, with his sword held at the ready, he said to Gordian, "There 5 are two risks you face, one here, the other in the future; one clearly predictable, the other open to the vagaries of chance. You must choose today whether you are to be safe with us and put your trust in the brighter prospects we all believe in, or whether you are going to die now at our hands. If you choose safety now, we have plenty of advantages to make us optimistic—the universal unpopularity of Maximinus, the desire to be rid of a cruel tyranny, the reputation of your past record, your celebrated name among the senate and people of Rome and your long distinguished position of honour. But, if you refuse 6 to join us, then this day will be your last, even though we have to die ourselves. For we have undertaken a deed of daring that needs a still greater act of desperation. The servant of the tyrant

---

[1] The extent to which the revolt was a spontaneous outburst or a carefully laid plot is discussed in 7.5.7n.

---

[3] ἡσυχ. τε προστάξας om Nauck   [4] πρόκοπον φi
[5] ἐλεύσεσθαι 1 γενέσθαι A   [6] Reisk πάθος Oi
[7] Mendelss ἀπαλλαγήσῃ A -λάξεις φi -λλάξεως Bekk
[8] Sylb -μήσεις Oi   [9] γνώσῃ O
[10] Steph τιμῆς Oi   [11] σήμερον Wolf
[12] προσαπ. O   [13] Stroth from P

ἡμῖν [1] συνάρῃ καὶ κοινωνὸς τῶν κινδύνων γένῃ,[2]
αὐτός τε τῆς ἐν βασιλείᾳ τιμῆς ἀπολαύσεις, τό τε
ἡμῖν προκείμενον ἔργον ἐπαινεθήσεται καὶ οὐ [3]
κολασθήσεται."

7   τοιαῦτά τινα λέγοντος τοῦ νεανίσκου οὐκ ἀνασχό-
μενον τὸ λοιπὸν πλῆθος, συνδραμόντων [4] ἤδη καὶ
πάντων τῶν κατὰ τὴν πόλιν ἐπειδὴ διεφοίτησεν ἡ
φήμη,[4] Σεβαστὸν Γορδιανὸν ἀναγορεύει. παραι-
τούμενος δὲ καὶ γῆρας προϊσχόμενος ἐκεῖνος,
ἄλλως δὲ φιλόδοξος ὤν, οὐδὲ ἀηδῶς ὑπέστη,
ἑλόμενος μᾶλλον τὸν μέλλοντα κίνδυνον ἢ τὸν

---

[1] ἡμῶν i   [2] om gl   [3] om φ
[4] συνδραμόντες ἤδη πάντες ἐπειδὴ διεφοίτησε κατὰ τὴν πόλιν
ἡ φήμη O

---

[1] That is, the *plebs urbana* of Thysdrus, a population
variously estimated as between 15,000 and 25,000 inhabitants;
cf. SHA, *Gord.* 7.4, *Max.* 14.3.

[2] For the date of this event, see 7.4.1n. The olive season
lasted from December to about February each year in Tunisia
(see 7.6.1n); Despoise, *Tunisie Orientale* 358. SHA, *Gord.*
23.2, says that an eclipse of the sun took place soon after
Gordian III became Caesar; since the only eclipses in 238
took place on 2nd April and 25th September (Ginzel, *Speziel.
Kanon d. Sonn. u. Mondfinsternisse* 83, 207) it is usually
assumed that the *vita* has made an error, and that the eclipse of
2nd April coincided with the arrival of the news of the African
revolt in Rome; i.e. that this revolt took place about 20th
March. But there is nothing inconsistent in H. or inscriptions,
etc., with assuming that the date in 7.4.1. is correctly stated and
that the revolt in Africa took place about 1st March, that the

has been struck down, paying the penalty for his cruelty by his murder at our hands. If you join us as a partner in our risks, your own reward will be the office of emperor, and we shall be praised, not punished, for the deed we propose to do.''

By now the whole population of the city [1] had 7 quickly gathered as the news spread. And when the young man finished his speech, the rest of the crowd, without waiting, acclaimed Gordian as Augustus.[2] Although Gordian declined the offer on the grounds of his old age, he was actually ambitious for power and not reluctant to accept it,[3] partly because he preferred to accept the future

Gordiani I and II were dead by 22nd March and the news reached Rome on 1st April, causing the election and elevation of Pupienus, Balbinus and Gordian III. It is only the other dates in the *vitae* and later chronicles which contradict such a chronology.

[3] G.'s willingness to accept the purple provides fuel for the theory of long planning and connivance in the plot to elevate Gordian. Several of the prominent protagonists of the events in Rome had African connections; e.g. L. Caesonius Lucillus Macer Rufinianus had served as *legatus* and *vice proconsulis* in the province and under Gordian III went back as proconsul; L. Flavius Honoratus Lucilianus was probably a native of Cuicul; an unnamed senator who may have been a member of the XXviri is honoured on an African inscription (*ILS* 8980), P. Aelius Secundinus probably originated from Thugga, Appius Claudius Julianus (if correctly associated with these events) had been *legatus* and proconsul in Africa. About 14% of senators were African in origin, but this does not necessarily prove an African faction in Rome began the revolt; on the other hand, the vigour of the action in Rome as soon as the revolt was announced would certainly argue for a planned revolt; cf. 7.10.3n for the names of the vigintivirate and Townsend, *YCS* 14 (1955) 49–105, for a discussion of the planning.

HERODIAN

παρόντα, ἔν τε γήρᾳ ἐσχάτῳ οὐ πάνυ τι δεινὸν
νομίζων, εἰ δέοι, ἐν βασιλικαῖς τιμαῖς καὶ τελευτῆ-
8 σαι. πᾶν δὴ τὸ Λιβύων ἔθνος εὐθέως ἐδεδόνητο,
καὶ τὰς μὲν τοῦ Μαξιμίνου τιμὰς καθῄρουν,
εἰκόσι δὲ καὶ ἀνδριᾶσι Γορδιανοῦ τὰς πόλεις
ἐκόσμουν, τῷ τε κυρίῳ αὐτοῦ ὀνόματι προσθέντες
Ἀφρικανὸν ἐκάλεσαν ἐφ᾽ ἑαυτῶν· οὕτω γὰρ
Λίβυες ὑπὸ [1] με σ ημβρίαν τῇ Ῥωμαίων φωνῇ
καλοῦνται.

6. ὁ δὲ Γορδιανὸς ἐνδιατρίψας τῇ Θύστρῳ, ἔνθα
ταῦτα ἐπράχθη, ἡμερῶν τιν ῶν, ἤδη φέρων βασιλέως

<hr>

[1] ⟨οἱ⟩ ὑπὸ Bekk

<hr>

[1] Cf. 6.8.6 for the same phrase. The whole scene of the
refus de pouvoir described here has similarities with that involv-
ing Maximinus—the surprise offer, the forcible acceptance, the
preference for present safety to the future risk. But in the
case of M. it is suggested that he might have contrived the
event.

[2] The effaced and mutilated inscriptions in the African
provinces are listed by Bersanetti, *Massimino* 68, Townsend,
YCS 14 (1955) 80; the cities which carried out this *abolitio*
were punished later (7.9.11, SHA, *Max.* 19.4, *Gord.* 9.3); note
CIL VIII. 757. 10047 with the name of M. obliterated and
then reinscribed.

[3] Roman coinage for both G. and his son gives them this
title; *imp. M. Ant(onius) Gordianus Afr(icanus) Aug.* and
imp. Caes. M. Ant(onius) Gordianus Afr(icanus) Aug.; *BMC*
VI. 114, Vogt. *Alex. Münz.* 1.190. In Asia and perhaps Africa
the title *Romanus* also appears (cf. *ILS* 493), perhaps a family
name (Birley, *Britain and Rome* 59 f.) but useful to publicize
the claims G. made to be the true legal emperor against a
barbarian usurper (cf. *Romae aeternae* on coins). About 90%

danger to the present one,[1] and partly because, being now an extremely old man, he did not find the prospect of a possible death while holding imperial honours such a terrible thing. The whole of Libya 8 was immediately rocked by revolt. All the honorary dedications to Maximinus were torn down,[2] and in their place the cities were adorned with portraits and statues of Gordian. In addition to his own title they gave him the name of Africanus after themselves,[3] the name given to Libyans in the south by those who speak the language of the Romans.[4]

6. For a few days Gordian remained at Thysdrus [5] where the events had taken place, by this time with

of senators came from Italy, Africa and the Greek-speaking provinces; Barbieri, *Albo* pp. 447, 453.

[4] The only place in the whole history that H. uses the name *Africanus* rather than the term Libyan for inhabitants of Africa. It is not clear whether (accepting the emendation of Bekker) H. is repeating Mela 1.4 that all the Libyans who live in the territory south of the Mediterranean are called Africans in Latin; or whether (as in the MSS) H. means this is the name that Latin-speaking Africans call themselves in the south, and that this was the origin of the name. In fact, the origin of the name *Africa* cannot be traced, though some have argued for a Berber source. It was used by the Romans, as the Greeks used the name *Libya*, either to refer to the political boundaries of the province, or as a general name for the whole Maghreb, or sometimes to mean the whole continent. See Gsell, *Hist. anc. de l'Afrique du Nord* VII. 2–8.

[5] El-Djem in present-day Tunisia, the centre of a rich agricultural region, producing chiefly olives and acting as the entrepôt for produce that was exported from Hadrumetum and Thaenae. The presence of the procurator was probably due to the collection of the *annona* levy of oil, the market for which was over by February each year. The proconsul would have been present to investigate complaints; Picard, *Karthago* 5 (1954) 212.

ὄνομα καὶ σχῆμα, ἀπάρας τε [1] τῆς Θύστρου ἐς τὴν
Καρχηδόνα ἠπείχθη, ἣν ᾔδει μεγίστην τε οὖσαν
καὶ πολυάνθρωπον, ἵν᾽ ὥσπερ ἐν Ῥώμῃ πάντα
πράττοι· ἡ γὰρ [2] πόλις ἐκείνη καὶ δυνάμει
χρημάτων καὶ πλήθει τῶν κατοικούντων καὶ
μεγέθει μόνης Ῥώμης ἀπολείπεται, φιλονεικοῦσα
πρὸς τὴν ἐν Αἰγύπτῳ Ἀλεξάνδρου πόλιν περὶ
2 δευτερείων. εἵπετο δὲ αὐτῷ πᾶσα ἡ βασιλικὴ
πομπή, τῶν μὲν στρατιωτῶν, οἵτινες [3] ἦσαν ἐκεῖ,
καὶ τῶν κατὰ τὴν πόλιν ἐπιμηκεστέρων νεανίσκων
ἐν σχήματι τῶν κατὰ τὴν Ῥώμην δορυφόρων
προϊόντων· αἵ τε ῥάβδοι ἐδαφνηφόρουν, ὅπερ ἐστὶ
σύμβολον ἐς τὸ διαγνῶναι τὰς βασιλικὰς ἀπὸ τῶν
ἰδιωτικῶν, τὸ δὲ πῦρ προεπόμπευεν, ὡς ὄψιν καὶ
τύχην ἔχειν πρὸς ὀλίγον, ὥσπερ ἐν εἰκόνι,[4] τῆς
Ῥώμης τῶν Καρχηδονίων τὴν πόλιν.

3 ὅ τε Γορδιανὸς γράμματά τε πάμπλειστα
ἐκπέμπει πρὸς ἕκαστον τῶν κατὰ τὴν Ῥώμην
πρωτεύειν δοκούντων, τοῖς τε τῆς συγκλήτου

---

[1] del Lange [2] γοῦν i
[3] aP εἴ τινες Ogl [4] ὥσπερ ἐν εἰκόνι del Lange ⁊

---

[1] In 4.3.7 Antioch is compared to Alexandria as the rival
for second city in the empire.
[2] A cohort of the urban troops was stationed at Carthage
(7.4.5); the main legionary force was in Numidia under the

the title and style of emperor. Then he left Thysdrus
and marched to Carthage, the largest and most
heavily populated city (as Gordian knew), so that
he could act exactly as if he were in Rome. The
city is the next after Rome in wealth, population
and size, though there is rivalry for second place
between it and Alexandria in Egypt.[1] With him 2
went the whole imperial escort, the soldiers stationed
there [2] and the tallest young men in the city acting
like the bodyguard in Rome.[3] The *fasces* were
garlanded with laurel, (a sign that distinguishes
an emperor from an ordinary man) and fire was
carried before him in procession,[4] so that for a short
time the city of Carthage was a kind of replica of
Rome in its prosperous appearance.

Gordian sent out a great many messages to all 3
whom he considered leading citizens in Rome, including letters to the most distinguished senators,

---

governor Capellianus, though a cohort of that legion probably
served the proconsul of Proconsularis; Cagnat, *L'armée rom.
d'Afrique* 57 ff., 211 ff. In 7.8.5 the speech of M. suggests
that none of the legionaries had defected to G., though there
was a later tradition that some did; SHA,*Max.* 13.6, 14.1,
Gord. 7.2, Zon. 12.16, Victor, *Caes.* 26.1, Eutrop. 11.2. In
order to explain how the tradition arose Townsend suggests
that it was veterans who joined G. that gave rise to the mis-
understanding; *YCS* 14 (1955) 61n; cf. 7.9.4n, 7.9.6n.
[3] The *iuvenes* (7.4.3n) were formed into a praetorian guard,
over whom, says Victor, *Caes.* 27.1, Gordian's son was made
prefect. This may be a confusion with the title of *princeps
iuventutis*, for which there is no direct evidence, but *IL Tun.*
111 (from Thysdrus) gives the heir the title *iunior*; (cf. Victor,
Caes. 26.7—*conscriptis iunioribus* in Italy).
[4] Cf. 1.8.4n.

δοκιμωτάτοις ἐπιστέλλει, ὧν ἦσαν αὐτῷ πλεῖστοι
φίλοι τε καὶ συγγενεῖς. ἐποίησε δὲ καὶ δημόσια
γράμματα πρός τε τὸν Ῥωμαίων δῆμον καὶ τὴν
σύγκλητον, δι' ὧν τήν τε Λιβύων ἐδήλου ἐς ἑαυτὸν
σύμπνοιαν, τῆς τε Μαξιμίνου ὠμότητος κατηγόρει
4 σφοδρότατα εἰδὼς μισουμένην, αὐτός τε πᾶσαν
πραότητα ὑπισχνεῖτο, συκοφάντας τε πάντας
φυγαδεύων καὶ παλινδικίαν ¹ διδοὺς τοῖς ἀδίκως
κατακριθεῖσι, τούς τε φυγάδας ἐς τὰς πατρίδας
ἐπανάγων· τοῖς δὲ στρατιώταις ὑπέσχετο ἐπίδοσιν
χρημάτων ὅσην οὐδεὶς πρότερον. τῷ τε δήμῳ
νομὰς ἐπήγγειλε. προυνοήσατο δὲ τοῦ πρότερον
ἀναιρεθῆναι τὸν κατὰ τὴν Ῥώμην τῶν στρατοπέδων
προεστῶτα· Βιταλιανὸς δὲ ἦν ὄνομα αὐτῷ. τοῦτον
ᾔδει ² τραχύτατα καὶ ὠμότατα πράττοντα, φίλτα-
τόν τε ὄντα ³ καὶ καθωσιωμένον τῷ Μαξιμίνῳ.
5 ὑποπτεύων οὖν μὴ τοῖς πραττομένοις γενναίως
ἀντιστῇ καὶ τῷ ἐκείνου φόβῳ μηδεὶς αὐτῷ
συνάρηται, πέμπει τὸν ταμίαν τοῦ ἔθνους, νεανίσκον

---

¹ ψῆφον δικαίαν A   ² ἤδη i   ³ om O

---

¹ Urgent news might travel direct from Carthage to Rome in
two to three days in the summer sailing season (Pliny, *NH*
19.3), but at this season must have gone by the Sicilian route
in seven to ten days; cf. 7.4.1n, 7.8.1n. The almost immediate
issue of coinage in Rome in the name of the Gordians (in a
reign of about three weeks) suggests that the dies were already
prepared and therefore that the revolt was anticipated, says

many of whom were his friends and relatives,[1]
and a public dispatch to the senate and people
of Rome. In the letters he informed them of his
unanimous support [2] in Libya and condemned the
brutality of Maximinus, which he knew they heartily
loathed. He promised that he would exercise great 4
clemency, send all informers into exile, grant retrials
to all who had been unjustly condemned and restore
exiles to their countries.[3] To the soldiers he
promised a bigger donative than ever before and to
the people he gave notice of a distribution of money.
First, he took precautions to have the commander
of the forces in Rome destroyed, a man called
Vitalianus.[4] Gordian was aware of the harsh, cruel
behaviour of this man, a completely devoted friend of
Maximinus, and he suspected that he would rigor- 5
ously resist his present activities; also, that no one
would join his own side for fear of Vitalianus. So he

Carson, *BMC* VI. 96–7; but it seems at least possible that
issues of the Gordians could have gone on after their death.

[2] The only occasion on which H. uses the word συμπνοία,
which exactly translates the Latin *consensus*; its stress under-
lines the importance of the ideology of the Republican principate in G.'s propaganda, while providing the senate with the
higher legality needed to justify the outlawing of M.; cf.
Goodenough, *YCS* 1 (1928) 90 ff., for Hellenistic parallels.
Was H. here copying some document he had seen?

[3] Cf. 2.14.3n for the regular formula expected of the
basileus in contrast to the *tyrannus*. But G. also had to
promise donatives and *congiaria*.

[4] Perhaps P. Aelius Vitalianus; if so, he was equestrian governor of Mauretania Caesariensis until at least 236; *AE* (1957)
278. The doubts about his status as prefect given by Howe,
Praet. Pref. no. 40 seem ill founded. The main body of the
praetorians and the other prefect were with M. at Sirmium
(8.5.9n).

193

φύσει εὔτολμον καὶ τὸ σῶμα οὐκ ἀγεννῆ καὶ τὴν
ἡλικίαν ἀκμάζοντα, πρόθυμόν τε ἐς τὸν ὑπὲρ
ἑαυτοῦ [1] κίνδυνον, παραδοὺς αὐτῷ ἑκατοντάρχας
καὶ στρατιώτας τινάς, οἷς ἔδωκε κατασεσημασμένα
γράμματα ἐν πτυκτοῖς [2] πίνακι, δι' ὧν τὰ ἀπόρρητα
καὶ κρυπτὰ ἀγγέλματα τοῖς βασιλεῦσιν ἐπιστέλλε-
6 ται. κελεύει δὲ αὐτοῖς πρὸ τῆς ἕω ἐς τὴν Ῥώμην
κατελθοῦσιν ἐπιστῆναι ἔτι ἰδιάζοντι [3] καὶ ἀνακε-
χωρηκότι τῷ Βιταλιανῷ ἐν τῷ τοῦ δικαστηρίου
οἰκίσκῳ, ἔνθα μόνος τὰ ἀπόρρητα καὶ κρυπτὰ
δοκοῦντα ὑπὲρ σωτηρίας τοῦ βασιλέως ἠρεύνα τε
καὶ ἐξήταζε, δηλῶσαί τε ὅτι φέρουσι γράμματα
πρὸς Μαξιμίνου [4] ἀπόρρητα, ἐπὶ τοῦτό τε παρ'
αὐτοῦ [5] πεμφθῆναι [6] ὑπὲρ ἀσφαλείας τοῦ βασιλέως·

---

[1] αὐτοῦ O   [2] πυκτοῖς φ al (g¹ in mg) πηκτοῖς A
[3] Stroth δικάζοντι Oi ἤδη δικάζοντι Gedike   [4] -ῖνον Oa
[5] παρὰ τοῦ gl παρά του a   [6] παραπεμφθῆναι.

---

[1] Zos. 1.14.1 says that among those sent to Rome by
Gordian was (P. Licinius) Valerianus, a man of consular rank,
who later became emperor (A.D. 253). Valerian is also
mentioned by SHA, *Gord.* 9.7, who says that he was *princeps
senatus.* Both statements are dubious, since a man of such
seniority is unlikely to have served as a *legatus* of Gordian in
Africa. But even if he had (just as G.'s son is said to have
been *legatus* to his father and of consular status, SHA, *Gord.*
18.5), he would surely not have been sent from Africa and
thus draw attention to the conspiracy. A suffect consul (Degrassi, *Fasti Consolari* 66) would not be *princeps senatus.* Later
Valerian's bid for the purple was supported by detachments
of legio III Augusta (reformed after its dispersal by Gordian
III; *ILS* 531, 2296) which now opposed and crushed the
Gordiani in Africa.

[2] Cf. 3.5.4 for the same attempted method of assassination.
If the revolt of G. took place on 1st March (7.4.1n, 7.5.7n), the

sent his provincial quaestor,[1] a young man who was
inherently brave, physically tough and in the prime
of his youth. He was also an enthusiastic supporter
for his cause. Gordian transferred to his command
some centurions and soldiers, to whom he gave a letter
sealed in folding tablets, the normal method used by
the emperor to send private, secret messages.[2] The 6
men were told to arrive before daybreak in Rome and
appear before Vitalianus while he was still on his own,
but after he had gone to the small room of the public
court in which he used to scrutinize carefully what
purported to be the private, secret dispatches concerning the safety of the emperor. They were to
inform him that they were bringing secret instruction
from Maximinus, sent by him[3] on this mission con-

news would have reached Rome about 11th March, and
Sirmium about 21st March (7.8.1n). The earliest rescript headings of 238 with the name of Gordian are dated to 1st Jan.
(*Cod. Just.* 5.70.2), 21st March (*ibid.* 7.26.5) and 29th March
(or 29th July, *ibid.* 7.43.2); the first must be an error, but the
other two might belong to Gordian I. *P. Yale* 156, which
records the name of the Gordians (I and II) on 20th June, was
written long after they were dead; but papyri scribes were
notoriously slow to react to changes in emperors. The detailed knowledge of events that H. displays probably indicates
that he was in Rome in 238.

[3] It is not clear from the Greek in the MSS (see *app. critic.*)
by whom the messages were purported to have been sent; the
emendations and adopted reading makes it clear that the
message was supposed to have come *from* Maximinus to
Vitalianus; cf. SHA, *Gord.* 10.6—*fictae sunt litterae Maximini.*
It is almost inconceivable that Vitalianus would otherwise
have exposed himself to a private meeting (cf. the reaction of
Albinus, 3.5.4). SHA, *Gord.* 10.5, most improbably places the
murder of Vitalianus after the senatorial decree recognizing
the Gordiani, and on the instructions of the senate.

7 προσποιήσασθαι δὲ βούλεσθαι καὶ διαλεχθῆναι
αὐτῷ ἰδιαίτερον ἀπαγγεῖλαί τε τὰ ἐντεταλμένα·
διασχολουμένῳ δὲ ἐκείνῳ περὶ [1] τὴν τῶν σφραγίδων
ἐπίγνωσιν προσποιουμένους [2] ὡς δὴ ἐροῦντάς τι,
οἷς εἶχον ὑποκολπιδίοις ξίφεσι φονεῦσαι. ἅπερ
πάντα προυχώρησεν ὡς ἐκέλευσεν. ἔτι γὰρ νυκτὸς
οὔσης, ὥσπερ [3] ἐκεῖνος εἰώθει πρὸ ἡμέρας προϊέναι,[3] ἐπέστησαν αὐτῷ ἰδιάζοντι, μηδὲ πολλοῦ
8 πλήθους παρόντος· οἱ μὲν γὰρ οὐδὲ προεληλύθεσαν,
οἱ δὲ προσαγορεύσαντες [4] πρὸ ἡμέρας ἀνακεχωρήκεσαν, ἡσυχίας τε [5] οὖν οὔσης ὀλίγων [6] τε πρὸ τοῦ
οἰκίσκου, δηλώσαντες αὐτῷ τὰ προειρημένα ῥᾳδίως
εἰσεδέχθησαν· ἐπιδόντες δὲ τὰ γράμματα, ἐκείνου
ταῖς σφραγῖσι τὰς ὄψεις ἐπιβάλλοντος προβαλόντες
τὰ ξιφίδια καὶ παίσαντες φονεύουσιν, ἔχοντές τε
9 αὐτὰ πρόκωπα [7] προπηδῶσιν. οἱ δὲ παρόντες
ἐκπλαγέντες ἀνεχώρησαν, οἰόμενοι Μαξιμίνου τὴν
κέλευσιν εἶναι· καὶ γὰρ ἐποίει τοῦτο πολλάκις καὶ
περὶ τοὺς δοκοῦντας εἶναι φιλτάτους. κατελθόντες
δὲ διὰ μέσης τῆς ἱερᾶς ὁδοῦ προτιθέασι τὰ πρὸς

---

[1] πρὸς Ol
[2] παρισταμένους conj Mendelss προσπ.—τι om P
[3] ὥσπερ—προϊέναι del Mendelss
[4] -εύοντες O
[5] om i
[6] ὀλίγον O
[7] πρόκοπα i

cerning a matter of imperial security. They were 7
further instructed to pretend they wanted a private
interview with Vitalianus to pass on their instructions.
Then, while he was busy examining the seals, they
were to act as if they were going to say something,
and kill him with the swords hidden under their
clothes. Everything went according to the instructions. While it was still dark (Vitalianus normally
left his house before daybreak), they appeared before
him while he was on his own, and no great number of
people were about. Some people had not yet come 8
out, and others had already gone home after making
their morning calls before dawn.[1] While the place
was quiet, and only a few people stood in front of the
chamber, the soldiers had no difficulty in getting an
audience by showing their letter. They gave
Vitalianus the letter, and while his attention was
turned to the seals, they drew their swords and
stabbed him to death. After this they rushed out of
the room with the swords in their hands. The by- 9
standers ran away in fright, because they thought the
murder was on Maximinus' orders—a not infrequent
action against even his supposedly closest friends.
The soldiers ran down the middle of the Sacred

[1] There are numerous references in Roman writers to the
early morning greetings (*salutatio matutina*). Poor clients
had the duty of paying a pre-dawn call (*officium antelucanum*)
by the first two hours of the day, Mart. 4.8.1; this often
necessitated rising in the middle of the night to be punctual,
Juv. 3.127, Luc. *Nig.* 22; cf. Hug, *RE* (salutatio). In the
third hour of the day the business of the courts began, according to Martial, 4.8.1. H. here seems to be saying that
the visit to the prefect was after the time for *salutatio* but
before the business of the day began.

τὸν δῆμον τοῦ Γορδιανοῦ γράμματα, τοῖς τε
ὑπάτοις καὶ τοῖς λοιποῖς τὰ ἐπεσταλμένα διδόασι·
διασκεδάννυταί τε ὑπ' αὐτῶν φήμη ὡς ἄρα καὶ
Μαξιμῖνος εἴη ἀνῃρημένος.

7. ὡς δὲ διεφοίτησε ταῦτα, εὐθέως πᾶς ὁ
δῆμος ὥσπερ ἐνθουσιῶν διέθει πανταχοῦ· καὶ
πάντες μὲν γὰρ ὄχλοι κοῦφοι πρὸς τὰ καινοτο-
μούμενα, ὁ δὲ ʿΡωμαίων δῆμος ἐν πλήθει
μεγίστῳ καὶ ποικίλῳ συγκλύδων τε ἀνθρώπων
πολὺ καὶ ῥᾴδιον ¹ ἔχει τὸ τῆς γνώμης εὐκίνητον.
2 πᾶσαι ἀνδριάντες οὖν καὶ εἰκόνες τιμαί τε
τοῦ Μαξιμίνου κατεσπῶντο, καὶ τὸ κρυπτὸν
πρότερον διὰ φόβον μῖσος ἀδεὲς καὶ αὐτεξούσιον
γενόμενον ἀκωλύτως ἐξεχεῖτο. ἥ τε σύγκλητος

---

¹ *longe ceteris mobilior* P πολὺ ῥᾶον Sylb

---

¹ The prefect had a tribunal at the *principia* of the Viminal
camp, Durry, *Cohortes prét.* 54, but the reference to a public
court (7.6.6) indicates that the court sessions (*auditoria*) were
being held in one of the courts of the city, perhaps that of the
urban prefect in the Forum Augusti; Carcopino, *Daily Life in
Anc. Rome* (Penguin) 189, though it might have been in the
imperial basilica on the Palatine (as is suggested by H.'s words
" ran down "); cf. SHA, *Gord.* 10.7, which mentions a portico,
and Dio (Xiph.) 69.18.2–4, recording the early morning judicial
hearings in the palace, which were held by Marcius Turbo,
prefect under Hadrian. The bystanders were probably other
soldiers of the prefect's escort. The age of the Severi was the
high-water mark of the judicial functions of the praetorian

Way[1] and displayed the letter written by Gordian
to the people, giving the consuls and the others their
messages, too. And they spread the rumour that
Maximinus had been destroyed as well.

7. As the rumour gained currency, the populace at
once began to rush around like people possessed.
Although every lower-class mob is quick to revolt,
the Roman population, made up of a vast, heterogene-
ous conglomeration of human beings, can change its
allegiances frequently and capriciously.[2] All the 2
statues, pictures and honorific dedications of Maximinus were torn down, letting loose a flood of hatred,
unrestrained by fear, but previously kept hidden
through intimidation. At a meeting of the senate,[3]

prefect, who, in addition to his own area of jurisdiction, acted
vice imperatoris (for the emperor), particularly with reference
to provincial affairs, and therefore as a final court of appeal;
Passerini, *Coorti pret.* 223–51, Durry, *op. cit.* 171–4. It is no
accident that during Maximinus' absence the praetorian
prefect was given more legislative power; *Cod. Just.* 1.26.2,
wrongly ascribed to Alexander.

[2] Cf. Salač, *Listy Filol.* 68 (1941) 206–8, who uses this
passage to prove that H. was using a source that was Roman
and hostile to provincial immigrants. One need not accept
the argument of a proto-Herodian to find traditional comments
of this sort about the Roman plebs; e.g. Sallust, *Cat.* 37.2–3,
id adeo more suo (sc. *plebs*) *videbatur facere. nam semper in
civitate . . . odio suarum rerum mutari omnia student; turba
atque seditionibus sine cura aluntur,* etc. The same comment
about foreign immigrants is made in 1.12.1. What H. does
indicate is a middle class outlook.

[3] According to SHA, *Gord.* 12.1, which claims to come from
Junius Cordus (who is probably fictitious, though Pasoli,
L'Uso di Erod. nella V. Max. 13 ff. believes he existed), the
decree of recognition was a *senatus consultum tacitum.* This
may be a misinterpretation of what H. says in 7.10.3, since
secret decrees are otherwise unknown.

συνελθοῦσα πρὶν τὸ ἀκριβὲς εἰδέναι περὶ τοῦ
Μαξιμίνου, ἐκ τῆς παρούσης τύχης τὰ μέλλοντα
πιστεύσαντες τὸν Γορδιανὸν ἅμα τῷ υἱῷ Σεβαστοὺς
ἀναγορεύουσι, τὰς δὲ τοῦ Μαξιμίνου τιμὰς ἀνατρέ-
3 πουσι. συκοφάνται τε οὖν καὶ οἱ γενόμενοι τινῶν
κατήγοροι ἢ ἔφευγον ἢ ὑπὸ τῶν ἀδικηθέντων
ἀνηροῦντο, ἐπίτροποί τε καὶ δικασταὶ οἱ τῆς
ἐκείνου ὠμότητος ὑπηρέται συρέντες ὑπὸ τοῦ
ὄχλου ἐς τοὺς ὀχετοὺς ἐρριπτοῦντο. φόνος τε οὐκ
ὀλίγος ἐγένετο καὶ μηδὲν ἀδικησάντων ἀνθρώπων·
δανειστὰς γὰρ ἑαυτῶν ἢ καὶ ἀντιδίκους ἐν πράγμα-
σιν ἀγοραίοις, καὶ εἴ τις πρός τινα βραχεῖαν αἰτίαν
εἶχε μίσους, ἐπαναβαίνοντες ταῖς [1] οἰκήσεσιν
ἀπροσδοκήτως, ἐπηρεάζοντες ὡς συκοφάντας ἐσύ-
4 λησάν τε καὶ ἐφόνευσαν. ἐν προσχήματι ἐλευθερίας ἀδείας τε εἰρηνικῆς ἔργα πολέμου ἐμφυλίου
ἐγένετο, ὡς καὶ τὸν τῆς πόλεως ἔπαρχοντα μετὰ

[1] τε φ i

---

[1] The collegality of G. and his son is attested on inscriptions
and coins; see *PIR*[2] A 833 and 834. On one coin (*BMC* VI.
247, no. 18 = pl. 42) and one inscription (from Bordeaux
perhaps, *ILS* 493) the son is given the title of *pontifex maximus*; if genuine this is the first example of complete collegality, but it is believed the coin is a hybrid and the inscription could refer to Gordian III. H. says nothing about
G. II being hailed as Augustus in Africa, though SHA, *Max.*
14.3, says this happened at Thysdrus, and *Gord.* 9.6 says it
took place at Carthage; the latter is said to derive from
Dexippus by Homo, *Rev. Hist.* 131 (1919) 227–32.

[2] The declaration of M. and his son as *hostes publici* is
recorded on *ILS* 1188 (restored in *PIR*[2] A 622—see 7.12.1n).
The formal deposition of a living emperor had happened only
to Nero and Julianus before this; H. makes it clear that there

before detailed information about Maximinus was available, they bestowed the title of Augustus on Gordian and his son [1] and stripped Maximinus of his honours,[2] confident of the future as a result of the present fortunate event. Informers and accusers 3 fled or were destroyed by the victims of their crimes. Procurators and jurymen who had acted as agents of Maximinus' brutality were seized by the mob and thrown into the sewers. There was widespread slaughter, even of innocent people, such as creditors or law-suit rivals or any person against whom one had a trivial reason for a grudge. Their homes were broken into without warning and they were insulted, robbed and murdered as informers. Ostensibly 4 in conditions of freedom and the security of peace-time, acts of civil war took place. When the urban prefect, named Sabinus,[3] a much experienced senior

was a formal *abrogatio imperii* and *hostis iudicatio*, the necessary preliminaries to declaration of *iustum bellum*. The questionable legality of such a step had to be justified in terms of *tyrannus* (*dominus*) ideology; cf. the discussion by Vittinghoff, *Staatsfeind in d. röm. Kaiserzeit* 99–101.

[3] His identity is not known, though he is certainly not Vettius Sabinus (a misnomer by SHA, *Max. et Balb.* 2.1, for C. Vettius Gratus Sabinianus, *Albo* 523). Nor is it clear whether he was killed for being a partisan of M. or simply while trying to maintain order (cf. *percussus in populo*, SHA, *Max.* 15.1); SHA, *Gord.* 13.2–9, implies that Sabinus was M.'s agent in Rome, but the passage is quite untrustworthy, and H.'s favourable description here would imply that he was not. There were several senior consulars named Sabinus: C. Octavius Appius Suetrius Sabinus, *amicus* of Caracalla (4.7.2n), *cos.* 214 (but he may be the *cos.* II of 240; cf. *CIL* VI. 37061 mutilated); L. Mantennius Sabinus, *cos. suff.* before 229, *legatus* of Moesia in 229 and son of an Egyptian prefect; Fabius Sabinus, said to have been an amicus of

HERODIAN

πράξεις πολλὰς ὑπατικάς (Σαβῖνος δὲ ἦν ὄνομα
αὐτῷ), βουλόμενον κωλῦσαι τὰ γινόμενα, ξύλῳ
παισθέντα κατὰ τοῦ κρανίου τελευτῆσαι.

καὶ ὁ μὲν δῆμος ἐν τούτοις ἦν, ἡ δὲ σύγκλητος
ἅπαξ ἀναρριφθέντος κινδύνου φόβῳ τοῦ Μαξιμίνου
πάντα ἔπραττεν ἐς τὸ ἀποστῆσαι αὐτοῦ τὰ ἔθνη.
5 πρεσβεῖαι τοίνυν πανταχοῦ πρὸς πάντας ἡγουμένους ἐξεπέμφθησαν, ἐπιλεχθέντων ἀνδρῶν ἔκ τε
τῆς συγκλήτου αὐτῆς καὶ τοῦ ἱππικοῦ τάγματος
οὐκ ἀδοκίμων, γράμματά τε πρὸς πάντας τὴν
Ῥωμαίων καὶ τῆς συγκλήτου γνώμην δηλοῦντα,[1]
προτρέποντά τε τοὺς ⟨μὲν⟩[2] ἡγουμένους συναί-
ρεσθαι ⟨τοῖς⟩[3] τῇ κοινῇ πατρίδι καὶ συνεδρίῳ
βουλεύουσι,[4] τὰ δ᾽ ἔθνη πείθεσθαι Ῥωμαίοις, ὧν
δημόσιον ἄνωθεν τὸ κράτος ἐστίν, αὐτά τε φίλα
6 καὶ ὑπήκοα ἐκ προγόνων. οἱ πλεῖστοι μὲν οὖν
προσήκαντο τὴν πρεσβείαν, καὶ τὰ ἔθνη ἀποστή-
σαντες ῥᾳδίως μίσει τῆς Μαξιμίνου τυραννίδος,

---

[1] om O [2] Bekk[2]
[3] Whit corrupt Stav [4] βουλῇ Steph

Severus Alexander (SHA, *Alex.* 68.1, though a poor authority;
cf. SHA, *Elag.* 16.2–3); P. Catius Sabinus, *cos.* II in 216 (*Albo*
126). Perhaps two Sabini are confused, one appointed after
Pupienus and Balbinus became emperors (*Max. et Balb.* 4.4)
and this man killed earlier. The solution may be in Victor,
Caes. 26.5, who says that this riot occurred as a result of the
encouragement given by a certain Domitius *after* the news of
Gordian's death; i.e. the incident caused by Domitius
Gallicanus in 7.11.3. If so, the problem is resolved, and

202

consular, attempted to put a stop to this, he was struck on the head with a club and killed.

With the populace in this state, the senate, once having risked the danger, from fear of Maximinus did their best to rouse the provinces.[1] Delegations 5 of special senatorial representatives [2] and well-known members of the equestrian order were sent in all directions to visit all provincial governors. Letters [3] also went out to explain the position of the Romans and the senate, and to urge governors to join sides with those who were planning for their common state and its senate; the provincial population was told to remain loyal to the Romans; the Roman people, they said, had exercised power [4] from ancient times while they, the provincials, had been friendly subjects from the time of their forefathers. As the 6 delegations were generally well received, the provincials rebelled from Maximinus unhesitatingly be-

Sabinus here was a supporter of the senatorial emperors who died in the rioting caused by the partisans of Gordian III, but three weeks after this date. Cf. the discussion by Cassola, *Att. Accad. Pont.* 6(1956/7)201–207.

[1] Replies from these delegations cannot have reached Rome before the death of the Gordiani (7.9.10).

[2] Often assumed to be the *vigintiviri*, but see 7.10.4n. This may, however, account for the appearance of the designation *a sena[tu electus*?] which appears on an inscription to an unknown senator in Africa, *ILS* 8980.

[3] The text of the letter is purported to be in SHA, *Max.* 15.6 ff., but is an evident forgery; similarly, the date of the senate's meeting (26th June) under the presidency of a suffect consul called Junius Silanus (*Max.* 16.1 ff.) is also fictitious. Hohl, *Maximini duo* (Kleine Texte f. Vorlesung. u. Übung., 1949) quotes Mommsen, *Ges. Schr.* VII. 308, 351, for the signs of invention.

[4] Cf. 2.8.4n.

τούς τε ἐκεῖσε πράττοντας, εἰ τὰ Μαξιμίνου φρο-
νοῖεν, ἀποκτείναντες προσέθεντο Ῥωμαίοις· ὀλίγοι
δέ τινες ἢ διεχρήσαντο τοὺς ἐλθόντας πρέσβεις ἢ
μετὰ φρουρᾶς πρὸς ἐκεῖνον παρέπεμψαν, οὓς
συλλαμβάνων ὠμῶς ἐκόλαζεν.

8. τὰ μὲν [1] κατὰ τὴν Ῥωμαίων πόλιν τε καὶ
γνώμην τοιαῦτα ἦν· ὡς δ' ἀπηγγέλη τῷ Μαξιμίνῳ
τὰ πεπραγμένα, σκυθρωπός τε ἦν καὶ ἐν μεγάλαις
φροντίσι, προσεποιεῖτο δὲ [2] αὐτῶν καταφρονεῖν.
τῆς μὲν οὖν πρώτης καὶ δευτέρας ἡμέρας ἔνδον
ἔμεινεν ἡσυχάζων καὶ τοῖς φίλοις περὶ τοῦ πρακ-
2 τέου κοινούμενος. τὸ δὲ στρατόπεδον πᾶν τὸ σὺν

[1] καὶ τὰ μὲν Jo τὰ μὲν οὖν A
[2] P τε Oi

---

[1] The extent of provincial reactions for or against M.
cannot be judged with any confidence by erased inscriptions
or coins issued in the name of the Gordiani, since in some cases
these were done retrospectively, after the death of M. However, Bersanetti, *Massimino* ch. IV, provides the following
list: the name of M. remained on inscriptions in Gallia
Lugdunensis, Aquitania, Hispania Tarrac., Lusitania, Baetica,
Mauretania Caesariensis, Arabia, Syria Palaestina, Cappadocia,
who also erased the names of P. and B. after their deaths; by
contrast inscriptions and coins of Gordian and his son exist
from Africa Proconsularis, Pontus-Bithynia, Galatia, Lycia-
Pamphylia, Egypt, Asia, Cilicia. Warning about accepting
such evidence as an accurate guide is given by Barbieri, *Epig.*
4 (1942) 90–3, and Townsend, *YCS* 14 (1955) 67, believes that
it can be shown that the Pannonias remained loyal to M., that
Cappadocia, Palestine, Arabia, Macedonia, Achaia, Syria,

cause they hated his tyranny.[1] They executed the
officials in the province who supported him, and they
joined the side of the Romans. But a few provinces
put the emissaries to death when they arrived, or
sent them under guard to Maximinus, who punished
them viciously as he got hold of them.

8. While this was the condition of the city and the
state of opinion in Rome, news of the events reached
Maximinus, making him an angry and extremely
worried man,[2] though he pretended to think them of
little importance. For the first two days he remained
inactive, in consultation with his council as to the best
course of action.[3] The whole of Maximinus' army 2

Thrace, Moesia Inferior went over to P. and B.; in Thrace
and Moesia Inferior, however, the governors' defection to the
senatorial side (cf. 8.5.3n) caused resistance from the troops
(e.g. 7.12.1n—the reluctance of legio VII Claudia, and in
Thrace the disturbances at Scaptopare, *IGRR* 1.674). Needless to say this is very speculative.

[2] Apart from any repercussions in Rome, Africa was vital
for the supply of corn and oil that came to Rome; Kotula,
Eos 50 (1959/60) 198. SHA, *Max.* 17, and *Gord.* 13.3 ff., agree
substantially with H., but elaborate with fictitious nonsense
about M.'s rage; according to the *vita Max.*, M. was angry
with his son also, maintaining that, had he been in Rome, there
would have been no revolt.

[3] The news from Africa must have reached M. about ten
days after it reached Rome; so M. must have heard about the
revolt at just about the same time that the Gordiani were
actually being defeated in Africa, i.e. about 21st March
(7.9.10). Since M. decided to march on Rome almost immediately (it was publicly announced on the " third day " = 23rd
March), the news of G.'s death and M.'s advance must have
arrived in Rome almost simultaneously; this much is made
clear in the confused chronology of SHA, *Gord.* 10, which says
that the envoys of M. were present in Rome at the same time
as the selection of the *XXviri* (see 7.10.4n).

αὐτῷ οἵ τε ἐπέκεινα πάντες ἄνθρωποι ἔγνωσαν μὲν
τὰ διαγγελθέντα, καὶ διοίδαινον πᾶσιν αἱ ψυχαὶ
τηλικούτων ἔργων εὐτόλμῳ [1] καινοτομίᾳ, οὐδέ
τις πρός τινα ἔλεγέ τι οὔτ' εἰδέναι τι προσεποιεῖτο·
τοσοῦτος γὰρ ἦν ὁ Μαξιμίνου φόβος ὡς μηδὲν
αὐτὸν λανθάνειν, παραφυλάττεσθαι δὲ πάντων οὐ
μόνον τὰ διὰ φωνῆς καὶ γλώττης προφερόμενα [2]
3 ἀλλὰ καὶ τὰ δι' ὄψεως νεύματα. ὁ μέντοι Μαξιμῖνος συγκαλέσας πάντα τὸν στρατὸν ἐς τὸ πρὸ τῆς
πόλεως πεδίον, προελθών [3] τε τῆς τρίτης ἡμέρας
ἀνελθών τε ἐπὶ τὸ βῆμα, ἐπιφερόμενος τὸ βιβλίον
ὅπερ ἦσαν αὐτῷ συντάξαντές τινες τῶν φίλων, ἐξ
ἀναγνώσεως ἔλεξε τοιάδε·

4   " ἄπιστα μὲν οἶδα καὶ παράδοξα λέξων πρὸς
ὑμᾶς, ὡς δὲ ἐγὼ οἴομαι, οὐ θαύματος ἀλλὰ
χλεύης καὶ γέλωτος ἄξια. ὅπλα ἐφ' ὑμᾶς καὶ
τὴν ὑμετέραν ἀνδρείαν οὐ [4] Γερμανοὶ αἴρονται,[5]
οὓς πολλάκις ἐνικήσαμεν, οὐ Σαυρομάται οἱ
περὶ εἰρήνης ἑκάστοτε ἱκετεύοντες· Πέρσαι τε

---

[1] Steph εὐτόλμων Oi   [2] προσφερόμενα Oag (eras in g)
[3] προσελθών φi   [4] οἱ O   [5] αἱροῦνται i

---

[1] A contrivance by H. to put a highly articulate and
rhetorical speech into the mouth of a supposedly " barbarian " emperor; SHA, *Max.* 18.1, records a very brief
contio militaris and *Gord.* 14.1–4 presents a quite different
speech (which is supposed to be Dexippus?). There is no
reason to think these speeches bore much relationship to the
actual words of M., but artistically the question of appro-
priateness was an important consideration; e.g. Luc. *How to*

and the local population knew the reports, and everyone's spirits were in a ferment at the bold, revolu-
tionary character of these important actions. But not
a word was spoken and everyone feigned ignorance.
Maximinus was so nervous that he let nothing go
unnoticed, keeping a close watch not only on people's
speeches and conversations but even on the flicker of
their eyes. On the third day Maximinus sum- 3
moned the entire army to the parade ground in front
of the city and went out to address them. After
he went up on to the rostrum, carrying a document which some of his advisers had composed for
him,[1] he read out the following speech:

"I am sure what I am going to say to you will be 4
incredible and unexpected; it is not in my opinion
so much a matter for astonishment as for laughter and
ridicule. Someone is pitting his arms against you
and your courage. But not the Germans, whom we
have defeated on many occasions, nor the Sarmatians,
who regularly come to beg for peace.[2] The Per-

Write History 58—the speech must be appropriate to the
person's character and his subject (cf. Dion. Hal. *de Thuc.* 37,
Quint. 10.1.101). Therefore the need for H.'s device here.
In 6.8.7–8 H. solves the problem by using indirect speech.

[2] The allusion shows that H. knew about the campaigns of
M. on the lower Danube in 236–7 (7.2.9n); although the
expeditio Dacica (*CIL* III. 3336, etc.) is recorded on inscriptions, and the titles *Sarmaticus Maximus* and *Dacicus
Maximus* are included on M.'s titles from 236, the total
absence of reference to the expeditions on M.'s coinage (apart
from his salutations as *imperator*) may indicate that the
battles were only to restore the frontier and had insufficient
importance to warrant special note. As far as H. is concerned, his main object was to show that M. was a good general,
Cassola, *Att. Accad. Pont.* 6 (1956/7) 192.

οἱ πάλαι Μεσοποταμίαν κατατρέχοντες νῦν ἡσυχά-
ζουσιν, ἀγαπητῶς ἔχοντες τὰ ἑαυτῶν, δόξης τε
τῆς ὑμετέρας ἐν τοῖς ὅπλοις ἀρετῆς τε,[1] πείρᾳ
τῶν ἐμῶν πράξεων, ἃς ἔγνωσαν ὅτε τῶν ἐπὶ
ταῖς ὄχθαις στρατοπέδων ἡγούμην, ἀνεχούσης
5 αὐτούς.[2] ἀλλὰ γὰρ (μή τι ἄρα καὶ καταγέλαστον
εἰπεῖν) Καρχηδόνιοι μεμήνασι, καὶ πρεσβύτην
ἄθλιον, ἐν ἐσχάτῳ γήρᾳ παραφρονοῦντα, πείσαντες
ἢ βιασάμενοι ὥσπερ ἐν πομπαῖς παίζουσι βασιλείαν,[3] τίνι θαρροῦντες στρατῷ, παρ᾽ οἷς ἐς τὴν
τοῦ ἡγουμένου ὑπηρεσίαν ἀρκοῦσι ῥαβδοῦχοι;
ποῖα φέροντες ὅπλα, παρ᾽ οἷς οὐδὲν πλὴν [4]
δορατίων οἷς [5] πρὸς θηρία μονομαχοῦσι· τὰ πολεμικὰ αὐτοῖς γυμνάσια χοροὶ καὶ σκώμματα καὶ
6 ῥυθμοί. μηδέ τινα ὑμῶν ἐκπληττέτω τὰ κατὰ
Ῥώμην ἀγγελθέντα. Βιταλιανὸς μὲν ἀνῃρέθη
δόλῳ καὶ ἀπάτῃ ληφθείς, τοῦ δὲ Ῥωμαίων δήμου
τὸ κοῦφον καὶ εὐμετάβολον οὐκ [6] ἀγνοεῖτε καὶ
μέχρι βοῆς θρασύ· εἰ δύο ἢ τρεῖς ὁπλίτας ἴδοιεν

[1] del Bekk
[2] edit. Basil αὐτῆς Oi
[3] βασιλεύειν? Whit
[4] Sylb πλέον Oi
[5] οἱ O
[6] οὐκ εἶναι O

[1] Unless M. is being made deliberately to falsify, H. knows
nothing of a further Persian invasion of Mesopotamia in the
reign of M. (6.6.6n). The absence of coinage from Nisibis and
Carrhae in his reign may be because Alexander never liberated
those cities (6.2.1n).
[2] See 6.8.1n. It is possible H. here refers to the post of
praefectus castrorum—a term applied to legionary com-

sians, after their invasion of Mesopotamia some time ago,[1] are now quiet and content with their own possessions. Keeping them in check is your reputation for bravery in fighting and their knowledge and experience of my activities when I was a commander of legions on the frontier banks of the river.[2] It is not they (and this surely is ludicrous news) but the Carthaginians who have gone mad. They have persuaded or forced a feeble, old man, who has taken leave of his senses in the extremity of old age, to be emperor, as though it were a game in a procession. But what sort of army are they relying on, when lictors are enough for them as attendants on their governor?[3] What sort of weapons will they use, when they have nothing but the lances used by gladiators in single combat against wild animals? Their only combat training is in choruses or witty speeches and rhythmic dances.[4] No one should be disturbed by the news from Rome. Vitalianus was caught and murdered by a deceitful trick, and you know perfectly well about the fickle infidelity of the Roman populace. But their bravery only extends to shouting. They have only to see

manders in Mesopotamia—or even *praefectus Mesopotamiae* (if στρατοπέδων is taken as truly plural), who commanded two legions; cf. Hohl, *RE* (Julius Verus 526) 857, *CAH* XII. 74 (Ensslin). But this may mean that M. held a special post during A.'s Persian Wars—as *dux ripae*, Gilliam, *TAPA* 72 (1941) 122.

[3] Cf. 7.6.2n. M.'s speech would naturally underrate the military support for Gordian.

[4] A reference to the various dramatic, rhetorical and musical contests that went to make up the *iuvenalia* (or *lusus iuvenum*) which constituted one of the activities of the municipal *iuventus*; cf. 7.4.3n.

μόνον, ὑπ' ἀλλήλων ὠθούμενοί τε καὶ πατούμενοι,
φεύγων ἕκαστος τὸν ἴδιον κίνδυνον τοῦ κοινοῦ
7 ἀμελῶς ἔχει. εἰ δὲ καὶ τὰ τῆς συγκλήτου τις
ὑμῖν [1] διήγγειλε, μὴ θαυμάζετε εἰ τὸ μὲν ἡμέτερον
σῶφρον τραχὺ αὐτοῖς δοκεῖ, τὸ δ' ὁμότροπον ἐν
ἀκολάστῳ βίῳ ἐκείνου προτιμᾶται, καὶ τὰ μὲν
ἀνδρεῖα καὶ σεμνὰ τῶν ἔργων φοβερὰ προσαγο-
ρεύουσι, τὰ δ' ἀνειμένα καὶ ἐκβεβακχευμένα ὡς
ἥμερα δι' ἡδονῆς ἔχουσι· διόπερ πρὸς τὴν ἐμὴν
ἀρχὴν οὖσαν ἐπιστρεφῆ καὶ κόσμιον ἀλλοτρίως
διάκεινται, ἥσθησαν δὲ τῷ Γορδιανοῦ ὀνόματι, οὗ
8 τὸν διαβεβλημένον βίον οὐκ ἀγνοεῖτε. πρὸς τούτους καὶ τοιούτους [2] ἡμῖν ὁ πόλεμος, εἴ τις οὕτως
αὐτὸν καλεῖν βούλοιτο. ἐγὼ μὲν γὰρ ἡγοῦμαι ὡς
οἱ πλεῖστοι καὶ σχεδὸν πάντες, εἰ μόνον Ἰταλίας
ἐπιβαίημεν, ἱκετηρίους [3] θαλλοὺς καὶ τέκνα προ-
τείναντες ὑποστρώσουσιν [4] αὐτοὺς τοῖς ἡμετέροις
ποσίν, οἱ δὲ λοιποὶ διὰ δειλίαν καὶ φαυλότητα
φεύξονται, ὡς ὑπάρξαι ἐμοί τε [καὶ] [5] ὑμῖν τὰ
ἐκείνων πάντα δοῦναι, ὑμῖν τε ἀδεῶς λαβοῦσι
καρποῦσθαι."
9 τοιαῦτά τινα εἰπών, βλάσφημά τε πολλὰ ἐς τὴν
Ῥώμην καὶ τὴν σύγκητον δι' ὧν παρεφθέγγετο
ἀπορρίψας, ταῖς τε διὰ χειρὸς ἀπειλαῖς καὶ
τραχέσι προσώπου νεύμασιν ὡς πρὸς παρόντας
ὀργισθείς, ἐπαγγέλλει τὴν ἐπ' Ἰταλίαν ἔξοδον.
διανείμας τε αὐτοῖς πάμπλειστα χρήματα, μιᾶς

two or three armed soldiers to be pushing and
trampling on each other, as each man runs away
from the threat to his own person, without a thought
for the common danger. If some of you have heard 7
about the senate's reactions, you should not be sur-
prised that our disciplined moderation is aggravating
for them, and that they prefer Gordian who shares
their dissolute habits. They say that courageous,
sober deeds are intimidation, whereas they favour
undisciplined incontinence as though it is toleration.
So, they are hostile to my rule because it is strict and
well-regulated, but welcome the sound of Gordian's
name—and you know the scandal of his past life.
These are the kinds of people against whom we 8
are at war, if war is the right name for it. I am
convinced that we only have to set foot in Italy for
almost everyone to hold out olive branches and bring
their children to us, begging for mercy and falling at
our feet. The rest will run away because they are
poor cowards. Then I shall be able to distribute all
their property to you, and you can take it and enjoy
it without restraint."

After this speech Maximinus made some passing 9
remarks, in which he abused Rome and the senate
roundly. Then, moving his hands around in threatening gestures and nodding his head ferociously, as
though he were venting his anger on the people in
front of him, he announced his departure for Italy.
A day later, after he had made an enormous cash

---

¹ ἡμῖν i   ² τοὺς τοιούτους   ³ Sylb ἱκετηρίας Oi
⁴ Sylb προτείναντας ὑποστρώσειν Oi
⁵ del Sylb

ἡμέρας διαλιπών, τῆς ὁδοῦ εἴχετο, πολύ τι πλῆθος
ἐπαγόμενος στρατοῦ, τήν τε ⟨πᾶσαν⟩ [1] ὑπὸ
10 Ῥωμαίοις δύναμιν. εἴπετο δὲ αὐτῷ καὶ Γερμανῶν
οὐκ εὐκαταφρόνητος ἀριθμός, οὓς τοῖς ὅπλοις
κεχείρωτο ἢ πείσας ἐς φιλίαν καὶ συμμαχίαν
ἐπῆκτο, μηχαναί τε καὶ πολεμικὰ ὄργανα, καὶ
ὅσα πρὸς τοὺς βαρβάρους ἰὼν [2] ἐπεφέρετο. αὐτὸς
μὲν σχολαιτέραν τὴν ὁδοιπορίαν ἐποιεῖτο διὰ τὴν
τῶν ὀχημάτων καὶ ἐπιτηδείων πανταχόθεν συγ-
11 κομιδήν· αἰφνιδίου γὰρ γενομένης τῆς ἐπ᾽ Ἰταλίαν
ὁδοῦ, οὐκ ἐκ προνοίας, ὥσπερ εἰώθει, ἀλλ᾽ ἐξ
αὐτοσχεδίου καὶ ἐπειγούσης ὑπηρεσίας τὰ χρειώδη
τῷ στρατῷ ἠθροίζετο. ἔδοξεν οὖν αὐτῷ προ-
πέμψαι τὰς τῶν Παιόνων φάλαγγας· ἐκείνοις γὰρ
μάλιστα ἐπίστευεν, οἵπερ αὐτὸν καὶ πρῶτοι

---

[1] Whit δὴ ⟨πᾶσαν⟩ Lange τε om O *universas . . . copias* P
[2] Steph ὤν l ὦν Oag

---

[1] M. set out from Sirmium, where he was still in winter
quarters; 7.2.9n, SHA, *Max.* 13.3. There is no reason to
believe that Victor, *Caes.* 27.3, is correct in saying M. began
his march from Thrace. The extent to which the northern
frontiers were denuded of troops can be judged from the
serious threat that developed in 238 from the invasions of the
Carpi and Goths in Moesia, and the attack on Istros in the
Dobrudja; SHA, *Max. et Balb.* 16.3, Stein, *Legaten v.
Moesien* 99, *CIL* III. 12455.

[2] That is, that the 300 (approx.) miles from Sirmium to

distribution to his men, he set out on his march at the head of a very large body of troops, the entire Roman force.[1] Quite a considerable number of Germans were under his command as well, people he had defeated in battle or whom he had persuaded to make a friendly treaty of alliance. Also, artillery and mechanical devices of war, all the equipment he was using in his expedition against the barbarians. The march was somewhat slow because of all the baggage carts and supplies choking all the roads.[2] The reason for this was that his expedition into Italy was a sudden decision without the usual advance planning; supplies for the army were being collected *en route* as aid was being rushed to him. So Maximinus decided to send ahead the Pannonian legions, in whom he had special confidence (they were the ones that first recognized him as emperor)[3] and who

Aquileia were completed at a much slower pace than the fast twenty miles per day commonly achieved by the Severan army. Including a difficult crossing of the Alps before the end of the winter snow, the journey cannot have taken less than twenty-five to thirty days. If M. left Sirmium about 24th March (7.8.1n), he would have reached Aquileia towards the end of April.

[3] The erasure of M.'s name from inscriptions in Pannonia and Dacia is stated by Bersanetti, *Massimino* 63 ff., to have occurred after the election of Pupienus and Balbinus; but it seems much more likely that the *abolitio* was a prudent measure after the death of M. later; Barbieri, *Epig.* 4 (1942) 91. The Pannonian troops supported M. to the end (8.6.1). The conclusion of Townsend, *YCS* 14 (1955) 72–4, that Dacia, Thrace and Moesia went over to the senate almost immediately, though not without resistance from the soldiers, goes much further than the evidence permits, but is at least possible if the main forces had been withdrawn for the march to Italy.

ἀνεῖπον βασιλέα ἐθελονταί τε ὑπὲρ αὐτοῦ κινδυνεύειν [1] ὑπισχνοῦντο. ἐκέλευσεν οὖν [2] αὐτοῖς
φθάσαι τὴν λοιπὴν δύναμιν καὶ τὰ ἐν Ἰταλίᾳ
χωρία προκαταλαβεῖν.

9. καὶ οἱ μὲν περὶ τὸν Μαξιμῖνον ὡδοιπόρουν,
ἐν δὲ τῇ Καρχηδόνι οὐχ ὡς ἠλπίκεσαν τὰ πράγματα
προυχώρει. Καπελιανὸς [3] γὰρ ἦν τις ὄνομα, τῶν
ἀπὸ συγκλήτου, ἡγεῖτο δὲ Μαυρουσίων τῶν ὑπὸ
Ῥωμαίοις, Νομάδων δὲ καλουμένων. τὸ δὲ ἔθνος
στρατοπέδοις πέφρακτο διὰ τὸ περικείμενον πλῆθος
Μαυρουσίων τῶν βαρβάρων, ὡς ἂν ἐπέχοι αὐτῶν
2 τὰς ἐξ ἐπιδρομῆς ἁρπαγάς. εἶχεν οὖν ὑφ᾽ ἑαυτῷ [4]
δύναμιν οὐκ εὐκαταφρόνητον στρατιωτικήν. πρὸς
δὴ τὸν Καπελιανὸν τοῦτον ὁ [5] Γορδιανὸς ἀπεχθῶς
διέκειτο [6] ἄνωθεν ἔκ τινος ἀγοραίου διαφορᾶς.
τότε τοίνυν ἐν τῷ τῆς βασιλείας γενόμενος ὀνόματι

---

[1] -ευσειν Mendelss   [2] om φ τε A
[3] OJo καπελλιανὸς ag καπετολινὸς lg[1] in mg (throughout)
[4] -τοῦ V -ὸν A (ὦ over ὸν A[1])   [5] καὶ ὁ i
[6] Sylb προσέκειτο Oi

---

[1] Apart from his association with this incident in H. and
the SHA, only *ILS* 8499 (see 7.9.11n) makes any reference to
Capellianus. He may be connected with the senator in the
age of Antoninus Pius, C. Iulius Gemin(i?)us Capellianus
(*PIR*[2] J 339), who in turn may be connected with the African
senatorial family of Geminius from Cirta, but both are dubious.

[2] Both SHA, *Max.* 19.1 and *Gord.* 15.1, make the error of
supposing Capellianus was governor of one of the provinces of
Mauretania (probably misled by what H. says here); only H.
gives the information that Capellianus was a senator and
legatus of Numidia. The organization of Numidia as a separate province by Septimius Severus, *c.* 198/9 is noted in
3.10.2n.

[3] The main legionary force was stationed at Lambaesis, but

had volunteered to take on a dangerous mission for him. They were instructed to proceed in advance of the main force and to be the first to occupy positions in Italy.

9. As Maximinus and his army made their march, events in Carthage had not gone as had been expected. A senator called Capellianus[1] was the commander of the part of Mauretania under Roman jurisdiction called Numidia.[2] The province was protected by military garrisons because of the numerous barbarian Mauretanians who lived all round the borders, the intention being to prevent them making marauding raids.[3] Thus Capellianus had 2 at his disposal a considerable army. Gordian was an old enemy of Capellianus over some legal dispute,[4] and, when he assumed the title of emperor, he

detachments of legionaries and *auxilia* were stationed in the various fortified outposts along the frontier, which had been extensively strengthened by Severus and Alexander. In one such fort on the southern Numidian frontier evidence shows that under A. it had been mainly garrisoned by oriental auxiliaries, who under M. had been replaced by detachments of legio III Augusta; Picard, *Castellum Dimmidi* 83, 115 ff. From this it is argued that one reason for the legion's hostility to Gordian was the fear that he would revert to A.'s policy of giving pride of place to *auxilia*. But the *auxila* had been withdrawn already, probably by A. in order to fight his wars; if the Severan system of defence in depth was gradually being replaced by fortified farms and auxiliary units it was *faute de mieux* through financial stringency rather than preference.

[4] All the sources state that the antagonism was personal and long-standing. The legionaries in Numidia apparently began by recognizing G., and only subsequently restored the inscriptions of Maximinus that had been first erased; Romanelli, *Province rom. Africa* 454 f., Picard, *Castellum Dimmidi* 115 ff.

HERODIAN

διάδοχόν τε [1] αὐτῷ ἔπεμψε καὶ τοῦ ἔθνους ἐξελθεῖν
3 ἐκέλευσεν. ὁ δὲ πρός τε ταῦτα ἀγανακτήσας, τῷ
τε Μαξιμίνῳ καθωσιωμένος,[2] ὑφ᾽ οὗ καὶ τὴν
ἡγεμονίαν πεπίστευτο, πάντα τὸν στρατὸν ἀθροίσας [3] ἀναπείσας τε Μαξιμίνῳ [4] τηρεῖν τὴν πίστιν
καὶ τὸν ὅρκον, κατῆλθεν ἐπὶ τὴν Καρχηδόνα
δύναμιν ἄγων μεγίστην τε καὶ γενναίων [5] ἀνδρῶν
ἡλικίαις ἀκμάζουσαν, καὶ παντοδαπῇ ὅπλων
παρασκευῇ ἐξηρτυμένην, ἐμπειρίᾳ τε πολεμικῇ καὶ
τῆς [6] πρὸς τοὺς βαρβάρους μάχης συνηθείᾳ
ἑτοίμην [7] πρὸς μάχας.

4 ὡς δὲ ἀπηγγέλη τῷ Γορδιανῷ ὁ στρατὸς προσιὼν
τῇ πόλει, αὐτός τε ἐν ἐσχάτῳ δέει ἦν, οἵ τε
Καρχηδόνιοι ταραχθέντες, οἰόμενοι [8] ἐν πλήθει
ὄχλου, οὐκ ἐν εὐταξίᾳ στρατοῦ τὸ εὔελπι τῆς
νίκης εἶναι, πανδημεὶ πάντες ἐξίασιν ὡς δὴ τῷ
Καπελιανῷ ἀντιταξόμενοι. Γορδιανὸς μὲν οὖν ὁ
πρεσβύτης, ὥς τινές φασιν, ἅμα τῷ [9] τῆς Καρχηδό-
νος ἐπιβῆναι ἐν ἀπογνώσει γενόμενος, ἐννοῶν τὴν
δύναμιν Μαξιμίνου, οὐδὲν δὲ ὁρῶν ἐν Λιβύῃ
ἀξιόμαχον ἰσόρροπον, ἀνήρτησεν ἑαυτὸν βρόχῳ·
5 κρυπτομένης δὲ αὐτοῦ τῆς τελευτῆς τὸν υἱὸν

---

[1] om O   [2] Steph καθοσιούμενος Oi *Suda*
[3] συναθ. O   [4] μαξίμω A
[5] -αν Ogl   [6] τῇ Bi om A
[7] corr in old edition Mendelss ἑτοίμη Oi
[8] οἰόμενοί τε Jo   [9] ⟨τὸν Καπελιανὸν⟩ τῷ Mendelss

---

[1] On the troops of Capellianus, see 7.9.6n.
[2] That is, the *plebs urbana* of Carthage, which had joined

216

sent a replacement for the commander, order-
ing him out of the province. The Numidian gover- 3
nor, a devoted servant of Maximinus, by whom he
had been entrusted with his command, was angry at
this treatment and concentrated all his troops together,[1] urging them to maintain their oath of
loyalty to Maximinus. Then he marched against
Carthage with a large force made up of excellent,
tough young men, all in the prime of life. They
were also fitted out with a full range of equipment and
ready for battle because of their war experiences in
regular fighting against the barbarians.

The news of the army's advance on the city reduced 4
Gordian to a complete panic and the Carthaginians to
a state of indiscipline. Imagining that their best
hope of victory lay in the size of their rabble [2] and not
in an army's discipline,[3] there was a mass exodus to
oppose Capellianus, as they imagined. Some sources
say that the moment the attack on Carthage took
place, Gordian grew desperate, because he knew the
power of Maximinus and the lack of any obviously
equal force capable of fighting against him in Libya,
and hanged himself.[4] His death was concealed, 5

Gordian; cf. SHA, *Gord.* 15.1, *omnis Carthaginiensium populus.*

[3] The extent of military support for Gordian was small (see
7.6.2n). The para-military organizations of the *iuventutes*
(7.4.3n) was probably the only sizeable disciplined force he
possessed.

[4] This version does not appear in any of the other sources;
it proves that H. had access to anti-Gordian sources; and by
repeating the story H. shows he is far from being a committed
supporter of G. himself, as is assumed by Townsend, *YCS* 14
(1955) 51 ff. Zos. 16.1, Zon. 12. 17D have other improbable
tales of G.'s death by shipwreck or after arrival in Rome.

αὐτοῦ στρατηγήσοντα δὴ τοῦ πλήθους εἵλοντο. γενομένης δὲ συμβολῆς οἱ μὲν Καρχηδόνιοι ὄχλῳ πλείους ἦσαν, ἄτακτοι δὲ καὶ πολεμικῶν ἔργων ἀπαίδευτοι ἅτε ἐν εἰρήνῃ βαθείᾳ τεθραμμένοι ἑορταῖς τε καὶ τρυφαῖς σχολάζοντες ἀεί, γυμνοί 6 τε ὅπλων καὶ ὀργάνων πολεμικῶν. ἕκαστος δὲ [1] ἐπεφέρετο οἴκοθεν ἢ ξιφίδιον ἢ πέλεκυν δοράτιά τε ἐκ κυνηγεσίων· βύρσας [2] τε τὰς ἐμπεσούσας περιτεμόντες καὶ ξύλα καταπρίσαντες ἐς τὰ παρατυχόντα σχήματα, ὡς ἕκαστος ἐδύνατο, πρόβλημα τοῦ σώματος ἐποιεῖτο. οἱ δὲ Νομάδες ἀκοντισταί τε εὔστοχοι καὶ ἱππεῖς ἄριστοι, ὡς καὶ χαλινῶν ἄνευ ῥάβδῳ μόνῃ τὸν δρόμον τῶν ἵππων 7 κυβερνᾶν. ῥᾷστα οὖν ἐτρέψαντο τῶν Καρχηδονίων τὸ πλῆθος, οἵπερ οὐχ ὑπομείναντες αὐτῶν τὴν

---

[1] γὰρ conj Mendelss from nam P
[2] Wolf χάρακας Irmisch βαρέας Oi

---

[1] The MSS reading is unintelligible, since it means either "flat-bottomed boats" or "towers." Politian uses the word sudes (stakes), which makes good sense, but he compresses the passage and may be translating the next words only. Irmisch, following Politian, suggests χάρακας, meaning "vineprops."

[2] A vexillatio Maurorum Caesariensium was stationed at Lambaesis; Cagnat, L'Armée rom. d'Afrique 206–7, CIL VIII. 2716; but Capellianus may have recruited the local coloni of the imperial estates in Numidia; cf. ILS 1400 (from Mauretania), ala I Aug(usta) Gem(ina) colonorum and ILS 9177 for

and his son chosen to lead the people. In the engagement that took place the Carthaginians had the advantage of numbers but were in disorder and untrained for war. They had been brought up in absolutely peaceful conditions, forever whiling away their time in festivals and easy living, completely divorced from weapons and instruments of war. Every man brought from home 6 a small sword, an axe and hunting spears. They cut up available skins,[1] and sawed up wood into any old shape, as best they could, to make shields for themselves. The Numidians were crack spearmen and expert riders, able to control their horses at the gallop without reins and using only a riding crop.[2] They had no difficulty at all in 7 routing the Carthaginian mob, who threw away all

a man who served in the reign of the Severi as *praepositus coh(ortis) II Fl(avia) Afr(orum) et n(umeri) col(onorum)*. The accomplishment of riding without reins is mentioned by a number of authors in connection with Numidian horsemen; e.g. Caes. *Bell. Afr.* 19.4. Moroccan horsemen are represented on Trajan's column with a spear, a small round buckler and riding their horses without saddles or bridles, though there is a halter round the neck of the horses; Cheesman, *Auxilia of the Rom. Imp. Army* 128-9. The emphasis that H. gives to the Numidian auxiliaries, rather than the legionaries (though they are mentioned below) gives colour to the theory that the legion was not wholly in support of Capellianus. But SHA, *Gord.* 15.1, which talks of a *tumultuaria manus*, is based on the assumption that Capellianus was governor of the *provincia inermis* of Mauretania; there is no evidence here to suggest a conflict between legion and *auxilia*, as suggested by Pflaum, *Jour. Sav.* (1949) 55-62. The disbanding of legio III Augusta by Gordian III and its title of *pia vindex Maximiniana* show the dominant part played by the legion in suppressing Gordian I; cf. *ILS* 4194.

ἐμβολήν, πάντα ῥίψαντες, ἔφυγον· [1] ὠθούμενοι δὲ
ὑπ' ἀλλήλων καὶ πατούμενοι, πλείους ὑπὸ τοῦ
οἰκείου πλήθους [2] ἐφθάρησαν ἢ πρὸς τῶν πολεμίων. ἔνθα καὶ ὁ τοῦ Γορδιανοῦ υἱὸς ἀπώλετο
οἵ τε περὶ αὐτὸν πάντες, ὡς διὰ πλῆθος πτωμάτων
μήτε νεκρῶν ἀναίρεσιν πρὸς ταφὴν γενέσθαι
δυνηθῆναι μήτε τὸ τοῦ νέου Γορδιανοῦ σῶμα
8 εὑρεθῆναι. οἱ μὲν γὰρ φεύγοντες, ὅσοι τε ἦσαν
εἰσρυέντες ἐς τὴν Καρχηδόνα ὅσοι τε λαθεῖν
ἠδυνήθησαν, σκεδασθέντες ἐς πᾶσαν τὴν πόλιν,
οὖσαν μεγίστην τε καὶ πολυάνθρωπον,[3] ὀλίγοι ἐκ
πολλῶν ἐσώθησαν· τὸ δὲ λοιπὸν πλῆθος περὶ ταῖς
πύλαις στενοχωρούμενον, παρεισδῦναι σπουδάζον-
τος ἑκάστου. βαλλόμενον τε ὑπὸ τῶν ἀκοντιστῶν
καὶ τιτρωσκόμενον ὑπὸ τῶν ὁπλιτῶν [4] διεφθείρετο.
9 πολλὴ δὲ οἰμωγὴ κατὰ τὴν πόλιν γυναικῶν τε καὶ
παιδίων,[5] ὧν ἐν ὄψει οἱ φίλτατοι ἀπώλοντο.
ἕτεροι δέ φασιν, ὡς δὴ ταῦτα οἴκοι μεμενηκότι
διὰ γῆρας τῷ πρεσβύτῃ Γορδιανῷ ἀπηγγέλη ὅ τε
Καπελιανὸς εἰσελαύνων ἐς τὴν Καρχηδόνα ἐδηλώθη,
ἐν ἀπογνώσει δὴ [6] πάντων γενόμενος, εἰσελθὼν
μόνος ἐς τὸν οἰκίσκον ὡς δὴ καθευδήσων, ἐξαρτήσας
ἧς ἐπεφέρετο ζώνης τὸν τράχηλον ἐν βρόχῳ, τοῦ
βίου ἀνεπαύσατο.
10 τοιούτῳ μὲν δὴ τέλει Γορδιανὸς ἐχρήσατο,
βιώσας τὰ πρῶτα εὐδαιμόνως, ἐν εἰκόνι τε
βασιλείας τελευτήσας· ὁ δὲ Καπελιανὸς ἐς

[1] ἔφευγον AJo
[2] πάθους A
[3] Mendelss πολλὴν Oi
[4] πολιτῶν φ πελταστῶν A
[5] παίδων ἐγίνετο Jo
[6] δε φ i

their equipment and ran without waiting for the charge. Pushing and trampling on each other, more were killed by their own side than by the enemy. In the battle Gordian's son and his entourage fell, but, because of the many dead, their bodies could not be brought back for burial, and the son's body was never found. A few of the many fugitives who were able 8 to dash back to Carthage and hide themselves by scattering throughout the large, populous city were saved. The remaining mass were picked off by the spearmen and butchered by the infantry as they crowded round the gates, each desperately trying to get inside. The whole city, women and children, mourned 9 their loved ones, cut down before their eyes. Different sources say that the news of these events and of Capellianus' entry into Carthage reached the elder Gordian at his house, where he had stayed behind because of his old age. In total despair he retired privately to his room, pretending that he was going to rest, and there he committed suicide by strangling himself in a noose made out of the girdle he was wearing.

So Gordian, to whom life had been fortunate in its 10 early stages, met his end masquerading as an emperor.[1] On his entry into Carthage, Capellianus

---

[1] The length of G.'s reign was twenty days according to the *Chronog. of 354* (Mommsen, *Chron. Min.* 1.147) and twenty-two days according to Zon. 12.17; assuming his accession was 1st March, he died about 22nd March (see 7.5.7n). The victory of Capellianus was probably the occasion for the *imp.* VII salutations of M., all of which are recorded in the year 238; Bersanetti, *Epig.* 3 (1941) 12. But the coins of 238 which record victories must relate to M.'s *imp.* VI salutation (which had been won in late 237 and is commemorated on

Καρχηδόνα εἰσελθὼν πάντας τε τοὺς πρωτεύοντας
ἀπέκτεινεν, εἴ τινες καὶ ἐσώθησαν ἐκ τῆς μάχης,
ἐφείδετό τε οὔτε ἱερῶν συλήσεως οὔτε χρημάτων
11 ἰδιωτικῶν τε καὶ δημοσίων ἁρπαγῆς. ἐπιών τε
τὰς λοιπὰς πόλεις ὅσαι τὰς Μαξιμίνου τιμὰς
καθῃρήκεσαν, τοὺς μὲν ἐξέχοντας ἐφόνευε, τοὺς
δὲ δημότας ἐφυγάδευεν, ἀγροὺς τε καὶ κώμας
ἐμπιπράναι λεηλατεῖν τε τοῖς στρατιώταις ἐπ-
έτρεπε, προσποιούμενος μὲν τιμωρίαν εἰσπράττειν
ἐφ' οἷς ἐς Μαξιμῖνον ἡμαρτήκεσαν, λανθανόντως
δὲ εὔνοιαν ἑαυτῷ παρὰ τῶν στρατιωτῶν μνώμενος,
ἵν' εἴ τι πταίσειεν τὰ Μαξιμίνου πράγματα, αὐτὸς
ἔχων δύναμιν εὐνοοῦσαν τῆς ἀρχῆς ἀντιποιήσαιτο.
τὰ μὲν δὴ κατὰ τὴν Λιβύην ἐν τούτοις ἦν.

10. ὡς δὲ ἐς τὴν Ῥώμην ἐδηλώθη ἡ τοῦ
πρεσβύτου [1] τελευτή, ἐν πολλῇ ταραχῇ καὶ ἀφασίᾳ
ὅ τε δῆμος ἦν ἥ τε σύγκλητος μάλιστα, Γορδιανοῦ [2]
τετελευτηκότος ἐς ὃν ἠλπίκεσαν· ᾔδεσαν γὰρ [3]

[1] γορδιανοῦ τοῦ πρεσβ. AP
[2] om P Wolf
[3] lacuna after γὰρ supplied by A τὸν Μαξιμῖνον ἐχθρὸν
αὐτοῖς ἄσπονδον οὔτέ τινος (sic) φεισόμενον

---

inscriptions of both 237 and 238) since M. would not have had
access to the Roman mint after the revolt.
   [1] One such person is recorded from near Theveste, *ILS* 8499,
*L. Aemilius Severinus qui et Phillyrio v(ixit) a(nnis) LXVI
p(lus) m(inus) et pro amore Romano quievit ab hoc Capeliano
captus.* Once again the propaganda emphasized that the
cause of Gordian was the true Roman cause against the
barbarian; cf. 7.5.8n, Kotula, *Eos* 50 (1959/60) 214. The

massacred any prominent person who had escaped
the battle, and had no compunction about robbing
temples or confiscating private and public funds.
He also attacked other cities that had destroyed dedi- 11
cations to Maximinus, killing the leading citizens[1] and
driving the lower class out of the territory. Fields
and villages[2] were turned over to his soldiers for
burning and plunder, on the grounds that this was
punishment for their offences against Maximinus,
though in fact Capellianus was quietly canvassing the
loyalty of the troops for himself. If anything were
to take a wrong turn in Maximinus' fortunes, he
intended to make a bid for the empire himself with
the aid of a loyal force of soldiers.[3]

After the events in Libya (10.) the news of the old
emperor's death reached Rome. The fact that
Gordian, on whom they had relied, was dead caused
stunned consternation among the people and
especially among the senate. For they knew

principes civitatum executed by Capellianus (SHA, *Max.* 19.4)
were the decurion class who had started the revolt (7.5.3n).

[2] Kotula (*op. cit.*) wrongly supposes this mention of villages
indicates extensive peasant support for Gordian; *vici*
commonly existed on private estates, inhabited by tenants
and clients of the owner; Rostovtzeff, *SEHRE* 685. SHA,
Gord. 7.5, in describing one of the leaders, says he canvassed
support *in agro suo.* Whether the farmer was a *colonus* or
not, the power of the patronage of rich landowners was bound
to be effective. There is a danger in trying to make Gordian's
revolt into an African nationalist movement; but the lists of
the legio III Augusta in 236/7 show that many recruits were
from local African cities, particularly from newly enfranchised
citizens; Picard, *Castellum Dimmidi* 116.

[3] The fate of Capellianus is unknown, but the legion was
disbanded.

HERODIAN

. . . αὐτὸν οὔτε φεισόμενον τινός· ὃς [1] γὰρ καὶ
φύσει ἀλλοτρίως καὶ ἀπεχθῶς πρὸς αὐτοὺς διέκειτο, τότε [2] καὶ ἐπ' εὐλόγοις αἰτίαις ὡς ὁμολογου-
2 μένοις ἐχθροῖς εἰκότως ὠργίζετο. ἔδοξεν οὖν
συνελθεῖν καὶ περὶ τῶν πρακτέων σκέψασθαι,
ἅπαξ τε ἀναρρίψαντας κίνδυνον πόλεμον ἄρασθαι,
προστησαμένους ἑαυτῶν χειροτονηθέντας βασιλέας,
οὓς [3] ἠθέλησαν μερίσαι τὴν ἀρχήν, ὡς μὴ παρ'
ἑνὶ οὖσα ἡ ἐξουσία ἐς τυραννίδα πάλιν [4] ἐξοκείλῃ.[5]
συνῆλθον οὖν οὐκ ἐς τὸ σύνηθες συνέδριον ἀλλ' ἐς
τὸν τοῦ Διὸς νεὼν ⟨τοῦ⟩ [6] Καπετωλίου, ὃν
3 σέβουσι Ῥωμαῖοι ἐν ἀκροπόλει. συγκλείσαντες
οὖν αὑτοὺς ἐν τῷ σηκῷ μόνους, ὥσπερ ὑπὸ
μάρτυρι τῷ Διὶ καὶ συνέδρῳ ἐπισκόπῳ τε τῶν

---

[1] Schott ὡς Oi
[2] τότε δὲ A διέκειτό τε καὶ ag διέκει τό τε καὶ φ
[3] εἰς οὓς A
[4] Stroth and Bekk μὴ πάλιν (πολλὴν A) ἰοῦσαν ἐξουσίαν Oi
[5] ἐξωκείλῃ O   [6] Bekk[2]

---

[1] A lacuna in the text (see *app. critic.* p. 222); MS Monacensis
(A) interpolates the words " they knew that Maximinus was an
implacable enemy of theirs and . . ."
[2] The *cella* of the Temple of Jupiter on the Capitol, where
the ancient *curia calabra* was held to announce the calendar and
induct new magistrates each year, though it was frequently
used on other occasions. The senate met here after the
murder of Gaius (Suet. *Cal.* 60), the occasion when there was
discussion about the restoration of a republic; which suggests
that the meeting-place had a special significance on this
occasion too; doubted by Mommsen, *StR* (3) 3.2.928. SHA,

that he (Maximinus) . . . and would spare no
one.[1] Not only was he naturally antagonistic
and hostile to them but he now had good
reason to be angry with them, since they were
openly declared enemies. They were resolved to hold 2
a meeting to discuss practical measures, for, now they
had staked their bid, they must fight a war. First,
they must choose and elect for themselves emperors, whom they proposed should share the rule,
to prevent the power reverting to a tyranny in the
hands of one man. The meeting therefore took
place, not in their normal chamber, but in the temple
of Jupiter Capitolinus,[2] the god whom the Romans
worship on their citadel. They held a closed session 3
in the inner sanctuary,[3] witnessed as it were by
Jupiter as their fellow councillor and guardian of

Max. et Balb. 1.1, says that this meeting took place in the
temple of Concordia on 9th July (238), but is certainly incorrect about the date and possibly about the place (next note).
[3] Private sessions behind closed doors were not unknown
under the republic, for which the *cella* of a temple proved
particularly convenient; cf. Cic. *Phil.* 2.44.112, 5.7.18 (in the
temple of Concordia, thus no doubt giving rise to the error of
SHA, *Max. et Balb.* 1.1; the SHA are particularly susceptible
to Ciceronian influence, 7.7.5n). On such occasions the clerical
staff probably left the meeting (Mommsen wrongly quotes
Cic. *Att.* 15.3.1). This is the basis of the description in SHA,
Gord. 12.1 ff., of an otherwise unknown *s.c. tacitum* (7.7.2n),
but H. says nothing about the passing of a resolution; cf.
Mommsen, *StR* (3) 3.2.931n, 1016n, 1017. It is important to
note that the *vita Gord.* places the *s.c. tacitum* after the news
of G.'s accession, whereas H. is quite clear about the date here.
It is ludicrous to argue, as Volckmann (see Introduction, pp.
xix–xx) that knowledge of this meeting proves H. was a
senator; information was bound to leak out, but this sooner
than most, as H. himself tells us in 7.10.5.

πραττομένων, ἐπιλεξάμενοι τῶν ἐν ἡλικίᾳ καὶ
ἀξιώματι προυχόντων οὓς ἐδοκίμαζον κατὰ ψηφο-
φορίαν, ἐχόντων καὶ ἄλλων [1] ψήφους, διακριθεισῶν
τε καὶ τοῦ πλείστου τῆς γνώμης Μάξιμόν τε καὶ
Βαλβῖνον [2] ἀνειπόντος [3] αὐτοκράτορας ἐποίησαν.
4 τούτων δ' ἦν ὁ μὲν Μάξιμος ἔν τε πολλαῖς στρατοπέδων ἀρχαῖς γενόμενος, τῆς τε Ῥωμαίων πόλεως
ἔπαρχος καταστὰς ἀνεπιστρόφως τε ἄρξας, καὶ
ἐν ὑπολήψει παρὰ τοῖς ὄχλοις φρενῶν τε καὶ
ἀγχινοίας καὶ βίου σώφρονος, ὁ δὲ Βαλβῖνος
γενόμενος μὲν εὐπατρίδης, ἐς δευτέραν τε ὑπατείαν
ἐληλακὼς ἐθνῶν τε ἡγησάμενος ἀμέμπτως, τὸ δ'
5 ἦθος ἁπλούστερος.[4] τῆς οὖν χειροτονίας ἐκεί-

---

[1] ἄλλους O
[2] ἀλβῖνον O almost throughout
[3] Schott -όντες Oi
[4] ἁπαλώτερος Peter cf. SHA, Max. 20.1 (moribus deli-
catiorem)

---

[1] Almost certainly a reference to the vigintiviri, a committee
of twenty consulars, chosen by the senate; although they are
explicitly mentioned in two inscriptions and in later authors,
it is usually assumed H. has omitted them; ILS 1186—L.
Caseonius Lucillus Macer Rufinianus, XXvir ex senatus consulto
r(ei) p(ublicae) curandae; ILS 8979—[V]alerius (or Galerius)
Claud[ius] (or -ianus) Acilius Priscilianus, inter XX cos.;
SHA, Max. 32.3, Gord. 10.1–2, Victor, Caes. 26.7, Zos. 1.14.2
(also SHA, Gord. 14.3, 22.1, which simply repeat the earlier
reference, once in a spurious speech). Of these references
only the vita Gord. (supposedly relying on Dexippus) says
unambiguously that the XXviri were appointed when news
of Gordian's revolt reached Rome; but the vita Max. ex-

their acts. After a preliminary selection of candidates from the men of seniority and distinction,[1] a vote was taken on them. Though many received votes, they were eliminated, and the majority of opinions came down in favour of Maximus and Balbinus, who were then appointed emperors. Maximus [2] had held many military commands and the prefecture of the city, an office he had exercised without bias; public opinion considered him an intelligent and shrewd man of sober habits. Balbinus [5] came from a patrician family, had held two consulships and had been a provincial governor, without giving cause for complaint; he was rather simpler in character than Maximus. After the vote 5

plicitly quotes Dexippus to agree with H.'s date, and SHA, *Gord.* 10.3–4, shows the confused chronology of the passage by stating that M.'s ambassadors were in Rome at the same time as the choice of the *XXviri*—which must mean about twenty days after news of G.'s revolt (ten days each way to Sirmium), just when news of G.'s death arrived. There is a danger of overestimating the significance of the committee, which H. may have considered like that of Alexander, elected by the senate (6.1.2n, 7.1.3n), but with added importance due to the emergency. Few names of *XXviri* are known for certain; a possible list is in Barbieri, *Albo* p. 791. Townsend, *YCS* 14 (1955) 98–105, and Theodorides, *Lat.* 6 (1947) 31–43, discuss the evidence, but Townsend goes too far in accepting the *vita Gord.* and the names in the SHA; also he assumes that the partisans of Gordian must have been the same as those of Pupienus and Balbinus, which is contradicted by H. (7.10.5).

[2] The careers of Pupienus (Maximus) and Balbinus are discussed below. The choice of the senate seems to have been determined by the need for representatives of both the military and civil divisions of the senate; divisions that were becoming increasingly clear cut. Cf. G. Alföldi, *Legionslegaten d. röm. Rheinarmeen* 114.

νους [1] ἀνειπούσης Σεβαστοί τε ἀνηγορεύθησαν,
καὶ πάσαις ταῖς βασιλικαῖς τιμαῖς ἡ σύγκλητος
διὰ δόγματος αὐτοὺς ἐκόσμησεν.

ὁ δὲ δῆμος τούτων ἐν τῷ Καπετωλίῳ πραττομένων, εἴτε ὑποβαλόντων τινῶν Γορδιανοῦ φίλων
καὶ οἰκείων εἴτε γνόντες ὑπὸ φήμης, παρειστήκεσαν
ταῖς πύλαις, φράξαντες πᾶσαν τὴν ἐς τὸ Καπετώλιον ἄνοδον τῷ πλήθει τῶν ὄχλων, λίθους τε
καὶ ξύλα ἐπεφέροντο, ἀντιπράττοντες τοῖς ὑπὸ
τῆς συγκλήτου ἐψηφισμένοις, καὶ μάλιστα τὸν
6 Μάξιμον παραιτούμενοι· στερρότερον ⟨γὰρ ἦρξε⟩ [2]
τῆς πόλεως, πολύ τε τὸ ἐπιστρεφὲς ἔσχε πρὸς
τοὺς φαύλους καὶ κούφους τῶν ὄχλων. ὅθεν δεδιότες ἀπηρέσκοντο αὐτῷ ἐβόων τε καὶ ἠπείλουν
ἀποκτενεῖν αὐτούς· ἠξίουν γὰρ τοῦ Γορδιανοῦ

---

[1] A Schott ἐκείνης φι
[2] Reisk following ⟨ἦρξέ τε γὰρ⟩ στερρότερον Wolf

---

[1] A clear indication of the internal intrigues and lack of
homogeneity among the opponents of M. The supporters of
Gordian I (and Gordian III) were not the same as the partisans
of Pupienus and Balbinus and the senatorial committee (see
7.10.3n). The faction of Gordian I was extensive says H.
(7.6.3), but only the connection with the descendants of Ti.
Claudius Atticus Herodes is certain (7.5.2n); G.'s wife is said
by SHA, *Gord.* 6.4, 17.4, to have been Fabia Orestilla, daughter
of Annius (Se)verus, great-granddaughter of Antoninus
(Pius?), but is untrustworthy—possibly she was related to the
family of Ti. Claudius Celsus Orestianus (whose wife was
Flavia Lycia); cf. *PIR*² II, p. 230 stemma, *Albo* 521. The
faction seems to have had strong control of the *plebs urbana*
(cf. Gallicanus and Maecenas, 7.11.3n). H., who approved
of the rule of Pupienus and Balbinus does not particularly
favour Gordian I (7.9.4n) and distinctly disapproves of the
manner of accession of Gordian III (8.8.7).

had selected these two, they were proclaimed as
Augustus and by decree the senate invested them
with full imperial honours.

During these transactions in the Capitol the
people began to gather at the gates of the temple,
possibly at the private prompting of some of Gordian's friends and relatives,[1] or because they had
got wind of the rumour. The mob filled the
entire approach road to the Capitol with their
numbers, all carrying stones and sticks and showing their antagonism to the men selected by the
senate's vote. They particularly disapproved of 6
Maximus,[2] who had been somewhat severe during
his urban prefectship and very strict with the un-
stable rabble of the lower class. Because they were
frightened of him, they did not like him, and began
to shout and make threats to kill the emperors. They
demanded that an emperor from Gordian's family

[2] The two emperors were M. Clodius Pupienus Maximus
(*PIR*[2] C 1179, *Albo* 1006) and D. Caelius Calvinus Balbinus
(*PIR*[2] C 126, *Albo* 99); both are stated by H. to be patricians,
though Pupienus probably within his own lifetime and
Balbinus for several generations (see 8.8.1n); remarkably
few details of their careers, as related in the *vita Max. et
Balb.*, can be substantiated, and some are improbable; the
following are the least disputed. Pupienus was *legatus* of one
of the Germanies (SHA, *Max. et Balb.* 5.9, says a special
command) under Caracalla (8.6.6, 8.7.8); he became proconsul of Asia, probably under Alexander, *c.* 222/234 (*AE*
(1902) 254 = *ILS* 8839); in 234 he became *cos.* II and
probably *praefectus urbi* at the same time. Balbinus cannot
be definitely assigned any provincial commands, not even
that of Asia (*AE* (1909) 175 is now discredited by Calder,
CR 27 (1913) 11), but he probably served in non-military
commands under Severus and reached *cos.* II in 213; cf.
SHA, *Max. et Balb.* 5.5.-9, 7.1-2.

γένους βασιλέα αἱρεθῆναι, τό τε τῆς αὐτοκρατο-
ρικῆς ὄνομα ἀρχῆς ἐκείνῳ τῷ οἴκῳ καὶ ὀνόματι [1]
7 μεῖναι. ὁ δὲ Βαλβῖνος καὶ Μάξιμος ἐκ τοῦ
ἱππικοῦ τάγματος νεανίας [2] τούς τε πάλαι στρατιώτας [2] οἳ ἐν Ῥώμῃ διέτριβον, περιστήσαντες
ἑαυτοῖς [3] ξιφηφόρους προελθεῖν τοῦ Καπετωλίου
ἐβιάζοντο, ὑπὸ δὲ πλήθους λίθων καὶ ξύλων
ἐκωλύθησαν, ἔστε δὴ ὑποβαλόντος [4] τινὸς
αὐτοὶ τὸν δῆμον ἐσοφίσαντο. ἦν τι παιδίον
νήπιον, τῆς Γορδιανοῦ θυγατρὸς τέκνον, τῷ
8 πάππῳ ὁμώνυμον. πέμψαντες τοίνυν τῶν σὺν
αὐτοῖς τινὰς κελεύουσι τὸ παιδίον κομισθῆναι. οἱ
δὲ εὑρόντες αὐτὸ ἄθυρον [5] οἴκοι, ἀράμενοι ἐπὶ τῶν
ὤμων, διὰ μέσου τοῦ πλήθους, δεικνύντες τοῖς
ὄχλοις Γορδιανοῦ τε ἔγγονον [6] λέγοντες καὶ τῇ
αὐτοῦ [7] προσηγορίᾳ ἀποκαλοῦντες, ἀνάγουσιν ἐς
τὸ Καπετώλιον εὐφημούμενον ὑπὸ τοῦ δήμου καὶ
9 φυλλοβολούμενον. τῆς τε συγκλήτου Καίσαρα
αὐτὸ ἀποδειξάσης, ἐπειδὴ διὰ τὴν ἡλικίαν οὐχ

---

[1] μόνῳ A   [2] Sylb τοὺς νεανίας πάλαι στρατιώτας τε Oi
[3] αὐτοῖς i   [4] Bekk ὑποβάλλοντος Oi lex Vindob
[5] Steph ἄθυρον Oi   [6] Bekk² ἔκγονον Oi
[7] αὐτῇ φgl

---

[1] Similar to the action of another senatorial emperor,
Galba, who enrolled a special bodyguard of equestrian
youths, and enrolled the provincial *iuventutes*; Suet. *Galba*
10.3, discussed by Rostovtzeff, *Klio* Beiheft 3 (1905) 74–8;
cf. 7.12.1n, Victor, *Caes.* 26.7 (*conscriptis iunioribus*), *ILS*

should be chosen, and that the imperial title should
remain in that family with someone of that name.
Balbinus and Maximus surrounded themselves with 7
all the young men [1] from the equestrian order and
those with previous military experience who were in
Rome, and with swords in hand they tried to force
their way out from the Capitol. But they were
checked by a shower of stones and sticks. Finally,
at someone's suggestion, they in turn tricked the
people.[2] There was a young lad, the son of Gordian's
daughter, named after his grandfather. So the 8
emperors sent some of their supporters to fetch the
boy, who was found playing at home. They lifted
him up on to their shoulders and carried him through
the crowd for the mob to see, proclaiming that this
was their heir of Gordian and calling him by Gordian's
name. As they made their way up to the Capitol,
the boy was cheered by the people and showered
with flowers. Once the senate had voted him the 9
title of Caesar (he was too young to be made head of

1188 (*tironibus legendis*) and the patronage of the *iuvenalia*
by Gordian I (7.4.3n). It seems probable that this special
guard drawn from the *iuventus* of equestrians (i.e. young men
from senatorial families as well as *equites*) was a source of
anger to the praetorians.

[2] Not clear how the people were tricked, perhaps because
someone not called Gordian was found. The daughter of G.
was Maecia Faustina, who had married the consular Junius
Balbus (if SHA, *Gord.* 4.2, is correct), perhaps the son of
the equestrian C. Junius Balbus, *subpraefectus vigilum* in 203
(*ILS* 2163). Dexippus apparently reported that the young
Gordian (III) was the son of Gordian II (SHA, *Gord.* 23.1,
Zos. 1.14.1), but inscriptions confirm H.; e.g. *ILS* 498, *M.
Antonio Gordiano divi M. Antoni Gordiani nep(oti) divi Antoni
Gordiani sororis fil(io)*; cf. *ILS* 500, *ILTun* 110, etc.

οἷός τε ἦν προΐστασθαι τῶν πραγμάτων, τῆς τε
ὀργῆς ὁ δῆμος ἐπαύσατο, ἠνέσχοντό τε προελθεῖν [1]
ἐς τήν βασίλειον αὐλήν.

11. συνέβη δὲ κατὰ τοὺς αὐτοὺς χρόνους
πταῖσμα ὀλέθριον τῇ Ῥωμαίων πόλει, ἀρχὴν καὶ
πρόφασιν λαβὸν [2] ἐξ εὐτόλμου θράσους δύο ἀνδρῶν
τῶν ἀπὸ συγκλήτου. συνεληλύθεσαν γὰρ ἐς τὸ
βουλευτήριον πάντες σκεψόμενοι περὶ τῶν καθ-
2 εστώτων· μαθόντες δ' οἱ στρατιῶται οὓς ἐν τῷ
στρατοπέδῳ Μαξιμῖνος καταλελοίπει (ἤδη γὰρ [3]
πρὸς ἄφεσιν [4] τῆς στρατείας ὄντες [5] καὶ δι'
ἡλικίαν οἴκοι μεμενηκότες [5]) ἦλθον μέχρι τῆς
εἰσόδου τῆς συγκλήτου, βουλόμενοι τὸ πραττόμενον μαθεῖν, ὅπλων μὲν γυμνοί, ἐν λιταῖς δὲ ἐσθῆσι
καὶ ἐφεστρίσιν, ἑστήκεσαν δὲ μετὰ τοῦ λοιποῦ
3 δήμου. καὶ οἱ μὲν ἄλλοι πρὸ τῶν θυρῶν ἔμενον,
δύο δέ τινες [6] ἢ τρεῖς περιεργότερον ἐπακοῦσαι

[1] προσελθεῖν O   [2] λαβὸν l λαβῶν AB
[3] om Agl   [4] ἄφιξιν φi
[5] -τας Bergl   [6] om i

[1] The one and only *congiarium* that took place in the reign
of Pupienus and Balbinus probably took place on this
occasion in association with Gordian Caesar, who appears on
the scene portrayed by the coins; *BMC* VI. 250, no. 5 = pl.
43, 251, no. 13 = pl. 43; cf. *RIC* IV. 2.177n and *BMC* VI.
252, no. 17A = pl. 44, where Gordian appears by himself with

state), the people's anger ended and they allowed the emperors to go to the imperial palace.[1]

11. But at this same time a fatal tragedy happened to the city of Rome, for which the impetuous bravado of two members of the senate was entirely to blame in the first instance. At the senate house there had been a mass gathering of people who wanted to find out about the current state of affairs. Some of the 2 soldiers belonging to the garrison left behind by Maximinus (men about to gain their discharge from the army, who had remained at Rome because of their age)[2] heard about the gathering and went up to the entrance of the senate house, hoping to find out what was going on.[3] They were unarmed, dressed in a simple uniform and cloak,[4] and standing with the rest of the people. Though most of the crowd 3 stopped at the entrance, two or three who were more

liberalitas, demonstrating the extent of the young boy's prestige. Gordian was thirteen years old (8.8.8).

[2] The discharge (*honesta missio*) of praetorians took place after sixteen years service, though sometimes postponed in times of emergency (as presumably on this occasion). These must be men left behind in 234 by Alexander; the main body of the guards was with M. in the North and at Aquileia (8.5.9), but, since they had declared allegiance to M., their comrades in Rome must have been viewed with suspicion.

[3] The mention of the senate house (*curia Julia*) shows that this was on a different occasion from the election of the emperors (7.10.2). Non-senators were barred from crossing the *curiae limen* (Livy 3.41.4) but could wait *in vestibulo curiae*, that is, outside the entrance doors. The statue of Victory was just inside the doors (5.5.7n). The doors of the senate house were normally left open while the senate was in session, and followers of individual senators often gathered at the doors; Mommsen, *StR* (3) 3.2.932.

[4] For praetorian dress, see 2.13.2n.

τῶν βουλευομένων¹ θελήσαντες ἐς τὸ συνέδριον
εἰσῆλθον, ὡς τὸν ἱδρυμένον βωμὸν τῆς νίκης
ὑπερβῆναι τούτους. τῆς δὲ συγκλήτου ἀνὴρ ἀπὸ²
ὑπατείας μὲν νεωστί, Γαλλικανὸς ὄνομα, Καρχηδό-
νιος δὲ τὸ γένος, καὶ ἕτερος στρατηγικὸς τὸ
ἀξίωμα, Μαικήνας³ καλούμενος, οὐδέν τι προσ-
δοκῶντας τοὺς στρατιώτας, ἔχοντας δὲ τὰς
χεῖρας ὑποκαθειμένας ταῖς ἐφεστρίσι, παίουσι
πληγαῖς κατακαρδίοις, ξίφεσιν οἷς ἐπεφέροντο
4 ὑποκολπίοις·⁴ πάντες γὰρ διὰ τὴν οὖσαν στάσιν
τε καὶ ταραχήν, οἱ μὲν φανερῶς οἱ δὲ καὶ κρύβδην,
ἐξιφηφόρουν, ἀμυντήρια δῆθεν φέροντες ἑαυτῶν
διὰ τοὺς αἰφνιδίως ἐπιβουλεύοντας ἐχθρούς. τότε
δὴ οἱ στρατιῶται πληγέντες καιρίως⁵ καὶ
ἀπροσδοκήτως⁶ προβαλεῖν οὐ δυνηθέντες⁶ πρὸ
5 τοῦ βωμοῦ ἔκειντο. οἱ δὲ λοιποὶ στρατιῶται
τοῦτο θεασάμενοι, ἐκπλαγέντες τῷ πάθει τῶν
συστρατιωτῶν, φοβηθέντες τοῦ δήμου τὸ πλῆθος

¹ βουλομένων i   ² ὑπὸ Vi
³ Maecenas P μαικύννας (-υνας A) O -ίννας i
⁴ οἷς—ὑποκολπίοις om P
⁵ Reisk καί πως φαl καί πως καὶ A καὶ πῶς g
⁶ ἀπροσδοκήτως—δυνηθέντες del Mendelss

¹ Probably L. Domitius Gallicanus Papinianus, whose
career has been found on an inscription from near Carthage;
ILAfr. 322, SHA, Max. 20.6, Gord. 22.8, Victor, Caes. 26.5.
His consulship date is unrecorded, but after this he held three
important military commands; PIR² D 148, Albo 1016. His

234

curious to hear the deliberations went so far inside the chamber that they passed beyond the altar of Victory which was standing there. One of the senators, a Carthaginian called Gallicanus,[1] who had recently held the consulship, and another of praetorian rank called Maecenas,[2] without any warning, while the soldiers had their hands under their cloaks, stabbed them in the heart with daggers they were carrying under the folds of their clothing. Because 4 of the rioting and unrest, everyone was carrying daggers, some openly and others secretly, alleging this was a protection against the sudden, treacherous attacks of their enemies. So, on this occasion the soldiers were fatally wounded while off their guard, without a chance to defend themselves, and lay there at the foot of the altar. When the other soldiers 5 saw this, they were horrified at the fate of their comrades, and ran away because they were apprehensive about the size of the crowd, while they were

Carthaginian origin seems to connect him with the original revolt of Gordian I; his present influence with the urban mob shows his association with the faction behind Gordian III.

[2] Otherwise unknown; perhaps the name is an error for P. Messius Augustinus Maecianus, another African senator, *AE* (1932) 34, and son of a distinguished Severan lawyer (3.13.1n); *Albo* 799. (Note the reading of the *i* group of MSS.) In SHA, *Max. et Balb.* 9-10, the rioting is dated after Pupienus had left Rome for the North and on two separate occasions; but the first incident seems to be a confusion with the elevation of Gordian as Caesar, and for the second there is no cause given for the outburst, though the *vita* may be correct in saying Pupienus was absent from the city (cf. 7.12.1, according to H. he left during the unrest). SHA, *Gord.* 22.7-9 quite incorrectly places the incidents after the death of Pupienus and Balbinus, and says that the *veterani* were unaware that Gordian III was by this time sole Augustus.

ἄνευ τε ὅπλων ὄντες ἔφυγον. ὁ δὲ Γαλλικανὸς
ἐκδραμὼν τῆς συγκλήτου ἐς τὸν δῆμον μέσον,
δεικνύς τε [1] τὸ ξίφος καὶ τὴν χεῖρα ἡμαγμένην,
διεκελεύετο διώκειν καὶ φονεύειν τοὺς ἐχθροὺς
μὲν συγκλήτου καὶ Ῥωμαίων, φίλους δὲ καὶ
6 συμμάχους Μαξιμίνου. ὁ δὲ δῆμος ῥᾷστα πεισθεὶς
τὸν μὲν Γαλλικανὸν εὐφήμει, τοὺς δὲ στρατιώτας
ὡς ἐδύναντο διώκοντες ἔβαλλον λίθοις. οἱ δὲ
φθάσαντες, ὀλίγων τινῶν καὶ τρωθέντων, ἐς τὸ
στρατόπεδον καταφυγόντες καὶ τὰς πύλας κλείσαντες, ὅπλα τε ἀναλαβόντες, ἐφρούρουν τὸ τεῖχος
τοῦ στρατοπέδου. ὁ δὲ Γαλλικανὸς ἅπαξ τολμήσας
ἔργον τηλικοῦτον, ἐμφύλιον πόλεμον καὶ ὄλεθρον
7 μέγαν ἤγειρε τῇ πόλει. τάς τε γὰρ δημοσίας
ἀποθήκας τῶν ὅπλων, εἴ τινες ἦσαν πρὸς πομπὴν
μᾶλλον ἢ μάχην ἐπιτήδειοι, ἀναρρῆξαι τοὺς ὄχλους
ἔπεισε, τό τε σῶμα ἕκαστον [2] φράττεσθαι ὡς οἷός
τε ἦν· τά τε τῶν μονομάχων καταγώγια ἀνοίξας
ἐξήγαγε τοῖς οἰκείοις ὅπλοις ἕκαστον ἐξηρτυμένον.

---

[1] τε τοῖς ὄχλοις A   [2] ἕκαστος φi

---

[1] Cf. 7.7.4n for the suggestion that it was on this occasion,
rather than three weeks earlier, that Sabinus, the urban
prefect was killed in the mob riots; this fits the evidence that
Pupienus and Balbinus appointed an urban prefect called
Sabinus, and it is plausible that he would have tried to quell
the disorder caused by the Gordiani partisans with his urban
cohorts.

[2] Cf. Cic. *pro Rab.* 7.20 for an occasion when weapons were
distributed to the people *ex aedibus sacris armamentariisque*;
ILS 333 records the clerks of the *armamentarium*, and *ILS*
5153 records a freedman in charge of the armoury at the Ludus
Magnus.   Apart from dedicatory weapons in the temples (and

unarmed. Gallicanus came running out of the senate house into the middle of the crowd, and showed them his blood-stained sword and hand, urging them to pursue and kill the enemies of the senate and Roman people who were friends and allies of Maximinus. The people were perfectly easily 6 persuaded, and cheered Gallicanus. They pursued the soldiers as far as they could with showers of stones. But the troops were too quick for them. In spite of a few casualties, they took refuge in their camp and shut the gates. Then they got hold of their weapons and defended the walls of the camp. Now that Gallicanus had dared to go so far, he began to stir up civil war and enormous destruction for the city.[1] He per- 7 suaded the mob to break into the public armouries (even though the weapons were meant for ceremonial purposes, not battles)[2] and to put on any protective covering they could. He threw open the gladiatorial barracks and marched all of them out armed with their individual weapons.[3] All spears, swords and

the armory in the praetorian camp) the public armouries were probably all in the gladiatorial schools.

[3] There were four main types of gladiators; the Samnites (*secutores*), the *murmillones* (*crupellarii*), the Thracians and the *retiarii*; cf. Dar.-Sag. (gladiator) 1583 ff., for a full discussion and illustrations. The gladiators were either freedmen or slaves, kept under strict discipline in the various schools. The main known schools were the Ludus Magnus, the Ludus Mututinus, the Ludus Dacicus and the Ludus Gallicus, all probably around the Colosseum in *regiones* II and III; the location of the Ludus Aemilius is not known; Platner-Ashby, *Top. Dict. Rome* 319–20. The number of gladiators in Rome obviously varied according to the occasion; Otho transferred 2,000 into his army (Tac. *H.* 2.11). At various festivals 1,200, 1,600 and even 10,000 appeared.

ὅσα τε ἦν ⟨ἐν⟩ [1] οἰκίαις ἢ ἐργαστηρίοις δόρατα
8 ἢ ξίφη πελέκεις τε, πάντα διηρπάζετο. ὅ τε
δῆμος ἐνθουσιῶν πᾶν τὸ ἐμπῖπτον ὕλης ἀξιομάχου
ἐργαλεῖον ὅπλον ἐποιεῖτο. ἀθροισθέντες οὖν ἐπ-
ῆλθον τῷ στρατοπέδῳ, καὶ ὡς πολιορκήσοντες
αὐτὸ δῆθεν προσέβαλλον ταῖς τε [2] πύλαις καὶ τοῖς
τείχεσιν. οἱ δὲ στρατιῶται μετὰ πολλῆς ἐμπειρίας
ὡπλισμένοι τε ⟨καὶ προβαλλόμενοι⟩ [3] τὰς ἐπάλξεις
καὶ τὰς ἀσπίδας,[4] τόξοις τε αὐτοὺς βάλλοντες καὶ
δόρασι μακροῖς ἀπείργοντες τοῦ τείχους ἀπεδί-
9 ωκον. ὡς δὲ καμὼν ὁ δῆμος οἵ τε μονομάχοι
τιτρωσκόμενοι ἤδη καὶ ἑσπέρας προσιούσης ἐπανελθεῖν [5] ἠθέλησαν, θεασάμενοι αὐτοὺς οἱ στρατιῶται
ἀπεστραμμένους [6] καὶ τὰ νῶτα δεδωκότας ἀπιόντας
τε ἀμελέστερον, οἰομένους μὴ τολμήσειν ἐπεξελθεῖν
ὀλίγους πλήθει τοσούτῳ, ἀνοίξαντες αἰφνιδίως τὰς
πύλας ἐπέδραμον τῷ δήμῳ, καὶ τούς τε μονομάχους
ἀπέκτειναν, τοῦ τε δήμου μέγα τι πλῆθος ἀπώλετο
ὠθούμενον. οἱ δὲ τοσοῦτον διώξαντες ὅσον μὴ
πολύ τι τοῦ στρατοπέδου ἀποστῆναι, πάλιν
ἐπανῆλθον ἐντός τε τοῦ τείχους ἔμενον.

12. ἐντεῦθεν μείζων ἡ ὀργὴ τοῦ τε δήμου καὶ
τῆς συγκλήτου ἐγένετο. στρατηγοί τε οὖν κατελέ-

---

[1] Steph   [2] Mendelss τε ταῖς Oi
[3] Steph *sese . . . protegentes* P
[4] ταῖς ἀσπισίσιν ἐσκέπαζον A   [5] ἀπελθεῖν V ἐπελθ. Ba
[6] edit. Basil ἐπεστρ. φὶ ἐστρ. A

---

[1] SHA, *Gord.* 10.2, says that the *vigintiviri* were each allocated a part of Italy to protect, probably referring to this
occasion, though the date in the *vita* is put earlier (see

axes were commandeered from houses and work-
shops. If they came across any kind of tool made 8
of material suitable for battle, the people in a frenzy
turned them all into weapons. Then, in a mass they
marched on the camp and launched an attack on the
gates and the walls, no doubt with the intention of
taking it by storm. With the advantage of long
experience and the protection of the turrets of the
walls and their shields, the soldiers drove the people
away from the walls by firing arrows at them and
fending them off with their long spears. In the end 9
the people and the gladiators decided to withdraw,
because they were exhausted and wounded and the
evening was closing in. But seeing the people
turning about and retreating somewhat over-
confidently, with their backs turned, because they
never dreamed a few men would dare come out and
attack such a large crowd, the soldiers suddenly
flung open the gates and charged at the people.
They killed the gladiators, and a large number of
people were lost in the scramble. After chasing
them away from the camp for a short distance, the
troops returned and stayed shut up behind the walls.

12. As a result of this incident the fury of the senate
and people increased. Commanders were chosen[1]

7.10.3n). Victor, *Caes.* 26.7, calls these men *potestatum vices*,
implying formal commissions by the senate; Theodorides,
Lat. 6 (1947) 41; confirmed by the title of Cripinus at Aquileia
(8.2.5n) who is recorded as [. . . *dux*] *ex s(enatus) c(onsulto)*;
cf. *ILS* 8980. These commanders may have been members
of the XXvirate, but were not necessarily so; it would be
more probable for the latter to remain beside the emperors as
advisers and *comites*; cf. *ILS* 8979 for the conjecture [*comes
Augg.*] *nn. inter XX cos.* as the position of Acilius Priscilianus.

HERODIAN

γοντο ἔκ τε πάσης Ἰταλίας λογάδες, ἥ τε νεολαία ¹
πᾶσα ἠθροίζετο, ὅπλοις τε αὐτοσχεδίοις καὶ τοῖς
προστυχοῦσιν ὡπλίζετο. τούτων δὴ τὸ μὲν πλεῖστον μέρος ὁ Μάξιμος σὺν αὑτῷ ἀπήγαγεν ὡς ²
δὴ Μαξιμίνῳ πολεμήσων· οἱ δὲ λοιποὶ ἔμειναν,
ὡς τὴν πόλιν φρουροῖέν τε καὶ προασπίζοιεν
2 αὐτῆς. ἑκάστοτε οὖν τῷ τείχει τοῦ στρατοπέδου
ἐγίνοντο ³ προσβολαί, ἔπραττον δὲ οὐδὲν προμα-
χομένων ἄνωθεν τῶν στρατιωτῶν· οἱ δὲ βαλλόμενοι καὶ τιτρωσκόμενοι κακῶς ἀπηλλάγησαν. ὁ δὲ
Βαλβῖνος οἴκοι μένων διάταγμά τε ⁴ προθεὶς
ἱκέτευε τὸν δῆμον ἐς διαλλαγὰς χωρῆσαι, τοῖς τε
στρατιώταις ὑπισχνεῖτο ἀμνηστίαν, ἄνεσίν ⁵ τε
3 πάντων ἐδίδου ἁμαρτημάτων. ἀλλ᾽ οὐδετέρους
ἔπειθε, τὸ δὲ δεινὸν ἑκάστοτε ηὔξετο, τοῦ μὲν
τοσούτου δήμου ἀπαξιοῦντος ὑπ᾽ ὀλίγων καταφρο-

¹ ῥώμη A ² εἰς Bi ³ ἐγένοντο φl ⁴ τι φi ⁵ ἄφεσίν A

¹ Note *ILS* 1188 (the text is improved in *PIR*² A 622), a
fragmentary and puzzling inscription, recording a senator in
242 named .....us Annianus, who had earlier had a com-
mission *missus adv(ersus) h(ostes) p(ublicos) in re[gionem trans
P]ad(um) tir(onibus) legend(is) et arm(is) fabr(icandis) in
[urb(e) Me]diol(anio)*; that is, a young senator (not yet a
consul) who was sent to organize recruiting and arms supply
in North Italy. He is wrongly believed by Townsend, *YCS*
14 (1955) 90, to be a member of the *XX viri*, but they were
senior consulars (see above note). At this time also a certain
Clodius Celsinus was sent to the *vexillationes Moesiae inferioris*

and recruits enrolled all over Italy.[1] All the youth groups[2] were called up and equipped with whatever makeshift weapons could be found. Maximus took most of the force with him to fight against Maximinus. The rest stayed behind to guard and protect the city. Regular attacks were made 2 against the camp fortifications, but without any success. The soldiers fought back from their superior height, and the attackers came off badly, as they were shot at and wounded. Balbinus, who had stayed behind, issued an edict begging the people to call a truce and promising the soldiers an amnesty, by offering them pardon for all their crimes. But 3 neither side listened, and every day the lawlessness grew worse. The people thought it a disgrace that

on a special mission to persuade them, after Maximinus had set out for Italy, to turn against him (*ad eradendum nomen saevissimae dominationis*); *AE* (1935) 164, Bersanetti, *RFIC* 20 (1942) 214–18.

[2] The exact relationship between the various organizations of young men is not certain; throughout Italy there were various *sodales*, *iuvenes*, *iuventutes* and *collegia iuvenum*; possibly the *iuventus* was only the young men within the wider *collegium* of *iuvenes* (all of military age); cf. at Mactar in Africa, where only sixty-nine names are on the *album* of the *collegium*; obviously not the whole extent of the *iuvenes* in the city; Picard, *Karthago* 8 (1957) 77–9. In Italy the importance of the *iuvenes* and *iuventutes* declined as the various *collegia iuvenum* on the Rhine, Danube and in Africa grew to meet the military requirements of the empire. In Rome the group of νεανίσκοι round the emperor (cf. 7.10.7) probably derived from the Hellenistic system of court pages, and was therefore encouraged by the emperors most influenced by the orient (Nero, Domitian, Commodus, Caracalla and Elagabalus); cf. 5.7.7 for a special officer under Elagabalus to control the equestrian *iuventus* at Rome; Rostovtzeff, *Klio, Beiheft* 3 (1905) 78.

νηθῆναι, τῶν δὲ στρατιωτῶν ἀγανακτούντων ὅτι
δὴ ταῦτα [1] ὑπὸ Ῥωμαίων ὡς ὑπὸ βαρβάρων
πάσχουσι.[1]

τὸ δὴ τελευταῖον, ἐπειδὴ τειχομαχοῦντες οὐδὲν
ἔπραττον, ἔδοξε τοῖς στρατηγοῖς ἐκκόψαι πάντας
τοὺς εἰσρέοντας ἐς τὸ στρατόπεδον ἀγωγοὺς
ὕδατος, σπάνει τε ποτοῦ καὶ ἐνδείᾳ ῥείθρων αὐτοὺς
4 παραστήσασθαι.[2] προσπεσόντες οὖν πᾶν τὸ ὕδωρ
τοῦ στρατοπέδου ἐς ἕτερα ῥεῖθρα μετωχέτευον,
ἐκκόπτοντες καὶ εἰσφράττοντες τὰς ἐς τὸ στρατόπεδον εἰσόδους αὐτοῦ. οἱ δὲ στρατιῶται ὁρῶντες
τὸν κίνδυνον καὶ ἐν ἀπογνώσει γενόμενοι, τὰς
πύλας ἀνοίξαντες ἐπεξῆλθον· μάχης τε καρτερᾶς
γενομένης καὶ φυγῆς τῶν δημοτῶν ἐπὶ πολὺ τῆς
5 πόλεως διώκοντες οἱ στρατιῶται προύβησαν. ἐπεὶ
δὲ οἱ ὄχλοι ταῖς συσταδὸν [3] μάχαις ἡττώμενοι,
ἀναπηδῶντες ἐς τὰ δωμάτια [4] τῷ τε κεράμῳ
βάλλοντες αὐτοὺς καὶ λίθων βολαῖς τῶν τε ἄλλων
ὀστράκων ἐλυμαίνοντο, ἐπαναβῆναι μὲν αὐτοῖς δι᾽
ἄγνοιαν τῶν οἰκήσεων οὐκ ἐτόλμησαν οἱ στρατιῶ-

[1] ea se a Romanis passos quae vix umquam a barbaris
exspectassent P
[2] περιστήσαντες φgl παραστήσαντες a
[3] συστάδην V συσταδὴν B
[4] δώματα ABi

[1] The water supply in the city was carried by open water
channels (canales), lead water pipes (fistulae) and ceramic pipes
(tubuli); Vitruv. 8.6.1; according to SHA, Max. et Balb.

their vast numbers were being defied by so few soldiers, and the soldiers were furious that Romans were behaving towards them like barbarians.

Finally, after the assaults on the wall proved futile, the commanders decided to cut off all the channels of water supply into the camp, so as to bring the soldiers to submission by a shortage of drinking and running water. During the course of an attack they diverted 4 the camp water supply into new channels by cutting and blocking up the pipes leading into the camp.[1] The danger was obvious to the soldiers, and, being in a desperate position, they threw open the gates and made an attack. A fierce battle took place, ending in the people running away and the soldiers advancing far into the city to pursue them. Although the 5 mob was no match for the soldiers in hand-to-hand fighting, they swarmed up into the upper rooms of houses and caused casualties among the soldiers by showering them with tiles and a hail of stones and broken pots.[2] The soldiers did not dare climb up after the people because of their unfamiliarity with

10.6, it was the *fistulae* that were blocked. The main supply came to the camp in the aqua Julia–Tepula–Marcia, which terminated at the Porta Collina; from there it was carried in pipes across the *campus cohortium praetoriarum*. The action described here took place on the *campus*. Cf. Nash, *Pict. Dict. Anc. Rome* I.48 ff.

[2] In spite of the repetition of the description of 1.12.8, and the Thucydidean antecedents of the passage (Thuc. 2.4.2), there is no reason to doubt the accuracy of H.'s description, which elsewhere (see above note) indicates a first-hand knowledge of events. The construction of ancient cities with narrow streets and overhanging houses must have meant that this kind of scene was a not uncommon occurrence; cf. Sallust, *Jug.* 67.1.

ται, κεκλεισμένων δὲ τῶν οἰκιῶν καὶ τῶν ἐργα
στηρίων ταῖς θύραις, καὶ εἴ τινες ἦσαν ξύλων
ἐξοχαί (πολλαὶ δὲ αὗται κατὰ τὴν πόλιν), πῦρ
6 προσετίθεσαν.[1] ῥᾷστα δὲ διὰ πυκνότητα τῶν
συνοικιῶν ξυλείας [2] τε πλῆθος ἐπάλληλον [5] μέγισ
τον μέρος τῆς πόλεως τὸ πῦρ ἐνεμήθη, ὡς πολλοὺς
μὲν ἐκ πλουσίων ποιῆσαι πένητας, ἀποβαλόντας
θαυμαστὰ καὶ ἀμφιλαφῆ κτήματα, ἔν τε προσόδοις
πλουσίαις καὶ ἐν ποικίλῃ [3] πολυτελείᾳ τίμια.
7 πλῆθός τε ἀνθρώπων σύγκατεφλέχθη, φυγεῖν μὴ
δυνηθέντων διὰ τὸ τὰς ἐξόδους ὑπὸ τοῦ πυρὸς
προκατειλῆφθαι. οὐσίαι τε ὅλαι πλουσίων ἀνδρῶν
διηρπάγησαν, ἐγκαταμιξάντων ἑαυτοὺς τοῖς στρα
τιώταις πρὸς τὸ ἁρπάζειν κακούργων καὶ εὐτελῶν
δημοτῶν. τοσοῦτον δὲ μέρος τῆς πόλεως τὸ πῦρ
ἐλυμήνατο ὡς μηδεμίαν τῶν μεγίστων πόλεων
ὁλόκληρον δύνασθαι τῷ μέρει ἐξισωθῆναι.
8 καὶ τὰ μὲν κατὰ τὴν Ῥώμην τοιαῦτα ἦν, ὁ δὲ
Μαξιμῖνος ἀνύσας τὴν ὁδοιπορίαν ἐπέστη τοῖς τῆς
Ἰταλίας ὅροις, θύσας τε ἐπὶ τῶν μεθορίων βωμῶν
τῆς ἐπ᾽ Ἰταλίαν εἰσβολῆς εἴχετο, ἐκέλευσέ τε
πάντα τὸν στρατὸν ἐν ὅπλοις εἶναι μετ᾽ εὐταξίας
προχωρεῖν.[4]

---

[1] προσετέθησαν φ
[2] ξυλ.—ἐπάλλ. om A
[3] πάσῃ A
[4] ΑΙΡ προσχωρεῖν φag

---

[1] In spite of building regulations to fire-proof walls of
insulae (housing blocks), the upper stories frequently projected
over the streets, making balconies (*maeniana*), usually part-

the houses, and the doors of the houses and shops were closed. So they set fire to the wooden balconies of such houses that possessed them (of which there were a lot in the city).[1] Because the buildings 6 adjoined each other very closely, and a great number of them in a row were made of wood, the fire very easily burned down most of the city. Many people who were rich were turned into paupers [2] by losing their magnificent accumulation of property, some of it valuable for the rich income it brought in, and some of it for its lavish workmanship. A great many 7 people were unable to run away because their escape route was cut off by the flames, and they were burned to death. The entire possessions of some rich men were looted by criminals and the lower class, who mixed with the soldiers in order to do just this. The section of Rome that burned down was wider in extent than the entire size of any of the largest cities elsewhere.

While this was going on in Rome, Maximinus had 8 completed his march and stood on the Italian frontier, where, after sacrificing on the altars at the border,[3] he began his invasion of Italy. Orders were given to the entire army to arm itself and proceed in good order.

timbered. Martial 1.86 says one could shake hands across the street from these upper floors; accidents often happened to passers by from objects thrown out of these rooms (Juv. 3.269) and in 368 a regulation was passed to prevent this kind of building (Amm. Marc. 27.9.10).

[2] Cf. 1.14.3n, 7.3.5n.

[3] Probably the altars of Fortuna Redux and Italia, both of which were publicized on imperial coinage as an emperor returned to Rome.

9   τὴν μὲν οὖν Λιβύης ἀπόστασιν καὶ τὸν κατὰ τὴν
Ῥώμην ἐμφύλιον πόλεμον, τά τε Μαξιμίνῳ
πραχθέντα καὶ τὴν ἐς Ἰταλίαν ἄφιξιν αὐτοῦ
ἐδηλώσαμεν· τὰ δὲ ἑπόμενα ἐν τοῖς ἑξῆς λεχθήσε-
ται.

This is my account of the revolt in Libya, the civil 9
war in Rome and of the activities of Maximinus up to
his arrival in Italy. What followed will now be
related in the next book.

BOOK EIGHT

ΒΙΒΛΙΟΝ ΟΓΔΟΟΝ

1. Τὰ μὲν δὴ Μαξιμίνῳ πραχθέντα μετὰ τὴν
Γορδιανοῦ τελευτήν, ἥ τε εἰς Ἰταλίαν ἄφιξις
αὐτοῦ, Λιβύης τε ἀπόστασις καὶ ἡ ἐν Ῥώμῃ τῶν
στρατιωτῶν πρὸς τὸν δῆμον διαφορὰ ἐν τοῖς πρὸ
τούτων λέλεκται· ὁ δὲ Μαξιμῖνος ἐπιστὰς τοῖς
ὅροις προύπεμψε σκοποὺς τοὺς ἐρευνήσοντας μή
τινες ἐνέδραι [1] ἐν κοιλάσιν ὀρῶν ἢ λόχμαις ὕλαις
2 τε κρύφιοι εἶεν. αὐτός δὲ καταγαγὼν ἐς τὸ
πεδίον τὸν στρατόν, τὰς μὲν τῶν ὁπλιτῶν φάλαγγας
ἐς τετράγωνα ἔταξε σχήματα, ἐπιμήκεις [2] μᾶλλον
ἢ βαθείας,[2] ὡς ἂν πλεῖστον τοῦ πεδίου διαλάβοιεν·
τὰ δὲ σκευοφόρα πάντα κτήνη [3] τε καὶ ὀχήματα [3]
ἐν μέσῳ τάξας, αὐτὸς ἅμα τοῖς δορυφόροις
3 ὀπισθοφυλακῶν εἵπετο. ἑκατέρωθεν δὲ παρέθεον
αἵ τε τῶν καταφράκτων ἱππέων ἶλαι καὶ Μαυρού-

---

[1] ἐνέδραις V ἐν ἐνέδραις (sic) B
[2] ἐπιμήκ.—βαθείας om P
[3] κτήνη—ὀχήματα om P

---

[1] For this recapitulation, see 3.1.1n.
[2] Presumably H. means the plain of the R. Save, up which
M. might have marched if he had been wintering at Sirmium
(7.2.9). But in that case, it is difficult to see why the army
should have marched so far in battle order, or from where they

BOOK EIGHT

1. In the previous book the activities of Maximinus following upon Gordian's death, his arrival in Italy, the revolt in Libya and the struggle in Rome between the soldiers and the people were related.[1] As Maximinus stood on the border he sent scouts on ahead to reconnoitre and see whether there were any hidden ambushes laid in the deep mountain valleys or dense woods. He himself led his army down to 2 the plain [2] and arranged the legions of infantry in a shallow, rectangular formation rather than in depth, so as to extend right across the plain.[3] All the equipment, including pack animals and carts, were allocated the centre, while he brought up the rear himself with the guards. On the wings rode the 3 squadrons of heavy cavalry,[4] the Mauretanian and

had been " led down ". The description is better suited to an approach from Sirmium up the Drave valley to Poetovio (perhaps to link up with the Upper Pannonian forces), and thence over the watershed to the Save valley, descending just north of Emona at the border post near Atrans; cf. Pavan, *Province rom. d. Pannonia Sup.* 429. This was in fact the main route from Sirmium, Mócsy, *RE* suppl. 9 (Pannonia) 661.

[3] Both SHA, *Max.* 21.1 and *Max. et Balb.* 2.4, says that M. came up to Emona in battle order (*quadrato agmine*), but the former assumes Emona is *post Alpes* and that M. has descended to the North Italian plain.

[4] Cf. 6.7.8. The heavy cavalry cataphracts are noted in 7.2.3n, though the Osrhoenian cavalry had been disbanded (7.1.9n).

σιοι ἀκοντισταὶ τοξόται τε οἱ ἀπὸ τῆς ἀνατολῆς.
καὶ Γερμανῶν ἱππέων μέγα τι πλῆθος [1] ἐπήγετο
συμμάχους· ἐκείνους γὰρ μάλιστα προυβάλλετο,
ἵν' ἐκδέχωνται τῶν πολεμίων τὰς πρώτας ἐμβολάς,
θυμοειδεῖς ὄντες καὶ εὔτολμοι ἐν ἀρχομένῃ μάχῃ,
εἰ δ' ἄρα καὶ κινδυνεύειν δέοι, εὐκαταφρόνητοι ὡς
4 βάρβαροι. ὡς δὲ πᾶν τὸ πεδίον διῆλθεν ὁ στρατὸς
μετ' εὐκοσμίας τε καὶ εὐταξίας, ἐπέστησαν πρώτῃ
Ἰταλίας πόλει ἣν καλοῦσιν Ἡμᾶν [2] οἱ ἐπιχώριοι·
πρόκειται δὲ αὕτη ἐπ' ἀκροτάτῳ πεδίῳ ἱδρυμένη
πρὸ τῆς ὑπωρείας τῶν Ἄλπεων. ἔνθα ὑπαντώμενοι τῷ Μαξιμίνῳ οἱ προφύλακες καὶ σκοποὶ τοῦ
στρατοῦ ἤγγειλαν κενὴν ἀνθρώπων εἶναι τὴν πόλιν
πανδημεί τε πεφευγέναι ἐμπρήσαντας τὰς θύρας
ἱερῶν τε καὶ οἰκιῶν, πάντα τε, ὅσα ἦν ἐν τῇ
πόλει ἢ τοῖς [3] ἀγροῖς, ἃ μὲν ἐκφορήσαντας ἃ δὲ
καταπρήσαντας, καὶ μήτε ὑποζυγίοις μήτε ἀνθρώ-
5 ποις καταλελεῖφθαι τροφάς. ὁ δὲ Μαξιμῖνος ἤσθη
μὲν ἐπὶ τῇ τῶν Ἰταλιωτῶν εὐθὺς φυγῇ, ἐλπίζων
πάντας τοὺς δήμους τοῦτο ποιήσειν οὐχ ὑπομένον-
τας τὴν ἔφοδον αὐτοῦ· ὁ δὲ στρατὸς ἤχθετο εὐθὺς
ἐν ἀρχῇ λιμοῦ πειρώμενος. διανυκτερεύσαντες οὖν

[1] χρῆμα ἐπήγετο ὡς A
[2] ἧμαν A Ἧμαν Mendelss Ἧμων Mommsen
[3] ἤτοι φὶ

---

[1] The German *auxilia* are noted in 7.8.10 and 8.4.3.
[2] Modern Ljubljana (Laibach), on the River Save, at the
foot of the Carnic Alps. The name of the city in ancient
authors is usually given as Emona or (H)aemona; Ptolemy
252

Eastern archers and a large body of allied German cavalry.[1] The Germans occupied a prominent forward position to take the first impact of an enemy attack, because they were daring, spirited fighters in the early stages of a battle, though when it came to a dangerous mission, being barbarians, they were of negligible value. As they travelled right across 4 the plain in orderly formation, the army reached their first Italian city, locally named Hema,[2] situated at the highest point of the plain at the base of Alpine foothills. At this point the advance guard and scouts met Maximinus, bringing the information that the city was deserted and that the entire population had fled, after burning the doors of their temples and houses; everything in the town and the countryside had been either taken away or burned, leaving no food supplies for transport animals or men. Maxi- 5 minus was delighted that the Italians had fled from him straight away, and was optimistic that all the population would follow suit without waiting for his arrival.[3] But the army was annoyed that at the

2.14.5, Pliny, *NH* 3.18.128, etc. The city was given colonial status, probably by Tiberius (colonia Iulia Emona, *CIL* II. 6087). Situated on the main route from Sirmium to Aquileia, it was originally part of Pannonia but was probably included in Italy during the Marcomannian Wars, *c.* 170. H. provides the first evidence that it was part of Italy now; Degrassi, *Il confine nord-orient. d. Ital. rom.* 109–113.

[3] An important factor in M.'s optimism must have been the news which reached him of the death of Gordian in Africa; the news would have arrived while he was on the march from Sirmium to Emona (perhaps about 10th April, if Gordian I died about 22nd March, 7.9.10n); cf. SHA, *Max.* 20.7–8, which says there was a gap between the news of Gordian's death and the election of Pupienus and Balbinus.

οἱ μὲν ἐν τῇ πόλει ἐν ἀθύροις καὶ κεναῖς [1] πάντων
οἰκίαις, οἱ δ' ἐν τῷ πεδίῳ, ἅμα ἡλίῳ ἀνίσχοντι
ἐπὶ τὰς Ἄλπεις ἠπείγοντο, ἅπερ ὄρη ὑπερμήκη
ὥσπερ τεῖχος Ἰταλίας ἡ φύσις ἤγειρεν, ὑπερνεφῆ
μὲν τὸ ὕψος, ἐπιμηκέστατα δέ, ὡς πᾶσαν Ἰταλίαν
διειληφότα καθήκειν ἐν μὲν τοῖς δεξιοῖς Ἰταλίας
μέρεσιν ἐς τὸ Τυρρηναῖον πέλαγος, ἐν δὲ τοῖς
6 λαιοῖς ἐς τὸν Ἰόνιον κόλπον. σκέπεται δὲ ὕλαις
δασείαις καὶ πυκναῖς, τὰς δὲ διεξόδους ἐστένωται
ἢ διὰ κρημνοὺς [2] ἐς βάθος μέγιστον ἀπερρωγότας [3]
ἢ διὰ πετρῶν τραχύτητα· στενωποὶ γάρ εἰσι χει-
ροποίητοι, μετὰ πολλοῦ καμάτου τοῖς πάλαι
Ἰταλιώταις εἰργασμένοι. μετὰ δέους οὖν πολλοῦ
διῄει ὁ στρατός, ἐλπίζοντες τάς τε ἄκρας κατει-
λῆφθαι πεφράχθαι τε τὰς διόδους ἐς κωλύμην τῆς
αὐτῶν διαβάσεως. ἤλπιζον δὲ καὶ ἐδεδοίκεσαν
εἰκότα, τῶν χωρίων τεκμαιρόμενοι τὴν φύσιν.

---

[1] κοιναῖς Oi many editions correct
[2] Steph κρημνοῦ Oi
[3] Ag (in g -ας over erasure) ἀπορρωγότας a ἀπερρωγότως l
ἀπορρωγότος φ

---

[1] H. is quoted (though not named) by SHA, *Max.* 21.3–5,
which says another version related that Emona was prepared
for a siege against M.; but that version is based on the
erroneous assumption that because Emona was in Italy it was
on the Italian side of the Alps.
[2] Cf. 2.11.8 for the commonplace; also Cic. *in Pis.* 81,
Prov. Cos. 34, Virgil, *Geor.* 3.474, Pliny, *NH* 3.31 (*saluberrimis
Romano imperio iugis*).

very start of the campaign they had to be short of food.[1]   After a night spent by some inside the city in the totally empty, doorless houses, and by others outside on the plain, at dawn they made for the Alps.   Nature has provided this long mountain range as a kind of fortification for Italy,[2] whose peaks reach above the clouds, and so extensive that it completely cuts off Italy, running from the Tyrrhenian Sea in the West to the Ionian Gulf in the East.   The moun- 6 tains are covered with dense, thick forests, and have passes hemmed in by overhanging cliffs [3] that end abruptly in precipitous drops, or by rocky outcrops. The narrow paths are artificially constructed as a result of the laborious toil of the ancient Italians. The army went through the area with considerable apprehension because they expected the heights to be occupied and the passes to be fixed to block their passage.   In view of the type of terrain, their expectations and fears were real possibilities.

[3] The route from Ljubljana via Longatico and Ajdovscina to the River Isontio (Gorizia) passes along the southern edge of the rocky escarpment of the Hrusĭca and Ternovan forests. Between Longatico and Ajdovscina there are two roads; the easier one along the Vipara valley, the watershed of which is only 2,000 feet, hardly fits the dramatic description given here by H.   But it is probable that M. crossed the watershed by the steeper, more direct route through the Selva di Piro, that rises to a height of 4,300 feet, which was the main Augustan road to Pannonia; see *Stud. 3. d. Militärgrenzen Roms* (6 Int. Limeskongress in S.-Deutschland) tafel 11.   The *Itin. Antonin.* and *Itin. Hierosol.* are no great help in solving the route precisely, but the latter, in describing the reverse route from the *mutatio Castra* to the *mansio Longatico*, says, *inde surgunt Alpes Iuliae ad Pirum summas Alpes*, which sounds like a description of the Selva di Piro; *Itin. Ant.* 128–9, *Itin. Hierosol.* 559–60, Mócsy, *RE* suppl. 9 (Pannonia) 659.

2. ὡς δὲ διέβησαν ἀκωλύτως μηδενὸς [1] ἐμποδὼν
γενομένου,[1] καταβαίνοντες ἐς τὸ πεδίον [2] ἤδη
ἀνεθάρρησάν τε καὶ ἐπαιάνισαν· ῥᾷστά τε αὐτῷ
πάντα προχωρήσειν ὁ Μαξιμῖνος ἤλπισεν Ἰταλῶν
μηδὲ ταῖς δυσχωρίαις τεθαρρηκότων, ἔνθα ἢ
κρύπτειν ἑαυτοὺς καὶ σώζειν ἠδύναντο ἢ δι᾽
ἐνέδρας ἐπιβουλεῦσαι, μάχεσθαί τε ἄνωθεν ἐξ
2 ὑπερκειμένων χωρίων. γενομένων δὲ αὐτῶν ἐν
τῷ πεδίῳ, οἱ σκοποὶ ἀπήγγειλαν πόλιν Ἰταλίας
τὴν μεγίστην, Ἀκυληίαν δὲ καλουμένην, κεκλεῖ-
σθαι, τὰς δὲ προπεμφθείσας φάλαγγας τῶν
Παιόνων προθύμως μὲν τειχομαχῆσαι, πολλάκις
δὲ προσβαλούσας [3] ἀνύειν οὐδέν, ἀπαγορεύειν δὲ
καὶ ἀναχωρεῖν βαλλομένους [4] λίθοις τε καὶ δόρασι
τόξων τε πλήθει. ὁ δὲ Μαξιμῖνος ἀγανακτήσας
πρὸς τοὺς στρατηγοὺς τῶν Παιόνων ὡς ἀμελεστε-
ρον μαχομένους, αὐτὸς σὺν τῷ στρατῷ ἠπείγετο,
ἐλπίζων ῥᾷστα αἱρήσειν τὴν πόλιν.

[1] μηδενὸς—γενομένου om Jo Mendelss
[2] AJo στρατόπεδον φi
[3] προβαλ. φ
[4] βουλομένους V βουλλομένους B

[1] The resistance of Aquileia and its adherence to the
senatorial cause may have been due to the influence of some
of the Aquileian aristocracy, rich trading families with
senatorial connections; e.g. the family of the Barbii (Calderini,
Aquileia romana (index) 467–8), a leading trading house with

2. When, however, they reached the other side without interference or anyone trying to stop them, their spirits rose again as they descended to the plain, and they sang with triumph. Maximinus was hopeful of an easy, sweeping success, if the Italians were lacking confidence even in difficult terrain, when they could have been safe by hiding, or have planned an ambush and attacked him from a position on the heights. Once on the plain, his recon- 2 naissance force brought him the news that Aquileia, the largest Italian city, had closed its gates [1] and that, although the advance force of Pannonian legions were vigorously attacking the fortifications, their repeated assaults were unsuccessful; they were now growing tired and withdrawing under a hail of stones, spears and arrows. Maximinus was very angry with the Pannonian generals for not putting their hearts into the battle, and he hurried there in person with his army, expecting to take the city without any difficulty.

ramifications all over the western provinces, who produced a *cos. suff.* in 140 (*AE* (1953) 190), probably connected with the Fulvii Aemiliani (*PIR*[2] F 530, though doubted by Pflaum, in spite of the name of the consul, M. Barbius Aemilianus), one of whom served under Alexander as recruiting officer (6.3.1n) and another became consul under Gordian III (*PIR*[2] F 529); the family may also have been connected with the Bruttii Praesentes, partisans of Alexander (7.1.5n, *PIR*[2] B 541); also note A.'s wife, Herennia Sallustia Barbia Orbiana (6.1.9n) from the Barbii family; cf. Pflaum, *Rev. Arch.* (1953) 72–6. Another important Aquileian family was the Statii (Calderini, *op. cit.* (index) 548–50), probably related to the senators M. Statius Longinus and M. Statius Patruinus, whose names also appear on the *album* of Canusium (see 7.1.5n, *Albo* 486, 1163–4).

3   ἡ δὲ Ἀκυληία καὶ πρότερον μέν, ἅτε μεγίστη
πόλις, ἰδίου δήμου ¹ πολυάνθρωπος ἦν, καὶ ὥσπερ
τι ἐμπόριον Ἰταλίας ἐπὶ θαλάττῃ προκειμένη καὶ ²
πρὸ τῶν Ἰλλυρικῶν ἐθνῶν πάντων ἱδρυμένη ² τά
τε ἀπὸ τῆς ἠπείρου διὰ γῆς ἢ ποταμῶν κατα-
κομιζόμενα παρεῖχεν ³ ἐμπορεύεσθαι τοῖς πλέουσι,³
τά τε ἀπὸ θαλάττης τοῖς ἠπειρώταις ἀναγκαῖα,
ὧν ἡ παρ' ἐκείνοις ⁴ χώρα διὰ χειμῶνας ⁵ οὐκ
ἦν εὔφορος, ἀνέπεμπεν ἐς τὴν ἄνω γῆν· πρὸς οἶνόν
τε μάλιστα πολύγονον χώραν γεωργοῦντες ἀφθονίαν ποτοῦ παρεῖχον ⁶ τοῖς ἄμπελον μὴ γεωργοῦσιν.
4   ἔνθεν πολύ τι πλῆθος ἐπεδήμει οὐ πολιτῶν μόνον
ἀλλὰ ξένων τε καὶ ἐμπόρων. τότε δὲ μᾶλλον
ἐπολυπλασιάσθη τὸ πλῆθος, τῶν ὄχλων πάντων
ἐξ ἀγρῶν ἐκεῖσε συρρυέντων,⁷ πολίχνας τε καὶ
κώμας τὰς περικειμένας καταλιπόντων, πιστευσάν-
των δὲ αὐτοὺς τῷ τε μεγέθει τῆς πόλεως καὶ τῷ
προβεβλημένῳ τείχει, ὃ παλαιότατον ⟨ὂν⟩ ⁸ ἐκ

---

¹ ἰδίου δήμου om P καὶ πάλαι οὖσα A
² καὶ πρὸ—ἱδρυμένη om A
³ παρεῖχεν εὐκόλως λαμβάνειν τοὺς πλέοντας A
⁴ παρ' ἐκείνης V παροῦσα A
⁵ Sylb χειμῶνα A χειμῶνος φi
⁶ Sylb παρεῖχε Oi
⁷ συρρεόντων φi   ⁸ Bekk

---

¹ The importance of Aquileia as the first trading port of
northern Italy dated from Augustus, after the Dalmatian
and Danube lands were opened up as a market for goods from

Aquileia has always been an important city with a 3
large local population. Sited as it is on the coast,
commanding the hinterland of the Illyrian territories,
it has acted as a trading port for Italy [1] by providing
sea traders with a market for goods that come from
inland by land and river.[2] Similarly, essential goods
which cannot be produced in the Illyrian countryside
because of the winters, come by sea and are sent from
Aquileia up country to the people of the interior.
They farm land which is particularly fertile for the
vine, and export a great quantity of wine to people
who do not grow grapes. As a result of this the city 4
is teeming with local citizens, aliens and traders. At
the time of Maximinus' invasion, the size of the
population was swollen by all the crowds swarming
in from the countryside, who had abandoned the little
towns and villages around Aquileia, seeking refuge
in the city because of its size and defensive wall.
Being very ancient, a large section of the wall had

Italy. A metal industry developed from the mines in Noricum, Raetia and Dalmatia; local sand produced high-quality
glass; the amber trade with Central Europe and the Baltic
increased. With an expanding market and excellent com-
munications (Rivers Save, Drave, Danube and the sea) much
of northern Italy turned from rearing pigs and sheep to viti-
culture, of which Aquileia was the centre; cf. Rostovtzeff,
SEHRE 548, 567, 610–11, for a full bibliography, Frank,
ESAR V. 111–5, Panciera, *Vita econ. di Aquileia, passim*, esp.
101 ff.

[2] Cf. Strabo 5.1.8 (214), " Aquileia has been given over as
an emporium for those tribes of the Illyrians that live near the
Danube; the latter load on wagons and carry inland the
products of the sea, and wine stored in wooden barrels, and
also olive oil, whereas the former get in exchange slaves, cattle
and hides." Cf. Strabo 4.6.9–10 (207) and 7.5.2 (314).

τοῦ πλείστου μέρους πρότερον μὲν κατερήριπτο,[1]
ἅτε μετὰ τὴν Ῥωμαίων ἀρχὴν μηκέτι τῶν ἐν
Ἰταλίᾳ πόλεων ἢ τειχῶν ἢ ὅπλων δεηθεισῶν,
μετειληφυιῶν δὲ ἀντὶ πολέμων εἰρήνην βαθεῖαν
καὶ τῆς παρὰ Ῥωμαίοις πολιτείας κοινωνίαν·
5 πλὴν τότε ἡ χρεία ἤπειξε τὸ τεῖχος ἀνανεώσασθαι
τά τ᾽ ἐρείπια ἀνοικοδομῆσαι, πύργους τε καὶ
ἐπάλξεις ἐγεῖραι. τάχιστα οὖν φράξαντες τῷ
τείχει τὴν πόλιν, τάς τε πύλας κλείσαντες,
πανδημεὶ ἐπὶ τῶν τειχῶν νύκτωρ τε καὶ μεθ᾽
ἡμέραν ἱδρυμένοι τοῖς προσιοῦσιν ἀπεμάχοντο.
ἐστρατήγουν δὲ αὐτῶν καὶ πάντα εἶχον διὰ
φροντίδος ἄνδρες δύο, ἀπὸ ὑπατείας μέν, ἐπιλε-
χθέντες δὲ ὑπὸ τῆς συγκλήτου· ὧν ὁ μὲν Κρισπῖνος
6 ὁ δὲ Μηνόφιλος [2] ἐκαλεῖτο. καὶ μετὰ πολλῆς
προνοίας τά [τε] [3] ἐπιτήδεια πάμπλειστα εἰσεκομί-
σαντο, ὡς ἐκτένειαν εἶναι, εἰ καὶ ἐπιμηκεστέρα
γένοιτο πολιορκία. ἦν δὲ καὶ ὕδατος ἀφθονία

---

[1] Sylb κατερήρειπτο Oi
[2] μηνίφιλος φi Menephilus P μινόφ. Jo
[3] del Whit following οἱ καὶ μετὰ π. προν. πάμπλειστα
ἐπιτήδεια conj Mendelss

---

[1] H. seems not to know of the siege of Aquileia during the
Marcomannian Wars (c. 170); Amm. Marc. 29.6.1, Lucian,
Alex. 48, though the date is much disputed, Fitz, Hist. 15
(1966) 339–42. But there is no reason to doubt that since
that date the walls had fallen into disrepair.

fallen into ruins by then because, after the extension of
the Roman empire, the cities of Italy did not need
walls or weapons any more, and in place of war enjoyed complete peace and a share of Roman citizenship.[1] Now through necessity the Aquileians were 5
forced to repair the wall by reconstructing the ruins
and erecting towers and parapets. After very rapidly
fortifying the city wall, they shut the gates, and, with
the entire population posted night and day on the
ramparts, they fought off the attacks of the enemy.
Two consulars, selected by the senate, named Crispinus [2] and Menophilus,[3] were the military commanders with overall responsibility for the whole
operation. With great foresight they had imported 6
a large stock of provisions into the city to ensure a
plentiful supply, even if the siege proved to be a long
one; there was unlimited water, too, from the many

[2] Rutilius Pudens Crispinus; *Albo* 1147, Stein, *Hermes* 65
(1930) 228–34. He had served in a military and civil career
under Alexander (6.5.2n), since when he had been *cos. suff.*
and proconsul of Achaia; the date of the last two offices is
uncertain, but must have extended into the rule of Maximinus
(7.3.5n). Crispinus' election by the senate to the defence of
Aquileia is confirmed by an inscription, *AE* (1929) 158,
[*electus dux?*] *ex s(enatus) c(onsulto) bello Aquil(eiensi)*; he was
very probably a member of the vigintivirate, though this title
is not included on the inscription. After the death of M. he
was appointed to serve in Spain, where a resistance to the rule
of Gordian III was continued for at least a year.

[3] Tullius Menophilus—the name now made certain; *AE*
(1962) 265, *Albo* 1071, Bersanetti, *RFIC* 72/3 (1944/5) 197,
quoting earlier references. Nothing is known of his earlier
career except what H. says here—that he had been *cos. suff.*;
it seems probable that he was a member of the vigintivirate,
and after this he took command of the important province of
Moesia Inferior until 241.

φρεατιαίου· πολλὰ γὰρ τὰ ὀρύγματα ἐν τῇ πόλει·
ποταμός ¹ τε παραρρεῖ ² τὸ τεῖχος, ὁμοῦ παρέχων
τε προβολὴν τάφρου καὶ χορηγίαν ὕδατος.

3. τὰ μὲν οὖν ἐν τῇ πόλει ¹ οὕτω παρεσκεύαστο·
τῷ δὲ Μαξιμίνῳ ἐπειδὴ ἀπηγγέλη φρουρουμένη
καὶ κεκλεισμένη γενναίως ἡ πόλις, ἔδοξε πέμψαι
ἐν σχήματι πρεσβείας τοὺς κάτωθεν διαλεξομέ-
νους, εἰ ἄρα πείσαιεν αὐτοὺς ἀνοῖξαι τὰς πύλας.
ἦν δὲ ἐν τῷ στρατῷ χιλίαρχος ᾧ πατρὶς μὲν ἡ
Ἀκυληία ἦν, τέκνα τε καὶ γυνὴ οἰκεῖοί τε πάντες
2 ἔνδον ἀποκέκλειντο. τοῦτον οὖν ἔπεμψε σὺν
ἑτέροις ἑκατοντάρχαις, ἐλπίσας ῥᾷστα πείσειν ὡς
πολίτην. ἀφικόμενοι δὲ οἱ πρέσβεις ἔλεγον ὅτι
ἄρα κελεύει Μαξιμῖνος ὁ κοινὸς βασιλεὺς ὅπλα
μὲν αὐτοὺς καταθέσθαι ἐν εἰρήνῃ, φίλον δὲ ἀντὶ
πολεμίου δέχεσθαι, σπονδαῖς δὲ μᾶλλον καὶ
θυσίαις σχολάζειν ἢ φόνοις, μηδὲ περιορᾶν πατρίδα
μέλλουσαν ἄρδην καὶ ἐκ θεμελίων ἀπόλλυσθαι,
ἐνὸν αὐτοῖς τε σῴζεσθαι καὶ τὴν πατρίδα σῴζειν,

¹ ποταμός—πόλει om A
² from P cf. 8.5.7 περιρρεῖ φi

¹ The River Natiso, up which ships could sail to the city
itself; Strabo 5.1.8 (214), Pliny, *NH* 3.127, Mela 2.4.15.
² The siege of Aquileia is discussed by Calderini, *Aquileia
romana* (Publ. Univ. Cattol. Sac. Cuore (5), sc. stor. 10 (1930))
53–61. Although the defence of the city was chiefly in the
hands of the citizens, they also had the service of the *iuventutes*
(see 8.4.1n) and some soldiers; SHA, *Max. et Balb.* 12.2,
confirmed by an interesting inscription found at Aquileia,

wells dug in the city; while the river which flows by the walls provided a defensive moat as well as a water supply.[1]

3. This was the state of preparation in Aquileia when Maximinus was informed that the city was securely defended and enclosed.[2] He therefore decided to send some of his men, under the guise of a diplomatic mission, to enter into negotiations from the foot of the walls, in an effort to persuade the citizens to open the gates. In his army he had a tribune who was a native Aquileian, with a wife, children and entire family shut up inside the city.[3] He was sent with an escort of centurions in the hopes that, as a citizen, he would persuade the people without any difficulty. When the mission arrived, they announced that Maximinus, the emperor they both acknowledged, ordered them to lay down their weapons peacefully and to receive him as a friend rather than an enemy. They should be occupied, he said, in making libations and sacrifices rather than participating in bloodshed. But they were warned not to forget that their city was on the point of being totally annihilated, though it

dedicated to Pupinus and Balbinus and Gordian Caesar by two equestrian officers, *Fl(avius) Servilianus a mil(itiis) et Fl(avius) Adiutor praef(ectus) coh(ortis) Ulpiae Galatarum praeposit(i* or *-us) militum agentium in protensione Aquileia* (sic), the latter perhaps retired from service with his cohort in Palestine, or in Italy on special duties; Brusin, *Scavi di Aquileia* 73–6.

[3] That is, a member of the senatorial or equestrian order, and therefore from one of the aristocratic families of the city; see 8.2.2n for the importance of this. A number of inscriptions record officers from Aquileia who served in the northern legions, but none can be dated to this particular period or incident; e.g. *ILS* 2403, 2638 (both centurions).

διδόντος αὐτοῖς χρηστοῦ βασιλέως ἀμνηστίαν [1]
συγγνώμην τε τῶν ἁμαρτηθέντων· οὐ γὰρ αὐτοὺς
3 αἰτίους γεγενῆσθαι ἀλλ' ἄλλους. οἱ μὲν οὖν
πρέσβεις τοιαῦτά τινα κάτω παρεστῶτες ἐβόων,
ὡς ἐξάκουστα εἴη· ὁ δὲ πλεῖστος δῆμος τῷ τείχει
καὶ τοῖς πύργοις ἐφεστώς, πλὴν τῶν τὰ λοιπὰ
μέρη φρουρούντων, ἐπήκουεν ἡσυχάζων τῶν λεγο-
4 μένων. ὁ δὲ Κρισπῖνος φοβηθεὶς μή πως ἅτε
ὄχλος ταῖς ὑποσχέσεσιν ἀναπεισθείς, εἰρήνην τε
ἀντὶ πολέμου ἑλόμενος, ἀνοίξῃ τὰς πύλας, περιθέων
τὸ τεῖχος ἐδεῖτο καὶ ἐλιπάρει μένειν τε θαρραλέως
καὶ ἀντέχειν γενναίως, μηδὲ προδιδόναι τὴν πρὸς
τὴν σύγκλητον καὶ Ῥωμαίων [2] δῆμον πίστιν,
σωτῆρας δὲ καὶ προμάχους Ἰταλίας πάσης
ἀναγραφῆναι, μὴ πιστεύειν δὲ ὑποσχέσεσι τυράννου
ἐπιόρκου τε καὶ ἀπατεῶνος, μηδὲ χρηστοῖς λόγοις
δελεασθέντας ὀλέθρῳ προύπτῳ παραδοθῆναι, ἐνὸν
5 πιστεῦσαι πολέμου ἀμφιβόλῳ τύχῃ· πολλάκις γὰρ
καὶ ὀλίγοι πλειόνων περιεγένοντο, καὶ δοκοῦντες
ἀσθενέστεροι καθεῖλον τοὺς ἐν ὑπολήψει ἀνδρείας

---

[1] ἀσυλίαν A   [2] τὸν Ῥωμαίων A

[1] The Aquileians might have been in two minds with good
reason, since M. seems to have been exceptionally generous to
the city in the past, among other things carrying out extensive
repairs of the roads all round the city to the benefit of the
city's trade; on the milestones M. was called *Aquileiensium
restitutor et conditor* (*ILS* 487, *AE* (1953) 31) and on one

was in their power to save themselves and their home-
land by accepting the offer of an amnesty and a
pardon for their errors from a noble emperor. In any
case, he said, it was not the people of Aquileia who
were guilty, but others. As the emissaries stood at 3
the foot of the walls, shouting up these terms for all
to hear, most of the people (apart from those on other
guard duties) were on the walls and towers listening
in silence. Crispinus was afraid that perhaps, being 4
common people, they would be taken in by these
promises and open up the gates because they preferred peace to war.[1] So he dashed round the ramparts, begging them again and again to stay firm,
keep up their fine resistance and not betray their
loyalty to the senate and Roman people. " Instead," he urged them, " earn yourselves the title
of saviours and defenders of all Italy. Do not
believe the promises of a tyrant who breaks his
word and deceives people. Do not be enticed by
fine words into surrendering yourselves to certain
destruction when you can rely upon even chances in
war. Numerically smaller sides often defeat bigger 5
armies; supposedly weaker sides frequently overthrow those with a reputation for greater bravery.[2]

(nameless) he is said to have made other benefactions—*inter
plurima indulgentiar(um) suar(um) in Aquileiens(es) pro-
videntissim(us) princeps*, ILS 5860. Therefore M. could have
expected his offer of an amnesty to be accepted, and was all
the more angry when it was rejected (8.4.1). Calderini,
Aquileia rom. 59 f., assumes all this repair work was done by
M.'s troops (*tirones*) during the siege for propaganda purposes—
surely impossible in the short time.

[2] A universal commonplace; cf. Thuc. 5.102, Sall. *Cat.* 7.7,
Jug. 67.2, Livy 21.43, etc.

μείζονος· μηδ' ἐκπλήττεσθαι τῷ πλήθει τοῦ
στρατοῦ. "οἱ μὲν γὰρ ὑπὲρ ἄλλου μαχόμενοι
καὶ τῆς παρ' ἑτέρῳ [1] ἐσομένης εὐδαιμονίας, εἴπερ
γένοιτο, μετριάζουσιν ἐν τῷ προθύμῳ τῆς μάχης,
εἰδότες ὡς τῶν μὲν κινδύνων αὐτοὶ μεθέξουσι, τὰ
δὲ μέγιστα καὶ κορυφαῖα τῆς νίκης ἄλλος καρπώσε-
6 ται· τοῖς δὲ ὑπὲρ τῆς [2] πατρίδος μαχομένοις καὶ
παρὰ τῶν θεῶν ἐλπίδες κρείττους, ἐπειδὴ οὐ τὰ
ἄλλων λαβεῖν ἀλλὰ τὰ αὐτῶν σώζειν εὔχονται.
τό τε ἐς τὰς μάχας πρόθυμον οὐκ ἐξ ἄλλου
κελεύσεως ἀλλ' ἐξ οἰκείας ἀνάγκης ἔχουσιν, ἐπεὶ
καὶ τῆς νίκης πᾶς ὁ καρπὸς αὐτοῖς περιγίνεται."
7 τοιαῦτά τινα λέγων ὁ Κρισπῖνος καὶ πρὸς ἑκάστους
καὶ [3] κοινῇ, φύσει μὲν καὶ ἄλλως αἰδέσιμος ὤν,
ἔν τε τῇ Ῥωμαίων φωνῇ εὐπρόσφορος [4] ἐν λόγοις,
ἐπιεικῶς τε αὐτῶν προεστώς, ἔπεισε μένειν ἐν
τοῖς προκειμένοις, τούς τε πρέσβεις ἀπράκτους
ἀπιέναι ἐκέλευσεν. ἐλέγετο δὲ τῇ ἐνστάσει τοῦ
πολέμου ἐμμεμενηκέναι πολλῶν ἔνδον [5] ὄντων περὶ
θυτικήν τε καὶ ἡπατοσκοπίαν ἐμπείρων, τά τε
ἱερὰ αἴσια ἀπαγγελλόντων· μάλιστα γὰρ τῇ
8 σκέψει ταύτῃ πιστεύουσιν Ἰταλιῶται. καὶ χρησμοὶ
δέ τινες ⟨δι⟩εδίδοντο [6] ὡς δὴ τοῦ ἐπιχωρίου θεοῦ
νίκην ὑπισχνουμένου· Βέλεν δὲ καλοῦσι τοῦτον,

---

[1] ἑτέρων Val
[2] om Agl
[3] om φgl
[4] εὐπροφ. A

So do not be disconcerted by the size of their army. Those who are fighting for the benefit of another person, and have to depend on him for any future happiness that might occur, are only moderately enthusiastic for a fight, because they know that, though they will have their share of the danger, someone else will reap the greatest benefits from the victory. Those 6 who are fighting for their own land[1] can expect more from the gods, because they are asking not to appropriate others' property but to save their own. Their motivation to fight is not someone else's order, but their own essential interest, since the entire fruits of victory will be for them." Crispinus, who was a 7 man that won respect naturally, was a fluent Latin orator[2] and a fair commander to them. His speech to individuals and to the general gathering persuaded the Aquileians to stick to their resolution, and the emissaries were told to go away empty-handed. It is reported that Crispinus persevered in prosecuting the war because there were a lot of people inside the city who were experts in the art of reading omens and entrails, and who announced that the signs were auspicious. The Italians place particular faith in this kind of divination. There were also some oracles 8 spread around to the effect that the local god was promising the Aquileians victory. The god, whose

[1] The antithesis between patriots and mercenaries is another favourite rhetorical scheme. One has to remember that not only does H. write his speeches in rhetorical clichés but the speeches themselves were delivered in clichés.

[2] A curious remark to make about a senator of Italian birth; *Albo* 1147.

---

[5] om OP   [6] Hercher *Hermes* 12 (1877) 150

σέβουσί τε ὑπερφυῶς, Ἀπόλλωνα εἶναι ἐθέλοντες.
οὗ καὶ τὴν εἰκόνα ἔλεγόν τινες τῶν Μαξιμίνου
στρατιωτῶν φανῆναι πολλάκις ἐν ἀέρι ὑπὲρ τῆς
9 πόλεως μαχομένην. ὅπερ εἴτε ἀληθῶς ἐφαντάσθη
τισίν, ἢ καὶ βουλομένοις μὴ ἀσχημονεῖν τοσοῦτον
στρατὸν πρὸς ὄχλον δημοτῶν πολὺ ἐλάττονα μὴ
ἀντισχόντα, δοκεῖν δὲ ὑπὸ θεῶν ἀλλὰ μὴ ὑπὸ
ἀνθρώπων νενικῆσθαι, εἰπεῖν οὐκ ἔχω· τὸ δὲ παράδοξον τῆς ἀποβάσεως ποιεῖ πάντα πιστεῦσαι.

4. πλὴν τῶν πρέσβεων ἀπράκτων πρὸς Μαξιμῖνον ἐπανελθόντων, ὀργῇ καὶ θυμῷ χρώμενος
πλείονι μᾶλλον ἠπείγετο. ἐπεὶ δὲ ἐγένετο πρός
τινι ποταμῷ μεγίστῳ, ἀπέχοντι τῆς πόλεως
σημεῖα ἑκκαίδεκα,[1] τὸ ῥεῖθρον εὗρε διά τε μεγίστου
2 βάθους καὶ πλάτους φερόμενον· τῶν γὰρ ὑπερκει-

---

[1] duodecim P

---

[1] Belinus or Belenus; a large number of inscriptions from
Aquileia testify to the god's popularity and his identification
with Apollo; *CIL* V. 732–55, 8212, etc., *ILS* 4867–74.
Probably a Celtic deity, since he was worshipped widely in
Noricum and Gaul; cf. Wissowa, *Relig. u. Kultus d. Rom.* (2)
297; according to SHA, *Max.* 22.1, Menophilus used the oracles
of the god to prevent the citizens of Aquileia from capitulating.
The inscriptions are collected by Calderini, *Aquileia rom.* 95 ff.,
who also quotes (p. 61) two inscriptions to *Belenus defensor*
and *Nemesis*, which he attributes to the divine aid the city is
supposed to have received in 238, though there is nothing to
prove such a date.
[2] Cf. 2.9.3 for H.'s scepticism about oracles and portents.
Here he adopts the paradoxical attitude that the incident is

worship is extremely popular, is called Beles [1] and
identified with Apollo.   Some of Maximinus' soldiers
said that his image appeared frequently in the sky
fighting for the city.   I am not sure whether the god 9
really appeared to some of the men or whether it was
their imagination.   They were anxious to avoid the
disgrace of being unable to resist a crowd of townsfolk
that was numerically smaller, and wanted it to appear
that they had been defeated by gods and not men.
The unusualness of the incident makes anything
credible.[2]

4. When the emissaries returned to Maximinus
after their unsuccessful mission, he became more
passionately angry and pressed on faster.[3]   But when
he arrived at a river sixteen miles distant from the
city, he found the current deep and broad;[4]   the 2

too incredible not to be believed, somewhat like the principle
of *difficilior lectio*.

[3] This seems to indicate that, although the advance guard of
Pannonian troops had left Emona immediately (8.1.5), M. and
the rest of the army had remained in Emona until news of
Italian reaction was received.

[4] The River Sontius (modern Isonzo); the bridge, where the
town of Gorizia now stands is frequently mentioned by ancient
writers.   The road from Aquileia to this bridge, the *via
Gemina*, was one of those repaired by M.'s orders by the
recruits of the *iuventus*; *ILS* 487, *AE* (1953) 31, *viam quoque
Geminam a porta usque ad pontem per tirones iuvent(utis) novae
Italicae suae dilectus posterior(is), longi temporis labe cor-
ruptam, munivit ac restituit*; this means that M. had used and
perhaps tried to reorganize the *iuventutes* of Italy, gearing
them to the same military purposes served by the *iuventutes*
of the provinces; part of the resistance to M. in Italy and
Aquileia may therefore be due to an aristocratic reaction
against the loss of control and militarization (hard labour) of
these traditionally equestrian strongholds; cf. 7.4.3n.

μένων ὁρῶν τὰς δι' ὅλου τοῦ χειμῶνος παγείσας
χιόνας λύουσα ἡ τοῦ ἔτους ὥρα παμμεγέθη τὸν
χειμάρρουν εἰργάζετο. ἄπορος οὖν ἦν ἡ [1] διάβασις
τῷ στρατῷ· τὴν γὰρ γέφυραν, ἔργον μέγα καὶ
κάλλιστον ὑπὸ τῶν πάλαι βασιλέων γεγενημένον
ἐκ τετραπέδων λίθων, στυλίσι [2] κατ' ὀλίγον
αὐξανομέναις [3] ὑπειλημμένον, διηρήκεσαν καὶ κατα-
λελύκεσαν οἱ Ἀκυλήσιοι. οὔτε οὖν γεφύρας οὔσης
οὔτε νεῶν ὁ στρατὸς ἐν ἀφασίᾳ καθειστήκει.
3 Γερμανοὶ δέ τινες οὐκ εἰδότες τῶν Ἰταλιωτῶν [4]
ποταμῶν τὰ σφοδρὰ καὶ καταρρηγνύμενα ῥεύματα,
οἰόμενοι δὲ σχολαίτερα ἐπινήχεσθαι τοῖς [5] πεδίοις
ὥσπερ παρ' αὐτοῖς (διὸ καὶ πήγνυται ῥᾳδίως, μὴ
σφοδρῶς κινουμένου τοῦ ῥεύματος), ἐπεισπηδή-
σαντες ἅμα τοῖς ἵπποις διανήχεσθαι [5] εἰθισμένοις,
παρενεχθέντες ἀπώλοντο.
4 δύο μὲν οὖν ἢ τριῶν ἡμερῶν σκηνοποιησάμενος
ὁ Μαξιμῖνος, τάφρου τῷ στρατῷ [6] περιβληθείσης
μή τινες ἐπέλθοιεν, ἔμεινεν ἐπὶ τῇ καθ' ἑαυτὸν [7]
ὄχθῃ, σκεψόμενος [8] ὅπως τὸν ποταμὸν γεφυρώσῃ. [9]
ἐπεὶ δὲ ξύλων ἦν ἀπορία καὶ νεῶν, ἃς ἔδει ζευχθεί-
σας [9] γεφυρῶσαι τὸ ῥεῖθρον, ὑπέβαλόν [10] τινες
τῶν τεχνιτῶν πολλὰ εἶναι κενὰ οἰνοφόρα σκεύη

---

[1] om φgl
[2] Gedike *pilis* P πυλίσι φι A[1] (in mg) πυλῶσι A
[3] -οις O   [4] ἰταλιωτικῶν gl
[5] τοῖς—διανήχεσθαι om A
[6] στρατοπέδῳ conj Mendelss
[7] αὐτῶν Va αὐτῶν B
[8] from P (*deliberabundus*) σκεψάμενος Oi
[9] γεφυρώσῃ—ζευχ. om φ
[10] Steph ἐπέβαλόν φι ἐπεβάλλοντό A

season of the year was melting the accumulated frozen snow of winter in the mountains overshadowing the city and turning it into a rushing torrent.[1]   There was no way for the army to cross, because the Aquileians had dismantled and broken down the bridge—a very large beautiful structure which had been built by earlier emperors out of rectangular blocks of stone and supported on gradually tapering piers.   Without a bridge or boats the army was faced with a problem.   Some Germans were unfamiliar with the 3 swift, rushing currents of Italian rivers, which they thought flowed gently into the plain, as in their own country (it is this slow moving current, incidentally, that causes the rivers to freeze so easily).   These men plunged into the river with their horses, which were used to swimming, but were swept away and lost.

Maximinus pitched camp and dug a ditch around 4 his force to prevent attacks.   Then he paused for two or three days on his own bank to decide how to bridge the river.   There was a shortage of timber, and ships would be needed to be joined together to bridge the torrent.   Some of the engineers, however, made the suggestion to Maximinus that there were a lot of empty, rounded, wooden wine-barrels in the

[1] The melting of the winter snow confirms that the date of M.'s approach to Aquileia was about late April, and that the general chronological framework of the events must be earlier than most of the dates in the SHA *vitae*; cf. 7.5.7n.   If M. had not reached Emona by 10th April (8.1.5n), he could not have been at Aquileia, allowing for the delay at the river and bad supply lines (7.8.10n), before about 20th April.   This gave about three weeks for the senate to organize the resistance of the city, though Pupienus was still at Ravenna collecting forces when the siege was over (8.6.5).

περιφεροῦς ξύλου ἐν τοῖς ἐρήμοις ἀγροῖς, οἷς
ἐχρῶντο μὲν πρότερον οἱ κατοικοῦντες ἐς ὑπηρεσίαν
ἑαυτῶν, ὡς ¹ παραπέμπειν τὸν οἶνον ἀσφαλῶς τοῖς
δεομένοις· ἅπερ ὄντα κοῖλα δίκην νεῶν, ἀλλήλοις
συνδεθέντα ἐπινήξεσθαι μὲν ἔμελλεν ὥσπερ σκάφη,
μὴ παρενεχθήσεσθαι δὲ διά τε τοῦ δεσμοῦ τὸ
ἐπάλληλον, φρυγάνων τε ἄνωθεν ἐπιβληθέντων,
χοῦ ² τε τῆς γῆς μετρίως ἐς αὐτὰ σωρευθέντος
5 χειρὶ πολλῇ καὶ σπουδῇ. ἐφεστῶτος οὖν αὐτοῦ
διαβὰς ὁ στρατὸς ² ἐπὶ τὴν πόλιν ἐχώρει. τὰ
μὲν ³ οἰκοδομήματα τῶν προαστείων ἔρημα εὕρισκον,⁴ ἀμπέλους μέντοι ⁵ καὶ δένδρα πάντα ἐξέκο-
πτον,⁶ ἃ δὲ ἐνεπίμπρασαν, καὶ τὴν πρότερον τοῖς
χωρίοις ὑπάρχουσαν ὥραν κατῄσχυνον. δένδρων γὰρ
στοίχοις ἴσοις ἀμπέλων τε πρὸς ἀλλήλας δέσει ⁷
πανταχόθεν ἠρτημένων ⁸ ἐν ἑορτῆς σχήματι, στε-
φάνῳ ⁹ ἄν τις τὴν χώραν κεκοσμῆσθαι ἐτεκμήρατο·
ἅπερ πάντα ῥιζόθεν ἐκκόψας ὁ στρατὸς ἐπὶ τὰ
6 τείχη ἠπείγετο. κεκμηκότι δὲ αὐτῷ προσβαλεῖν
εὐθέως οὐκ ἔδοξε· μείναντες δὲ ἔξω τοξεύματος
καὶ διαιρεθέντες κατὰ λόχους καὶ φάλαγγας περὶ
πᾶν τὸ τεῖχος, ὡς ἑκάστοις κατὰ μέρος προστέ-
τακτο, μιᾶς ἡμέρας ἀναπαυσάμενοι, τοῦ λοιποῦ
εἴχοντο τῆς πολιορκίας.

μηχανάς τε οὖν παντοίας προσέφερον, καὶ

---

¹ Irmisch καὶ Οἱ καὶ ⟨εἰς τὸ⟩ etc. conj Steph Reisk
² χοῦ—στρατὸς corrupt Mendelss
³ μὲν ⟨οὖν⟩ conj Mendelss μέντοι ? Whit
⁴ εὑρίσκων A   ⁵ μὲν A   ⁶ ἐξέκοπτεν V
⁷ Steph δέσεις Οἱ   ⁸ ἠρτυμένων φα ἠρτημένας A
⁹ probably l Wolf στεφάνων φαg -οις A

deserted fields, which had previously been used by the local inhabitants for their own needs in transporting wine safely to the customer.[1] These barrels were rounded and hollow like vessels and, if tied together, were likely to float like ships. They would not be swept away, because they would be linked to each other after brushwood had been laid on top of them and soil piled up evenly on top of that by many willing helpers. Under Maximinus' supervision the 5 army got across and marched against the city of Aquileia. They found the houses in the outlying districts deserted, but they cut down and burned all the vines and trees, wrecking the natural beauty that once belonged to the countryside. The even rows of trees and the vines,[2] all linked and joined together, as in a festival procession, adorned the country like a crown, one might say. But all this was uprooted and cut down as the army advanced towards the city walls. It was decided that in their state of exhaus- 6 tion the army should not make an immediate assault; so they stayed out of bowshot range, and in their various sections and legionary divisions encircled the fortification, in the sector allocated to each. Then, after one day's rest they put the city under continuous siege.

After bringing up the complete range of siege

[1] Cf. 8.2.3n. Strabo says the barrels were larger than houses!

[2] Athen. *Deipn.* 3.82 C says that Aquileia was famous for apples; its olives were exported throughout the Danube basin; Strabo 5.1.8(214). The vines were grown in among the rows of trees, which then served as props for the tendrils.

τειχομαχοῦντες παντὶ σθένει οὐδὲν παρέλειπον
7 εἶδος πολιορκίας. πολλῶν δὲ καὶ σχεδὸν ἑκάστης
ἡμέρας γινομένων [1] προσβολῶν, καὶ παντὸς τοῦ
στρατοῦ ὥσπερ σαγηνεύσαντος [2] τὴν πόλιν, μετὰ
πολλῆς βίας καὶ προθύμου μάχης τειχομαχοῦντες
ἀντεῖχον οἱ Ἀκυλήσιοι, νεὼς μὲν καὶ οἰκίας
ἀποκλείσαντες, πανδημεὶ δὲ ἅμα παισὶ καὶ
γυναιξὶν ἄνωθεν ἐξ [3] ἐπάλξεών τε καὶ πύργων
ἀπομαχόμενοι. οὐδέ τις οὕτως [4] ἦν ἄχρηστος
ἡλικία ὡς μὴ μετέχειν τῆς ὑπὲρ τῆς πατρίδος
8 μάχης. τὰ μὲν γὰρ προάστεια, καὶ εἴ τι τῶν
πυλῶν ἔξωθεν ἦν, ὑπὸ τοῦ Μαξιμίνου στρατοῦ
κατέστραπτο, τῇ τε ξυλείᾳ τῶν οἰκοδομημάτων
ἐς τὰς μηχανὰς κατεκέχρηντο. ἐβιάζοντο δὲ τοῦ
τείχους κἂν μέρος τι καθελεῖν, ἵν᾽ ἐπεισελθὼν ὁ
στρατὸς πάντα τε διαρπάσῃ καὶ κατασκάψας τὴν
πόλιν μηλόβοτον καὶ [5] ἔρημον τὴν χώραν κατα-
λίπῃ. [6] οὐδὲ γὰρ ἄλλως [7] αὐτῷ τὴν ἐπὶ Ῥώμην
ὁδὸν εὐπρεπῆ καὶ ἔνδοξον ἔσεσθαι, μὴ τῆς πρώτης
ἐν Ἰταλίᾳ πόλεως ἀντιστάσης καθαιρεθείσης.
9 ὑποσχέσεσί τε οὖν δωρεῶν καὶ δεήσεσιν αὐτός τε
καὶ ὁ υἱὸς [8] αὐτοῦ, ὃν πεποιήκει Καίσαρα, περι-

---

[1] Bekk² γενομένων	[2] σαγηνεύοντος Jo	[3] om ABi
[4] ὄντως φ	[5] μηλόβ. καὶ φὶ καὶ πολιορκήσας A	
[6] καταλείπῃ φa	[7] ὅλλως B ὅλως V	[8] παῖς AJo

---

[1] The same simile is used by H. five times (2.13.5, 4.9.6, 4.15.4, 6.5.9).

[2] Conventional terms to describe total annihilation; Isoc. *Plataic.* 31 (302C), Appian *BC* 1.24 (Carthage) and perhaps the famous passage of Tac. *Agric.* 30.

[3] C. Julius Verus Maximus; *PIR²* J 620. The name Maximinus is incorrectly given in the SHA *vitae* and Victor,

engines, they assaulted the fortifications in full
strength, leaving no aspect of siege warfare untried.
Practically every day there was a number of attacks 7
launched, and the entire army kept the city encircled in a tight net.[1] But the people of Aquileia
fought back vigorously and enthusiastically from
the walls; temples and houses were shut, and the
entire population, including women and children,
joined in the resistance from the battlements and
turrets up on the wall. No one was too young or old
to play a useful part in the defence of his country.
Outlying districts and parts of the city outside the 8
walls had been levelled by Maximinus' army and
timber taken from buildings was used for the siege
engines. A strenuous attempt was made to break
down at least a section of the wall so that the army
could get inside and plunder the whole place.
Then, when they had devastated the city, they would
turn the whole region into deserted gazing land.[2] For
if they did not demolish this, the first city in Italy to
oppose them, they could not decently make their
triumphant march on Rome. So Maximinus and 9
his son (whom he had made Caesar) [3] rode round the

Caes. 25.2. He was made Caesar officially in 236 (7.1.3n),
though it seems possible that this was the date of senatorial
confirmation of the title that had been given in 235 when M.
won his second imperial salutation (7.2.9n). There is one
instance of the title of Augustus for him alone on a bronze
coin of Amisus (almost certainly incorrect; Babelon-Reinach,
Monnaies grec. d'Asie 1.92, no. 130d), though he is frequently,
according to current, occasional practice, called Augustus
together with his father—which does not mean he had
received the title; *BMC* VI. 95, 242, nos. 229–31, *ILS* 490;
the same applied to the title of *imperator*, though he did
receive the other honorifics of his father.

θέοντες ἵπποις ἐποχούμενοι, τὸν στρατὸν ἀνέπειθον
λιπαροῦντες ἐς προθυμίαν τε ἐγείροντες. οἱ δὲ
Ἀκυλήσιοι λίθοις τε ἔβαλλον ἄνωθεν, καὶ κιρνῶντες
θείῳ τε καὶ ἀσφάλτῳ πίσσαν ἔλαιόν τε,[1] κοίλοις
σκεύεσιν ἐμβαλόντες λαβὰς ἐπιμήκεις ἔχουσι καὶ
πυρώσαντες, ἅμα τῷ προσπελάζειν τοῖς τείχεσι
τὸν στρατὸν κατεσκεδάννυσαν, καταχέοντες ὄμβρου
10 δίκην ὁμοθυμαδόν. φερομένη δὲ ἡ πίσσα σὺν οἷς
προείρηται, δυομένη τε διὰ τῶν γεγυμνωμένων
μερῶν τοῦ σώματος, ἐς πᾶν ἐχεῖτο, ὥστε τοὺς
θώρακας αὐτοὺς πεπυρωμένους ἀπορρίπτειν καὶ
τὰ λοιπὰ ὅπλα, ὧν ὁ σίδηρος ἐθερμαίνετο, τά τε
ἐκ βυρσῶν τε καὶ ξύλων ἐφλέγετο καὶ συνείλκετο.
ἦν γοῦν ἰδεῖν γεγυμνωμένους[2] τοὺς στρατιώτας
αὐτοὺς ὑφ’[3] ἑαυτῶν, καὶ σκύλων ὄψιν ὅπλα
παρεῖχεν ἐρριμμένα, σοφίᾳ τέχνης ἀλλ’ οὐκ ἀνδρείᾳ
11 μάχης περιῃρημένα. ἔκ τε τοῦ τοιούτου πάμπλειστον πλῆθος τοῦ στρατοῦ τάς τε ὄψεις[4]
ἐπηροῦντο[5] καὶ τὸ πρόσωπον ἠκρωτηριάζετο,
τὰς χεῖρας[4] καὶ εἴ τι γυμνὸν ἦν τοῦ σώματος.
ἀλλὰ μὴν καὶ ταῖς μηχαναῖς προσαγομέναις δᾷδας
ἐπέβαλλον[6] ὁμοίως πίσσῃ καὶ ῥητίνῃ[7] δεδευμένας
ἐπί τε τῷ ἄκρῳ βελῶν ἀκίδας ἐχούσας· αἱ
ἀναφθεῖσαι φερόμεναι, ἐμπαγεῖσαι ταῖς μηχαναῖς
καὶ προσπεφυκυῖαι ῥᾳδίως αὐτὰς κατέφλεγον.

---

[1] Gedike Stroth πίτταν ἐλόντες Οἱ καὶ πίσσῃ καὶ ἐλαίῳ Jo
[2] old correction Mendelss γυμνωμένους φα γυμνουμένους Agl
[3] ἐφ’ a followed by ἑαυτοῖς A

army on horseback making promises of rewards and issuing appeals, trying constantly to encourage the soldiers and keep up their enthusiasm. The Aquileians fired down rocks from the walls and prepared a concoction of pitch and oil mixed with sulphur and bitumen, which they poured into empty jars with long handles. As soon as the army approached the walls, they set fire to the mixture and poured it out, showering it all together like rain on the besiegers. The pitch mixed with the other ingredients (see 10 above), when poured out, penetrated through the exposed parts of the body and spread all over the person. Men tore off their burning breast-plates and other armour because the metal was getting red-hot, and the leather and wooden parts were burning and shrinking. And so one had the spectacle of soldiers who had actually stripped themselves, and of weapons that had been abandoned, looking like spoils of war— all this achieved not by military prowess, but by scientific skill. As a result of this incident a great 11 number of soldiers lost their eyesight; or their faces and hands and any other exposed parts of their bodies were disfigured. The townsfolk also fired down torches soaked in pitch and resin, which were tipped with arrow heads, against the siege machines being brought up to the walls. After being lighted, these arrows were fired off and embedded themselves fast in the machines, thereby sending them up in flames without any difficulty.

---

⁴ ὄψεις—τὰς χεῖρας om A corrupt passage cf. ὥστε . . . διαφθείρεσθαι τά τε πρόσωπα καὶ τὰς χεῖρας ἀκροτηριαζομένους (sic) Jo   ⁵ ἐπηροῦτο Steph   ⁶ ἐπέβαλον φgl   ⁷ ῥιτίνη φi

5. τῶν μὲν οὖν πρώτων ἡμερῶν ἀντίπαλός πως καὶ ἰσόρροπος ἔμενεν ἡ τύχη τῆς μάχης· χρόνου δὲ ἐγγενομένου [1] ὅ τε στρατὸς τοῦ Μαξιμίνου ὀκνηρὸς ἐγίνετο,[2] καὶ πταίων τῆς ἐλπίδος ἀθύμως διέκειτο· οὓς γὰρ ἠλπίκεσαν μηδεμίαν ὑπομενεῖν προσβολήν, τούτους εὕρισκον οὐκ ἀντέχοντας 2 μόνον ἀλλὰ καὶ ἀνθεστῶτας. οἱ δὲ Ἀκυλήσιοι ἐπερρώννυντό τε καὶ προθυμίας πάσης ἐνεπίμπλαντο, τῇ τε συνεχείᾳ τῆς μάχης πεῖραν καὶ θάρσος ὁμοῦ προσλαμβάνοντες κατεφρόνουν τῶν στρατιωτῶν, ὡς καὶ ἀποσκώπτειν ἐς αὑτούς, ἐνυβρίζειν τε τῷ Μαξιμίνῳ περινοστοῦντι, ἔς τε αὐτὸν καὶ τὸν παῖδα ἀπορρίπτειν δυσφήμους καὶ αἰσχρὰς βλασφημίας, ἐφ᾽ αἷς ἐκεῖνος κε 3 νούμενος ὀργῆς μᾶλλον ἐνεπίμπλατο. χρῆσθαι δὲ κατὰ τῶν πολεμίων οὐ δυνάμενος, ἐκόλαζε τοὺς πλείστους τῶν ἡγουμένων τῶν ἰδίων στρατιωτῶν [3] ὡς ἀνάνδρως καὶ ῥᾳθύμως προσφερομένους τῇ τειχομαχίᾳ. ὅθεν αὐτῷ περιεγένετο πρὸς μὲν τῶν οἰκείων μῖσός τε καὶ ὀργή, παρὰ δὲ τῶν ἀντιπάλων πλείων ἡ καταφρόνησις.

συνέβαινε δὲ τοῖς Ἀκυλησίοις πάντα ὑπάρχειν ἔκπλεα καὶ ἐπιτηδείων ἀφθονίαν, ἐκ πολλῆς παρασκευῆς ἐς τὴν πόλιν πάντων σεσωρευμένων ὅσα ἦν ἀνθρώποις καὶ κτήνεσιν ἐς τροφὰς καὶ ποτὰ ἐπιτήδεια· ὁ δὲ στρατὸς πάντων ⟨ἦν⟩ [4] ἐν σπάνει, τῶν τε καρποφόρων δένδρων ἐκκεκομ 4 μένων καὶ τῆς γῆς ὑπ᾽ αὐτοῦ δεδῃωμένης. μέ

---

[1] Mendelss ἐγγινομένου Oi γενομένου Jo
[2] ἐγένετο φJo   [3] στρατῶν   [4] Wolf ὑπῆρχεν Jo

5. For the first few days each side had a fairly evenly divided share of the luck of the battle. But, as time went on, Maximinus' army became apathetic and dejected because its hopes were disappointed. The people whom they had not expected to stand up to a single attack were now found to be not only holding out but even fighting back. By contrast, the 2 inhabitants of Aquileia were growing stronger and becoming full of enthusiasm.[1] They were gaining experience and confidence from the continuous fighting, and began to become contemptuous of the army, shouting jibes at them and making fun of Maximinus as he rode around, by calling out terrible, foul insults against him and his son. Being devoid of all resources, Maximinus grew more and more angry, but could do nothing against the enemy. So he punished a great number of commanders on 3 his own side for cowardly lack of effort in their conduct of the siege. The result was that hatred and anger began to grow among his own soldiers and his enemies grew still more contemptuous.

It turned out that the people of Aquileia had no shortage of anything, but were well supplied because of their careful preparation in building up stocks in the city of all the provisions needed to feed and water men and beasts. The army, on the other hand, was suffering from a shortage of everything because the fruit trees had been cut down and the countryside devastated by themselves. Some of them were 4

[1] On three occasions the SHA *vitae* repeat the colourful but conventional story that the women of Aquileia supplied their hair as bow strings, a tale that derived from Dexippus; *Max. et Balb.* 16.5; cf. *ibid.* 11.3, *Max.* 33.1.

νοντες δὲ ὑπὸ σκηναῖς αὐτοσχεδίοις, οἱ δὲ πλεῖστοι
ὑπὸ γυμνῷ τῷ ἀέρι, ὄμβρων τε καὶ ἡλίου ἠνείχοντο,
λιμῷ τε διεφθείροντο, μηδὲ ἐπεισάκτου τροφῆς
αὐτοῖς τε καὶ ὑποζυγίοις εἰσκομιζομένης. πανταχόθεν γὰρ τὰς τῆς Ἰταλίας ὁδοὺς παραφράξαντες
ἦσαν οἱ Ῥωμαῖοι τειχίων τε ἐγέρσεσι καὶ πυλίδων
5 ἀσκήσεσιν. ἄνδρας τε ὑπατευκότας ἐξέπεμψεν
ἡ σύγκλητος σὺν ἐπιλέκτοις καὶ λογάσιν ἀπ᾽
Ἰταλίας πάσης ἀνδράσιν, ἵν᾽ αἰγιαλοί τε πάντες
καὶ λιμένες φρουρῶνται καὶ μηδενὶ [1] ἔκπλους
συγχωρῆται, ὡς ἄπυστα [2] καὶ ἄγνωστα εἶναι
Μαξιμίνῳ τά ἐν Ῥώμῃ πραττόμενα· αἵ τε
λεωφόροι ὁδοὶ καὶ ἀτραποὶ πᾶσαι ἐφυλάττοντο
ὡς μηδένα διαβαίνειν. συνέβαινε δὲ [3] τὸν στρατὸν
δοκοῦντα πολιορκεῖν αὐτὸν πολιορκεῖσθαι, ἐπεὶ
μήτε τὴν Ἀκυληίαν ἑλεῖν ἐδύνατο, μήτε ἀποστὰς
ἐκεῖθεν ἐπὶ τὴν Ῥώμην χωρῆσαι διά τε νηῶν καὶ
ὀχημάτων ἀπορίαν· ἅπαντα γὰρ προκατείληπτο
6 καὶ συνεκέκλειστο. φῆμαι δὲ μείζους ἐξ ὑποψίας [4]
ἀληθείας ⟨δι⟩εδίδοντο,[5] ὅτι πᾶς ὁ δῆμος ὁ
Ῥωμαίων ἐν ὅπλοις εἴη, Ἰταλία τε πᾶσα συμπεπ-
νεύκοι, πάντα τε [6] ἔθνη Ἰλλυρικὰ καὶ βάρβαρα τά

---

[1] μηδὲν φ μηδεὶς A   [2] ἄπιστα O
[3] δὲ καὶ Jo δὴ P (ita)   [4] ἐξ ὑποψίας μείζους Leisn Stav
[5] Sylb ἐδίδοντο Oi
[6] old correction Mendelss πάντα τὰ φι καὶ πάντα τὰ A

---

[1] Some of the delegates were perhaps members of the
vigintivirate (7.10.3n), who, according to the SHA, had been

under improvised shelters, but the majority were out
in the open air, enduring the rigours of rain and sun,
and dying of hunger because of the breakdown in
supplies of even the imported food for themselves
and the pack animals. The Romans had blockaded
roads all over Italy by constructing barriers and
operating gate controls. The senate sent ex-consuls 5
accompanied by selected men of distinction [1] from all
over Italy, to ensure a guard over the coast and the
ports and allow no one to sail out.[2] Maximinus was
therefore without news or information of developments in Rome. All public highways and footpaths
were guarded to prevent anyone passing through.
Thus, the army supposedly mounting a siege was
actually being besieged,[3] since it could not capture
Aquileia, and yet could not leave and make for Rome
without any ships or wagons. All of them had been
previously commandeered and blocked. Exaggerated 6
rumours were spread, because there was a hint of
truth, when it was said that the entire Roman people
were up in arms and had been joined by the whole of

allocated sectors of Italy (7.12.1n); but SHA, *Max.* 23.3, says
that the emissaries were *praetorios et quaestorios*, which
follows what H. says here.

[2] Some of the *vigintiviri* were Italian and exercised patronage
among the Italian communities; e.g. Rufinianus had been
curator of the port of Puteoli sometime earlier (*c.* 228), *ILS*
1186; Crispinus had estates at Ostia (*CIL* XV. 2192), and
Pupienus himself was holding the naval base of Ravenna
(8.6.5).

[3] A rhetorical commonplace; Thuc. 4.29.2, 7.11.4, Florus
4.2.27, etc. (see Irmisch, *Herod. hist. ad loc.*); although
frequently quoted to prove H.'s imitation of Thucydides,
Stein, *Dexip. et Herod.* 139, rightly says, *magis exercitationes
rhetorum olent quam Thucydidis imitationem.*

HERODIAN

τε ὑπ᾽ ἀνατολαῖς καὶ μεσημβρίαις στρατὸν ἀγείρει,[1]
μιᾷ τε γνώμῃ καὶ ψυχῇ ὁμοίως Μαξιμῖνος
μεμίσηται. ὅθεν ἐν ἀπογνώσει ἦσαν καὶ πάντων
σπάνει οἱ στρατιῶται, σχεδὸν καὶ ὕδατος αὐτοῦ.
7 ὃ γὰρ ἦν μόνον ἐκ τοῦ παραρρέοντος ποταμοῦ
ποτόν, αἵματι καὶ φόνοις μεμιασμένον ἐπίνετο· οἵ
τε γὰρ Ἀκυλήσιοι τοὺς ἐν τῇ πόλει τελευτῶντας
οὐκ ἔχοντες ὅπως θάψωσιν, ἐς τὸν ποταμὸν
ἀπερρίπτουν, οἵ τε ἐν τῷ στρατῷ φονευόμενοι ἢ
διαφθειρόμενοι νόσῳ ἐδίδοντο τῷ ῥεύματι, οὐκ
ἐχόντων αὐτῶν τὰ πρὸς ταφὰς [2] ἐπιτήδεια.
8   παντοδαπῆς οὖν ἀπορίας καὶ δυσθυμίας τὸν
στρατὸν κατεχούσης, αἰφνιδίως ἀναπαυομένου τοῦ
Μαξιμίνου ἐν τῇ σκηνῇ, καὶ τῆς ἡμέρας ἐκείνης
ἐν ἀνέσει τοῦ πολέμου οὔσης, τῶν τε πλείστων ἐς
τὰς σκηνὰς καὶ τὰ ἐγκεχειρισμένα τῆς φρουρᾶς
χωρία ἀνακεχωρηκότων, ἔδοξε τοῖς στρατιώταις
οἳ πρὸς τῇ Ῥωμαίων πόλει στρατόπεδον εἶχον
ὑπὸ τὸ καλούμενον ὄρος Ἀλβανόν, ἔνθα παῖδας
καὶ γυναῖκας καταλελοίπεσαν, φονεῦσαι τὸν Μα-

[1] ἀγείροι al
[2] g² (in mg) τροφὰς φι ταφὴν A inopia ciborum confecti P

[1] Note the senatorial delegate sent to Viminacium to
persuade the troops of Moesia Inferior to desert M., 7.12.1n.
[2] The legio II Parthica. Evidence of the legion at Aquileia
is provided by a soldier who died and is commemorated on an
inscription, probably dating from this time; ILS 2361,
Calderini, op. cit. 206.
[3] One of the long-range effects of permitting soldiers to

Italy. Or, that the Illyrians[1] and the barbarian
nations in the East and South were raising an army.
Everyone, it was said, was animated by a single
thought—their hatred of Maximinus. As a result of
Roman action the soldiers were in a desperate position, short of everything. They were practically
running out of water even, since their only supply of 7
drinking water, which came from the nearby river,
was being used while contaminated with blood and
dead bodies. The Aquileians were throwing those
who had died inside the city out into the river,
because they had no way of burying them. Members
of the army that were killed or died from sickness
were thrown into the river, too, because the troops
lacked the wherewithal for funerals.

These were the prevailing conditions of extreme 8
privation and low morale, when a sudden change
occurred. Maximinus was resting in his quarters,
and there was a break in the fighting that day. Most
of the soldiers, too, had retired to their shelters or to
the guard post allotted to their charge. Suddenly
the soldiers from the camp on Mount Alba near
Rome [2] (where they had left behind wives and children)[3] decided to murder Maximinus, so that they

marry during their service was the pressures that could be
brought upon them by their wives and families (3.8.5n); Durry
alleges that praetorians did not share this privilege of legal
conubium, but offers no dated evidence, and in any case cohabitation was widespread; *Cohortes prét.* 294 ff. In this
case, concerning the Parthian legion, one cannot doubt that
the families of the soldiers had been under pressure from the
recent rioting and anti-Maximinus feeling in Rome; cf.
Whittaker, *Hist.* 13 (1964) 364n, for other examples of a
similar kind; cf. 7.3.6n.

ξιμῖνον, ὡς παύσαιντο μὲν χρονίου καὶ ἀπεράντου
πολιορκίας,[1] μηκέτι δὲ πορθοῖεν Ἰταλίαν ὑπὲρ
9 τυράννου [1] κατεγνωσμένου καὶ μεμισημένου. τολ-
μήσαντες οὖν ἐπίασι τῇ σκηνῇ αὐτοῦ περὶ μέσην
ἡμέραν, συναραμένων δὲ αὐτοῖς καὶ τῶν φρουρούντων δορυφόρων τάς τε εἰκόνας ἐκ τῶν σημείων
κατασπῶσι, καὶ αὐτὸν σὺν τῷ παιδὶ προελθόντα
τῆς σκηνῆς, ὡς δὴ ἄρα διαλέξαιτο αὐτοῖς, οὐκ
ἀνασχόμενοι ἀναιροῦσι. φονεύουσι δὲ καὶ τὸν
ἔπαρχον [2] τοῦ στρατοῦ [3] πάντας τε τοὺς ἐκείνῳ
θυμήρεις φίλους· ῥίψαντές τε τὰ σώματα τοῖς
βουλομένοις ἐνυβρίζειν καὶ πατεῖν εἴασαν κυσί τε
καὶ ὄρνισι βοράν. τοῦ δὲ Μαξιμίνου καὶ τοῦ
παιδὸς τὰς κεφαλὰς ἐς τὴν Ῥώμην ἔπεμψαν.

τοιούτῳ μὲν δὴ τέλει ὁ [4] Μαξιμῖνος καὶ ὁ παῖς
αὐτοῦ ἐχρήσαντο,[5] δίκας πονηρᾶς ἀρχῆς ὑποσχόν-
τες· 6. ὁ δὲ στρατὸς πᾶς ὡς ἐπύθετο τὰ γενόμενα,
ἔν τε ἀφασίᾳ ἦσαν καὶ οὐ πάνυ τι [6] τῷ πραχθέντι

---

[1] πολιορκίας—τυράννου om φ
[2] ἐπάρχοντα Jo
[3] στρατοπέδου conj Mendelss
[4] om Oag
[5] ἐχρήσαντο βασιλεύσαντες ἔτη γ΄ add Jo
[6] τοι AV

---

[1] The praetorians joined the Parthian legion in the revolt;
only they carried the *imagines* of the emperor on their
standards; Durry, *Cohortes prét.* 206, 391. The rapprochment

284

could abandon the long, interminable siege, and stop laying waste Italy for the benefit of a tyrant who was condemned and hated. With great daring the 9 men went to Maximinus' tent about mid-day, and tore down his portrait from the standards with the assistance of the bodyguards.[1] When Maximinus and his son came out of their hut to try and negotiate, the soldiers killed them without listening. The military prefect [2] was also killed, and all Maximinus' close advisers. Their bodies were thrown out for anyone to desecrate and trample on, before being left to be torn to pieces by dogs and birds. The heads of Maximinus and his son were sent to Rome.

And so Maximinus and his son died, punished for their disgraceful rule.[3] 6. When the whole army heard the news, they were nonplussed and by no means all pleased at the event. This particularly

between praetorians and Parthian legion may have been due in some cases to close relatives serving in each organization; cf. *CIL* VI. 2579, 3277 for brothers in the two different troops.

[2] Unknown. The name Anolinus (Anullinus?) is only a gloss in the text of the *vita Max.*; cf. Passerini, *Coorti pret.* 332, Dessau, *Hermes* 29 (1894) 412. According to SHA, *Max.* 32.4–5, Dexippus related that the prefect and M.'s son were killed before M.'s eyes; other historians declared that M. himself committed suicide. But as the *vita* says earlier (31.4), there were a number of fictitious tales about the siege of Aquileia.

[3] The date cannot be fixed; calculations based on the inadequate evidence available are uncontrolled. Evidently the siege of Aquileia was not long because: (*a*) the supply line of the besiegers broke down rapidly, though there was plenty of food left in the city; (*b*) Maximus had still not left Ravenna, where he was mustering a force. I am inclined therefore to put the siege at about one month long, ending about late May (cf. 8.4.2n).

πάντες ἠρέσκοντο, καὶ μάλιστά γε οἱ Παίονες
καὶ ὅσοι βάρβαροι Θρᾷκες, οἳ καὶ τὴν ἀρχὴν
αὐτῷ ἐγκεχειρίκεσαν. πλὴν τοῦ ἔργου ἅπαξ
γεγονότος ἄκοντες μέν, ἔφερον δέ· ἀνάγκη τε ἦν
συνήδεσθαι τοῖς πραχθεῖσιν ὑποκρινομένοις.¹
2 καταθέμενοί τε τὰ ὅπλα ἐν εἰρηνικῷ σχήματι
προσῄεσαν τοῖς τείχεσι τοῖς Ἀκυλησίων, ἀγγέλλοντες τὸν φόνον τοῦ Μαξιμίνου· τὰς δὲ πύλας
ἀνοίγειν ἠξίουν, δέχεσθαι τε ² φίλους τοὺς χθὲς ³
ἐχθρούς. οἱ δὲ τῶν Ἀκυλησίων στρατηγοὶ τὰς
μὲν πύλας ἀνοῖξαι οὐκ ἐπέτρεψαν, προθέντες δὲ
τὰς εἰκόνας Μαξίμου καὶ Βαλβίνου Γορδιανοῦ τε
Καίσαρος στεφάνοις καὶ δάφναις κεκοσμημένας
αὐτοί τε εὐφήμουν,⁴ καὶ τοὺς στρατιώτας ἠξίουν
γνωρίσαι καὶ ἀνειπεῖν εὐφημῆσαί τε τοὺς ὑπὸ
Ῥωμαίων καὶ συγκλήτου ἀναδειχθέντας αὐτοκρά-
3 τορας. Γορδιανοὺς δὲ ἔλεγον ἐκείνους ἐς οὐρανὸν
καὶ θεὸν ⁵ ἀνακεχωρηκέναι. προύθεσάν τε ὑπὲρ
τῶν τειχῶν ἀγοράν, ὤνιον παρέχοντες πάντων ⁶
τῶν ἐπιτηδείων ⁶ τροφῶν τε παντοδαπῶν καὶ
ποτῶν ἀφθονίαν, ἐσθῆτός τε καὶ ὑποδημάτων, καὶ
ὅσα ἐδύνατο παρέχειν ἐς χρῆσιν ἀνθρώποις πόλις
4 εὐδαιμονοῦσα καὶ ἀκμάζουσα. ὅθεν καὶ μᾶλλον
ἐξεπλάγη ὁ στρατός, συνεὶς ὅτι τοῖς μὲν πάντα
αὐτάρκη ἦν, εἰ καὶ ἐπὶ πλέον πολιορκοῖντο, αὐτοὶ
δὲ ἐν σπάνει πάντων τῶν ἐπιτηδείων θᾶττον ⁷
⟨ἂν⟩ διεφθάρησαν ἢ εἷλον πάντα ἔχουσαν πόλιν.

¹ -μένους Stav   ² ὡς A
³ πρὶν OP   ⁴ ἠξίουν O
⁵ θεοὺς conj Steph

applied to the Pannonians and barbarian Thracians, [1] who had been responsible for Maximinus' elevation to power. But, now that the deed was done, they accepted it, however unwillingly. They had to pretend that they were pleased about what had happened. After putting aside their weapons, they 2 approached the walls of Aquileia, dressed as in peacetime, and told the inhabitants of Maximinus' murder, requesting them to open the gates and admit their former enemies as friends. The Aquileian commanders, however, refused to allow the gates to be opened. Instead they brought out pictures of Maximus, Balbinus and Gordian Caesar wreathed in crowns of laurel, which they cheered. Then they demanded that the soldiers too should acknowledge and recognize by acclaim the emperors elected by the senate and Roman people. The two older Gordians, 3 they declared, had gone to join the gods in heaven. The people then set up a market on the ramparts, and offered to sell any amount of every commodity, all kinds of food and drink, clothes and shoes—all the things a prosperous, flourishing city might offer to satisfy peoples wants. The troops were even more 4 astonished at this sight, because they realized that the Aquileians had plenty of supplies left to withstand a longer siege, while they themselves, suffering as they were from a shortage of all supplies, would

---

[1] " Barbarian " is used almost as a conventional epithet for Thracians, though they were Roman citizens; cf. 6.8.1n.

---

[6] πάντων—ἐπιτηδείων del Bekk[2]
[7] om O ⟨ἄν⟩ Bekk[2]

HERODIAN

ὁ δὲ στρατὸς ἔμενε περὶ [1] τοῖς τείχεσιν, ἔχων τὰ χρειώδη, ἅπερ ἀπὸ τῶν τειχῶν ἐλάμβανον, ὅσα ἕκαστος ἐβούλετο· διελέγοντό τε [2] ἀλλήλοις. καὶ ἦν εἰρήνης μὲν καὶ φιλίας διάθεσις, σχῆμα δὲ ἔτι πολιορκίας, τῶν τειχῶν κεκλεισμένων καὶ τοῦ στρατοῦ περὶ αὐτὰ διαιτωμένου.

5 τὰ μὲν οὖν κατὰ τὴν ᾿Ακυληίαν ἐν τούτοις ἦν· οἱ δ᾿ ἱππεῖς οἱ τὴν Μαξιμίνου κεφαλὴν κομίζοντες ἀπὸ τῆς ᾿Ακυληίας ὡδοιπόρησάν τε [3] μετὰ πάσης ἐπείξεως, καὶ [4] ἐπιφοιτῶσιν αὐτοῖς τὰς λοιπὰς πόλεις ⟨αἱ⟩ [5] πύλαι ἀνεῴγνυτο,[6] καὶ δαφνηφοροῦντες αὐτοὺς οἱ δῆμοι ὑπεδέχοντο. ὡς δὲ διέπλευσαν τάς τε λίμνας καὶ τὰ [7] τενάγη [μεταξὺ ᾿Αλτίνου [8] καὶ ῾Ραβέννης] [9] περιέτυχον Μαξίμῳ αὐτοκράτορι διατρίβοντι ἐν ῾Ραβέννῃ, ἔνθα τούς τε ἀπὸ ῾Ρώμης ἐπιλέκτους καὶ τοὺς ἀπὸ τῆς ᾿Ιταλίας

6 λογάδας ἤθροιζεν. ἀφῖκτο δὲ αὐτῷ καὶ Γερμανῶν

---

[1] παρὰ a   [2] τοῦ gl (but τε g[2] in mg)
[3] Stroth ὁδοιπορήσαντες μετὰ πάσης ἐπείξεως i (though Stroth follows order μ. π. ἐπ. ὁδοιπορήσαντες O)
[4] οἷς a   [5] Bekk   [6] ἀνοίγν.φi
[7] om i τενάγη ⟨τὰ⟩ Reisk   [8] ἀκτίνου al
[9] del Whit

---

[1] The omission of the relative article (supplied by Reisk) and the repetition of the name of Ravenna indicate that this is a glossator's marginal explanation that has crept into the text; H.'s geography is rarely so exact. The marsh and lagoon are the present-day Laguna Veneta and the Valli di Comacchio. The horsemen embarked at Altinum near Venice and went by waterways to Ravenna; cf. Strabo 5.1.7 (214), Tac. *H.* 3.6, *Itin. Ant.* pp. 126, 128, 244, 281. The same waterway is referred to again in 8.7.1 as the *septem maria*; cf. Pliny, *NH* 3.119.

have died before they captured this well-stocked
city. The army remained in its position around the
city walls, with all their individual needs supplied by
their purchases from up on the walls. The two sides
communicated with each other in conditions of peace
and friendship, even though it looked like a siege
still because the defences were kept shut and the
army was all around them.

While this situation existed in Aquileia, the horse- 5
men bringing Maximinus' head were travelling as
fast as they could from the city. As they reached
other cities on their way, gates were opened, and the
people welcomed them waving laurel branches.
After they had been ferried across the marshes and
lagoons [separating Altinum from Ravenna],[1] they
found the emperor Maximus waiting in Ravenna,
where he was mustering his special units from Rome
and Italy. A number of German allies[2] joined him 6

[2] The German *vexillationes* were probably part of the Rhine
army auxiliaries, who had served under Pupienus when he
was governor of one of the German provinces and were later
used by him as a counterweight to the praetorians; 8.7.8,
8.8.2, 8.8.5, 8.8.7. They were not the same as Caracalla's
specially recruited *equites extraordinarii* (4.13.6n). If the
troop had come in response to the call for recruits soon after
the accession of Pupienus and Balbinus in early April
(7.12.1), they could not have arrived at Ravenna before mid-
May (ten days for fast post from Rome to Germany, thirty days
minimum for rapid light-armed troop movements from
Germany to Ravenna); no doubt this was why Pupienus was
delaying at Ravenna. Cf. Domaszewski, *RhM* 57 (1902)
509–10, on the German troops. SHA, *Max.* 24.6, says incorrectly that Pupienus dismissed the Germans as soon as he
received news of M.'s death; but they are probably confused
with the German auxiliaries of M.'s army (8.1.3n); Hohl,
Maximini duo 37.

289

οὐκ ὀλίγη συμμαχία, πεμφθεῖσα ὑπ' αὐτῶν κατ'
εὔνοιαν ἣν εἶχον πρὸς αὐτὸν ἄνωθεν, ἐξ οὗπερ ἦν
αὐτῶν ἐπιμελῶς ἄρξας. παρασκευάζοντι οὖν αὐτῷ
τὴν δύναμιν ὡς πολεμήσουσαν τῷ Μαξιμίνου
στρατῷ προσίασιν οἱ ἱππεῖς τὴν κεφαλὴν τοῦ τε
Μαξιμίνου καὶ τοῦ παιδὸς φέροντες, νίκην τε καὶ
εὐπραγίαν ἀγγέλλοντες, ὅτι τε ἄρα ὁ στρατὸς τὰ
Ῥωμαίων φρονεῖ, καὶ σέβει αὐτοκράτορας οὓς ἡ
7 σύγκλητος ἐποίησε. τούτων δὲ παρ' ἐλπίδα ἀγ-
γελθέντων θυσίαι τε βωμοῖς εὐθὺς προσήγοντο,
καὶ νίκην ἐπαιάνιζον πάντες ἣν ἀκονιτὶ ἐνίκησαν·
ὁ δὲ Μάξιμος καλλιερήσας ἐκπέμπει τοὺς ἱππεῖς
ἐς τὴν Ῥώμην ἀγγελοῦντάς τε τὰ πραχθέντα τῷ
δήμῳ καὶ τὴν κεφαλὴν κομίζοντας.[1] ἐπεὶ δὲ
ἀφίκοντο εἰσέπεσόν τε ἐς τὴν πόλιν δεικνύντες
τὴν κεφαλὴν τοῦ πολεμίου ἀνεσκολοπισμένην, ὡς
πᾶσι περίοπτος εἴη, οὐδ' εἰπεῖν ἔστι λόγῳ ἐκείνης
8 τῆς ἡμέρας τὴν ἑορτήν. οὔτε γὰρ ἡλικία τις ἦν
ἢ μὴ πρὸς τοὺς βωμούς τε καὶ τὰ ἱερὰ ἠπείγετο,
οὔτε τις ἔμενεν οἴκοι, ἀλλ' ὥσπερ ἐνθουσιῶντες
ἐφέροντο συνηδόμενοί τε ἀλλήλοις καὶ ἐς τὸν
ἱππόδρομον συνθέοντες ὥσπερ ἐκκλησιάζοντες ⟨ἐν⟩
τῷ [2] χωρίῳ. ὁ δὲ Βαλβῖνος καὶ αὐτὸς ἑκατόμβας

---

[1] Οἱ Jo κομιοῦντας Mendelss
[2] Whit following ⟨ἐν ἐκείνῳ⟩ τῷ Steph τῶ χώρω A χωρίω φι
⟨εἰώθεσαν ἐν τῷδε⟩ τῷ Sylb ὥσπερ—χωρίῳ spurious Mendelss

---

[1] The phrase is suspected by Mendelssohn, but the circus was
frequently used as a meeting-place for the *plebs urbana*; cf.

there, sent by their states because of their warm feeling for Maximus ever since his conscientious term as
their governor. While he was in the middle of these
preparations against Maximinus' army, the horsemen
arrived carrying the head of Maximinus and his son.
They passed on the news about the successful victory, and told him that the army now agreed with
Rome and recognized the emperors elected by the
senate. This unexpected news was at once cele- 7
brated with sacrifices on the altars, and everyone
joined in singing hymns for a victory they had won
without any effort. After favourable omens in the
sacrifice Maximus sent the horsemen on to Rome
with the heads, to tell the people the news. It is
impossible to describe the scenes of celebration that
day after the arrival of the messengers, and their
sudden entry into the city with the head of the
enemy stuck on a pole for all to see. People of all 8
ages ran to the altars and the temples; no one stayed
indoors. They were swept along as though a spirit
was in control of them, congratulating each other and
all rushing together to the circus, as though there
were a public assembly there.[1] Balbinus actually in

2.7.5 and Whittaker, *Hist.* 13 (1964) 348-69, esp. 362. SHA,
Max. 25.3 ff., says that the message arrived three days after
leaving Ravenna and reached Rome during some *dies ludorum*,
when it was taken to Balbinus and Gordian at the theatre;
immediately after the games the senate met to record its
acclamations. Though the wording of the *acclamatio* is
suspect, the circumstantial detail may be substantially true;
the mover of the motion is said to have been Cuspidius
Celerinus, perhaps Cuspidius Flaminius Severus, who became
governor of Cappadocia in this year under Pupienus and
Balbinus; Hohl, *Maximini duo* 38, *Albo* 1011, 1544.

HERODIAN

ἔθυεν, ἀρχαί τε πᾶσαι καὶ σύγκλητος, ἕκαστός τε
ὥσπερ ἀποσεισάμενος πέλεκυν τοῖς αὐχέσιν ἐπικεί-
μενον ὑπερευφραίνετο· [1] ἔς τε τὰ ἔθνη ἄγγελοι
καὶ κήρυκες δαφνηφόροι διεπέμποντο.

7. καὶ τὰ μὲν κατὰ τὴν Ῥώμην ἑορτῆς [2] εἶχεν
οὕτως, ὁ δὲ Μάξιμος ἀπὸ τῆς Ῥαβέννης ⟨ἀπ⟩άρας [3]
ἐπέστη Ἀκυληΐᾳ, διαβὰς τὰ τενάγη, ἃ ὑπό τε [4]
Ἠριδανοῦ ποταμοῦ πληρούμενα καὶ τῶν περι-
κειμένων ἑλῶν ἑπτὰ στόμασιν ἐς θάλασσαν
ἐκχεῖται· ἔνθεν καὶ τῇ ⟨ἰδίᾳ⟩ φωνῇ [5] καλοῦσιν οἱ
ἐπιχώριοι Ἑπτὰ πελάγη τὴν λίμνην ἐκείνην.
2 εὐθὺς οὖν οἱ Ἀκυλήσιοι τὰς πύλας ἀνοίξαντες
ὑπεδέχοντο, αἵ τε ἀπὸ [6] Ἰταλίας πόλεις πρεσβείας

---

[1] -φραίνοντο O
[2] om l Mendelss
[3] Mendelss
[4] Steph ἅ τε ὑπό Oi
[5] Steph (or ⟨ἑαυτῶν⟩ or ⟨πατρίῳ⟩) from patria lingua P
[6] del Mendelss ἀπὸ τῶν a

---

[1] Cf. SHA, *Max. et Balb.* 11.4–7, for a learned but incorrect
discussion on hecatombs. The word was applied to a large
sacrifice.
[2] Perhaps the delegation noted in SHA, *Max. et Balb.*
12.4, sent to congratulate Pupienus (again twenty men, whose
names were supposedly recorded by Junius Cordus). It was
probably soon after this that there was a major reappraisal of
provincial appointments, since many changes occurred in
238, of which some must have been made by Pupienus and
Balbinus. This means that some of the provincial governors
would have been supporters of the senatorial emperors but
not of Gordian III, between whom there was an uneasy compromise. Townsend, *YCS* 14 (1955) 83–96, quite wrongly

person sacrificed hecatombs,[1] while all the magistrates, the senate and every ordinary man was bursting with joy, as though he had shaken off a sword that was hanging over his head. Messengers and agents wearing laurel wreaths were sent out to the provinces.[2]

7. While the scene in Rome took on the appearance of a festival, Maximus left Ravenna and came to Aquileia by going through the lagoons into which the River Eridanus and the surrounding swamps empty, before they flow into the sea by seven channels. The local inhabitants call the lake the Seven Seas (in their own language).[3] The Aquileians opened their gates straight away and welcomed

assumes that supporters of Pupienus and Balbinus must be identical with those of Gordian III (see 7.10.5, 8.8.7), dismissing the *abolitio memoriae* of the names of the former as only "strange." Yet many of the men appointed to the provinces in 238 disappear from any office by 241, the date when Gordian III and his prefect father-in-law, Timesitheus, were strong enough to establish their independence of the senate; e.g. M. Asinius Sabinianus, who probably replaced Timesitheus himself in Asia (7.1.4n; Timesitheus was demoted to *procurator* in Gaul), replaced *c.* 240/1; Cuspidius Flaminius Severus (see above note), no further career known; Menophilus (8.2.6) appointed to Moesia and replaced in 241; Crispinus (8.2.6) appointed to Hispania Superior–Gallaecia and then no further governorship; L. Vettius Juvenis appointed to Thrace, no further career known; Q. Axius Aelianus stayed on in office in Dacia Apulensis, then no further career known; M. Domitius Valerianus appointed to Arabia, no further career known. Naturally some of these were quite ready to serve any emperor or were replaced normally. On the counter-revolution under Timesitheus, see Introduction, pp. xiv and xxix.

[3] See 8.6.5. The allusion to " their own language " may mean dialect, or simply be Latin.

ἔπεμπον τῶν πρωτευόντων παρ᾽ [1] αὐτοῖς ἀνδρῶν,
οἱ λευχειμονοῦντες καὶ δαφνηφόροι θεῶν πατρίων
ἕκαστοι προσεκόμιζον ἀγάλματα καὶ εἴ τινες ἦσαν
στέφανοι χρυσοῦ ἐξ ἀναθημάτων, εὐφήμουν τε καὶ
ἐφυλλοβόλουν [2] τὸν Μάξιμον. ὁ δὲ στρατὸς ὁ [3]
τὴν Ἀκυληίαν πολιορκήσας [4] προῄει [5] καὶ αὐτὸς
ἐν εἰρηνικῷ σχήματι δαφνηφόρος, οὐκ ἐξ ἀληθοῦς
μὲν διαθέσεως πᾶς, προσποιήτῳ δὲ εὐνοίᾳ καὶ
τιμῇ διὰ τὴν παροῦσαν ἐξ ἀνάγκης τῆς βασιλείας
3 τύχην. οἱ πλεῖστοι γὰρ αὐτῶν ἠγανάκτουν καὶ
λανθανόντως ἤλγουν τὸν [6] μὲν ὑπ᾽ αὐτῶν ἐπιλε-
χθέντα βασιλέα [7] καθῃρημένον, κρατοῦντας δὲ
τοὺς ὑπὸ συγκλήτου ᾑρημένους. ὁ δὲ Μάξιμος ἐν
τῇ Ἀκυληίᾳ γενόμενος πρώτης μὲν καὶ δευτέρας
ἡμέρας ἱερουργίαις ἐσχόλαζε, τῇ δὲ τρίτῃ τῶν
ἡμερῶν συγκαλέσας ἐς τὸ πεδίον πάντα τὸν
στρατόν, βήματός τε αὐτῷ κατασκευασθέντος,
ἔλεξε τοιάδε·

4 " ὅσον μὲν ὑμᾶς ὤνησε μεταγνόντας τε καὶ τὰ
Ῥωμαίων φρονήσαντας, πείρᾳ μεμαθήκατε, ἀντὶ
πολέμου μὲν εἰρήνην ἔχοντες πρὸς θεοὺς [8] οὓς
ὀμωμόκατε, καὶ [9] νῦν φυλάσσοντες τὸν στρατιωτικὸν ὅρκον, ὅς ἐστι τῆς Ῥωμαίων ἀρχῆς σεμνὸν

[1] ἐν O	[2] -βολοῦντο i
[3] om φι	[4] πορθήσας Jo
[5] PJo προσήει Oi	[6] ⟨ὁρῶντες⟩ τὸν Mendelss from Jo
[7] βασιλεύειν Jo	[8] ⟨δὲ⟩ θεοὺς Wolf [9] del Stav

[1] The Greek *mysterion* and Latin *sacramentum* are both
used in the sense of " secret." The military *sacramentum*,
normally taken *in nomen principis*, was, if not reinforced by a
iusiurandum (as Livy suggests, 22.38.1–5, and apparently

Maximus in. The Italian cities sent delegations of
their prominent citizens dressed in white, wearing
laurel wreaths and all bringing with them the statues
of their local gods and any golden crowns that were
among their dedications. They paid their homage
to Maximus and showered him with flowers. The
army that had been besieging Aquileia came out, too,
dressed for peace and carrying laurel branches. Not
all of them acted from genuine feeling, but they pretended to show their loyalty and to honour the emperor of necessity, because of the prevailing conditions
in the principate. The majority were resentful and 3
privately angry that their own choice of emperor had
been destroyed, while the senatorial choices were in
power. For the first two days in Aquileia Maximus did
nothing except perform sacrifices. On the third day
he marshalled the whole army on the plain, and then
mounted a specially constructed dais to give them
the following address:

"You now know from experience the value of 4
changing your minds and falling into line with Roman
policy. In place of war you are at peace with the
gods in whose name you took your oaths, and you are
now being true to your military vow, which is the
sacred secret of the Roman empire.¹ For the

confirmed here by H.), regarded by this time as having the
force of a formal oath, the violation of which rendered the
culprit *nefas* (liable to execution). The oath was taken *in
nomen* of the emperor, but in 69 a mutinous legion had demanded to take the oath *in nomen senatus*, Suet. *Galba* 16;
there is therefore nothing new or strange about the constitutional principle involved in the oath demanded by Pupienus
here; suggested by Mullens, *G & R* 17 (1948) 76. For the
military oath, see Dar.-Sag. (sacramentum) 951-2.

HERODIAN

μυστήριον. χρὴ δ' ὑμᾶς καὶ τοῦ λοιποῦ διὰ
παντὸς τούτων ἀπολαύειν, τὰ πιστὰ τηροῦντας
Ῥωμαίοις τε καὶ συγκλήτῳ καὶ αὐτοκράτορσιν
ἡμῖν, οὓς ἐξ εὐγενείας καὶ πολλῶν πράξεων [καὶ] [1]
μακρὰς διαδοχῆς ὥσπερ κατ' ἀκολουθίαν ἐπὶ
τοῦτο ἀναβάντας [2] κρίναντες ὁ δῆμος καὶ ἡ
5 σύγκλητος ἐπελέξαντο. οὐ γὰρ ἑνὸς ἀνδρὸς ἴδιον
κτῆμα ἡ ἀρχή, ἀλλὰ κοινὸν τοῦ Ῥωμαίων δήμου
ἄνωθεν, καὶ ἐν ἐκείνῃ τῇ πόλει ἡ τῆς βασιλείας [3]
ἵδρυται τύχη· ἡμεῖς δὲ διοικεῖν καὶ διέπειν τὰ
τῆς ἀρχῆς σὺν ὑμῖν ἐγκεχειρίσμεθα.[4] ταῦτα δὲ [5]
μετ' εὐταξίας τε καὶ κόσμου τοῦ πρέποντος,
αἰδοῦς τε καὶ τιμῆς πρὸς τοὺς ἄρχοντας, ὑμῖν μὲν
εὐδαίμονα καὶ πάντων ἀνενδεῆ παρέξει βίον, τοῖς
δ' ἄλλοις πᾶσιν ἀνθρώποις κατά τε ἔθνη καὶ κατὰ
πόλεις εἰρήνην καὶ πρὸς τοὺς ἡγουμένους πειθώ.
βιώσεσθέ [6] τε [καὶ] [7] κατὰ γνώμην ἐν τοῖς
6 οἰκείοις, οὐκ ἐν ἀλλοδαπῇ κακοπαθοῦντες. ὑπὲρ
δὲ τοῦ καὶ τὰ βάρβαρα ἡσυχάζειν ἔθνη, διὰ
φροντίδος ἡμεῖς ἕξομεν. δύο μὲν γὰρ ὄντων

---

[1] del Wolf [2] ἀναβάντες O-των l
[3] ἡ τῆς βασιλείας i ἃς φ καθ' ἦν A [4] -ισμένα O
[5] ταῦτα δὲ ⟨γιγνόμενα⟩ Reisk [6] βιώσεσθαί Ogl
[7] del Bergl lacuna after τε Steph perhaps βιώσεσθαι δ' ἔσται
Whit (δὲ from *autem* P)

---

[1] See 7.10.6n for what is known of Pupienus' career. H.'s
stress upon a *cursus honorum* leading to the principate, as an
alternative qualification to high birth (cf. 7.5.2—Gordian I),
represents a theoretical compromise between *virtus* and *nobilitas*
suited to the new Antonine and Severan aristocracy of his own
day; cf. Wickert, *RE* (princeps) 2194, 2205.

future you must always enjoy these benefits by keeping your pledges to the Romans and the senate and to us your emperors. The senate and the Roman people decided to choose us because of our noble birth and many achievements in a long series of offices, which we held like graded promotions before reaching this final position.[1] The empire is not the private property of a single man but by tradition the common possession of the Roman people.[2] It is in the hands of the city of Rome that the fate of the principate is placed. We have been given the task to govern and administer the empire with your assistance. If this is done in a disciplined and properly ordered way, with respect and honour shown to the rulers, you will find a pleasant life which lacks nothing. And in the provinces and cities everyone will live in peace and obedience to their governors. You will live as you want in your own homes, not in foreign lands undergoing privations. It will be our care to see that the barbarian nations keep the peace.[3] There are two of us emperors, so there will

[2] Cf. 2.8.4, 5.1.6 for the contrast between the *tyrannus* who rules the empire " as though it were his private property " and the *optimus princeps* who regards his rule as a *commune imperium*, a public *tutela* that the *princeps* exercises on behalf of the people. Inevitably under the régime of the two senatorial *principes*, Pupienus and Balbinus, the slogans of the *libera res publica* appear in the speech. Cf. Wickert, *RE* (princeps) 2080 ff., on " Prinzipat und Freiheit." The great defect in the rule of Pupienus and Balbinus was the breakdown of their *concordia* (8.8.4).

[3] Closely parallel to the civil concept of *tutela* and *cura* was the military ideology of the *princeps* who kept to his *statio* (guard post); cf. Béranger, *Recherches* 184-6, Wickert, *RE* (princeps) 2230.

βασιλέων εὐμαρέστερον καὶ τὰ ἐν τῇ Ῥώμῃ
διοικήσεται καὶ εἴ τι [1] ἐπὶ τῆς ἀλλοδαπῆς ἐπείγοι,[2]
πρὸς τὴν χρείαν ἀεί του [3] πρὸς τὰ καλοῦντα
ῥᾳδίως παρόντος. μηδέ τις ὑμῶν οἰέσθω τῶν
πεπραγμένων εἶναί τινα μνήμην, εἴτε ὑφ᾽ ἡμῶν
(ἐκελεύεσθε [4] γὰρ) εἴτε ὑπὸ Ῥωμαίων ἢ τῶν
ἄλλων ἐθνῶν, οἳ ἀδικούμενοι ἀπέστησαν· ἀλλὰ γὰρ
ἔστω πάντων ἀμνηστία, καὶ σπονδαὶ [5] φιλίας
βεβαίου, εὐνοίας τε καὶ εὐκοσμίας πίστις αἰώνιος."
7 τοιαῦτά τινα εἰπὼν ὁ Μάξιμος, νομάς τε
χρημάτων μεγαλοφρόνως αὐτοῖς ἐπαγγείλας,
ὀλίγων ἡμερῶν διατρίψας [6] ἐν τῇ Ἀκυληίᾳ τὴν ἐς
Ῥώμην ἐπάνοδον συγκροτεῖ. καὶ τὸ μὲν ἄλλο
στρατιωτικὸν ἀπέπεμψεν ἔς τε τὰ ἔθνη καὶ τὰ
οἰκεῖα στρατόπεδα, αὐτὸς δὲ ἐπανῆλθεν ἐς τὴν
Ῥώμην σύν τε [7] τοῖς δορυφόροις, οἳ τὴν βασίλειον
φρουροῦσιν αὐλήν,[8] σύν τε τοῖς ὑπὸ Μαξιμίνῳ
8 ἐστρατευμένοις.[9] ἐπανῆλθον δὲ καὶ οἱ ἀπὸ Γερμα-

---

[1] τις O   [2] ἐπείγοιτο O
[3] Wolf ἀεὶ τοῦ Oi ἀεὶ τοῦ ⟨ἑτέρου⟩ Steph
[4] ἐκέλευσε   [5] σπονδαὶ φ
[6] ἐνδιατρίψας i   [7] om O   [8] ἀρχὴν i
[9] Whit (see notes) βαλβίνω στρατευομένοις Oi

---

[1] According to SHA, Max. et Balb. 13.5, there were plans
for two military expeditions during the brief rule; one was to
be against the " Germans," the other against the " Parthians,"
the first led by Balbinus and the other by Pupienus. The
" Germans " refer to the Carpi and Goths, who Dexippus
says had attacked Istros (SHA, Max. et Balb. 16.3; cf. Pick,
Antik. Münz. v. Moesien u. Dacien 1.147) and Marcianopolis
(Müller, FGH Dexippus frag. 18, Jord. Get. 16.92). But the
only confirmation of a " Parthian " (= Persian) crisis is Zon.

be more efficient rule at Rome and abroad if any emergency arises. One of us will always be quickly on the spot for service as it is demanded.[1] None of you should imagine that there is any recrimination for the past on our part (since you were under military orders), nor on the part of the Romans or the rest of the nations that rebelled when they were unjustly treated. There must be a complete amnesty, a firm treaty of friendship and a pledge of loyalty and discipline for ever."[2]

With these words Maximus announced a generous 7 distribution of money. Then, after a few days' wait in Aquileia, he organized the return trip to Rome. Most of the army was returned to the provinces where they had their own camps, but Maximus took the palace guards and those who had served under Maximinus [3] back on his return trip. With him also 8

12.18, who says that they had occupied Nisibis and Carrhae; this is contrary to 7.8.4, apart from it being improbable that two campaigns would be planned within one and a half months.

[2] The coins of Pupienus and Balbinus lay stress on *pax publica* and the constitutional aspects of the rule (*patres senatus*) which are emphasized in this speech; *BMC* VI. 100–103. The double principate, however, forms the main theme of the issues (8.8.4).

[3] The MSS all read "those serving under Balbinus," which I have emended as above. There is no other reference to troops under Balbinus, who must be assumed to have stayed in Rome. Here there are two parallel clauses—"the guards who protect the palace" and "those . . . under Maximinus (or Balbinus)"; the former are the praetorians and perhaps the *equites singulares*; the others are the Parthian legion, who did not guard the palace but who did return to Rome. The phrase was however misunderstood by SHA, *Max. et Balb.* 12.7, which says that Pupienus took Maximinus' army with him to Rome. The German *auxilia* are discussed in 8.6.6n.

νίας ἐληλυθότες σύμμαχοι· ἐθάρσει γὰρ αὐτῶν
τῇ εὐνοίᾳ ἅτε καὶ τοῦ ἔθνους ἐπιεικῶς πρότερον
ἄρξας, ὅτε ἰδιώτευεν. εἰσιόντι δὲ αὐτῷ ἐς τὴν
Ῥώμην ὅ τε Βαλβῖνος ὑπήντετο, ἐπαγόμενος
Γορδιανὸν Καίσαρα, ἥ τε σύγκλητος καὶ ὁ δῆμος
εὐφημοῦντες ὥσπερ θριαμβεύοντα [1] ὑπεδέχοντο.

8. ἦρχον δὲ τοῦ λοιποῦ τῆς πόλεως μετὰ πάσης
εὐκοσμίας τε καὶ εὐταξίας, ἰδίᾳ τε καὶ δημοσίᾳ
πανταχοῦ εὐφημούμενοι· ἔχαιρέ τε ὁ δῆμος
αὐτοῖς, σεμνυνόμενος εὐπατρίδαις καὶ ἀξίοις τῆς
βασιλείας αὐτοκράτορσιν. οἱ μέντοι στρατιῶται
διοίδαινον τὰς ψυχάς, καὶ οὔτε ταῖς εὐφημίαις τοῦ
δήμου ἠρέσκοντο, ἐβαροῦντό τε αὐτῶν αὐτὴν τὴν
εὐγένειαν, καὶ ἠγανάκτουν ὅτι ἄρα ἔχοιεν ἐκ
2 συγκλήτου βασιλέας. ἐλύπουν δὲ αὐτοὺς καὶ οἱ

---

[1] Jo -οντας i -σαντες O

---

[1] A longer account of the administration of Pupienus and
Balbinus is given in SHA, *Max. et Balb.* 13.4–5, including
the publication of laws and military dispositions. But there
can have been very little time for all this (8.8.4n). The re-
introduction of the double denarius, abandoned by Alexander,
perhaps indicates the inflationary tendency of the period; it
was tariffed at about twenty to the aureus probably, an
attempt to return to the real value of the silver content
because of loss of confidence in the poor denarii in circulation;
BMC VI. 20n.

[2] All sources (except a manifest error in Eutrop. 9.2.1) are
agreed on the patrician status of Balbinus; he was probably

went the German auxiliary allies, in whose loyalty
Maximus was confident because of his fair administration as governor of the territory at an earlier
period before becoming emperor. As he approached
Rome, Balbinus with Gordian Caesar came to meet
him, accompanied by the senate and people, who
welcomed him back with cheers as though he were
celebrating a triumph.

8. From now on the emperors ruled the city extremely efficiently and sensibly,[1] which was well
appreciated by individuals and by the state as a
whole. The people liked them because they respected
emperors of patrician status [2] who were also worthy
of the principate. The soldiers, however, were
seething with anger inside; they disliked the acclaim given by the people, actually disapproved of
the noble birth of the two men and hated having
emperors chosen by the senate. The presence of 2

descended from the Spanish family of the Coelii, related to the
emperors Trajan and Hadrian, under whom they had achieved
patrician rank; the Coelii were also related to the Greek
senatorial family of the Vibulli, who may have been related
to the family of Herodes Atticus (as was the family of Gordian,
7.5.2n); cf. *PIR*[2] C 1241, *Albo* 652b; thus Balbinus stemmed
from the heart of the Antonine aristocracy. Pupienus'
status is contrasted with that of Balbinus, which probably gave
rise to the stories that he was of low birth; SHA, *Max. et
Balb.* 5.1, 14.1, 16.2, Eutrop. 9.2.1. But H. insists on his
patrician rank in 238 and it is possible that the Clodii were an
old Tibur family related to the Pinarii (cf. Pinarius Valens,
SHA, *Max. et Balb.* 4.4, 5.5, alleged to be Pupienus'
praetorian prefect) who were a senatorial family from Tibur;
see Townsend, *YCS* 14 (1955) 83n. But from his military
career, it seems more probable that Pupienus was a *novus
homo* who had been given patrician status in his own lifetime;
see 8.8.4n.

Γερμανοὶ παρόντες τῷ Μαξίμῳ ἔν τε τῇ Ῥώμῃ
διατρίβοντες· ἀντιπάλους γὰρ ἕξειν ἤλπιζον, εἴ
τι τολμῷεν, καὶ ἐφεδρεύειν αὐτοῖς ὑπώπτευον, εἴ
τινι δόλῳ ἀποζωσθεῖεν, ἐκεῖνοι δὲ ἅτε [1] παρόντες
ῥᾳδίως ὑποκατασταῖεν· τό τε Σεβήρου ὑπόδειγμα,
ὃς τοὺς Περτίνακα ἀποκτείναντας ἀπέζωσεν,
εἰσῄει αὐτούς.

3 ἐπιτελουμένου δὲ ἀγῶνος τοῦ τῶν Καπετωλίων,
πάντων τε περὶ τὴν πανήγυριν καὶ τὰς θέας
ἀσχολουμένων, αἰφνιδίως ἣν εἶχον γνώμην λανθά-
νουσαν ἐξέφηναν, καὶ τοῦ θυμοῦ μὴ κρατήσαντες,
ὁρμῇ δὲ ἀλόγῳ χρησάμενοι, ἀνῆλθον ὁμοθυμαδὸν
ἐς τὰ βασίλεια, τοῖς τε πρεσβύταις βασιλεῦσιν
4 ἐπεισῆλθον. συνέβαινε δὲ κἀκείνους μὴ πάνυ τι
ἀλλήλοις ὁμονοεῖν, ἀλλ' οἷα περ μοναρχίας ἐπιθυμίᾳ
καὶ τὸ ἀκοινώνητον ἐν ταῖς ἐξουσίαις εἴωθε

---

[1] Reisk ἐκείνῳ ἅτε O ἐκεῖνο ἅτε gl ἐκεῖνο καὶ ἅτε a

---

[1] Said in SHA, *Max. et Balb.* 14.8, to have had their
quarters *extra urbem*. See 8.6.6n.

[2] The only more or less exact date given in H. for the whole
sequence of events of 238 ironically cannot be identified. The
games are almost certainly the quinquennial *agon Capitolinus*
(i.e. held every four years; cf. 1.9.2n). Since 184, when H.
records the games, they appear to have been held regularly;
Dio 79.10.2 notes them in 220, and they would thus fall due in
238. But the day and month of the games is not known—if

the German troops at Maximus' side, living in Rome,[1] made them furious, because they expected them to constitute a counter force to any bold action by themselves. They also suspected that the emperors were on the watch to disarm them treacherously, and that the Germans would then easily take over the guard themselves, since they were on the spot. The example of how Severus disarmed the murderers of Pertinax served as a reminder to them.

The soldiers' hidden attitude became suddenly 3 clear during the celebrations of the Capitoline games, [2] while everyone was busy with the festival and the shows. No longer controlling their emotions, in a black fit of anger they all rushed to the palace and burst in on the old emperors. In practice the two 4 men were not in complete agreement; [3] it was a typical result of the desire for sole rule and the in-

there was a fixed day; Friedländer, *Sitt. Roms* (10) 2.150, Dar-Sag. (ludi) 1377 (which gives the approximate date of June or July, but based on this incident). Victor, *Caes.* 27.7, says that the quinquennial games started by Nero (probably an error for Domitian) were enlarged by Gordian III (i.e. they were still in existence, which was not true of Nero's *quinquennalia*) and given a fixed date. This would refer to the *agon Capitolinus*, which commemorated the *dies imperii* of Gordian; cf. Hartke, *RE* (Neronia) 46-7.

[3] The theme of *concordia* figures largely in the coin issues, with slogans like *fides mutua, pietas mutua, amor mutuus, caritas mutua*. The equality of both men is shown by the fact that each held the title of *pontifex maximus* (cf. 7.7.2n). The rivalry between them broke out almost at once, before Pupienus even reached Rome; SHA, *Max. et Balb.* 12.5-6. Pupienus can hardly have reached Rome before late May or early June (8.6.6n) and a month later both emperors were dead. For H. this, and the concomitant unrest among the praetorians, were the flaws in the ideal rule.

ποιεῖν,[1] ἕκαστος πρὸς αὐτὸν τὴν δύναμιν ἀνθεῖλκεν,
ὁ μὲν Βαλβῖνος κατ' εὐγένειαν καὶ διπλῆν προά-
γουσαν ὑπατείαν πρωτεύειν [2] ἀξιῶν, ὁ δὲ Μάξιμος
διά τε τὸ ἔπαρχος [3] τῆς πόλεως γεγονέναι καὶ
ἔχειν ὑπολήψεις ἐμπειρίας πραγμάτων· [4] [ἑκατέ-
ρωθέν τε εὐγενεῖς καὶ [5] εὐπατρίδαι καὶ γένους
πλῆθος αὔταρκες ἐς ἐπιθυμίαν μοναρχίας ἔπειθεν.][6]
5 ὅπερ αὐτοῖς καὶ μάλιστα γέγονεν ἀπωλείας αἴτιον.
ὡς γὰρ ἐπύθετο ὁ Μάξιμος ἀφικνεῖσθαι ἐπ'
ὀλέθρῳ αὐτῶν τοὺς πραιτωριανοὺς καλουμένους,
ἐβούλετο μεταπέμψασθαι τοὺς Γερμανοὺς συμμάχους, ὄντας ἐν Ῥώμῃ, αὐτάρκεις ἐσομένους
ἀντιστῆναι τοῖς ἐπιβουλεύουσιν.[7] ὁ δὲ Βαλβῖνος
οἰόμενος δόλον τινὰ εἶναι καθ' αὑτοῦ [8] καὶ σόφισμα

---

[1] Jo εἴωθε ποιεῖν om Oi
[2] old correction Mendelss πρωτεύσειν Oi
[3] ἔπαρχον i   [4] γραμμάτων AB   [5] om i
[6] del Mendelss ἑκατέρωθέν τε εὐγενὴς καὶ εὐπατρίδης καὶ
γένους πλῆθος αὔταρκες ἔχων· ταῦτα ἑκάτερον ἐρᾶν τῆς μοναρχίας
ἔπειθεν A   [7] πραιτωριανοῖς AP
[8] κατ' αὐτοῦ ABagJo

---

[1] It was orthodox political doctrine that the supreme power
could be shared but not divided, though the *sententia* is most
commonly found in the condemnation of *regnum*; Tac. *A.*
12.47, Lucan 1.92–3, Sallust, *Cat.* 54.4, etc. But as the post-
Trajanic principate took on the garments of Greek philosophy,

divisible nature of supreme power [1] that each man began a tug-of-war for personal power. Balbinus considered that he took precedence because of his noble birth and earlier second consulship, Maximus because of his term as urban prefect and his reputation as an experienced administrator. [Both men were of noble, patrician status, and the adequate size of their family backing persuaded them to aim for sole rule].[2] This proved the chief reason for their destruction. 5 When Maximus heard that the praetorians (as they were called) had come to kill him, he was all for summoning the German auxiliaries who were in Rome,[3] since they would be strong enough to resist the plot. But Balbinus was opposed to this because he thought

the term *princeps* was regarded both as the Roman republican *primus inter pares* (who did not rule at all) and the Stoic natural *basileus* (who by definition could not be equalled).

[2] The text has been corrupted by the intrusion of a marginal gloss that is historically incorrect; cf. 8.8.1n. Balbinus had been *cos.* II in 213, over twenty years before Pupienus reached his second consulship in 234. Although Zon, 12.17 says Balbinus was sixty and Pupienus seventy, their ages must be reversed to make sense; therefore Balbinus was the older man, a patrician of long-standing (cf. *CIL* VI. 1981 which records him as a member of the Salii some time after 191) and with more extended family ramifications among the senatorial aristocracy. Pupienus had risen through military service, probably as a *novus homo*, and had only become a patrician under Alexander, but his military reputation gave him greater prestige; in inscriptions and papyri his name always appears first.

[3] According to SHA, *Max. et Balb.* 14.3 ff. some of the German guard were actually on the Palatine at the time, but with Balbinus, who refused to send them to the aid of Pupienus; the *vita* does not make clear how Balbinus lost their protection after that.

(ἤδει γὰρ τοὺς Γερμανοὺς τῷ Μαξίμῳ [1] εὐνοοῦν-
τας) ἐκώλυε, φάσκων οὐκ ἐς κωλύμην οὐδ' ἐς
ἀντίστασιν αὐτοὺς τῶν πραιτωριανῶν ἀφίξεσθαι,
ἀλλ' ἐς τὸ περιποιῆσαι τῷ Μαξίμῳ τὴν μοναρχίαν.

6 ἐν ᾧ δὲ περὶ [2] τούτων διαφέρονται,[3] εἰσδραμόντες
οἱ στρατιῶται ὁμοθυμαδὸν ἅπαντες, ἐκστάντων
αὐτοῖς τῶν περὶ τὰς αὐλείους εἰσόδους φυλασ-
σόντων, ἁρπάζουσι τοὺς πρεσβύτας, περιρρήξαντες
δὲ ἃς εἶχον περὶ τοῖς σώμασιν ἐσθῆτας λιτὰς ἅτ'
οἴκοι διατρίβοντες, γυμνοὺς τῆς βασιλείου αὐλῆς
ἐξέλκουσι μετὰ πάσης αἰσχύνης καὶ ὕβρεως·
παίοντές τε καὶ ἀποσκώπτοντες τοὺς ἀπὸ συγκλήτου βασιλέας, γενείων τε καὶ ὀφρύων σπαραγμοῖς
καὶ πάσαις τοῦ σώματος λώβαις ἐμπαροινοῦντες,
διὰ μέσης τῆς πόλεως ἐπὶ τὸ στρατόπεδον ἀπῆγον,
οὐ θελήσαντες οὐδ' ἐν τοῖς βασιλείοις ἀποκτεῖναι
ἀλλὰ ζῶσιν ἐνυβρίσαι, ἵν' ἐπὶ πλέον ὧν πάσχουσιν
αἴσθοιντο.

7 ἐπεὶ δὲ ταῦτα πυθόμενοι οἱ Γερμανοί, λαβόντες
ὅπλα, ἠπείγοντο ὡς ἀμυνοῦντες αὐτοῖς, μαθόντες
οἱ πραιτωριανοὶ ἀφικνουμένους φονεύουσιν ἤδη πᾶν

---

[1] Μαξιμίνῳ V
[2] om Agl
[3] διεφέροντο Jo τούτων δὴ περὶ τούτων διεριζόντων A

it was a clever trick designed against him, knowing that the Germans were loyal to Maximus. He alleged that the Germans would not come to stop or resist the praetorians, but to put the sole rule in the hands of Maximus. While they were arguing, the soldiers all 6 burst in together, as the guards at the entrance to the palace abandoned their posts.[1] The two old men were seized, stripped of the simple clothes they had on for indoor wear and dragged naked from the imperial palace, to the accompaniment of absolutely degrading indignities. After beating and jeering at these senatorial emperors, the praetorians mal-treated them by pulling out their beards and eye-brows and mutilating their bodies, before dragging them through the city to their camp. They were not even prepared to kill them in the palace;[2] instead they wanted to torture them alive, so that they would feel their agony longer.

As the Germans heard the news, they collected 7 their weapons and rushed to the aid of the two men, but, after the praetorians were informed of their approach, they murdered the emperors, whose bodies

---

[1] That is the *auliculi*, or palace attendants; cf. 2.5.2–3. The whole description of the death of Pertinax in 2.5 must have been written with the events of 238 very much in mind.

[2] SHA, *Max. et Balb.* 5–6, substantially agrees with H., though it clearly derived some detail from another source. Victor, *Caes.* 27.6, Eutrop. 9.2 say that Pupienus and Balbinus were killed in the palace. Thus there were at least two traditions upon which the *vita* drew, one Herodian and one behind the third-century Latin writers; cf. Homo, *Rev. Hist.* 132 (1919) 5–8, though he refuses to accept that the *vita* could have drawn direct from H., in spite of an almost exact similarity of one phrase (next note).

HERODIAN

τὸ σῶμα λελωβημένους τοὺς βασιλέας. καὶ κατα-
λιπόντες τὰ σώματα ἐρριμμένα ἐπὶ τῆς λεωφόρου,
ἀράμενοι δὲ τὸν Γορδιανὸν Καίσαρα ὄντα,
αὐτοκράτορά τε ἀναγορεύσαντες, ἐπειδὴ πρὸς
τὸ παρὸν ἄλλον οὐχ εὗρον, βοῶντές τε πρὸς τὸν [1]
δῆμον ὅτι ἄρα εἴησαν ἀπεκτονότες οὓς ὁ δῆμος
ἐν ἀρχῇ οὐκ ἐβούλετο ἄρξαι, Γορδιανόν τε
ἐπελέξαντο ἐκείνου τε ἀπόγονον καὶ ὃν [2] αὐτοὶ
Ῥωμαῖοι ἐξεβιάσαντο, ἔχοντες αὐτὸν [3] ἀπελθόν-
τες [4] ἐς τὸ στρατόπεδον, κλείσαντες [5] τὰς πύλας
ἡσύχαζον. οἱ δὲ Γερμανοὶ μαθόντες ἀνηρημένους
τε καὶ ἐρριμμένους ὧν χάριν ἠπείγοντο, οὐχ
ἑλόμενοι πόλεμον μάταιον ὑπὲρ ἀνδρῶν τεθνηκό-
των, ἐπανῆλθον ἐς τὸ ἑαυτῶν καταγώγιον.

8   τέλει μὲν δὴ τοιούτῳ ἐχρήσαντο ἀναξίῳ τε

[1] om Bi   [2] οἷον Jo   [3] οὖν αὐτὸν καὶ A
[4] ἀπῆλθον Jo   [5] καὶ κλείσ. Jo

[1] Translated by SHA, *Max. et Balb.* 15.7, *quia non erat
alius in praesens.* Thus Gordian was neither the choice of a
large number of senators, nor was he a particular preference
of the soldiers. How far the action of the soldiers was
fomented by the partisans of Gordian must be a matter for
speculation. If Zon. 12.17 is correct, the two senatorial
emperors had been plotting the assassination of young
Gordian. Jord. *Rom.* 282 says Gordian was responsible for
the murder of the two emperors. After the murders, the
names of Pupienus and Balbinus were erased (even in
Aquileia), a sure sign of the revisionist character of the rule
of Gordian III. SHA, *Gord.* 22.5–9, 23.1–3, is totally confused about the sequence of events, placing the incident of

were by now totally mutilated. Their bodies were left exposed out on the road, while the soldiers lifted up Gordian (who held the title of Caesar) and proclaimed him as the emperor, for want of someone else at this stage.[1] They shouted out to the people that the men whom the people did not want to rule in the first place were now dead, and that they had chosen Gordian as emperor, the descendant of the first Gordian, whom the Romans themselves had forced to rule. Then they took Gordian with them back to the camp, shut the gates and remained inactive. Once the Germans heard that the men to whose assistance they were hurrying were destroyed and lying out in the road, they saw no point in fighting a senseless war for dead men. They preferred to return to their own quarters.[2]

This was the end of Maximus and Balbinus,[3] a 8

Gallicanus (7.11.3) after the murder of Pupienus and Balbinus.

[2] Cf. 8.8.2n.

[3] The date was some time before 29th August 238, since coins of Alexandria with year 1 of Gordian's reign must have been issued before that date (and therefore the news from Rome had arrived before that date). The length of the rule of Pupienus and Balbinus is given by the *Chron. of 354* (Mommsen, *Chron. Min.* 1.147) as ninety-nine days, and by the *Chron. Pasc.* (1.501 Bonn) as one hundred days; cf. Zon. 12.17 who says three months. If they had acceded on 1st April (7.5.7n), the date of their deaths would have been 8th/9th July—the date given by SHA, *Max. et Balb.* 1.1 (emended text), for the accession. If they had died on 9th July, the news would have been in Alexandria about 1st August (twenty-eight days for travel), allowing about twenty-eight days for the first coin issue after making new dies; since the first issue was very brief this fits with the small number of coins actually found.

ἅμα καὶ ἀνοσίῳ σεμνοὶ καὶ λόγου ἄξιοι πρεσβῦται,
εὐγενεῖς τε καὶ κατ᾽ ἀξίαν ἐπὶ τὴν ἀρχὴν ἐληλυ-
θότες· ὁ δὲ Γορδιανὸς περὶ ἔτη που γεγονὼς
τρισκαίδεκα αὐτοκράτωρ τε ἀνεδείχθη καὶ τὴν
Ῥωμαίων ἀρχὴν ἀνεδέξατο.

[1] This sombre conclusion to the history can hardly have
been written during the reign of Gordian III. Furthermore,
H. makes clear his dislike of very young emperors, against
whom the philosophic objection (*dii avertant principes pueros!*
SHA, *Tac.* 6.5) was reinforced by his own bitter experience of

death that was undeserved and desecrated for two respected and distinguished old men, who had come to power through their high birth and by their own merits. Gordian, aged about thirteen, was saluted as emperor and took over the Roman empire.[1]

Commodus, Caracalla, Elagabalus and even Alexander; the latter was corrupted by the domination of his mother, just as Gordian III was dominated by his mother; see Introduction, pp. xii ff.

INDEX TO HERODIAN

INDEX OF NAMES

All names are listed, as far as possible, in the form in which they appear in the text. References are to books and sections. Interpolated references are in square brackets.

Abgar (King of Osrhoene): takes refuge with Severus, III.9.2

Achilles (Homeric hero): Caracalla's imitation of, IV.8.4, 9.3; tomb of, IV.8.4–5

Acilius (M'. Acilius Glabrio, see Glabrio)

Adiabene (country east of Euphrates): Severus in, III.9.3

Adventus (M. Oclatinius Adventus, praetorian prefect c. 212–217): prefect of Caracalla, IV.12.1; refuses to be emperor, IV.14.2

Aegean Sea: as limit of Persian claims, VI.2.2, 4.5

Aelius (P. Aelius Hadrianus, see Hadrian)

Aelius (P. Aelius Vitalianus, see Vitalianus)

Aemilianus (Asellius Aemilianus, consul c. 180): governor of Asia, III.2.2; governor of Syria, III.2.3; general of Niger, III.2.2; accused of betraying Niger, III.2.3

Aemilius (Q. Aemilius Laetus, see Laetus)

Aeneas (mythical founder of Rome): Romans descended from, I.11.3; ancestor of Glabrio, II.3.4

Aesculapius: Caracalla at shrine of, in Pergamum, IV.8.3

Africa (see also Libya): procurator of, killed, VII.4.3–6, 5.6; Gordian I, governor of, VII.5.1–2

Africanus: title of Gordian I, VII.5.8

Alban Mount: soldiers from, VIII.5.8

Albinus (D. Clodius Albinus, named Caesar 193): ancestry of, II.15.1, III.5.2; friends and supporters of, III.5.2, 5.5, 8.1, 8.6; governor of Britain, II.15.1; made Caesar by Severus, II.15.2–4; coins of, II.15.5;

partnership of, with Severus, III.6.2–5; character and life of, III.6.7, 7.1; army of, II.15.1, III.6.6; plot against, by Severus, III.5.2–8; declared hostis, III.6.8; defeated at Lugdunum, III.7.2–7; death of, III.7.7–8: head of, III.7.7, 8.1

Alexander (the Great, King of Macedon 336–323 B.C.): conquests of, VI.2.6; defeats Darius, III.4.3, VI.2.2, 2.6; at Issus, III.4.3; admired and imitated by Caracalla, IV.8.1–2, 9.3–4; city of, visited by Caracalla, IV.8.6–9; name taken by Severus Alexander, V.7.3; successors of, I.3.2, VI.2.6–7; cf. also VII.6.1

Alexander (M. Aurelius Severus Alexander, emperor 222–235): age and youth of, V.3.3, 8.10; alleged son of Caracalla, V.3.10, 7.3; name of, V.3.3, 7.3; education and teachers of, V.7.5, 7.6, 8.2; as Caesar, V.7.1–2, 7.4, 8.4; as consul with Elagabalus, V.7.4; adopted by Elagabalus, V.7.4; plots against, by Elagabalus, V.8.2–4; reinstated by Elagabalus, V.8.6; rumours of death of, V.8.5; saluted emperor, V.8.10, VI.1.1; character and faults of, VI.1.6, 1.10, 7.3, 8.3, 9.8; dislikes war, VI.2.3; rule and reforms of, VI.1.1–4, 1.6–7, 9.8; length of rule of, VI.2.1, 8.4, 9.3, 9.8, VII.1.1; controlled by Mamaea and Maesa, V.8.10, VI.1.1, 1.5–6, 1.10, 5.8–9, 8.3, 9.4–5; opposes and blames mother, VI.1.8, 1.10, 9.6; wife and father-in-law of, VI.1.9–10; council and friends of, VI.1.2, 1.4, 2.3, 5.1, VII.1.3, 1.9; staff of, VII.1.4;

315

INDEX OF NAMES

loved by people, VI.4.2; troops of, VI.4.3, 5.1, 7.8; support of, by troops, V.8.2, 8.5–7; donative of, to troops, VI.4.1, 6.4; parsimony of, to troops, VI.8.4, 9.4–5; anger of troops against, VI.6.1, 6.4, 7.3, 7.10, 8.3, 9.4–5; mutiny of troops against, VI.4.7, 9.1–4; deserted by troops, VI.9.5; speech of, to troops, VI.3.2–7; speech of, to senate, VI.4.1; in Rome and departure from, VI.3.1, 4.1–2; in Antioch, VI.4.3, 6.2–4, 6.6; diplomatic contacts of, with Artaxerxes, VI.2.3–5, 3.5, 4.4, 4.6; preparations for and strategy of, in eastern wars, VI.3.1, 4.3, 4.7, 5.1–2, 5.4; leadership of, in eastern wars, VI.5.2, 5.7–8; failure of, in East, VI.5.8; receives news of German invasion, VI.7.2–3; German expedition of, VI.7.5–6, VII.2.2; peace offer of, to Germans, VI.7.9–10; camp of, in Germany, VI.8.8; gives position to Maximinus, VI.7.2; plan to murder, VI.8.4, 8.7; death of, VI.9.6–8, VII.1.1

Alexandria (near Issus): Niger defeated near, III.4.3

Alexandria (in Egypt): considered by Geta as capital, IV.3.7; character of people of, IV.8.7–9, 9.2–3; Caracalla in, IV.8.6–9.8; massacre of people in, IV.9.4–8; Nile at, IV.9.8; size and wealth of, VII.6.1

Alexianus: family name of Severus Alexander, V.3.3, 7.3

Alps (mountains of N. Italy): description of, II.11.8, VIII.1.5–6; Julianus advised to block, II.11.8; Severus controls passes of, III.6.10; Emona at foot of, VIII.1.4; Maximinus crosses, VIII.1.5–2.1

[Altinum] (city near Venice): lagoon at, VIII.6.5

Anchises (father of hero Aeneas): ancestor of M'. Acilius Glabrio, II.3.4

Annius (M. Annius Verus, see Verissimus)

Annia (Annia Galeria Faustina, see Faustina)

Antigonus ("Monophthalmos," King of Macedon): behaviour of, as successor to Alexander, I.3.3

Antioch (leading city of Syria): temples of, II.8.6; festivals and spectacles of, II.7.9, 8.9; rivalry with Laodicea, III.3.3, 6.9; character of people of, II.7.9, 10.7; Niger at II.8.7, 8.9, 14.6, III.2.10, 3.4, 4.6; Niger's troops from, III.1.3, 4.1; Severus' opinion and treatment of, II.10.7, III.6.9; Geta considers as capital, IV.3.7; Caracalla at, IV.8.6, 9.8; ashes of Caracalla sent to Julia Domna at, IV.13.8; Marcrinus at, IV.15.9, V.1.1, 2.3, 4.1; Severus Alexander at, VI.4.3, 6.2–4, 6.6

Antoninus (M. Aurelius Antoninus, see Caracalla)

Antoninus (M. Aurelius Antoninus, see Elagabalus)

Antoninus (M. Commodus Antoninus, see Commodus)

Antoninus Pius (T. Aurelius Fulvus Boionius Arrius Antoninus, emperor 138–161): father of Faustina, Commodus' mother, I.7.4

Antonius (M. Antonius, triumvir in 43 B.C.): wars against, III.7.8; children of, III.13.3

Antonius (M. Antonius Gordianus, see Gordian III)

Antonius (M. Antonius Gordianus Sempronianus Romanus, see Gordian I and Gordian II)

Apollo (Greek god): Beles in Aquileia identified with, VIII.3.8

Aquileia (city of N.E. Italy): description and size of, VIII.2.2–4; wine production of, VIII.4.4; oracles and gods of, VIII.3.8; siege of, VIII.4.6 ff., 7.2; provisions of, for siege, VIII.2.6, 5.3, 6.4; rejects Maximinus and his envoys, VIII.2.2, 3.7, 4.1; hastily fortified, VIII.2.5; ordered to surrender, VIII.3.2; successfully resists Maximinus, VIII.4.7, 5.5; countryside around, ravaged, VIII.4.5, 4.8; bridge near, destroyed, VIII.4.2; growing strength of, VIII.5.2; military tribune from, VIII.3.1–2; burial of dead at, VIII.5.7; peace negotiations of, with northern army, VIII.6.2–4; welcomes and admits Maximus, VIII.7.1–3, 7.7

INDEX OF NAMES

INDEX OF NAMES

VIII.6.6, 7.4, 8.1; portraits of, VIII.6.2; joint rule of, with Maximus, VIII.7.5–6, 8.1; forced to accept Gordian III as Caesar, VII.10.7–9; unable to control disorder in Rome, VII.12.2–3; soldiers' dislike of, VIII.8.1–3; celebrates news of Maximinus' death, VIII.6.8; meets Maximus on his return, VIII.7.8; breakdown of concord of, with Maximus, VIII.8.4–6; plot against, by praetorians, VIII.8.5; death of, VIII.8.6–8

Barsemius (King of Hatra): supports Niger, III.1.3, 9.1

Beles (Belinus, god worshipped in Aquileia): identified with Apollo in Aquileia, VIII.3.8

Berytus (city in Syria): rivalry of, with Tyre, III.3.3

Bithynia (Roman province in Asia Minor): Nicomedia in, III.2.9; Chalcedon in, IV.3.6; Niger's garrison in, III.2.9; Severus' forces invade and overrun, III.2.6, 3.1; Caracalla travels through, IV.8.6; Macrinus captured in, V.4.11

Britain, British (Roman province and/or territory beyond in northern Scotland): description of, III.14.6–8; size of army in, II.15.1, III.6.6; courage and fighting skill of, II.15.1, III.7.2; Albinus, governor of, II.15.1; Albinus crosses from, III.7.1; danger of, to Severus, II.15.5; success for Albinus at Lugdunum, III.7.3; division of province by Severus, III.8.2; rebellion in, III.14.1–2; Severus' expedition to, III.14.2–10; end of expedition against, III.15.6–8

Britannicus (half-brother of Emperor Nero): quoted as an example by Caracalla, IV.5.6

Bruttia (Bruttia Crispina, see Crispina)

Byzantium (city on European shore of the Bosphorus): walls of, III.1.6–7, 2.1; falls to Niger, III.2.1; Niger attempts to occupy, III.1.5–6; siege and capture of by, Severus, III.6.9; subject status of, III.6.9; Caracalla's army in, IV.3.6; Macrinus almost reaches, V.4.11

Caelius (D. Caelius Calvinus Balbinus, see Balbinus)

Caesar (title of emperor's heir or children): Albinus as, II.15.3, III.5.2, 7.8; Diadumenianus as, V.4.12; Severus Alexander as, V.7.1, 7.4, 8.4; Maximinus' son as, VIII.4.9; Gordian III as, VII.10.9, VIII.6.2, 7.8, 8.7

Caesar (C. Julius Caesar, murdered 44 B.C.): civil wars of, III.7.8

Campus Martius (in Rome): deification ceremony of emperors in, IV.2.6

Campania (Italian plain south of Latium): Severus' property in, III.13.1

Capellianus (Roman senator, otherwise unknown): governor of Numidia, VII.9.1–3; enmity of, against Gordian I, VII.9.2; supporter of Maximinus, VII.9.3; defeats Gordian I, VII.9.2–11; entry of into Carthage, VII.9.9–10; imperial ambitions of, VII.9.11; punishes African cities, VII.9.11

Capitol (hill in Rome): Caracalla's statues on, VII.8.1; crowds gather at, to coerce senate, VII.10.5–8

Capitoline: festival of Jupiter in Commodus' reign, I.9.2; games celebrated under Maximus and Balbinus, VIII.8.3

Cappadocia (Roman province on Euphrates): climate of, III.3.7; Taurus mountains divide from Cilicia, III.1.4; Severus in, III.3.1

Caracalla (M. Aurelius Antoninus, co-emperor with his father Septimius Severus 198–208, with his brother Geta 211–212, sole rule 212–217; referred to throughout as Antoninus, see also Severus (sons of)): Bassianus original name of, III.10.5; noble birth of, V.1.6; character of, III.11.1, 13.2, IV.3.3–4, 12.8; physical strength and appearance of, IV.7.2, 7.4, 7.6–7; statues of, IV.8.1–2; loves chariot racing, shows, circuses, hunting, III.10.3–4, 13.2, IV.6.2, 6.4, 7.2, 11.9, 12.7; and oracles, IV.12.3; and Alexander the Great, IV.8.1–2, 8.6–7, 8.9, 9.3; and Achilles, IV.8.4–5, 9.3; admires Sulla and Hannibal, IV.8.5;

INDEX OF NAMES

created Augustus by Severus, III.9.1; attempts to become emperor, III.15.1–2; joint rule of, with Geta, III.15.7 ff.; partitions empire with Geta, IV.3.5–7; saluted as sole emperor, IV.4.8; friends and flatterers of, III.13.6, V.1.3; mother of (see also Julia Domna), III.15.6; brother of (see Geta); Maesa at court of, V.3.2, 3.10; alleged father of Elagabalus and Severus Alexander, V.3.10, 3.11, 4.3–4, 7.3; wife of (see also Plautilla), III.13.2; hates wife, III.12.8, 10.8; plots against wife, III.13.2; victories of, VI.3.6; military life of, IV.12.2; and the army, IV.7.7, 13.7, 14.4–5; attempts to win over troops, III.15.5; popularity of, with troops, V.2.5; donatives and pay of, to troops, IV.4.7, 5.1, 7.4; murders Geta, IV.4.2–3; announces Geta's death to troops, IV.4.4–6; suspected of slandering Plautian, III.12.3–4; kills Plautian, III.12.10–12; executions of, III.15.4, IV.5.7–6.4; addresses senate, IV.5.1–7; administration of, IV.7.1–2; in Britain with Severus, III.14.9 ff.; makes peace with British, III.15.6; in the northern provinces, IV.7.1–8.3; in Asia, IV.8.3–6; visits Alexandria in Egypt, IV.8.6 ff.; anger of, against Alexandrians, IV.9.1–3; massacres Alexandrians, IV.9.4–8; in Syria (Antioch), IV.8.6, 9.8; in Parthia, IV.11.2–8; marriage proposals of, to Artabanus, IV.10.1–11.4; massacres Parthians, IV.11.5–8; claims conquest of Parthia, IV.11.8–9; at Carrhae in Mesopotamia, IV.13.3; plots against, IV.12.3–5, 14.2; assassination of, IV.13.3–6, 15.8, V.1.1, 3.2; ashes of, IV.13.8; senate's reaction to death of, V.2.1–2; Macrinus disowns actions of, V.1.2–3; length of rule of, IV.13.8

Caria (southern Asia Minor): once a Persian satrapy, VI.2.2; claimed by Persians, VI.4.5

Carrhae (town in N. Mesopotamia): Caracalla murdered near, IV.13.3

Carthage, Carthaginians (main city in province of Africa): foundation of,

V.6.4; size and wealth of, VII.6.1; resembles Rome, VII.6.2; rich families of, VII.4.3; Urania's statue from, V.6.4; procurator of, causes revolt, VII.4.2; revolt of, VII.8.5; Gordian I marches to, VII.6.1–2; Gordian I defeated at, VII.9.1–10; entry of Capellianus into, VII.9.9–10; undisciplined mob of, VII.9.4–7; slaughter of, VII.9.8–10; Gallicanus, senator from, VII.11.3

Celts (see also Gaul): territory of, overrun by Maternus, I.10.2

Chalcedon (city on Asian side of the Bosphorus): proposal for Geta's army to be stationed at, IV.3.6; capture of Macrinus at, V.4.11

Cilicia (territory between Asia Minor and Syria): Taurus mountains separate from Cappadocia, III.1.4; Severus' army invades, III.3.8

Claudius (Ti. Claudius Pompeianus, see Pompeianus)

Claudius (Claudius Pompeianus Quintianus, see Quintianus)

Cleander (M. Aurelius Cleander, freedman chamberlain of Emperor Commodus, executed 190): rise to power of I.12.3 ff.; causes famine in Rome, I.12.3–4; buildings by, I.12.4; riots against, I.12.5 ff.; feared, I.13.1; execution of, I.13.4, 13.6; friends and sons of, executed, I.13.6

Clodius (D. Clodius Albinus, see Albinus)

Clodius (M. Clodius Pupienus Maximus, see Maximus)

Colossus (statue near the Colosseum in Rome): Commodus replaces head of, I.15.9

Commodus (M. Commodus Antoninus, originally L. Aelius Aurelius Antoninus, and later a reversion to this same name; son of M. Aurelius and co-emperor 178–180, sole rule 180–192): noble birth and ancestry of, I.5.5, 7.4, 15.7, V.1.6; son of M. Aurelius, I.2.1 ff.; education of, I.2.1; youth of, at accession, I.3.5; appearance of, I.7.5; brothers and sisters of (see also children of M. Aurelius, Verissimus, Lucilla, Fadilla), IV.6.3; sister's (Lucilla's)

INDEX OF NAMES

same year): as Caesar, V.4.12; execution of, V.4.12

Didius (M. Didius Severus Julianus, *see* Julianus)

Dido (legendary foundress of Carthage), V.6.4

Dionysius (tyrant of Syracuse 367/6–345 B.C., son of Dionysius I): excesses of, I.3.2

Dionysus (Greek God): imitated by Antigonus of Macedon, I.3.3; Elagabalus resembles statues of, V.3.7

Domitian (T. Flavius Domitianus, emperor 81–96, son of T. Flavius Vespasianus, emperor 69–79): cruel behaviour of, I.3.4; quoted as an example by Caracalla, IV.4.6

Domitius (L. Domitius Ahenobarbus Nero, *see* Nero)

Domitius (L. Domitius Gallicanus Papinianus, *see* Gallicanus)

Domna (Julia Domna, *see* Julia)

Eclectus (full name unknown, perhaps L. Aurelius Eclectus, once a freedman of the Emperor L. Aurelius Verus; then a freedman of M. Ummidius Quadratus (*q.v.*) and finally freedman of the Emperor Commodus, and his chamberlain in 192): Egyptian origins of, I.17.6; ordered to arrange Commodus' transfer to the gladiators' barracks, I.16.5; death warrant of, I.17.4; plots the death of Commodus, I.17.6–11; action of, after Commodus' death, in selecting Pertinax, II.1.3 ff.; persuades soldiers to accept Pertinax, II.2.4 ff.; friend of Pertinax, II.1.10

Egypt, Egyptian (*see also* Alexandria): Eclectus shows typical characteristics of, I.17.6; troops from mutiny, VI.4.7; Alexandria in, VII.6.1

Elagabalus (the Syrian god Baal, worshipped under the Graeco-Phoenician name of *Helio*(-sun)-*gabalus*, a cult of which flourished at Emesa in Syria-Phoenice, the home of the Syrian wife of Severus): cult of, at Emesa, V.3.4 ff.; cult stone of, V.3.5; grandsons of Maesa as priests of, V.3.3, 3.6 ff., 5.6–7; sacrifices to and worship of, in

Rome, V.5.7, 6.6–10; divine marriage of, V.6.3–5

Elagabalus (the nick-name given to M. Aurelius Antoninus, emperor 218–222; originally named Bassianus by H., but Avitus by Dio; son of Sex. Varius Avitus and Soemias Bassiana, he took the name Antoninus, by which H. refers to him throughout, when claiming to be the son of Caracalla): youth of, V.3.3, 3.7, 5.1; appearance and dress of, V.3.7–8, 5.3–4, 6.10, 8.1; character of, V.7.1; vices of, V.6.10; alleged son of Caracalla, V.3.10, 3.11, 4.3–4, 7.3; named Bassianus, V.3.3; marriages of, V.6.1–2; mother of (*see* Soaemis); as a priest, V.3.2, 3.6, 3.8, 5.3–4, 5.8–6.1; painting of, as priest, V.5.6–7; buildings of, V.6.6; temple of, V.5.8–9, 6.6; games, donatives, festivals of, V.5.8, 6.6–10; arranges marriage for his god, V.6.3–5; rejects Maesa's advice, V.5.6; friends and company of, V.5.1, 5.6; appointments of, V.7.6–7; executions by, V.6.1; saluted emperor by Syrian troops, V.3.12; causes desertion of troops, V.4.2, 4.6; troops of, V.3.8–12, 4.2–5, 4.8–10, 5.1; anger of soldiers against, V.8.1–2, 8.5–8; fights against Macrinus, V.4.6–7; pursues Macrinus, V.4.10–11; winters in Nicomedia, V.5.3; adopts and shares consulship with Severus Alexander, V.7.4; regrets adoption, V.7.5–6; plots against Severus Alexander, V.8.2–4; spreads rumours of Severus Alexander's death, V.8.5; forced to reinstate Severus Alexander, V.8.6; murder of, V.8.8–10, VI.1.1; length of rule of, V.8.10

Emesa (principal city of Syria-Phoenice): home of Maesa, V.3.2–4; cult of Elagabalus at, V.3.4–5; military garrison near, V.3.9

Emona (*see* Hema)

Eridanus (river near Ravenna), VIII.7.1

Ethiopia: Commodus imports wild beasts from, I.15.5

Euphrates (river on eastern frontier

INDEX OF NAMES

of Roman empire): boundary of Syria, II.7.4; ambassadors from beyond come to Niger, II.8.8; confluence with Tigris the aim of Severus Alexander's expedition, VI.5.2

Europe: Asia opposite, II.8.7, 14.7, VI.2.2, 4.5; straits between Asia and, III.1.6; news of Niger spreads through land opposite, II.8.7; land opposite, claimed by Persians, VI.4.5; Caracalla plans to rule in, IV.3.5; senators from, plan to remain in Rome, IV.3.6; Macrinus makes for, V.4.11

Fadilla (daughter of Emperor M. Aurelius (*q.v.*), married to M. Peducaeus Plautius Quintillus, almost certainly survived Commodus): warns Commodus of Cleander's plot, I.13.1–4

Faustina (Annia Galeria Faustina, the younger, wife of Emperor M. Aurelius, daughter of Emperor Antoninus Pius): mother of Commodus, I.7.4

Festus (Marcius Festus, chamberlain and secretary of Caracalla): died and buried at Ilium, IV.8.4–5

Flavius (T. Flavius Domitianus, *see* Domitian)

Flavius (Flavius Maternianus, *see* Maternianus)

Flavius (Ti. Flavius Sulpicianus, *see* Sulpicianus)

Flavius (T. Flavius Vespasianus, *see* Titus)

Forum (in Rome): bronze equestrian statue of Severus in, II.9.6

Fulvius (C. Fulvius Plautianus, *see* Plautian)

Fulvia (Publia Fulvia Plautilla, *see* Plautilla)

Galatia (Roman province in Asia Minor): Niger's forces flee to, III.2.6; Severus in, III.3.1

Gallicanus (probably L. Domitius Gallicanus Papinianus, consul before 238, from Carthage): leader of a pro-Gordian faction, VII.11.3–7; stirs up civil war in Rome, VII.11.6–7

Gallus (river in Phrygia), I.11.2

Ganymede (mythical cup-bearer of the gods): the rape of, causes a battle, I.11.2

Gaul (refers throughout to the provinces of Tres Galliae, *see also* Celts): Albinus crosses from Britain to, III.8.2; Caracalla and Geta land in, III.15.8

Germany, Germans (imprecise term used to refer to tribes beyond the Rhine and/or Danube): habitations of, VII.2.3–4; river borders of, VI.7.6; tactics of, against the Romans, VII.2.5–6; training and tactics of the Romans against, VI.7.8, VII.2.2; as daring fighters, VIII.1.3; M. Aurelius fears rising of, I.3.5; Pertinax's wars against, II.1.4, 9.9; Caracalla loved by, IV.7.3; clothes and hair of, worn by Caracalla, IV.7.3, 13.6; body-guard of Caracalla, IV.7.3, 13.6; invasion of, into Illyricum and threat to Italy, VI.7.2–4; Severus Alexander's expedition against, VI.7.5–6, 8.3; Severus Alexander's peace offer to, VI.7.9–10; cavalry of, in Maximinus' army, VIII.1.3, 4.3, 8.10; Maximinus' campaigns against, VII.1.5–8, 2.1–8, 8.4; total conquest of, intended by Maximinus, VII.2.9; troops under Maximus, made into a body-guard, VIII.6.6, 7.8, 8.2, 8.5, 8.7; as barbarians, II.1.4, IV.7.4, VII.2.9, VIII.1.3; *see also the following references to barbarians*, I.3.5, 5.8, 6.5, 6.6, 6.8–9, 13.2, 15.7, II.2.8, 4.3, 9.1, 10.5, VII.3.1

Germanicus (triumphal title): Commodus abandons title of, I.15.9; brother of Tiberius?, IV.5.6

Geta (P. Septimius Geta, younger son of Severus, made Caesar in 198 and Augustus in 209, co-emperor with Caracalla 211–212 before being murdered by him: *see also* Severus (sons of)): character and interests of, III.10.3–4, IV.3.2–3; appointed Augustus by Severus, III.9.1; civil administration of, in Britain, III.14.9; council and supporters of, III.13.6, 14.9, IV.3.2–3; supporters and servants of, executed, III.15.4, IV.5.7–6.4; alleged plots of, against

INDEX OF NAMES

Caracalla, IV.5.4; proposes division of empire, IV.3.5–7; lands east of Libya allocated to, IV.3.8; chooses Antioch or Alexandria as future capital, IV.3.7; senators from East to accompany, IV.3.6; Alexandrians refer to, IV.4.3, 13.8; murder of, IV.9.2–3; mourning for, IV.6.3; declared a public enemy, IV.4.6, 4.8, 5.6

Glabrio (M'. Acilius Glabrio, consul II 186, senior senatorial friend of Commodus): offers principate to Pertinax, II.3.3–4

Gordian I (M. Antonius Gordianus Sempronianus Romanus Africanus, born c. 159, consul c. 222; after several governorships he became governor of Africa by 238, and emperor in an African revolt in the same year, but defeated after three weeks rule; father and grandfather of the two below): age, previous career and nobility of, VII.5.2, 5.5, 5.7, 8.5; governor of Africa, VII.5.2; son, daughter and grandson of (see also Gordian II, Gordian III), VII.7.2, 10.7, 10.8; chosen emperor at Thysdrus (Africa), VII.5.3–8; speech of young man to, VII.5.5–6; refuses power, VII.5.4, 5.7; hailed Augustus by senate, VII.7.2; friends and relatives of, in Rome, VII.6.3, 10.5; supported by senate and people in Rome, VII.5.2, 5.5, 8.7; messages of, to Rome, VII.6.3–4, 6.9; promises, of, for rule, VII.6.4; promises donative to soldiers, VII.6.4; laxity of, VII.8.7; plans assassination of Vitalianus, VII.6.4–7; quaestor of, sent to Rome, VII.6.5; at Thysdrus, VII.6.1; marches to Carthage, VII.6.1–2; statues of, in Africa, VII.5.8; title of Africanus, VII.5.8; enmity of, with Capellianus, VII.9.2; defeated at Carthage, VII.6.1–2; stories of death of, VII.9.4–5, 9.9; death of, VII.9.10, VIII.1.1; deification of, VIII.6.3; member of his family demanded as emperor, VII.10.6

Gordian II (M. Antonius Gordianus Sempronianus Romanus, son of the above, made Augustus with his father and died fighting in 238): hailed Augustus by senate, VII.7.2; succeeds Gordian I, VII.9.5; death of, VII.9.7; deification of, VIII.6.3

Gordian III (M. Antonius Gordianus, grandson of Gordian I by his daughter, made Caesar under mob pressure and chosen Augustus by the praetorians in 238, ruled as emperor 238–244, when succeeded by Philip the Arab): age of, VIII.8.8; portraits of, VIII.6.2; made Caesar by mob support, VII.10.7–9, VIII.8.7; as Caesar, VIII.6.2, 7.8, 8.7; meets Maximus on his return to Rome, VIII.7.8; proclaimed emperor by soldiers, VIII.8.7; saluted as emperor, VIII.8.8

Greece, Greek (used generally of Greek-speaking inhabitants of the Roman empire, especially of Greece and Asia): M. Aurelius loves literature of, I.2.3; law, I.3.3; education, VII.5; dress, V.5.4; statues, V.3.5; rivalries and weakness of, III.2.8; origin of word Latium, I.16.2; information for about Magna Mater, I.11.1; wars of Italy against, II.11.4; athletes compared to Maximinus, VII.1.12

Hadrian (P. Aelius Hadrianus, emperor 117–138): great-grandfather of Commodus, I.7.4

Hannibal (Carthaginian leader in third century B.C.): admired by Caracalla, IV.8.5

Hatra, Atreni (independent city-kingdom in central Mesopotamia, near the River Tigris, successfully resisted both Severus in 197–198 and the Persians in c. 229; allied with and garrisoned by the Romans in 232): Barsemius, king of, III.1.3, 9.1; Niger requests and receives help from, III.1.2–3, 5.1; siege of, by Severus, III.9.3–7, 9.9

Helvius (P. Helvius Pertinax, see Pertinax)

Hema (name given to Emona, mod. Ljubljana at the eastern foot of the Carnic Alps, included within the boundaries of Italy, probably c.

INDEX OF NAMES

170): first city in Italy reached by Maximinus, VIII.1.4

Hercules (the Greek form Heracles used throughout): Commodus named after, I.14.8, 15.8; names of months refer to, I.14.9

Ilium (Roman colony near site of ancient Troy): Palladium from, I.14.4, V.6.3; Caracalla visits, IV.8.4–6

Illyria, Illyricum, Illyrian (general name applied to the provinces on the north-eastern border of the Roman empire): power of army, II.11.7, III.4.1; army, III.1.1; courage of soldiers, III.7.2; provinces in Roman empire, VI.7.4; bordering Italy, VI.7.2; plot of Perennis with army, I.9.1, 9.4; sons of Perennis command province, I.9.1; popularity of Pertinax as governor, II.9.8–9, 10.1; army against Niger, II.8.10, 14.6, III.2.2, 4.5; army supports Severus, II.10.1, 10.8–9, 11.9, 15.5; news of Niger's accession reaches, II.9.1; Niger fails to go to, for support, II.8.10, victory of troops at Cyzicus, III.2.2; victory of troops at Issus, III.4.5; troops disarm praetorians, II.13.10; Severus Alexander visits provinces, VI.4.3; sickness of soldiers in East, VI.6.2; anger of soldiers against Severus Alexander, VI.7.3; governor asks for Severus Alexander's aid, VI.7.2; Aquileia port for, VIII.2.3; rumours of resistance to Maximinus, VIII.5.6

Ilus the Phrygian (mythical character): battle of, against Tantalus, I.11.2

India: animals from used by Commodus, I.15.5

Ionia (seaboard of Asia Minor): once under Persia, VI.2.2; claimed by Persians, VI.4.5

Ionian Gulf (Adriatic Sea): Alps run from, VIII.1.5

Issus (bay on the northern border of Syria, *mod.* Iskenderun): battle of, III.4.2–5

Ister (*see* Danube)

Italy, Italians (only named references given): rivers of, VIII.4.3; climate

of, I.6.2; passes into, II.6.10; Alps, natural barrier of, II.11.8, VIII.1.5; constructed ancient road across Alps, VIII.1.6; unwarlike character and history of, II.11.3–5; unfortified cities of, VIII.2.4; cities of, I.7.2–3; Aquileia, first city in, largest city of, port for, II.2.2, 2.3, 4.8; Emona, first city in, VIII.1.4; VIII.3.7; Palladium brought to, I.14.4; Saturnalia legend of, I.16.1–2; Illyrians border, VI.7.2; separation from East, VI.7.4; relieved of military duties by Augustus, II.11.5; recruiting from, II.14.6–7 (Severus), VI.3.1 (Alexander), VII.12.1, VIII.6.5 (Maximus); plague in, I.12.1; attendance of, at special games, I.15.1, III.8.10; Perennis, native of, I.8.1; Perennis' sons reach, I.9.9; Pertinax, native of, II.1.4; Pertinax in, II.4.6; Severus crosses frontier of, II.11.3; Severus feared by, II.11.6; Caracalla leaves, IV.7.2; instructed to celebrate Elagabalus' (god) divine marriage, V.6.5; German threat to, VI.7.4; Maximinus' expedition to, VII.8.9 ff.; Maximinus forecasts collapse of, VII.8.8; Maximinus at borders of, VII.12.8; Maximinus feared in, VIII.1.5; Emona deserted by, VIII.2.1; Aquileia urged to save, VIII.3.4; notable men from, assist defence against Maximinus, VIII.5.5; blockade of roads in, VIII.5.4; rumours of resistance to Maximinus, VIII.5.6; Alban soldiers dislike laying waste, VIII.5.8; cities of, honour Maximinus, VIII.7.2

(Janus): *see note at I.16.1 for probable reference in a lacuna*

Jocasta (legendary queen, mother of Oedipus, committed incest by marrying him): Julia Domna referred to as, IV.9.3

Julia (Julia Avita Mamaea, *see* Mamaea)

Julia (Julia Maesa, *see* Maesa)

Julia (Julia Soemias, *see* Soaemis)

Julia (Julia Domna, Syrian wife of Emperor Septimius Severus, be-

INDEX OF NAMES

came Augusta on Severus' accession in 193, later receiving many other titles; survived both Severus and her son Caracalla; died 218): sister of Maesa, V.3.2, [8.3]; attempts to reconcile her sons, III.15.6, IV.3.4; present at imperial council, III.15.6, IV.3.5; protests at proposed division of the empire, IV.3.8–9; at Geta's murder, IV.4.3, 5.4; mourns Geta's death, IV.6.3; travels of, III.15.6 (Britain), IV.13.8 (Antioch); referred to as Jocasta in Alexandria, IV.9.3; suicide of, IV.13.8

Julianus (M. Didius Severus Julianus, became emperor in 193 after the death of Pertinax, by an auction of the empire, but ruled for less than three months; executed by order of the senate on the approach of Severus): character, behaviour and career of, II.6.6, 7.1; persuaded to bid for empire, II.6.7–9; supported by soldiers, II.6.11, 6.13; promises freedom to soldiers, II.6.10; soldiers turn against, II.7.1–2, 7.6, 8.5, 11.7–8; anger of people against, II.6.13, 7.2–3, 7.5–6, 11.7, 12.2; promises to restore Commodus' name, II.6.10; neglects his duties, II.7.1; fortifies Rome, II.11.9; despair of and failure to stop Severus, II.11.7 ff., 12.1 ff.; wishes to abdicate, II.12.5; denigrated by Severus, II.10.4–5; proposes to negotiate with Severus, II.12.3; Severus' children during reign of, III.2.4; condemned by senate, II.12.4–7; death of, II.12.7, 13.1, III.1.1, 7.8

Julianus (Ulpius Julianus, supporter and praetorian prefect of Macrinus, killed in 218): as praetorian prefect sent against Elagabalus, V.4.3; killed by soldiers, V.4.4

Julius (C. Julius Caesar, see Caesar)
Julius (Julius? Laetus, see Laetus)
Julius (Julius Martialis, see Martialis)
Julius (C. Julius Maximinus Verus, see Maximinus)
Julius (C. Julius Verus Maximus, see Maximinus' son)

Jupiter (god, given Greek name of Zeus throughout; a temple of

Capitoline Jupiter stood on the Capitol in Rome): Magna Mater statue from, I.11.1; and Ganymede, I.11.2; Cronos flees from, I.16.1; Heracles son of, I.14.8; creator of sole rulers, IV.5.7; temple of, in Rome, visited by emperors, I.7.6 (Commodus), II.3.11 (Pertinax), II.14.2, III.8.4 (Severus); senate meet in temple of, VII.10.2–3; Capitoline games of (see Capitoline)

Laconia (see Sparta)

Laetus (Q. Aemilius Laetus, appointed praetorian prefect c. 190; plotted the murder of Commodus, supported Pertinax, then Severus; executed by Julianus in 193): ordered to arrange Commodus' stay in the gladiatorial barracks, I.16.5; death warrant of, I.17.4; plots to kill Commodus, I.17.7–11; selects Pertinax as emperor, II.1.3 ff.; friend of Pertinax, II.2.1; gains praetorian support for Pertinax, II.2.1, 2.5 ff.

Laetus (Julius? Laetus, general of Severus, probably the same as the man later executed at Hatra in 198): at battle of Lugdunum, III.7.3–5

Laodicea (city in Syria): rivalry with Antioch, III.3.3; attacked by Niger, III.3.5; dominates Antioch, III.6.9

Latin: education, V.7.5; language, VIII.3.7

Latium (plain around Rome): origin of name, I.16.2

Laurentum (city south of Rome): Commodus withdraws to, I.12.2; origin of name, I.12.2

Liberty: statue of, I.15.1

Libya, Libyans (see also Africa, but the Greek name is used throughout; usually refers to the Roman province of Africa Proconsularis only): called Africa by Romans, VII.5.8; population and farmworkers of, VII.4.4; worship of Urania in, V.6.4; Hannibal, native of, IV.8.5; Severus, native of, II.9.2, III.10.6; Plautian, native of, III.10.6; included in western lands allocated to Caracalla, IV.3.7; wife of Severus

INDEX OF NAMES

Alexander exiled to, VI.1.10; rapacity of procurator of, VII.4.3; Maximinus' strength in, VII.9.4; revolt of, VII.4.1 ff., 5.8, 12.9, VIII.1.1; events of 238 in, VII.9.11; support of, for Gordian I, VII.6.3

Lucilla (Annia Aurelia Galeria Lucilla, second daughter of M. Aurelius, married the co-emperor L. Verus in 164 and Ti. Claudius Pompeianus in 169, exiled and later executed for a plot in 182): marriage of, to L. Verus, I.8.3; marriage of, to Pompeianus, I.6.4, 8.3; eldest of children of M. Aurelius in 182, I.8.3; honours of, I.8.4; anger of, against Crispina, I.8.4; plots against Commodus, I.8.4 ff.; execution of, I.8.8; son of, executed by Caracalla, IV.6.3

Lucius Verus (L. Aurelius Verus, co-emperor with M. Aurelius in 161, married Lucilla, M. Aurelius' daughter, died suddenly in 169): victories of, in East, VI.2.4; marriage of, and partnership of, with M. Aurelius, I.8.3; death of, I.8.3; murder of, by M. Aurelius, alleged by Caracalla, IV.5.6

Lugdunum (main city of Tres Galliae, *mod.* Lyon): battle of, III.7.2–6; ravaged, III.7.7

Macedon, Macedonia: Alexander the Great of (*see also* Alexander), V.7.3, VI.2.2, 2.6; Ptolemy breaks law of, I.3.3; Antigonus rejects customs of, I.3.3; dominates Greece, III.2.8; controls Asia, VI.2.6–7; troops of, under Caracalla, IV.8.2, 9.4; Caracalla in dress of, IV.8.2; Caracalla visits Thrace adjacent to, IV. 8.1

Macedo (name otherwise unknown): part of, in plot of Quartinus against Maximinus, VII.1.10–11

Macrinus (M. Opellius Macrinus, praetorian prefect of Emperor Caracalla, whom he succeeded in 217; defeated in 218 and executed by Elagabalus): son of (*see* Diadumenianus); equestrian origin of, V.1.5–7; character of, V.1.2–3; dress of, V.2.4–5; idleness, laxness, effeminacy of, IV.12.2, V.2.4–6, 4.2, 5.2; imitates M.

Aurelius, V.2.4; as praetorian prefect and legal experience of, IV.12.1, 12.7; plots against Caracalla, IV.12.5–7, 13.1–2, 14.2; conceals Maternianus' letter of accusation, IV.12.7–8; pretends ignorance of Caracalla's death, IV.13.7–8; praises Caracalla, IV.14.4–5; disowns Caracalla's actions, IV.15.7, V.1.2–3; selected as emperor, IV.14.2–3; concludes peace with Artabanus, IV.15.6–9; letter of, to senate, V.1.1–2.1; promises to senate, V.1.4, 1.8; senate's reaction to accession of, V.2.1–2; orders Maesa to return home, V.3.2; at Antioch, IV.15.9, V.1.1, 4.1; troops of, IV.14.3, 15.1, V.4.8–10; errors of, over the army, V.2.3; unpopularity of, with the army, V.2.4–3.1, 4.2; bribes troops, V.3.11; troops of, mutiny, V.4.4; mobilizes troops, V.4.5; troops desert, V.4.6; speech of, to troops, IV.14.4–8; receives news of Elagabalus' rebellion, V.4.1–2; fights against Elagabalus, V.4.6–7; flight of, V.4.7–8, 4.10–11; fails to reach Rome, V.4.11–12; execution of, V.4.11–12; length of rule of, V.2.2, 3.1

Maecenas (otherwise unknown): praetorian senator in 238): leader of pro-Gordian faction, VII.11.3

Maesa (Julia Maesa, sister of Julia Domna and grandmother of Elagabalus and Severus Alexander; in a powerful position during the reigns of Elagabalus and Alexander; died *c.* 225): daughters of (*see also* Soaemis *and* Mamaea), V.3.3; claims Caracalla as father of Elagabalus and Severus Alexander, V.3.10, 7.3; wealth of, V.3.11; clients of, V.3.9; controls administration, V.5.1; controls Severus Alexander, V.8.10, VI.1.1; at court of Severus and Caracalla, V.3.2, 3.10, [8.3]; banished to Phoenicia, V.3.2–3; discourages Elagabalus from priestly dress, V.5.5–6; intrigues for Severus Alexander, V.7.1–3; frustrates Elagabalus' plot, V.8.2–4; death and deification of, VI.1.4

326

INDEX OF NAMES

Magna Mater (goddess brought from Asia Minor to Rome): spring festival of, I.10.5; reasons for Roman veneration of, I.11.1 ff.

Magnus (probably C. Petronius Magnus, ex-consul, executed 235): plots against Maximinus, VII.1.5–8

Mamaea (Julia Avita Mamaea, daughter of Maesa and wife of Gessius Marcianus, mother of Severus Alexander; gained power and named Augusta when Alexander became emperor in 222, and was murdered with him in 235): family of, V.3.3; mother of Severus Alexander, V.7.1; claims Caracalla is the father of Severus Alexander, V.7.3; faults of, VI.1.8, 9.8; educates and protects Severus Alexander, V.7.5, 8.2; controls and restrains Severus Alexander, V.8.10, VI.1.1, 1.5, 1.10, 5.8, 8.3, 9.4–5; blamed and opposed by Severus Alexander, VI.1.10, 9.6; bribes soldiers, V.8.3; anger of, against Severus Alexander's wife, VI.1.9–10; charged by father-in-law of Severus Alexander, VI.1.9; murder of, VI.9.6–8

Marcius (Marcius Festus, *see* Festus)

Marcia (Marcia Aurelia Ceionia Demetrias, freedwoman of Lucius Verus (?), Quadratus and Commodus; mistress of Commodus, whom she murdered in 192, and subsequently married Eclectus): honours to, as mistress of Commodus, I.16.4; attempts to dissuade Commodus from going to gladiators' barracks, I.16.4; finds death warrant, I.17.4–5; affair of, with Eclectus, I.17.6; plots to kill Commodus, I.17.6–11; persuades Narcissus to kill Commodus, I.17.11; selects Pertinax as emperor, II.1.3

Marcus Aurelius (M. Aurelius Antoninus, earlier called M. Aelius Aurelius Verus after adoption by Pius, co-emperor with L. Verus 161–180, died at Vienna and succeeded by his son, Commodus): family of, I.7.4; not of noble birth, V.1.8; character of, I.2.2–5; wide reading of, I.3.2; children of (*see also* Commodus, Fadilla, Lucilla,

Verissimus), I.2.1–2, IV.6.3; marriage of daughters of, I.2.2; daughter of, executed by Caracalla IV.6.3; relation of, marries Elagabalus, V.6.2; son-in-law (L. Verus of, I.8.3, IV.5.6; generalship of I.1.5, 5.7; political ability of, I.1.5, ideal reign of, VI.1.7; history before and since, I.1.4, 2.5; concern over Commodus, I.3.1 ff., 3.5; education of Commodus, I.2.1; German tribes cause concern to, I.3.5; illness and death of, I.3.1, 4.7–8, 17.12; death-bed speech of, I.4.2–6; arrangements for funeral of, I.5.1; burial place of, IV.1.4; praised in empire, I.4.8; deification of, I.5.6; friends and councillors of, I.4.1 ff., 5.1, 6.1, 6.3 ff., 6.4 (Pompeianus), 8.1–3, II.1.4 (Pertinax), 1.7 (Pertinax); Perennis accuses old advisers of, I.8.2; Commodus rejects family name of, I.14.8; Pertinax serves under, II.9.9; Pertinax copies, II.4.2; praised and claimed as a model by Severus, II.10.3, 14.3; name of, taken by Caracalla, III.10.5; Macrinus imitates, V.2.4

Marius (C. Marius, republican leader in first century B.C.): civil wars of, III.7.8

Martialis (Julius Martialis, officer in Caracalla's escort in 217): persuaded by Macrinus to kill Caracalla, IV.13.1–2; plots against Caracalla, IV.13.7; murders Caracalla, IV.13.5–6

Maternianus (Flavius Maternianus, acting as urban prefect in 217): in charge of Rome, IV.12.4, 13.1; warns Caracalla of a plot, IV.12.5–6

Maternus (otherwise unknown): leader of a rebellion in 187 in Gaul and Spain): plots against Commodus, I.10.1–7, 11.5

Morocco (-an), Mauretanian, Moorish (Greek name Maurousi used throughout; probably refers usually to the Mauretanian provinces, but sometimes also includes Numidia): ostriches, I.15.5; javelin teachers of Commodus, I.15.2; troops, III.3.4–5 (Niger), IV.15.1 (Caracalla and Macrinus), IV.7.8 (Severus

INDEX OF NAMES

Alexander), VII.2.1 (Severus Alexander and Maximinus), VIII.1.3 (Maximinus); bordering Numidia, VII.9.1; Numidia part of, VII. 9.1; lands allocated to Caracalla, IV.3.7; *see also references to barbarians*, VII.9.1, 9.3

Maximinus (C. Julius Verus Maximinus, emperor 235-238; chosen by soldiers after the murder of Severus Alexander, remained for three years on the northern frontier and murdered at Aquileia when marching on Rome): humble origins of, VI.8.1, VII.1.1-2; son of, VIII.4.9, 5.2, 5.9, 6.6; early life and previous career of, VI.8.1, 9.1, VII.8.4; bravery of, VII.2.6-8; greed of, VII.3.1, 3.3, 3.5, 4.2; character and appearance of, VII.1.2, 1.6, 1.12; oracles and dreams of, VI.8.6; oppressive rule of, VII.1.1-2, 3.1-6, 6.3; portraits and paintings of, VII.2.8, VII.5.9; dedications and titles of, VII.2.8, 5.8, 7.1, 9.11; approach of, against Severus Alexander, VII.9.3, 9.5; blamed by Severus Alexander, VI.9.1; murders Severus Alexander, VI.9.6-7; declared emperor, VI.8.4-6, 9.5-6, VII.1.1; dismisses friends and staff of Severus Alexander, VII.1.3-4; council of, VII.8.1; northern campaigns and intentions of, VII.2.9, 8.4; against Germans, VII.1.5-8, 2.1-8; in Pannonia, VII.2.9, 3.4; rapacity of officials of, VII.4.2; revolt in Africa against, VII.5.1; dedications of, in Africa, destroyed, VII.5.8; privations and loss of morale of troops, VIII.5.1, 5.3-8, 6.4; unpopularity of, with troops, VIII.3.6, 6.3; anger of, with Pannonian generals, VIII.2.2; sol-

diers of, in Rome, VII.11.2; anger of soldiers at murder of, VII.6.1, 7.3; soldiers of, claim divine intervention, VIII.3.8-9; invasion of, and arrival in Italy, VII.8.9-11, 9.1, 12.8-9, VIII.1.1-3, 2.4; finds Emona deserted, VIII.1.4-5; crosses Alps, VIII.1.5-6; confident of victory in Italy, VIII.2.1; sends mission to demand surrender of Aquileia, VIII.3.1-3; crosses river before Aquileia, VIII.4.1-5; besieges Aquileia, VIII.4.6 ff.; ravages country round Aquileia, VIII.4.5, 4.8; insulted by Aquileians, VIII.5.2; fails to take Aquileia, VIII.5.5; plots against, VII.11.5.5; false orders from, to Vitalianus, VII.6.6, 6.8; Vitalianus assumed to be assassinated by, VI.6.9; unpopularity of, VII.3.5-6, 5.5, 6.3; honours and dedication of removed, VII.7.1-2; abuses Rome and senate, VII.8.9; fears in Rome of revenge by, VII.10.1; army of Maximus against, VII.12.1, VIII.6.6; troops of, return to Rome with Maximus, VIII.7.7; rumours of death of, VII.6.9-7.1; murder of, VII.5.8-9, 6.2; head of, sent to Rome, VIII.5.9, 6.5-7; length of rule of, VII.4.1

Maximinus' son (C. Julius Verus Maximus, never named by H., created Caesar 235/236, assassinated with his father 238): created Caesar, VIII.4.9; insulted by Aquileians, VIII.5.2; murdered at Aquileia, VIII.5.9; head of, sent to Rome, VIII.5.9, 6.6-7

Maximus (M. Clodius Pupienus Maximus, co-emperor with Balbinus 238): nobility of, VIII.7.4, 8.1, 8.4; character of, VII.10.4; portraits of, VIII.6.2; previous career of, VII.10.4, 10.6, VIII.7.4, 8.4, 10.4;

INDEX OF NAMES

INDEX OF NAMES

INDEX OF NAMES

peror after the death of Commodus 193; ruled for only a few months before being murdered by the praetorians): inferior birth of, II.3.1–2, V.1.8; previous career of, II.1.4; service of, under M. Aurelius, II.9.9; friend of M. Aurelius, II.1.4, 1.7; earlier campaigns of, against Germans and barbarians, II.2.8, 4.3, 9.8–9; popularity of, in Illyricum and on frontiers, II.2.8, 9.8–9, 10.1; military distinction of, II.3.2; son of, II.4.9, IV.6.3; Sulpicianus, relative of, II.6.9; Laetus and Eclectus, friends of, II.1.10; selected as emperor by Marcia, Laetus and Eclectus, II.1.3 ff.; people informed of choice of, as emperor, II.2.2; people fear praetorian opposition to, II.2.4 ff.; attempts to gain praetorian support, II.2.5 ff.; titles of acclaimed by senate and people, II.2.9, 3.3, 3.11; fears senatorial opposition, II.3.1 ff.; persuaded by Glabrio, II.3.3–4; speech of, to senate, II.3.5–10; sacrifices at temple of Jupiter, II.3.11; emulates M. Aurelius, II.4.2; administrative reforms of, II.4.1 ff.; land reforms of, II.4.6; and imperial property, II.4.7; and finance and taxes, II.3.9, 4.7; banishes informers, II.4.8; restrains praetorians, II.4.1, 4.4; opposition of praetorians to, II.4.5 ff., 5.1 ff.; murder of, II.5.1–9, 13.12, III.1.1, VIII.8.2; news of death of, angers senate and people, II.6.1; Niger possesses qualities of, II.7.5; Severus swears allegiance to, II.9.5; Severus claims to avenge, II.9.8, 13.1, 14.3; appears in Severus' dream, II.9.5–6; Severus takes name of, II.10.1, 10.9, 14.3; praised by Severus, II.10.4; son of, executed by Caracalla, IV.6.3; length of rule of, II.4.5

Pescennius (C. Pescennius Niger Justus, *see* Niger)

Pessinous (Pessinus, town on borders of Phrygia): statue of Magna Mater found at, I.11.1–5

Petronius (C. Petronius Magnus, *see* Magnus)

Pharos (name for lighthouses), IV.2.8

Philocommodus: boy-servant of Commodus, I.17.3–4

Phoenicia, Phoenician (part of province of Syria until 195, when made into a separate province, Syria-Phoenice): dress, V.5.4, 5.10; law, V.6.9; worship of Astroarche, V.6.4; cult of Elagabalus, V.3.4; women in Rome, V.5.9; garrison, V.3.9; rivalry of cities, III.3.3; Dido from, V.6.4; under Syria in Niger's governorship, II.7.4; battle on borders of, V.4.6

Phrygia (included in province of Asia): statue of Magna Mater from, I.11.1–3; Aeneas from, I.11.3; *cf. also* Ilus; Cleander from, I.12.3; Persian diplomats settled in, VI.4.6

Pitanetai (*see* Sparta)

Plautian (C. Fulvius Plautianus, praetorian prefect under Severus *c.* 197–205, acquired enormous power and his daughter married Caracalla; executed for a plot in 205): African origin and rise of, III.10.5–7; character of, III.10.7, 12.12; Severus' friendship with, III.10.6, 12.3–4; ambition and honours of, III.11.1–3, 12.10; as praetorian prefect, III.10.5, 10.7, 11.4, 11.8; Caracalla's hatred of, III.10.8, 12.4; fears Caracalla, III.11.1; controlled by Severus, III.11.3–4; plots against Severus and Caracalla, III.11.4–12.12; execution of, by Caracalla, III.12.12; daughter of (*see* Plautilla)

Plautilla (Publia Flavia Plautilla, not named in the text, daughter of Plautian, married to and executed by Caracalla): daughter of Plautian, III.10.5; married to Caracalla, III.10.5–7; exiled and executed by Caracalla, III.13.2–3, IV.6.3

Pompeianus (Ti. Claudius Pompeianus, senior senator and friend of M. Aurelius, married to Lucilla, retired under Commodus): marriage to Lucilla, I.8.3; devotion to Commodus, I.8.4; urges Commodus to remain on northern front, I.6.4–7; guides Commodus, I.6.7

Pompey (Cn. Pompeius Magnus, statesman of first century B.C.):

INDEX OF NAMES

civil wars of, III.7.8; sons of, III.7.8

Pontus (Black Sea, but apparently including the Propontis): limit of Persian territorial claims, VI.4.5

Propontis (Sea of Marmara): site of Byzantium on, III.1.5; division between empires of Geta and Caracalla, IV.3.6, 3.8; Macrinus crosses, V.4.11; Persian claims to extent of, VI.2.2

Ptolemy (probably Ptolemy II Philadelphus, ruler of Egypt 308–246 B.C.): recalled as an example by M. Aurelius, I.3.3

Pupienus (M. Clodius Pupienus Maximus, see Maximus)

Pyrrhic Dance: at deification of emperors, IV.2.9

Quadratus (probably named Ummidius Quadratus, son of Cn. Claudius Severus and adopted by M. Ummidius Quadratus; young noble in 182): plots with Lucilla against Commodus, I.8.4–5; executed, I.8.8

Quintianus (Claudius Pompeianus Quintianus, step-son or nephew of Lucilla, betrothed to Lucilla's daughter, perhaps quaestor c. 180): plots with Lucilla against Commodus, I.8.5–6

Quartinus (Titius? Quartinus, ex-consul c. 236): plots against Maximinus, VII.1.9–10

Ravenna: Maximus at, VIII.6.5, 7.1; lagoon at, [VIII.6.5]

Rhine (north-western boundary river of Roman empire): description of, VI.7.6–8; news of Niger's claim reaches, II.9.1; German invasion across, VI.7.2; Severus Alexander reaches, VI.7.6

Rome, passim

Romulus (mythical founder of Rome): action against brother quoted by Caracalla, IV.5.5

Rutilius (Rutilius Pudens Crispinus, see Crispinus)

Sabinus (identity uncertain; urban prefect 238): killed in riots in Rome, VII.7.4

Sacred Way (Via Sacra, principal route through Roman Forum to the Palatine): Palladium carried along, I.14.5; Severus dreams that Pertinax falls on, II.9.5; effigy of dead emperors carried along, IV.2.4; assassins of Vitalianus run down, VII.6.9

Sarmatians (tribes north of River Danube): Maximinus campaigns against, VII.8.4

Saturnalia (late December festival in Rome): festival explained, I.16.1–2; approach of festival, II.2.2

Saturninus (tribune? of praetorian guard 205): Syrian origin of, III.11.8; commissioned by Plautian as assassin, III.11.4–7; pretends to assist Plautian, III.11.8–9; betrays Plautian, III.12.1–3; proves Plautian's guilt, III.12.4–8

Saturn (Greek form Cronos used; ancient pre-Olympian God): legend of concealment of, I.16.1

Sebastos (see Augustus)

Secular Games: under Severus, III.8.10

Selele (moon-goddess, confused with Mesopotamian male god Sin): temple of, near Carrhae, IV.3.3; cf. also Urania

Septimius (P. Septimius Aper, see Severus)

Septimius (P. Septimius Geta, see Geta)

Septimius (L. Septimius Severus, see Severus)

Serapis (Egyptian God, not named in the text): venerated by Caracalla, IV.8.6–7

Seres (the Chinese), V.5.4

Seven Seas (lagoons between Ravenna and Venice), VIII.7.1

Severus (probably P. Septimius Aper, named Severus in the text, consul 207): executed by Caracalla, IV.6.3

Severus (L. Septimius Severus, later took title of Pertinax; emperor 193–211 after defeating Julianus, Niger and Albinus; won distinguished victories in the East and in Britain, reorganized some of the provinces of the empire and planned for the joint rule of his sons, Caracalla and Geta; died of old age 211): poor

INDEX OF NAMES

African origins of, III.10.6; character and qualities of, II.9.2, 14.2, III.8.3, 8.7–8; toughness of, II.11.1–2; deception of, II.9.10, 9.13; autobiography of, II.9.4; historians of, II.15.6–7; oracles and dreams of, II.9.3 ff., 9.7; titles of, II.12.6, III.1.1, 9.12; advisers of, IV.3.5; in command of whole of Pannonia, II.9.2; allegiance of, to Pertinax, II.9.5; praises and takes name of Pertinax, II.10.4, 14.3; wishes to avenge Pertinax, II.9.8, 9.10–11, 13.1, 14.3; denigrates Julianus, II.10.4–5; praises M. Aurelius and excuses Commodus, II.10.3, 14.3; decides to seize empire, II.9.3; canvasses and supported by northern troops, II.9.7 ff., 9.11–12, 10.1, 10.9; declared emperor by troops, II.9.11, 10.9; speech of, to northern troops, II.10.2–9; Julianus attempts to resign in favour of, II.12.5; receives news of Julianus' execution, II.13.1; supported by senate, II.12.3–5, 14.1–2; voted power by senate, II.12.6, III.1.1; speech of, to senate, II.14.3; mistrusted by senate, II.14.4; attacks friends of Niger and Albinus, III.4.7, 8.1–3, 8.6–7; reaches Italian frontier, II.11.3; orders army to march on Rome, II.12.1–2; entry of, into Rome, II.14.1, 14.5, III.1.1; supported by Roman people, II.12.2, 14.1–2; feared by Roman people, II.12.2, 14.1; feared by Italians, II.11.6; distributes money to people, II.14.5, III.8.4, 10.2; games, shows and festivals of, in Rome, II.14.5, III.8.9–10, 10.1–2; disarms praetorian guard, II.13.1 ff., VIII.8.2; speech of, to praetorians, II.13.5–9; occupies praetorian camp, II.13.12; new praetorians of, II.14.5; preparations and march of, against Niger, II.14.5–7, 15.5, III.1.1, 2.1–2; holds governors' children as hostages in Rome, III.2.3–5; acts against Niger's generals, III.5.6; supported by eastern cities, III.2.9 (Nicomedia), III.3.3 (Laodicea and

Tyre); defeats Aemilianus at Cyzicus, III.2.2; troops of, enter Bithynia, III.2.6; victory of, at Nicaea, III.2.10; checked at Taurus Pass, III.3.1–2; victory of, at Taurus Pass, III.3.6–8; victory of, at Issus, III.4.1–5; effect of victories on cities III.2.7; postpones plans against Hatra and Parthia, III.4.1; settlement of, in East, III.5.1; eastern wars of, III.9.1–11; Parthian victory and titles of, III.9.12, VI.2.4, 3.6; wins over Albinus, III.5.2–8; plots against Albinus, III.5.2–8; speech of, against Albinus, III.6.1–7; marches from Asia to Gaul, III.6.10; victory of, at Lugdunum, III.7.2–7; victories and victory monuments of, III.7.7–8; campaign of, in Britain, III.14.2–10; divides Britain, III.8.2; military achievement of, III.3.1, 6.6, 7.2–7; gives privileges to soldiers, III.8.4–5; gives donative to soldiers, II.11.1, 14.5, III.6.8; garrison of, in Rome, II.14.5, III.13.4; soldiers honour wishes of, III.15.5; affection of, for Plautian, III.10.6, 12.3–4; reduces Plautian's power, III.11.3–4; plot of Plautian revealed to, III.12.2–3; suspects Caracalla of incriminating Plautian, III.12.3–4; arrests Plautian, III.12.9–10; wife of (see Julia); sons of (see also Caracalla and Geta), III.9.1, 10.1; dissolute life of sons of, III.14.1–2; rivalry of sons of, III.13.1–6, IV.1.1–2, 3.1–4.2; attempts to reconcile sons, III.13.3–6; sons of, divide palace, IV.1.2, 1.5; sons of, plan to divide empire, IV.3.5–9; Maesa at court of, V.3.2, cf. 3.10, 8.3; treasuries and resources of, III.13.4, IV.4.7; administration of, III.10.2, 13.1; appoints two prefects, III.13.1; quarters of, in the palace, III.12.1; lives outside Rome, III.13.1; as an old man, II.15.4, III.11.1, 14.2–3; illness and death of, III.15.1–2, IV.13.8; length of rule of, III.15.3, IV.1.1, 4.7; ashes of, taken to Rome, III.15.8, IV.1.3–4; burial and

333

INDEX OF NAMES

deification of, IV.2.1–3.1; summary of rule of, III.15.3

Sicily: Dionysius of, I.3.2; Plautilla exiled to, III.13.3, IV.6.3

Sirmium (principal city of Lower Pannonia): Maximinus winters at, VII.2.9

Soaemis (Julia Soemias Bassiana, wife of Sex. Varius Marcellus and mother of Emperor Elagabalus, gained power with her son and murdered with him in 222): family of, V.3.3; as Augusta, V.8.8; murder of, V.8.8–10

Spain: overrun by Maternas, I.10.2

Sparta: Caracalla's cohort from (called Pitanetai), IV.8.3, 9.4

Sulla (L. Cornelius Sulla, aristocratic leader in first century B.C.): civil wars of, III.7.8; admired by Caracalla, IV.8.5

Sulpicianus (Ti. Flavius Sulpicianus, father-in-law of Pertinax and urban prefect 193, made a vain bid for the empire on Pertinax's death; finally executed 197): father-in-law and urban prefect of Pertinax, II.6.8; bids for empire, II.6.8–9

Syria, Syrian (Roman province, separated from Phoenicia in 195; principal city Antioch (q.v.)): character, II.7.9, 10.6–7, III.11.8; Niger and Aemilianus as governors of, III.2.3, 7.4; Niger in, III.3.3–6; Severus urges troops to disregard events in, II.10.6–8; rivalry of cities, III.3.3; battle on borders, V.4.6.; Elagabalus leaves, V.5.3; claimed by Persians, VI.4.5; threatened by Artaxerxes, VI.2.1; governor of, warns Severus Alexander, VI.2.1; troops mutiny, VI.4.7

Tantalus the Lydian (mythical character): battles against Ilus, I.11.2

Taurus (mountains separating Cilicia from Cappadocia): Niger fortifies, III.1.4; Niger's forces flee across and defend, III.2.6, 2.10; pass of, defended and lost by Niger, III.3.1–2, 3.6–8

Thrace (province to the east of Macedonia): Illyrian troops cross to join

Severus, II.14.6; Byzantium in, III.1.5; Caracalla marches to, IV.8.1; Maximinus a native of, VI.8.1, VII.1.2; troops from, support Maximinus, VIII.6.1; troops from, anger at Maximinus' death, VIII.6.1

Thysdrus (city in Byzacium district of Africa Proconsularis, *mod.* El Djem): Gordian I at, VII.5.3; population of, force Gordian's accession, VII.5.7

Tiber (river): statue from Pessinus transported to, I.11.3; bodies of Elagabalus and Soaemis thrown into, V.8.9

Tiberius (emperor 14–37): quoted as an example by Caracalla, IV.5.6

Tigidius (Tigidius Perennis, *see* Perennius)

Tigris (river on the eastern boundary of Mesopotamia): ambassadors from beyond come to Niger, II.8.8; deserters cross, III.4.7; as boundary of Roman empire, VI.2.1; crossed by Artaxerxes, VI.2.1; confluence with Euphrates the objective of Severus Alexander, VI.5.2

Titius (Titius? Quartinus, *see* Quartinus)

Titus (T. Flavius Vespasianus, emperor 79–81): quoted as an example by Caracalla, IV.5.6

Trajan (M. Ulpius Traianus, emperor 98–117): great-grandfather of Faustina (Commodus' mother), I.7.4; victories of, in East, VI.2.4

Troy (*see* Ilium)

Tullius (Tullius Menophilus, *see* Menophilus)

Tyre (city of Phoenicia): rivalry with Berytus, III.3.3; supports Severus and is attacked by Niger, III.3.3, 3.5

Tyrrhenian Sea: Alps run from, VIII.1.5

Ulpius (Ulpius Julianus, *see* Julianus)

Ulpius (M. Ulpius Traianus, *see* Trajan)

Ummidius (Ummidius Quadratus, *see* Quadratus)

Urania (*see also* Astroarche): Libyan name for Astroarche, V.6.4; statue sent for from Carthage, V.6.4–5

INDEX OF NAMES

Printed in Great Britain by
Richard Clay (The Chaucer Press) Ltd.,
Bungay, Suffolk

THE LOEB CLASSICAL LIBRARY

VOLUMES ALREADY PUBLISHED

Latin Authors

AMMIANUS MARECLLINUS. Translated by J. C. Rolfe. 3 Vols.

APULEIUS: THE GOLDEN ASS (METAMORPHOSES). W. Adling-
ton (1566). Revised by S. Gaselee.

ST. AUGUSTINE: CITY OF GOD. 7 Vols. Vol. I. G. E.
McCracken Vol. II. W. M. Green. Vol. III. D. Wiesen.
Vol. IV. P. Levine. Vol. V. E. M. Sanford and W. M.
Green. Vol. VI. W. C. Greene.

ST. AUGUSTINE, CONFESSIONS OF. W. Watts (1631). 2 Vols.

ST. AUGUSTINE, SELECT LETTERS. J. H. Baxter.

AUSONIUS. H. G. Evelyn White. 2 Vols.

BEDE. J. E. King. 2 Vols.

BOETHIUS: TRACTS and DE CONSOLATIONE PHILOSOPHIAE.
Rev. H. F. Stewart and E. K. Rand.

CAESAR: ALEXANDRIAN, AFRICAN and SPANISH WARS. A. G.
Way.

CAESAR: CIVIL WARS. A. G. Peskett.

CAESAR: GALLIC WAR. H. J. Edwards.

CATO: DE RE RUSTICA; VARRO: DE RE RUSTICA. H. B. Ash
and W. D. Hooper.

CATULLUS. F. W. Cornish; TIBULLUS. J. B. Postgate; PER-
VIGILIUM VENERIS. J. W. Mackail.

CELSUS: DE MEDICINA. W. G. Spencer. 3 Vols.

CICERO: BRUTUS, and ORATOR. G. L. Hendrickson and H. M.
Hubbell.

[CICERO]: AD HERENNIUM. H. Caplan.

CICERO: DE ORATORE, etc. 2 Vols. Vol. I. DE ORATORE,
Books I. and II. E. W. Sutton and H. Rackham. Vol. II.
DE ORATORE, Book III. De Fato; Paradoxa Stoicorum;
De Partitione Oratoria. H. Rackham.

CICERO: DE FINIBUS. H. Rackham.

CICERO: DE INVENTIONE, etc. H. M. Hubbell.

CICERO: DE NATURA DEORUM and ACADEMICA. H. Rackham.

CICERO: DE OFFICIIS. Walter Miller.

CICERO: DE REPUBLICA and DE LEGIBUS; SOMNIUM SCIPIONIS.
Clinton W. Keyes.

2

Greek Authors

ACHILLES TATIUS. S. Gaselee.

AELIAN: ON THE NATURE OF ANIMALS. A. F. Scholfield. 3 Vols.

AENEAS TACTICUS, ASCLEPIODOTUS and ONASANDER. The Illinois Greek Club.

AESCHINES. C. D. Adams.

AESCHYLUS. H. Weir Smyth. 2 Vols.

ALCIPHRON, AELIAN, PHILOSTRATUS: LETTERS. A. R. Benner and F. H. Fobes.

ANDOCIDES, ANTIPHON, Cf. MINOR ATTIC ORATORS.

APOLLODORUS. Sir James G. Frazer. 2 Vols.

APOLLONIUS RHODIUS. R. C. Seaton.

THE APOSTOLIC FATHERS. Kirsopp Lake. 2 Vols.

APPIAN: ROMAN HISTORY. Horace White. 4 Vols.

ARATUS. Cf. CALLIMACHUS.

ARISTOPHANES. Benjamin Bickley Rogers. 3 Vols. Verse trans.

ARISTOTLE: ART OF RHETORIC. J. H. Freese.

ARISTOTLE: ATHENIAN CONSTITUTION, EUDEMIAN ETHICS, VICES AND VIRTUES. H. Rackham.

ARISTOTLE: GENERATION OF ANIMALS. A. L. Peck.

ARISTOTLE: HISTORIA ANIMALIUM. A. L. Peck. Vols. I.–II.

ARISTOTLE: METAPHYSICS. H. Tredennick. 2 Vols.

ARISTOTLE: METEOROLOGICA. H. D. P. Lee.

ARISTOTLE: MINOR WORKS. W. S. Hett. On Colours, On Things Heard, On Physiognomies, On Plants, On Marvellous Things Heard, Mechanical Problems, On Indivisible Lines, On Situations and Names of Winds, On Melissus, Xenophanes, and Gorgias.

ARISTOTLE: NICOMACHEAN ETHICS. H. Rackham.

ARISTOTLE: OECONOMICA and MAGNA MORALIA. G. C. Armstrong; (with Metaphysics, Vol. II.).

ARISTOTLE: ON THE HEAVENS. W. K. C. Guthrie.

ARISTOTLE: ON THE SOUL. PARVA NATURALIA. ON BREATH. W. S. Hett.

ARISTOTLE: CATEGORIES, ON INTERPRETATION, PRIOR ANALYTICS. H. P. Cooke and H. Tredennick.

ARISTOTLE: POSTERIOR ANALYTICS, TOPICS. H. Tredennick and E. S. Forster.

ARISTOTLE: ON SOPHISTICAL REFUTATIONS.
On Coming to be and Passing Away, On the Cosmos. E. S. Forster and D. J. Furley.

ARISTOTLE: PARTS OF ANIMALS. A. L. Peck; MOTION AND PROGRESSION OF ANIMALS. E. S. Forster.

ARISTOTLE: PHYSICS. Rev. P. Wicksteed and F. M. Cornford. 2 Vols.

ARISTOTLE: POETICS and LONGINUS. W. Hamilton Fyfe; DEMETRIUS ON STYLE. W. Rhys Roberts.

ARISTOTLE: POLITICS. H. Rackham.

ARISTOTLE: PROBLEMS. W. S. Hett. 2 Vols.

ARISTOTLE: RHETORICA AD ALEXANDRUM (with PROBLEMS. Vol. II). H. Rackham.

ARRIAN: HISTORY OF ALEXANDER and INDICA. Rev. E. Iliffe Robson. 2 Vols.

ATHENAEUS: DEIPNOSOPHISTAE. C. B. GULICK. 7 Vols.

BABRIUS AND PHAEDRUS (Latin). B. E. Perry.

ST. BASIL: LETTERS. R. J. Deferrari. 4 Vols.

CALLIMACHUS: FRAGMENTS. C. A. Trypanis.

CALLIMACHUS, Hymns and Epigrams, and LYCOPHRON. A. W. Mair; ARATUS. G. R. MAIR.

CLEMENT of ALEXANDRIA. Rev. G. W. Butterworth.

COLLUTHUS. Cf. OPPIAN.

DAPHNIS AND CHLOE. Thornley's Translation revised by J. M. Edmonds; and PARTHENIUS. S. Gaselee.

DEMOSTHENES I.: OLYNTHIACS, PHILIPPICS and MINOR ORATIONS. I.–XVII. AND XX. J. H. Vince.

DEMOSTHENES II.: DE CORONA and DE FALSA LEGATIONE. C. A. Vince and J. H. Vince.

DEMOSTHENES III.: MEIDIAS, ANDROTION, ARISTOCRATES, TIMOCRATES and ARISTOGEITON, I. AND II. J. H. Vince.

DEMOSTHENES IV.–VI.: PRIVATE ORATIONS and IN NEAERAM. A. T. Murray.

DEMOSTHENES VII.: FUNERAL SPEECH, EROTIC ESSAY, EXORDIA and LETTERS. N. W. and N. J. DeWitt.

DIO CASSIUS: ROMAN HISTORY. E. Cary. 9 Vols.

DIO CHRYSOSTOM. J. W. Cohoon and H. Lamar Crosby. 5 Vols.

DIODORUS SICULUS. 12 Vols. Vols. I.–VI. C. H. Oldfather. Vol. VII. C. L. Sherman. Vol. VIII. C. B. Welles. Vols. IX. and X. R. M. Geer. Vol. XI. F. Walton. Vol. XII. F. Walton. General Index. R. M. Geer.

DIOGENES LAERTIUS. R. D. Hicks. 2 Vols.

DIONYSIUS OF HALICARNASSUS: ROMAN ANTIQUITIES. Spelman's translation revised by E. Cary. 7 Vols.

EPICTETUS. W. A. Oldfather. 2 Vols.

EURIPIDES. A. S. Way. 4 Vols. Verse trans.

EUSEBIUS: ECCLESIASTICAL HISTORY. Kirsopp Lake and J. E. L. Oulton. 2 Vols.

GALEN: ON THE NATURAL FACULTIES. A. J. Brock.

THE GREEK ANTHOLOGY. W. R. Paton. 5 Vols.

GREEK ELEGY AND IAMBUS with the ANACREONTEA. J. M. Edmonds. 2 Vols.

THE GREEK BUCOLIC POETS (THEOCRITUS, BION, MOSCHUS). J. M. Edmonds.

GREEK MATHEMATICAL WORKS. Ivor Thomas. 2 Vols.

HERODES. Cf. THEOPHRASTUS: CHARACTERS.

HERODIAN. C. R. Whittaker. 2 Vols.

HERODOTUS. A. D. Godley. 4 Vols.

HESIOD AND THE HOMERIC HYMNS. H. G. Evelyn White.

HIPPOCRATES and the FRAGMENTS OF HERACLEITUS. W. H. S. Jones and E. T. Withington. 4 Vols.

HOMER: ILIAD. A. T. Murray. 2 Vols.

HOMER: ODYSSEY. A. T. Murray. 2 Vols.

ISAEUS. E. W. Forster.

ISOCRATES. George Norlin and LaRue Van Hook. 3 Vols.

[ST. JOHN DAMASCENE]: BARLAAM AND IOASAPH. Rev. G. R. Woodward, Harold Mattingly and D. M. Lang.

JOSEPHUS. 9 Vols. Vols. I.–IV.; H. Thackeray. Vol. V.; H. Thackeray and R. Marcus. Vols. VI.–VII.; R. Marcus. Vol. VIII.; R. Marcus and Allen Wikgren. Vol. IX. L. H. Feldman.

JULIAN. Wilmer Cave Wright. 3 Vols.

LIBANIUS. A. F. Norman. Vol. I.

LUCIAN. 8 Vols. Vols. I.–V. A. M. Harmon. Vol. VI. K. Kilburn. Vols. VII.–VIII. M. D. Macleod.

LYCOPHRON. Cf. CALLIMACHUS.

LYRA GRAECA. J. M. Edmonds. 3 Vols.

LYSIAS. W. R. M. Lamb.

MANETHO. W. G. Waddell: PTOLEMY: TETRABIBLOS. F. E. Robbins.

MARCUS AURELIUS. C. R. Haines.

MENANDER. F. G. Allinson.

MINOR ATTIC ORATORS (ANTIPHON, ANDOCIDES, LYCURGUS, DEMADES, DINARCHUS, HYPERIDES). K. J. Maidment and J. O. Burtt. 2 Vols.

NONNOS: DIONYSIACA. W. H. D. Rouse. 3 Vols.

OPPIAN, COLLUTHUS, TRYPHIODORUS. A. W. Mair.

PAPYRI. NON-LITERARY SELECTIONS. A. S. Hunt and C. C. Edgar. 2 Vols. LITERARY SELECTIONS (Poetry). D. L. Page.

PARTHENIUS. Cf. DAPHNIS and CHLOE.

PAUSANIAS: DESCRIPTION OF GREECE. W. H. S. Jones. 4 Vols. and Companion Vol. arranged by R. E. Wycherley.

PHILO. 10 Vols. Vols. I.–V.; F. H. Colson and Rev. G. H. Whitaker. Vols. VI.–IX.; F. H. Colson. Vol. X. F. H. Colson and the Rev. J. W. Earp.

PHILO: two supplementary Vols. (*Translation only.*) Ralph Marcus.

PHILOSTRATUS: THE LIFE OF APOLLONIUS OF TYANA. F. C. Conybeare. 2 Vols.

PHILOSTRATUS: IMAGINES; CALLISTRATUS: DESCRIPTIONS. A. Fairbanks.

PHILOSTRATUS and EUNAPIUS: LIVES OF THE SOPHISTS. Wilmer Cave Wright.

PINDAR. Sir J. E. Sandys.

PLATO: CHARMIDES, ALCIBIADES, HIPPARCHUS, THE LOVERS, THEAGES, MINOS and EPINOMIS. W. R. M. Lamb.

PLATO: CRATYLUS, PARMENIDES, GREATER HIPPIAS, LESSER HIPPIAS. H. N. Fowler.

PLATO: EUTHYPHRO, APOLOGY, CRITO, PHAEDO, PHAEDRUS. H. N. Fowler.

PLATO: LACHES, PROTAGORAS, MENO, EUTHYDEMUS. W. R. M. Lamb.

PLATO: LAWS. Rev. R. G. Bury. 2 Vols.

PLATO: LYSIS, SYMPOSIUM, GORGIAS. W. R. M. Lamb.

PLATO: REPUBLIC. Paul Shorey. 2 Vols.

PLATO: STATESMAN, PHILEBUS. H. N. Fowler; ION. W. R. M. Lamb.

PLATO: THEAETETUS and SOPHIST. H. N. Fowler.

PLATO: TIMAEUS, CRITIAS, CLITOPHO, MENEXENUS, EPISTULAE. Rev. R. G. Bury.

PLOTINUS: A. H. Armstrong. Vols. I.–III.

PLUTARCH: MORALIA. 16 Vols. Vols. I.–V. F. C. Babbitt. Vol. VI. W. C. Helmbold. Vols. VII. and XIV. P. H. De Lacy and B. Einarson. Vol. VIII. P. A. Clement and H. B. Hoffleit. Vol. IX. E. L. Minar, Jr., F. H. Sandbach, W. C. Helmbold. Vol. X. H. N. Fowler. Vol. XI. L. Pearson and F. H. Sandbach. Vol. XII. H. Cherniss and W. C. Helmbold. Vol. XV. F. H. Sandbach.

PLUTARCH: THE PARALLEL LIVES. B. Perrin. 11 Vols.

POLYBIUS. W. R. Paton. 6 Vols.

PROCOPIUS: HISTORY OF THE WARS. H. B. Dewing. 7 Vols.

PTOLEMY: TETRABIBLOS. Cf. MANETHO.

QUINTUS SMYRNAEUS. A. S. Way. Verse trans.

SEXTUS EMPIRICUS. Rev. R. G. Bury. 4 Vols.

SOPHOCLES. F. Storr. 2 Vols. Verse trans.

STRABO: GEOGRAPHY. Horace L. Jones. 8 Vols.

THEOPHRASTUS: CHARACTERS. J. M. Edmonds. HERODES, etc. A. D. Knox.

THEOPHRASTUS: ENQUIRY INTO PLANTS. Sir Arthur Hort, Bart. 2 Vols.

THUCYDIDES. C. F. Smith. 4 Vols.

TRYPHIODORUS. Cf. OPPIAN.
XENOPHON: CYROPAEDIA. Walter Miller. 2 Vols.
XENOPHON: HELLENICA. C. L. Brownson. 2 Vols.
XENOPHON: ANABASIS. C. L. Brownson.
XENOPHON: MEMORABILIA AND OECONOMICUS. E. C. Marchant.
 SYMPOSIUM AND APOLOGY. O. J. Todd.
XENOPHON: SCRIPTA MINORA. E. C. Marchant and G. W.
 Bowersock.

IN PREPARATION

Greek Authors

ARISTIDES: ORATIONS. C. A. Behr.
MUSAEUS: HERO AND LEANDER. T. Gelzer and C. H.
 WHITMAN.
THEOPHRASTUS: DE CAUSIS PLANTARUM. G. K. K. Link and
 B. Einarson.

Latin Authors

ASCONIUS: COMMENTARIES ON CICERO'S ORATIONS.
 G. W. Bowersock.
BENEDICT: THE RULE. P. Meyvaert.
JUSTIN–TROGUS. R. Moss.
MANILIUS. G. P. Goold.

DESCRIPTIVE PROSPECTUS ON APPLICATION

London   WILLIAM HEINEMANN LTD
Cambridge, Mass.   HARVARD UNIVERSITY PRESS